5.95

THE IRONY OF VIETNAM

Leslie H. Gelb
with Richard K. Betts

THE IRONY OF VIETNAM:
THE SYSTEM WORKED

The Brookings Institution
Washington, D.C.

Library of Congress Cataloging in Publication Data:

Gelb, Leslie H
  The irony of Vietnam.

  Includes bibliographical references and index.
  1. United States—Foreign relations—Vietnam.
2. Vietnam—Foreign relations—United States.
3. Vietnamese Conflict, 1961–1975. I. Betts, Richard K.,
1947– joint author. II. Title.
E183.8.V5G4   327.73'0597   78-26563
ISBN 0-8157-3072-1
ISBN 0-8157-3071-3 pbk.

9 8 7 6 5 4 3 2 1

THE BROOKINGS INSTITUTION is an independent organization devoted to nonpartisan research, education, and publication in economics, government, foreign policy, and the social sciences generally. Its principal purposes are to aid in the development of sound public policies and to promote public understanding of issues of national importance.

The Institution was founded on December 8, 1927, to merge the activities of the Institute for Government Research, founded in 1916, the Institute of Economics, founded in 1922, and the Robert Brookings Graduate School of Economics and Government, founded in 1924.

The Board of Trustees is responsible for the general administration of the Institution, while the immediate direction of the policies, program, and staff is vested in the President, assisted by an advisory committee of the officers and staff. The by-laws of the Institution state: "It is the function of the Trustees to make possible the conduct of scientific research, and publication, under the most favorable conditions, and to safeguard the independence of the research staff in the pursuit of their studies and in the publication of the results of such studies. It is not a part of their function to determine, control, or influence the conduct of particular investigations or the conclusions reached."

The President bears final responsibility for the decision to publish a manuscript as a Brookings book. In reaching his judgment on the competence, accuracy, and objectivity of each study, the President is advised by the director of the appropriate research program and weighs the views of a panel of expert outside readers who report to him in confidence on the quality of the work. Publication of a work signifies that it is deemed a competent treatment worthy of public consideration but does not imply endorsement of conclusions or recommendations.

The Institution maintains its position of neutrality on issues of public policy in order to safeguard the intellectual freedom of the staff. Hence interpretations or conclusions in Brookings publications should be understood to be solely those of the authors and should not be attributed to the Institution, to its trustees, officers, or other staff members, or to the organizations that support its research.

Foreword

The American experience in Vietnam was the greatest trial of U.S. foreign policy since the Second World War. Among its legacies is a strong desire by many citizens to understand the process by which decisions were made to increase the scope and intensity of American operations in Vietnam.

Only recently have the perspective of time and the opening of documentary sources made possible a comprehensive study of that process. This book relies heavily on the official records published in the Defense Department's history of U.S.-Vietnam relations, known as the Pentagon Papers. In addition, it is the first comprehensive scholarly work to make combined use of recently released parts of the Pentagon Papers dealing with secret negotiations, as well as declassified portions of White House files on Vietnam that are now available in the Lyndon B. Johnson and John F. Kennedy presidential libraries. The analysis marshals these official documents and many secondary studies and memoirs to explain the history and logic of U.S. decisionmaking about Vietnam.

Leslie H. Gelb conceived the book and wrote the bulk of it while a senior fellow in the Brookings Foreign Policy Studies program. His research was informed by his prior U.S. government experience as director of the Pentagon Papers project. He is grateful to Morton H. Halperin, Richard Holbrooke, Anthony Lake, Richard H. Ullman, and his wife, Judith C. Gelb, for helpful comments as the writing progressed, and to Len Ackland, Lee Niedringhaus Davis, and Sally Shelton for research assistance in the early stages. Richard K. Betts wrote the introduction and chapters 3, 4, and 5 and contributed to other parts of the book as well. He began his work while on the faculty of Harvard University and completed it as a Brookings research associate.

Both authors give special thanks to Henry Owen, director of the Brookings Foreign Policy Studies program from 1969 to 1978, for his perseverance in driving this book to a conclusion. They are also grateful to Tadd Fisher, who edited the manuscript, and to Judy L. Cameron, who verified its factual content. Florence Robinson prepared the index, and the figures were drawn by Clare and Frank Ford. More typists than can be acknowledged performed heroically through many drafts of the manuscript; the authors especially thank Delores Burton.

The views expressed in this book are those of the authors, and should not be ascribed to the trustees, officers, or other staff members of the Brookings Institution.

BRUCE K. MACLAURY
President

December 1978
Washington, D.C.

Contents

Table

Figures

Abbreviations

AID	Agency for International Development
ARVN	Army of the Republic of [South] Vietnam
CIA	Central Intelligence Agency
CINCPAC	Commander in Chief, Pacific
CIP	Counterinsurgency Plan
COMUSMACV	Commander, U.S. Military Assistance Command, Vietnam
DRV	Democratic Republic of [North] Vietnam
EDC	European Defense Community
FSO	Foreign Service officer
GVN	Government of [South] Vietnam
ISA	Office of International Security Affairs
JCS	Joint Chiefs of Staff
MAAG	Military Assistance Advisory Group
MACV	Military Assistance Command, Vietnam
NATO	North Atlantic Treaty Organization
NIE	National Intelligence Estimate
NLF	National Liberation Front
NSAM	National Security Action Memorandum
NSC	National Security Council
NSSM	National Security Study Memorandum
NVA	North Vietnamese Army
NVN	North Vietnam
OPLAN	Operations plan
OSD	Office of the Secretary of Defense
OSS	Office of Strategic Services
PAVN	People's Army of [North] Vietnam
POL	Petroleum, oil, lubricants
RVN	Republic of [South] Vietnam
SAM	Surface-to-air missile
SEATO	Southeast Asia Treaty Organization
SNIE	Special National Intelligence Estimate
SVN	South Vietnam
VC	Vietcong
VN	Vietnam

Introduction

The title of this book must strike any intelligent reader, at first glance, as ridiculous. America's war in Vietnam was obviously a failure. Whether the failure was strategic, tactical, conceptual, operational, military, political, diplomatic, moral, or all these, will remain in dispute. But after decades of commitment to prevent Communist domination of the country, at the cost of many billions of dollars and many thousands of American and Vietnamese lives, virtually no one can credibly maintain that the effort was successful.

By what seemingly perverse logic, then, can we argue that the system worked? That ironic logic is the central reason for this book, for now that the dust has finally settled, the conventional wisdom of most postmortems still holds that America's failure in Vietnam was the failure of America's foreign policy decisionmaking system. Somehow the process of assessment, consultation, and decision must have gone awry. Given the results of the war, common sense suggests that U.S. leaders could not have realized what they were doing when they decided to do it. But this commonsense interpretation is simpler, and in a way more dangerously comforting in its implications, than the reality that those making decisions to increase U.S. involvement were aware that victory would probably not be the result. Of all the lessons of the war for Americans—and many of these lessons will prove to be as simplistic, confining, and misleading as the earlier ones of World War II and the cold war that

The genesis of this book is an article by Leslie H. Gelb, "Vietnam: The System Worked," in *Foreign Policy*, vol. 3 (Summer 1971), pp. 140–67. Copyright © 1971 by the Carnegie Endowment for International Peace. Passages from this article appear in chapters 1, 6, 7, 8, 10, 12, and 13. In addition, material is used in chapters 7 and 10 from Gelb's article, "The Essential Domino: American Politics and Vietnam," in *Foreign Affairs*, vol. 50, no. 3 (April 1972), pp. 459–75. Copyright © 1972 by the Council on Foreign Relations, Inc.

prompted commitment in Vietnam—this paradox is the most fundamental. Without recognizing this point, it will be impossible to perceive accurately or to appreciate the other lessons of the war. Our argument is not a perfect one—the evidence indicates exceptions, particular ways in which the system did not work—but in general, and at the most crucial junctures, the argument is depressingly valid.

The paradox is that the *foreign policy* failed, but the *domestic decisionmaking system* worked. It worked as it usually does, in the way that most constitutionalists and democratic pluralists believe it should work. Vietnam was not an aberration of the decisionmaking system but a logical culmination of the principles that leaders brought with them into it.

Radicals believe that the system produced bad policy because capitalism requires imperialism and counterrevolution. Reactionaries believe that the system produced bad policy because democracy requires compromise, and that overly accountable leaders lacked the autonomy and security to go to the unpopular extremes of either withdrawal or unlimited war. Both agree, in short, that the system worked yet produced bad policy because it was a bad system. For liberals, conservatives, and most Americans, however, the argument that a good system produced disastrous policy is understandably galling. But the painful reality is that if the system failed, it did so in ways almost unavoidable in a democratic regime and representative institutional pattern of policymaking, or because no system can compensate for errors of judgment (or felt needs to gamble on unlikely possibilities) if those errors are pervasive among authorities. Failure of policy cannot automatically be the same as failure of the system; otherwise substance and process are indistinguishable.

The three general criteria by which the U.S. system can be said to have worked are (1) the core consensual goal of postwar foreign policy (containment of communism) was pursued consistently; (2) differences of both elite and mass opinion were accommodated by compromise, and policy never strayed very far from the center of opinion both within and outside the government; and (3) virtually all views and recommendations were considered and virtually all important decisions were made without illusions about the odds for success.

The first point is the most basic and will be made again and again throughout our analysis. This repetition is unavoidable because the remarkable continuity of basic objectives is the key to the history of progressive escalation in the face of progressive failure of policy.

The second point would be questionable if, as some intellectuals believed in the late 1960s, the war went on despite the public's desire for withdrawal. The public, it is true, did not want the war—certainly not the prolonged one that it got. But throughout the period covered by this book, those who sought to end the war by escalation outnumbered those who sought to end it by letting the Communists win. The intensity of the latter group's dissent, however, was greater by 1967. In this sense, the balancing of opposition views by the Johnson administration underwrote the compromise course of gradual escalation.

The third point is, with hindsight, the hardest to believe. The logic of the conventional wisdom that sees the expansion of military operations as a deluded journey into a morass is that realistic pessimism about the chances of victory would necessarily have yielded a decision to get out. While American leaders may have been deluded about many things, however, each time they turned the ratchet of escalation up another notch they did not believe that the increase would provide victory in the classic sense of decisive defeat of the enemy. At best they *hoped* they might be lucky, but they did not *expect* to be. Opponents of this argument often point to the pessimists who warned that U.S. policy was not bringing the situation closer to a successful conclusion and that the nation was sinking into an infinite involvement, as if these doves were Cassandras who were ignored and overridden. But they were not ignored. Those who opposed them heard them out and were usually pessimistic themselves. And although the doves within the government agonized and doubted more than their other colleagues, they were not really overridden. With very few exceptions, even the most reticent of these men, seeing what they did and haggling on the margins of options, *supported* the critical decisions on aid, troops, and bombing. They did this because of the compelling precedence of the first point: the consensus that containment required preventing the Communists from taking full control of Vietnam.

If the decisionmaking system failed, it did so in ways that were not unique to the issue of Vietnam but only seem so because the consequences were so horrendous. The system did not prevent willingness to take risks, wishfulness, and the fatal tendency to let hope override expectation. But no system can transcend the dynamics of human psychology. Perhaps it is most significant that the system did not force a definitive early decision on what the tolerable limits of eventual total costs would be. One astute critic of our argument, Herbert Schandler, was half correct when he asserted: "Since the cost of not intervening in Vietnam was deemed to be greater than the cost of intervening, the ultimate military cost of that intervention was not measured. The only cost that had to be considered was continued public support."[1] But the *possible* ultimate costs were measured (see especially the latter part of chapter 4), and continued public support was a cost that was anticipated in assessing nonintervention as well. With hindsight, it seems evident that the costs of the strategy of preventing defeat were incalculable. But at the time of the crucial decisions the costs of *accepting* defeat appeared to be incalculable. The system in this case coped as democracies usually do: by compromising between extreme choices, satisfying the partisans of neither extreme of opinion within the government but preventing the total alienation of either.

Democratic governments are inherently maladapted to the sort of decisive long-range planning that forces the resolution of conflicting costs. Democracy requires frequent accountability of leaders, and this forces them to place a high premium on near-term results; it is not conducive to the independence and psychological freedom that would facilitate accepting apparently disastrous losses in the short run in the interest of avoiding larger losses in the long run. Lest this be interpreted simply as an indictment of the American foreign policy system, it is necessary to remember that freedom from conflicting domestic constituencies is a two-edged sword. If presidents had not felt constrained by the anticipated price of public support at critical points of decision, especially Lyndon Johnson in 1965, they would have had more domestic freedom to disengage. But by the same token they would have had more strategic freedom to escalate further.

This book is an exploration of the history of the decisionmaking process that produced steady increases in American involvement in Vietnam. It is about what happened in Washington from World War II until the decision to cease escalation in 1968. The reader will have to look elsewhere for a full understanding of the complexity of the war itself: the background of Vietnamese history;[2] the development of the

1. Herbert Y. Schandler, *The Unmaking of a President: Lyndon Johnson and Vietnam* (Princeton University Press, 1977), p. 335. Schandler concluded: "Only when the cost had *already* become too high were the objectives that were being pursued and the strategy being followed to attain them matched to see if they were in accord. This was the failure of the decision-making process" (p. 338).

2. See, for example, David G. Marr, *Vietnamese Anticolonialism: 1885–1925* (University of California Press, 1971); John T. McAlister, Jr., *Viet Nam: The Origins of Revolution* (Knopf, 1969); and Dennis J. Duncanson, *Government and Revolution in Vietnam* (New York: Oxford University Press, 1968), chaps. 2–5.

internal politics of the South Vietnamese regime and the Communist revolution;[3] the sociological, economic, organizational, and cultural factors that affected the conflict;[4] and the operational history of the war.[5] These issues are considered here only insofar as they affected U.S. policymaking. We also do not deal in detail with the 1969–75 period of phased withdrawal, negotiation, "peace" accord, and defeat. The story of Richard Nixon and Gerald Ford's Vietnam policy is an important story but a different one, the story of how the United States got out rather than how it got in. We seek to explain the growth in U.S. involvement, not the decline. Moreover, the documentary sources needed to

3. See Joseph Buttinger, *Vietnam: A Dragon Embattled*, 2 vols. (Praeger, 1967); Robert Shaplen, *The Lost Revolution: The U.S. in Vietnam 1946–1966*, rev. ed. (Harper Colophon, 1966); idem, *The Road from War: Vietnam 1965–1970* (Harper and Row, 1970); and idem, *Time Out of Hand: Revolution and Reaction in Southeast Asia* (Harper and Row, 1969), chap. 8; Douglas Pike, *Viet Cong: The Organization and Techniques of the National Liberation Front of South Vietnam* (MIT Press, 1966); and idem, *War, Peace, and the Viet Cong* (MIT Press, 1969); Bernard B. Fall, *The Two Viet Nams: A Political and Military Analysis*, 2d rev. ed. (Praeger, 1967); idem, *Viet-Nam Witness, 1953–66* (Praeger, 1966), and idem, *Last Reflections on a War* (Doubleday, 1967); Allan E. Goodman, *Politics in War: The Bases of Political Community in South Vietnam* (Harvard University Press, 1973); and Lucien Bodard, *The Quicksand War: Prelude to Vietnam*, Patrick O'Brian, trans. (Atlantic–Little, Brown, 1967).

4. See Jeffrey Race, *War Comes to Long An: Revolutionary Conflict in a Vietnamese Province* (University of California Press, 1972); Robert L. Sansom, *The Economics of Insurgency in the Mekong Delta of Vietnam* (MIT Press, 1970); W. P. Davison, *Some Observations on Viet Cong Operations in the Villages* (Rand Corporation, March 1967); Michael Charles Conley, "The Communist Insurgent Infrastructure in South Vietnam: A Study of Organization and Strategy," 2 vols. (American University Center for Research in Social Systems, July 1967; processed); Gerald C. Hickey, *Village in Vietnam* (Yale University Press, 1964); James B. Hendry, *The Small World of Khanh Hau* (Aldine, 1964); and Paul Mus, *Viêt-Nam: sociologie d'une guerre* (Paris: Editions du Seuil, 1952). The latter classic is partially translated in John T. McAlister, Jr., and Paul Mus, *The Vietnamese and Their Revolution* (Harper and Row, 1970).

5. See Admiral U. S. G. Sharp, USN, Commander in Chief, Pacific, and General William C. Westmoreland, USA, Commander, U.S. Military Assistance Command, Vietnam, *Report on the War in Vietnam (as of 30 June 1968)* (Government Printing Office, 1969); U.S. Military Assistance Command, Vietnam, *Command History* (Saigon: MACV, 1964–68); William R. Corson, *The Betrayal* (Norton, 1968); Bernard B. Fall, *Street Without Joy: Insurgency in Indochina 1946–63*, 4th ed. (Stackpole, 1964); and Guenter Lewy, *America in Vietnam* (New York: Oxford University Press, 1978). Numerous topical studies have been produced by the historical offices of the military services, and official service histories of the war will be forthcoming.

analyze the post-1968 phase properly will not be available for some time.[6]

This, then, is a history and an analysis of how the U.S. decisionmaking system worked while policy failed. The story is a tangled web of facts and themes, and a full understanding of the realities requires an appreciation of the record in both chronological and topical terms. Thus some repetition of documentary material is necessary, but such overlapping is warranted by the greater clarity that results from presenting both complementary approaches. The chronological treatment is presented in part I, with an outline of the basic conceptual approaches to the subject. The topical analyses follow in parts II–IV.

6. For the Johnson administration and earlier, we have the rich lode of the official record in the Pentagon Papers (including the negotiations volumes), the complementary unofficial and anecdotal history by David Halberstam, *The Best and the Brightest* (Random House, 1972), and a portion of previously classified White House files. No comparable sources are likely to be available in the near future for the Nixon and Ford administrations. See the bibliographical note on p. 375 for an explanation of our use of the Pentagon Papers and other official sources.

PART ONE

Decisions: Getting into Vietnam

CHAPTER ONE

Patterns, Dilemmas, and Explanations

Writing history, especially history as recent and controversial as the Vietnam War, is a treacherous exercise. One picks away at the debris of evidence only to discover that it is still alive, being shaped by bitterness and bewilderment, reassurances and new testimony. Consequently answers to certain questions will forever remain elusive. Were U.S. leaders right or wrong in involving the nation in Vietnam? Did they adopt the best strategy for fighting the war? Were they genuinely seeking a compromise peace? Each succeeding generation of historians will produce its own perspective on the rights and wrongs of the war, and each perspective will be different from the others. This has happened with every other war, and it will happen with Vietnam.

What the historian can legitimately seek to do at this point is to begin to piece together the whats and whys. What were the patterns that characterized the war in Vietnam? What policy dilemmas did U.S. leaders face? Why were their choices indeed dilemmas? Why did they choose the way they did?

Patterns

Four basic and recurring patterns marked what was happening in Vietnam from 1947 to 1969.

The first pattern was that of the French, the Saigon government, and their military forces. The military forces always got better, but they never got good enough. Each Vietminh or North Vietnamese offensive, whatever the immediate results, showed again and again that first the French and then the Saigon forces could not defend themselves without

ever larger doses of massive American assistance. (The invasion of
South Vietnam by the North Vietnamese across the demilitarized zone
in 1972 was a partial exception.) These anti-Communist forces could
never translate their advantages in total air superiority, dominance in
mobility and firepower, and a sizable edge in manpower into victory. In
fact they spent most of the time on the defensive until mid-1968. Something was wrong somewhere. Something always was wrong..

Military power without political cohesiveness and support is an
empty shell. The non-Communist Vietnamese, to be sure, invariably had
a solid strike against them: it could not be an easy task to coalesce the
forces of nationalism while depending militarily on the French or the
Americans. Yet the non-Communist groups never were able to submerge
their own differences in a single, unified purpose and to gather support
from the peasant masses. Before the end, the regime of President
Nguyen Van Thieu gained in stability but seemingly not in legitimacy.
Without this legitimacy—and the quest for it seemed never-ending—the
anti-Communist Vietnamese perpetually required American support.

A second pattern characterized the Vietminh and later the Hanoi
government. While the annual hopeful prediction was that the Communists were about to expire, their will to fight seemed undiminished
and they kept coming back. When the going got rough in Vietnam, they
would divert temporarily to Laos and Cambodia. One need not glorify
the Communists to face this fact. The brutality of their methods of warfare matched, if not exceeded, Saigon's.[1] And certainly Hanoi received
massive doses of aid from the Soviet Union and China, although only a
fraction of the aid the United States gave to France and Saigon. But
something always went right for them somewhere.

1. Descriptions of South Vietnamese and American atrocities can be found
throughout press accounts of the late 1960s, particularly in radical journals, such as
Ramparts, and in Vietnam Veterans Against the War, *The Winter Soldier Investigation: An Inquiry into American War Crimes* (Beacon Press, 1972). Communist
cadres were often able to take political advantage of such incidents. Samuel Popkin
commented on the phenomenon of "political judo" in "The Myth of the Village:
Revolution and Reaction in Vietnam" (Ph.D. dissertation, Harvard University,
1969). For a defense of the American record, see Guenter Lewy, "Vietnam: New
Light on the Question of American Guilt," *Commentary,* vol. 65 (February 1978).
A detailed analysis of Vietcong terrorism, which was sometimes more discriminating
and politically calculated than that of the American and South Vietnamese forces,
can be found in Stephen T. Hosmer's Rand Corporation study, *Viet Cong Repression
and its Implications for the Future* (Heath Lexington, 1970); and in Douglas Pike,
*Viet Cong: The Organization and Techniques of the National Liberation Front of
South Vietnam* (MIT Press, 1966), chap. 13.

The Communist leaders always had their differences, but they could put them aside in the pursuit of their goal of an independent and unified Vietnam. Although as dictatorial as their foes, if not more so, they were nevertheless able to organize and marshal their efforts effectively year after year. They were, in short, more *effectively* dictatorial than the Saigon mandarins, especially because after World War II they captured much of the banner of nationalism. The non-Communist nationalists never achieved the same degree of ideological cohesion, organizational discipline, and grass roots activism. For these reasons the Communists crept near to victory on several occasions.

Victory would have been theirs on these occasions had it not been for a third pattern—that of increasing American involvement. As U.S. involvement increased, appearing at times to raise the possibility of a Communist defeat, the Soviet Union and China would step up aid to their ally. Whenever one Vietnamese side or the other in this conflict was in danger of losing, one of the superpowers would step in to redress the balance. The war could not end as long as these outside powers wanted to keep their clients from losing.

The upshot was a fourth pattern—stalemate. From time to time negotiating initiatives were launched, serving only to emphasize that the war was basically a civil war in which neither side would risk genuine compromise. Each side tried more force. The other side would match it. The anti-Communist Vietnamese, though inefficient and corrupt, always had enough support and resiliency to hang on. The Communist Vietnamese, though battered, always possessed the determination to drive on. Death fast became a way of life in Vietnam as stalemate continued but the war got bigger.

Dilemmas

Back in Washington, these patterns created, and were in part created by, the conflicting goals that posed a rack of interlocking policy dilemmas.

Stakes versus leverage. U.S. stakes in avoiding a Communist takeover in Vietnam were as great as the stakes of Paris and Saigon. Thus, occasional threats from Washington to "shape up or else" were never taken seriously, for leaders in Paris and Saigon realized that the United States stood to lose as much as they from withdrawal. As the stakes grew, leverage shrank. American goals and strength were therefore paradoxically a fundamental source of bargaining weakness.

Pressure versus collapse. At various times U.S. leaders believed that neither the French nor the South Vietnamese would undertake necessary reforms without hard pressure from Washington, and that pressing too hard might lead to complete collapse of the anti-Communist position. If the Americans pushed the French into granting genuine independence to Vietnam, France would have no incentive to continue the fight against communism and would withdraw. If the Americans pushed the Saigon government too hard on land reform, corruption, and the like, Saigon's administrative structure would become overburdened, its power base would be placed in jeopardy, and its ever-fragile unity might come apart. Thus the weakness of the French and the South Vietnamese was the source of their bargaining strength.

Vietnamese reform versus American performance. Truman, Eisenhower, Kennedy, and Johnson each made clear that reforms would be a precondition for further U.S. assistance. Each violated his own preconditions. The dilemma was this: if the United States performed before the French and the Saigon government reformed, they would never reform, but if the United States did not perform first and the situation further deteriorated, reforms would become academic. Thus at the end of 1964 American leaders concluded that the Saigon government was too precarious to warrant additional U.S. help but was unlikely to survive without it.

Involvement or not—a loss either way. U.S. strategists recognized over the years that greater involvement by outside powers was sure to run against the grain of Vietnamese nationalism, thereby making the war unwinnable. Eisenhower realized that getting further involved in France's colonial war was a losing proposition. Kennedy saw in 1961 that sending in American combat troops and making the American presence more visible could only transform the situation into "a white man's war," again a losing proposition.[2] But Eisenhower, Kennedy, and the other presidents also believed that France and Saigon were certain to fail without greater U.S. involvement.

Restraint versus signals. U.S. leaders correctly calculated that increas-

2. Arthur M. Schlesinger, Jr., *A Thousand Days: John F. Kennedy in the White House* (Houghton Mifflin, 1965), p. 547.

ing American involvement in Vietnam would trigger heightened domestic criticism of the war. Thus each President sought to postpone and then to downplay escalatory actions or even to conceal the significance of those actions as long as possible. But at the same time, they calculated with equal correctness that restraint for domestic political purposes would convey the wrong signal to the Vietminh, Hanoi, and their supporters. It could only be read by the Communists as a sign of U.S. weakness and ultimate irresolution.

The damned if do, damned if don't dilemma. At bottom, the presidents acted as if they were trapped no matter what they did. If they escalated to avoid defeat, they would be criticized. If they failed to escalate, they would be criticized for permitting defeat. Theirs was the most classic of all dilemmas: they were damned if they did and damned if they didn't. There seemed to be no course of action that would not risk domestic support, although until 1968 criticism for softness seemed less bearable than criticism for excessive involvement. The dilemma lay not only in balancing left-wing domestic constituencies against right-wing ones, but also in the contradictory demands of the Right. Republican rightists at various times criticized Democrats both for being the "war party" *and* for "selling out" countries to communism.

In sum, given the constant goal of a non-Communist South after the Korean War, these six U.S. dilemmas in Vietnam melded into three historically phased ones. At first, U.S. leaders realized that there was no chance of defeating the Vietminh unless France granted true independence to Vietnam, but that if France did so, it would not remain and fight the war. So the United States could not win with France and could not win without it. Then American leaders recognized that although President Ngo Dinh Diem was losing the support of the people, he nevertheless represented the only hope of future political stability. So the United States could not win with Diem and could not win without him. Later the American view was that the Saigon regime would not reform with U.S. aid and could not survive without massive U.S. involvement, and that the North Vietnamese effort seemed able to survive despite U.S. efforts. Once again, the war could neither be won with U.S. help nor without it. Why, then, did the United States continue throughout these phases to put its resources into an ever-expanding and never-ending war?

A Range of Explanations

Nations at war and after a war, win or lose, try to scratch away at the traditions or values that hold their societies together to see what they are made of. Are they wise and just nations? Or are they foolish and aggressive? Merciless or humane? Well led or misled? Vital or decadent? Hopeful or hopeless? It is arguable whether a society should indulge in such self-scrutiny. Societies are, as Edmund Burke wrote, "delicate, intricate wholes" that are more easily damaged than improved when subjected to the glare of grand inquisitors.

But in the case of the United States and the war in Vietnam, many people have sought answers to which they are entitled, and many others are only too eager to fill in the blanks. The families and friends of those who were killed and wounded want to know whether it was worth it. This answer is clear to most by now: No. Intellectuals still want to know "Why Vietnam?" Policy analysts want to know whether the failure was conceptual and strategic (the realm of ends) or organizational and operational (the realm of means).[3] The answers to these questions will themselves become political facts and forces, shaping the U.S. role in the world and the lives of Americans at home for years to come.

Central to this inquiry are the wide-ranging explanations of U.S. involvement given in the Vietnam War literature. Nine seem to stand out. Different authors combine them in different ways, although none presents a complete answer. The nine basic explanations are as follows:

1. *The arrogance of power—idealistic imperialism.* Richard Hofstadter has argued that Americans have had a misleading historical experience with warfare, and that unlike the Europeans, they have not learned to live with minor setbacks and limited successes, since they have known only victory. This led to the "illusion of American omnipotence" in U.S. foreign policy.[4]

3. See the debates in Richard M. Pfeffer, ed., *No More Vietnams? The War and the Future of American Foreign Policy* (Harper and Row for the Adlai Stevenson Institute of International Affairs, 1968); and in W. Scott Thompson and Donaldson D. Frizzell, eds., *The Lessons of Vietnam* (Crane, Russak, 1977).

4. Richard Hofstadter, "Uncle Sam Has Cried 'Uncle' Before," *New York Times Magazine*, May 19, 1968, p. 30. See also J. William Fulbright, *The Arrogance of Power* (Random House, 1966).

This view holds that a driving force in American involvement in Vietnam was that the United States is a nation of enormous power and, like comparable nations in history, sought to use this power at every opportunity. To have power is to want to employ it and, eventually, is to be corrupted by it. The arrogance derived from the belief that to have power is to be able to do anything. It was also an idealistic arrogance, an imperialism more ingenuous than malevolent, a curious blend of Wilsonianism and realpolitik that sought to make the world safe for democracy even if this meant forcing Vietnam to be free. Power invokes right and justifies itself. Vietnam was there, a challenge to this power and an opportunity for its exercise, and no task was beyond accomplishment.

2. *The rapacity of power: economic imperialism.* This explanation, a variant of the domestic politics interpretation given below, is that special-interest groups, such as the industrial and financial elite, maneuvered the United States into war. This elite's goal was to capture export markets and natural resources at public expense for private economic gain. Gabriel Kolko's neo-Marxist analyses are the best examples of this approach.[5]

Michael Klare, mixing the power elite model of C. Wright Mills with the economic determinism of Noam Chomsky, put the argument this way:

U.S. policy in general and U.S. intervention in Vietnam in particular were "the predictable outcome of an American drive to secure control over the economic resources of the non-Communist world." American businessmen held key posts in the executive branch. Senators, congressmen, academics, scientists, think-tankers, and the military were their hirelings. They all longed for the almighty dollar. They could not make enough "honest dollars" in the United States, so they enlisted the power of Washington to guarantee foreign markets for the export of goods and capital and access to raw materials. They hoodwinked the rest of the nation into believing that the protection of their profits was in the U.S. national interest. They needed military capability. The military-industrial complex responded with sensors, defoliants, automatic battlefields,

5. Gabriel Kolko, *The Roots of American Foreign Policy: An Analysis of Power and Purpose* (Beacon Press, 1969); idem, *The Politics of War: The World and United States Foreign Policy, 1943–1945* (Random House, 1968); and Joyce and Gabriel Kolko, *The Limits of Power: The World and United States Foreign Policy, 1945–1954* (Harper and Row, 1972).

helicopters, and the like, and tested them in the laboratory of Vietnam. Put it all together with an adversary who would do everything he could to resist, and you have a war without end.[6]

3. *Bureaucratic politics.* There are several, not mutually exclusive, approaches within this view. One, a quasi-Freudian version, has it that national security bureaucrats—the professionals who make up the military services, civilians in the Defense Department, the Agency for International Development, the State Department, and the Central Intelligence Agency (CIA)—are afflicted with the curse of machismo, the need to assert and prove manhood and toughness. This instinct compounded misunderstanding and organizational failure. The bureaucrats' career advancement and acceptability within the government depended on showing that they were not afraid to propose the use of force. Another more conspiratorial approach has it that bureaucrats purposefully misled their superiors about the situation in Vietnam and carefully constructed policy alternatives so as to circumscribe their choices, thus forcing further involvement in Vietnam.

The first approach has been set forth by Richard Barnet and James C. Thomson, Jr. According to Barnet, the national security manager quickly learns that "toughness is the most highly prized virtue."[7] Thomson drove the point home: "Those who doubted our role in Vietnam were said to shrink from the burdens of power, the obligations of power, the uses of power, the responsibility of power. By implication such men were soft-headed and effete." Citing the lack of informed judgment on Indochina because of the "banishment of real expertise" on Asia, the "domestication of dissenters," the "effectiveness trap" whereby bureaucrats refrain from protesting for fear of losing their influence, the "curator mentality," and "bureaucratic detachment" from moral issues, Thomson observed that the conflict was bound to lead to "a steady give-in to pressures for a military solution."[8]

Of the second approach, Stavins, Barnet, and Raskin noted:

The deliberate inflation and distortion of issues in the advocacy process leads to what I call the bureaucratic model of reality . . . the final purpose of which is to induce the President to do something or to make him feel comfortable

6. Michael T. Klare, *War Without End: American Planning for the Next Vietnams* (Knopf, 1972), pp. 5 (quotation), 7 ff. See also Noam Chomsky, *At War with Asia* (Pantheon, 1970).

7. Richard Barnet, "The Game of Nations," *Harper's*, November 1971, p. 55.

8. James C. Thomson, Jr., "How Could Vietnam Happen? An Autopsy," *Atlantic Monthly*, April 1968, p. 52.

about something the bureaucracy has already done. . . . The shrewd adviser tailors his advice to the President's prejudices as best he knows them.[9]

David Halberstam emphasized this bureaucratic duplicity, particularly in regard to the role of military reporting from the field in the early 1960s.[10] A similar variant of bureaucratic politics is posed by the Committee of Concerned Asian Scholars: "The Indochina war is in large part a product of sheer institutional momentum."[11] According to this interpretation, bureaucrats develop a stake in their solution to a problem; a change in the solution is difficult because it means a repudiation of a previous chain of decisions and is therefore an admission of personal failing in the past. As another analyst argued, the crisis managers advising the President became so involved they "would not, perhaps could not, let go."[12] This fairly unified vision of bureaucracy contrasts with a fourth and final view of organizational determinism: bureaucratic bargaining. In this explanation the cautious approach of the State Department and the CIA gradually lost out in the councils of decision to the arguments of the professional military.[13]

4. Domestic politics. This explanation is quite complicated, and authors argue their cases on several different levels. The magnanimous view sees American presidents fending off the Communists in Vietnam in order to save the country from another round of right-wing McCarthyism and to retain domestic support for a continuing U.S. role in the world. Chroniclers who have been close to presidents have stressed this interpretation.[14]

Another more complex portrait was sketched by Daniel Ellsberg, who saw domestic politics as putting U.S. leaders in a bind between

9. Ralph Stavins, Richard J. Barnet, and Marcus G. Raskin, *Washington Plans an Aggressive War* (Vintage, 1971), pp. 207, 217.

10. David Halberstam, *The Best and the Brightest* (Random House, 1972).

11. Committee of Concerned Asian Scholars, *The Indochina Story: A Fully Documented Account* (Bantam, 1970), p. 248.

12. Melvin Gurtov, "Beyond the Pentagon Papers," *Ramparts,* February 1972, p. 61.

13. See Robert L. Gallucci, *Neither Peace nor Honor: The Politics of American Military Policy in Viet-Nam,* Washington Center of Foreign Policy Research, School of Advanced International Studies, Studies in International Affairs, 24 (Johns Hopkins University Press, 1975).

14. See Schlesinger, *A Thousand Days;* Harry McPherson, *A Political Education: A Journal of Life with Senators, Generals, Cabinet Members and Presidents* (Little, Brown, 1972); W. W. Rostow, *The Diffusion of Power: An Essay in Recent History* (Macmillan, 1972); and Theodore C. Sorensen, *Kennedy* (Harper and Row, 1965).

two conflicting imperatives: "Rule 1 . . . *Do not lose the rest of Vietnam to communist control before the next election,*" and "Rule 2 . . . *Do not commit U.S. ground troops to a land war in Asia, either.*" The former drove the presidents on and the latter constrained them. The presidential rule that *"this is a bad year for me to lose Vietnam to Communism,"* said Ellsberg, along with rules 1 and 2,

amounts to a *recurrent* formula for calculating Presidential decisions on Vietnam realistically, given inputs on alternatives, any time from 1950 on. The mix of motives behind this judgment can vary with circumstances and Presidents, but since 1950 a variety of domestic political considerations have virtually always been present. These have been *sufficient* underpinning even in those years when . . . "strategic" concerns were not also urgent.[15]

These constraints can also be seen as reinforced by the underlying urge, especially in Johnson's case, not to be "the first President to lose a war."

5. *Pragmatic security managers.* This interpretation is closely linked to the bureaucratic and arrogance-of-power explanations. It is the view that U.S. leaders over the years were not inspired by any particular ideology but were essentially pragmatists weighing the evidence and looking at each problem on its merits. According to this perspective, these leaders knew they were facing tough choices, and their decisions always were close ones. But having decided 51 to 49 to go ahead, they tried to sell and implement their policies 100 percent.

Pragmatists are problem-solvers, and in the words of Joseph Kraft: "The war is peculiarly the war of the Whiz Kids and their friends and supporters in the liberal, business, and academic community. It is the war of those of us who thought we could manage force, and tune violence finely."[16]

6. *Ethnocentricity and misperception.* Some analysts emphasize the naiveté and insensitivity of policymakers who did not understand the significance of cultural differences, and who therefore did not see that America's Vietnamese allies would not and could not live up to U.S. expectations. Communist revolution in the context of Vietnamese society was simplistically and falsely equated with the earlier challenges in Western Europe. Policymakers assumed that the stakes and solutions were similar, ignoring the complexity, uniqueness, and much greater

15. Daniel Ellsberg, *Papers on the War* (Simon and Schuster, 1972), pp. 101–02 (emphasis in the original).

16. Joseph Kraft, "After McNamara," in Robert Manning and Michael Janeway, eds., *Who We Are: An Atlantic Chronicle of the United States and Vietnam* (Little, Brown, 1969), p. 251.

foreignness of the Vietnamese setting. The United States failed in Vietnam because Americans thought they could treat it like any other Western country and were oblivious to the constraints of the traditional Vietnamese culture and character and to the reasons for the vitality of Vietnamese communism.[17] A related view is that which stresses misunderstanding of Hanoi's and the Vietcong's motives and the miscalculation of policy based on this misperception.[18] Better anthropology and psychology would have helped. In short, had the United States really known who it was dealing with and had it really comprehended how *they* viewed the war, it would not have gotten in so deeply.

7. *The slippery slope.* Tied to the pragmatic approach, the balance of power, and the arrogance of power, but attributing more to the process than to the underlying assumptions, is the explanation that holds that U.S. involvement in Vietnam is the story of the slippery slope. According to this view Vietnam was not always critical to U.S. national security; it became so over the years as each succeeding administration piled commitment on commitment. Each administration not quite knowingly slid further into the Vietnam quagmire, not really understanding the depth of the problems in Vietnam and convinced that it could win. The catchwords of this view are optimism, miscalculation, and inadvertence.

The most vocal advocate of this thesis has been Arthur M. Schlesinger, Jr., who in 1967 expressed it as follows:

And so the policy of 'one more step' lured the United States deeper and deeper into the morass. In retrospect, Vietnam is a triumph of the politics of inadvertence. We have achieved our present entanglement, not after due and deliberate consideration, but through a series of small decisions. It is not only idle but unfair to seek out guilty men. President Eisenhower, after rejecting American military intervention in 1954, set in motion the policy of support for Saigon which resulted, two Presidents later, in American military intervention in 1965. Each step in the deepening of the American commitment was reasonably regarded at the time as the last that would be necessary. Yet, in retrospect, each step led only to the next, until we find ourselves entrapped today in that nightmare of American strategists, a land war in Asia—a war which no President, including President Johnson, desired or intended. The Vietnam story is a tragedy without villains.[19]

17. See Frances FitzGerald, *Fire in the Lake: The Vietnamese and the Americans in Vietnam* (Atlantic–Little, Brown, 1972).

18. See Ralph K. White, *Nobody Wanted War: Misperception in Vietnam and Other Wars* (Doubleday, 1970).

19. Arthur M. Schlesinger, Jr., *The Bitter Heritage: Vietnam and American Democracy, 1941–1966* (Houghton Mifflin, 1967), pp. 31–32.

Schlesinger went on to say: "By continually increasing what the Pentagon calls the 'quotient of pain,' we can, according to the administration theory, force Hanoi at each new stage of widening the war to reconsider whether the war is worth the price." But "the theory that widening the war will shorten it . . . appears to be based on three convictions: first, that the war will be decided in North Vietnam; second, that the risk of Chinese or Soviet entry is negligible; and third, that military victory in some sense is possible" (at least in suppressing the resistance in the South).[20] All these convictions, he concluded, were dangerous forms of illusion and self-deception. Marvin Kalb and Elie Abel agreed when they stated that America stumbled "step by downward step, into the longest, most costly, and most disruptive war Americans have ever fought, in the misguided belief that when things go wrong anywhere in the world the commitment of sufficient American dollars and—if need be—of American soldiers, must surely put them right."[21]

Other writers have been less charitable. Bernard Fall, referring to Schlesinger's theory that "error creates its own reality," said that "it would not be unfair to state that the official reports on the situation from 1954 to the present depict a well-nigh unbroken series of seemingly 'unavoidable' decisions, all made with the best of intentions and for the noblest of purposes—but each gone awry at the last moment because of outside factors beyond one's control."[22] He added, however, that "official reactions to warnings about the surely catastrophic end results of the course upon which the Saigon authorities—both Vietnamese and American—were embarked fell upon both deaf and resentful ears, as differences of view between the trained outside observers and officialdom became irreconcilable."[23]

According to Theodore Draper:

As a result of one miscalculation after another, we have gradually been drawn into making an enormous, disproportionate military and political investment in Vietnam. This investment—not the vital interests of the United States in Vietnam—has cast a spell on us. The same thing would happen if we should

20. Ibid., pp. 32–34. See also Schlesinger's "Eyeless in Indochina," *New York Review of Books,* October 21, 1971, pp. 23–32.
21. Marvin Kalb and Elie Abel, *The Roots of Involvement: The U.S. in Asia, 1784–1971* (Norton, 1971), p. 11.
22. Bernard B. Fall, *Viet-Nam Witness, 1953–1966* (Praeger, 1966), pp. 4–5.
23. Ibid., p. 11.

decide to put 500,000 troops in Mauritania or even Ruritania. Once American resources and prestige are committed on such a profligate scale, the "commitment" develops a life of its own and, as the saying goes, good money must be thrown after bad.[24]

8. *International power politics and containment—policing the world.* The desire to maintain some perceived balance of power among nations is an explanation that is intimately related to that of pragmatism but places more emphasis on the traditional imperatives of international relations. According to Donald Zagoria: "For the Americans—as for the Russians and Chinese—Vietnam has been a pawn in a global ideological and power struggle." The United States, he said, was "intent—particularly after the Korean War—on drawing a Cold War line in Asia."[25]

The principal considerations in pursuing the balance-of-power goal were seeing that "the illegal use of force" was not allowed to succeed, honoring commitments, and keeping credibility with allies and potential adversaries. The underlying judgment was that failure to stop aggression in one place would tempt others to aggress in ever more dangerous places. As the most powerful non-Communist nation, the United States had no choice but to serve as the world's policeman. Intervention in Vietnam, in this view, was not aggressive, adventurous, idealistic, or naive, but simply the ineluctable result of the American power position in the world, the same response that great powers have historically made to challenges from other powers.

Kalb and Abel, for example, noted that after Lyndon Johnson won his election, he *could* have considered changing U.S. policy. But he was determined not to lose Vietnam and thus rejected the possibility of a quiet withdrawal. "To him, that would have meant going back on the nation's pledged commitment."[26] Townsend Hoopes described numerous times during the period October 1967 through March 1968 when pressures were brought to bear on the President that might have changed U.S. policy. But the President's reaction was that the struggle was a test of wills between Washington and Hanoi and that the United States must not relent. Relenting was regarded as tantamount to a resounding defeat to worldwide U.S. policy and prestige and as a green light to the

24. Theodore Draper, *Abuse of Power* (Viking, 1967), p. 161.
25. Donald S. Zagoria, *Vietnam Triangle: Moscow, Peking, Hanoi* (Pegasus, 1968), p. 29.
26. Kalb and Abel, *Roots of Involvement*, p. 176.

Soviet Union and China to foster more Communist wars of national liberation around the world.[27]

9. *Ideological anticommunism.* The analysts who offer this explanation hold that anticommunism was the central fact of U.S. foreign policy from at least 1947 until the end of the 1960s. After World War II global competition between East and West began. An ideology whose very existence seemed to threaten basic American values had combined with the national force of first Russia and then China. This combination caused American leaders to see the world in "we-they" terms and to insist that peace was indivisible. Going well beyond balance-of-power considerations, every piece of territory became critical and every besieged nation a potential domino. Communism came to be seen as an infection to be quarantined rather than a force to be judiciously and appropriately balanced. Vietnam in particular became the cockpit of confrontation between the Free World and totalitarianism; it was where the action was for twenty years.

Hoopes, for example, observed that although the United States was confronted by a genuine and serious Soviet threat following World War II (and one aggravated in particular by the Korean War), unfortunately "the American response to the cold war generated its own momentum and, in doing so, led us . . . beyond the rational requirements of our national security." Anticommunism degenerated into a religious obsession despite numerous indications that the Communist bloc was no longer monolithic. U.S. aid to Vietnam continued to be based on the conviction that any Communist expansion threatened the security of the United States. The graduated escalation of the war, beginning around 1965, reflected the continuing influence of the cold war beliefs and resulted in wanton destruction grossly disproportionate to the goal sought.[28]

Chester Cooper, in tracing the history of U.S. involvement in Vietnam since World War II, showed how the anti-Communist strain evolved through the different administrations. The residue of democratic antitotalitarian militancy of World War II, directed against fascism, carried over into cold war anticommunism.

27. Townsend Hoopes, *The Limits of Intervention: An Inside Account of How the Johnson Policy of Escalation Was Reversed* (McKay, 1969). This view was reinforced by rhetoric from revolutionaries, such as Che Guevara's exhortations for "two, three, many Vietnams."

28. Townsend Hoopes, "Legacy of the Cold War in Indochina," *Foreign Affairs*, vol. 48 (July 1970), pp. 601–16 (quotation, p. 606).

The issue of the "Free World vs. International Communism" made decisions about international relations seem simple and, what is more, cast a mantle of morality and righteousness over all our actions abroad. The Soviet Union and its friends, by their deeds and their words, provided the spark that launched an American crusade to save the world from Communism.[29]

Stereotypes Fail

Each of these explanations provides some insight into particular issues, particular people, and the workings of bureaucratic organizations at certain times. But however these explanations are combined, they are better as answers to the question of why the United States originally became involved and committed in Vietnam than as analyses of the process of involvement, the strategy for fighting the war, and the strategy for ending it.

The most prevalent and popular combination of explanations—pragmatic security managers, domestic politics, anticommunism, and slippery slope—is misleading in three crucial respects: it sees commitment as essentially stemming from involvement, the stakes building with each successive escalation—the simple investment trap model; it does not sufficiently emphasize the constraints in fighting the war, nor does it tie these constraints in a coherent way to the strategy of gradualism; and in stressing the factor of Washington's optimism about victory, it seriously distorts official American appraisals of, and expectations about, the war. Explanations 8 and 9, which see involvement as the rational product of given premises about the international balance of power and American ideals, are closer to the mark if any are. But Vietnam, according to most observers, is a story about how the U.S. system failed because the people who ran it blundered. According to this conventional wisdom the American leaders were a collection of moderate pragmatists and cold war ideologues who were trapped by their own philosophies and their ignorance of Vietnam. Pragmatists and ideologues alike foundered, so the stories go, because neither understood that Vietnam was an endless war, a quagmire.

Both stereotypes are compelling in some ways. The pragmatic one gives comfort to those who see where the United States wound up in

29. Chester L. Cooper, *The Lost Crusade: America in Vietnam* (Dodd, Mead, 1970), p. 409.

Vietnam and conclude that no one could have wished this result. It must have been a mistake. The ideological one offers proof to those who look at Vietnam as one more act in the American drama about communism. It was necessary to fill the bill. These general pictures of blundering and blustering are also compelling in a sense as glimpses of the organizational minds of the State Department and the armed services.

Yet the stereotypes fail. They fail because the decisionmaking system they purport to describe *did achieve its stated purpose* of preventing a Communist victory in Vietnam until the domestic balance of opinion shifted and Congress decided to reduce support to Saigon in 1974–75— that is, until the consensus, and hence the purpose, changed and the United States decided to let Vietnam go.

The system worked. The story of U.S. policy toward Vietnam is either far better or far worse than supposed. Presidents and most of those who influenced their decisions did not stumble into Vietnam unaware of the quagmire. U.S. involvement did not stem from a failure to foresee that the war would be a long and bitter struggle. Vietnam was indeed a quagmire, but most American leaders knew it. Of course, there were periods when many were genuinely optimistic. But these infrequent and short-lived periods (late 1953, 1957–59, 1962 and early 1963, and late 1967) were invariably followed by deep pessimism. Very few persons, to be sure, envisioned what the Vietnam situation would be like by 1968. Most realized, however, that the light at the end of the tunnel was very far away, if not unreachable. Nevertheless, the presidents persevered. Given the international compulsions to "keep our word" and "save face," domestic prohibitions against losing, and high personal stakes, U.S. leaders did "what was necessary," did it about the way they wanted to, were prepared to pay the costs each administration could foresee for itself, and plowed on with a mixture of hope and doom. They saw no acceptable alternative until 1968, when the President decided to deescalate, and again in 1974–75, when Congress decided to trim the aid cord.

Summary: Three Propositions

The remainder of this book is built around three propositions. Part Two will develop the first proposition, Part Three will develop the second, and Part Four will expand on the third. The first proposition tells why and how the United States became involved in Vietnam. The second explains both why "winning" strategies could not be adopted and why the process of involvement was gradual. The third offers answers about expectations.

Proposition 1. U.S. involvement in Vietnam is not mainly a story of inadvertent descent into unforeseen quicksand but of why U.S. leaders considered it vital not to lose Vietnam by force to communism. They believed Vietnam to be vital, not for itself, but for what they thought its "loss" would mean internationally and domestically. Previous involvement made further involvement harder to avoid, and to this extent initial commitments were compounded. But the basic pressures, stakes, and objectives, and the judgments of Vietnam's vitalness—after the fall of China and beginning with the Korean War—were sufficient in themselves to set the course for escalation.

Proposition 2. The presidents, Congress, public opinion, and the press all both reinforced the stakes against losing and introduced constraints against winning. Until the summer of 1965 the presidents did less than those who were urging military victory recommended and rejected policies that could lead to disengagement—in effect they did what they deemed to be minimally necessary at each stage to keep Vietnam and later South Vietnam out of Communist hands. After the summer of 1965, as the war dragged on and the consensus began to dissipate, President Johnson remained a true believer and pushed for the maximum feasible, given diplomatic and domestic constraints as he saw them. Throughout, however, the presidents met the pressures of the system as brakemen, doing less than what they were being told was necessary for victory. While each President was one of the key architects of this consensus, he also was a part and a prisoner of the larger political system that fed on itself, trapping all its participants in a war they could not afford to lose and were unable to win quickly.

Proposition 3. The presidents and most of their lieutenants were not deluded by reports of progress and did not proceed on the basis of optimism about winning a near-term or even longer-term military victory. A feeling of pessimism characterized most of these men most of the time. Occasional optimism or flushes of hope that took temporary precedence over actual analysis only punctuated the general atmosphere of resignation. Policymakers recognized that the steps they were taking were inadequate to win the war and that unless Hanoi relented they would have to do more and more. In effect they chose a course of action that promised stalemate, not victory or peace. The presidents, at times, sought to escape the stalemated war through a negotiated settlement but without fully realizing (though realizing more than most of their critics) that a civil war cannot be ended by political compromise. Their strategy was to persevere in the hope that their will to continue—if not the practical effects of their actions—would cause the Communists to relent.

CHAPTER TWO

Recurrent Patterns and Dilemmas from Roosevelt to Eisenhower

The Vietnam War was a secret hot potato in the United States for twenty years (1945–65), passed on quietly but pointedly from administration to administration. To many it appeared that the potato could be juggled by each President and tossed to the next with little danger of anyone getting burned. Not until the escalation of 1965 when the war exploded into living rooms and headlines did many outside the inner circle perceive it as a central issue, something that could not be left to simmer. But a succession of presidents of the United States had known this all along. No sooner did they assume the burdens of office than they were confronted with the "Indochina problem."

"Hot Potato" Briefings

On his first full day in office President Harry Truman asked the State Department for a paper on the "principal problems" of world diplomacy. That same day, he received a memo covering U.S. relations with the United Kingdom and the Soviet Union and the issues of the postwar status of Eastern Europe and a war settlement with Germany. The second item on the memo dealing with France read as follows:

The best interests of the United States require that every effort be made by this Government to assist France, morally as well as physically, to regain her strength and her influence.

It is recognized that the French Provisional Government and the French people are at present unduly preoccupied, as a result of the military defeat of 1940 and the subsequent occupation of their country by the enemy, with

27

questions of national prestige. They have consequently from time to time put forward requests which are out of all proportion to their present strength and have in certain cases, notably in connection with Indochina, showed unreasonable suspicions of American aims and motives. It is believed that it is in the interest of the United States to take full account of this psychological factor in the French mind and to treat France in all respects on the basis of her potential power and influence rather than on the basis of her present strength.[1]

On November 18, 1952, President-elect Dwight D. Eisenhower was invited to the White House to hear a briefing from Secretary of State Dean Acheson on *only* the most important international problems. These problems included Korea, the oil situation in Iran, French-German complications in the North Atlantic Treaty Organization (NATO), and Indochina. During the Indochina briefing, Acheson reported:

We had been concerned for a long time about the course of action in Indo-China. There was a strong body of opinion in France which regarded this as a lost cause that was bleeding France both financially and by undermining the possibility of French-German equality in European defense.

There had been a noticeable lack of French aggressive attitude from a military point of view in Indo-China. The central problem in Indo-China was the fence-sitting by the Population. They would never come down on one side or another until they had a reasonable assurance of who would be the victor and that their interests would be served by the victor.

We are helping France to the extent of carrying between one-third and one-half of the financial burden of the Indo-Chinese war. We have had military discussions between the five powers—the United States, the United Kingdom, France, Australia and New Zealand—which had not been effective in devising agreed military solutions against the contingency of overt Chinese intervention in Indo-China. The French now sought political discussions to carry the matter forward.

This is an urgent matter upon which the new administration must be prepared to act.[2]

On January 19, 1961, the day before President-elect John F. Kennedy's inauguration, Eisenhower set up a briefing for Kennedy and his team. According to Clark Clifford, "the deteriorating situation in Southeast Asia" was the first item on the agenda. Berlin, Cuba, and strategic nuclear arms followed. The outgoing President himself led off with Laos, which he said was "the key to the entire area of Southeast Asia." Clifford's account of President Eisenhower's statements is thus far undisputed.

1. Harry S. Truman, *Memoirs*, vol. 1: *Year of Decision* (Doubleday, 1955), pp. 14–15.

2. Ibid., vol. 2: *Years of Trial and Hope* (Doubleday, 1956), p. 519.

He said that if we permitted Laos to fall, then we would have to write off all of the area. He stated that we must not permit a Communist take-over. He reiterated that we should make every effort to persuade member nations of SEATO [Southeast Asia Treaty Organization] or the International Control Commission to accept the burden with us to defend the freedom of Laos.

As he concluded these remarks, President Eisenhower stated that it was imperative that Laos be defended. He said that the United States should accept this task with our allies, if we could persuade them, and alone if we could not. He added, "Our unilateral intervention would be our last desperate hope in the event we were unable to prevail upon the other signatories to join us."[3]

Eisenhower, however, did not mention Vietnam.

On November 23, the day after President Kennedy's assassination, President Lyndon B. Johnson listened to a worldwide intelligence briefing. He later wrote that "the international front was about as peaceful as it ever gets in these turbulent times," and that "only South Vietnam" had given him "real cause for concern." (Although it was not a central problem in the first days of the administration, Johnson devoted an increasing amount of attention to it.) "Lodge was optimistic," arguing that the new Saigon government "was an improvement" over that of the recently assassinated Ngo Dinh Diem and his brother Ngo Dinh Nhu. John McCone, the director of central intelligence, "was much less encouraging," arguing that Vietcong attacks were being stepped up and that political "difficulties" lay down the road. Secretary of State Dean Rusk and Defense Secretary Robert McNamara "expressed some reservations," but "reaffirmed the estimate that we could begin withdrawing some of our military advisers by the end of the year and a majority of them by the end of 1965." All the advisers, Johnson concluded, agreed on the necessity of "continuity of policy." On November 27, before a joint session of Congress, the President declared: "We will keep our commitments from South Vietnam to West Berlin."[4]

By means of these White House briefings, each new President was being let in on the secret and told where the problem stood for him. For Truman, Indochina was to be a one-finger exercise of dealing with French sensibilities, a colonial problem—at least until the fall of China and the Korean War. For Eisenhower, the issue was not how to ease the

3. Clark M. Clifford, "A Viet Nam Reappraisal," *Foreign Affairs*, vol. 47 (July 1969), p. 604.

4. The quotations in this paragraph are from Lyndon Baines Johnson, *The Vantage Point: Perspectives of the Presidency, 1963–1969* (Holt, Rinehart and Winston, 1971), pp. 22, 43–46.

French out of a troublesome colonial holding but how to keep them in
Indochina fighting against communism and how to organize a counter-
interventional alliance in the event of Chinese intervention—at least
until France departed from Indochina after the Geneva Conference of
1954. For Kennedy, Indochina was portrayed as a Communist watershed test of the American resolve, a place where the United States might
have to go it alone. For Johnson, other world problems had subsided,
Indochina had narrowed to Vietnam, and American involvement was a
prominent and unrelenting public matter.

The "Asian Berlin"

All these briefings at the moment of change of power, except for the
last, would have come as a surprise to everyone but a few dozen
Washington insiders. It was not that Southeast Asia or Indochina or
Vietnam were unknown to the American public. Quite the contrary;
there had been a steady stream of newspaper and magazine stories right
along. The surprise would have been over the persistent prominence of
the matter. While few of the general public focused on the steady
stream of stories, Indochina was always at or near the top of the White
House list of international problems, keeping company with such head-
line-grabbing issues as Soviet affairs, China policy, missiles, and Berlin.
Indochina was where the fighting was year after year. Sometimes quiet
or near collapse or near a peaceful settlement or near a great power
confrontation, it was there and in trouble. For twenty years, Indochina
had been the Asian Berlin.

Most American leaders came to think about South Vietnam the same
way they had thought of West Berlin, even explicitly. Both problems
seemingly took root in the ashes of World War II when the exigencies of
maintaining Big Power harmony held precedence over considerations
of the immediate fate of any particular country. Thus Germany and
Berlin were divided to stay on friendly terms with Russia, and Vietnam
was divided between Nationalist China and Great Britain. Arrange-
ments in both countries were thought to be temporary. The occupying
powers were to facilitate enemy surrender in their zones, then remove
themselves after a political settlement. But the settlements never materialized. Moscow and Washington installed their own regimes in
Germany. Chiang Kai-shek allowed the Vietminh, known to be nation-

alistic and Communist-led, to establish themselves in northern Vietnam (although he supported Kuomintang-oriented nationalists), while the British facilitated the French return to southern Vietnam. In both nations the antagonistic regimes emerged as defenders of the faith in a continuing confrontation between East and West. As such, they were each in a position to make endless claims against their sponsors, and each was a constant testing ground of Big Power resolve. In this way West Berlin and South Vietnam were accorded an importance far transcending local circumstances. Each in a sense was deemed to be the pivot of the other and a source of pressure on the United States. West Berlin, to be sure, was for twenty years the more glamorous and vital of the two—always in the news, always the publicly prominent bastion, but South Vietnam eventually caught up. Kennedy linked them rhetorically on many occasions, for example, twice in his State of the Union Address on January 14, 1963.

The parallelism between West Berlin and South Vietnam should not be carried too far. U.S. leaders recognized key differences. In fact, the differences provide the key to why Vietnam and not Berlin eventually dragged the United States into war. While both had roots in the cold war, Vietnam's also went deep into a colonial past. Conventional and nuclear deterrence governed the outcome in Berlin; in Vietnam the internal dynamics of revolution were more salient. West Berlin's prominence as a cold war sore thumb left no doubt about the American commitment, at least after 1948, whereas South Vietnam's relative obscurity was bound to leave open some questions about Washington's ultimate intent. Finally, in West Berlin, Russians and Americans stood nose to nose, while in Vietnam they never had to face each other directly. Thus in Berlin neither side had much leeway. Too much Soviet pressure to gain control of the city or too heavy-handed an American response could rapidly ignite a general war. But in Vietnam both sides, particularly the side that was losing, had room to maneuver, escalate, and even use force. The narrow margin for error in Berlin militated against taking chances; the wide margins in Vietnam allowed for miscalculation.

Putting aside all these differences and similarities, West Berlin and South Vietnam shared one quality that made both the highest affairs of state. They were perceived as at once vital and intractable. The United States could not take action to solve either problem except at unacceptable cost and risk. To make West Berlin truly secure necessitated the reunification of Germany, and the reunification of Germany on terms acceptable to the West meant war with the Soviet Union. But on the other hand, to liquidate the point of vulnerability by abandoning West Berlin to the Russians was seen as inviting the erosion of NATO and eventually bringing on war with the Russians anyway. Similarly, to ensure the safety of South Vietnam required the destruction of the North Vietnamese regime, which in turn made war with China and Russia seem a near certainty. On the other hand, to disengage from South Vietnam was certain to mean its conquest by North Vietnam, which in turn was believed to be the trigger to a general Asian collapse, again leading to war with China and Russia. In the case of both outposts, then, it was thought, or at least said, that there was no way to win and no way to get out without another world war.

The United States paid dearly in different ways to avoid these Hobson's choices. In order to deter a Soviet grab of West Berlin, Washington spent billions of dollars each year after the end of World War II on maintaining hundreds of thousands of U.S. fighting men in Europe and at home for a European contingency. After the 1948 airlift Washington never swerved from brinkmanship in Berlin to reinforce the deterrent effect of the American presence. To prevent Hanoi's victory over Saigon, Washington went to war, paying the costs in lives and domestic upheaval as well as in billions of dollars.

With hindsight, either or both of these policies appear to many to have been miscast or tragically wrong and unnecessary. But hindsight is the gift of time past, and the story of U.S. involvement in Vietnam must also be told as it was seen by the men who acted in what was then the present. Because these men abjured decisive action to win or to get out of Vietnam, they condemned themselves to recycle the past. For the history of U.S. involvement in Vietnam is one of recurrent patterns and dilemmas, of choices American leaders could not make in the pursuit of objectives they could not bring themselves to abandon—men caught in the grip of pressures they had helped to create.

The Roosevelt Administration

As the United States and Japan drifted toward war in the summer of 1941, the problem for President Franklin Delano Roosevelt was how to deter the Japanese from making military thrusts into British and

Dutch possessions in Southeast Asia. Almost a year before, Toyko had pressured Vichy France into granting Japan certain military rights and facilities in Tonkin. And then the Japanese had swooped down to occupy the remainder of French Indochina. President Roosevelt answered by cutting off the vital flow of American oil to Japan. He and Secretary of State Cordell Hull took this drastic action anticipating that it would not quell the Tokyo hawks unless it had public backing in the United States.

Hull instructed Under Secretary of State Sumner Welles to "make clear" in a July 24 press release that "the occupation of Indochina by Japan possibly means one further important step to seizing control of the South Sea area, including trade routes of supreme importance to the United States controlling such products as rubber, tin and other commodities." He stressed that this was "of vital concern to the United States" and that failure to "bring out this point" would leave Americans with no understanding of "the significance of this movement into Indochina."[5] These same problems concerned FDR later that August. He was quite explicit about them to Sumner Welles.

He [FDR] did . . . make it very plain to me that he thought the immediate danger was an attack by Japan upon some British possession in the Far East, or even more probably upon the Netherlands East Indies. What worried him deeply was that, though this would immediately threaten our own vital interests, it might be impossible to persuade either the Congress or the American people that it was tantamount to an attack upon our own frontiers and justified military measures of self-defense.[6]

Roosevelt and Hull correctly saw the remoteness of Indochina from the American experience. Accordingly the executive branch leaders advanced a rationale, resting on access to natural resources, for the importance of Southeast Asia to U.S. national security. In an inversion of Marxist theory, economic interest was used as a cloak for political interest, and seeing the importance of Indochina to the American people evolved into a pattern for future American presidents.

Indochina's remoteness was to plague the policymakers themselves. In their minds Vietnam cum Indochina was a geographical abstraction.

5. "Memorandum by Mr. Cecil W. Gray, Assistant to the Secretary of State," July 24, 1941, in *Foreign Relations of the United States: Diplomatic Papers, 1941*, vol. 4: *The Far East* (Government Printing Office, 1956), p. 341. See also *The Memoirs of Cordell Hull* (MacMillan, 1948), vol. 2, pp. 1013–14.

6. Sumner Welles, *Seven Decisions that Shaped History* (Harper, 1951), p. 89. This conversation took place in early August 1941, just before the Atlantic Charter meeting.

This was not surprising, since little was known in Washington about the colonies of the Western European powers. Indochina was just another colony—perhaps somewhat less than that because U.S. trade and cultural relations with it had at best been insignificant. But the consequences of U.S. decisions concerning this geographical abstraction were tragic for the people of Indochina, since what American officials saw when confronted with an issue in this part of the world was not a nation or a culture or a history, but merely a place. To them, the entities of French Indochina—Vietnam, Laos, and Cambodia—were submerged in the whole; there was no life, only landscape. But within that landscape lay a Vietnam peopled with Hoa Hao, Cao Dai, Catholics, Buddhists, Montagnards, Francophiles, Francophobes, peasants, and aristocrats intermixed in the historically distinct divisions of Tonkin in the north, Annam in the center, and Cochin China in the south. Unfortunately the mental picture of landscape, not life, dominated and distorted U.S. policy in Vietnam from President Roosevelt to President Nixon.

Most important, Indochina remained little more than a geographical abstraction to President Roosevelt himself. Returning from the Yalta Conference in 1945, he related the following remarkable exchange with Chiang Kai-shek: "The first thing I asked Chiang was, 'Do you want Indo-China?' He said, 'It's no help to us. We don't want it. They are not Chinese.' " [7]

What FDR was really doing about Indochina was a matter of controversy in 1945 and remains so now. To most observers, because of his death an opportunity was irretrievably lost to have changed history, to have prevented the French return to Indochina, or at least to have paved the way for independence, thereby sparing all the agony of more than a quarter-century of war. To others, his death changed little, for they believe he had already surrendered the principle of anticolonialism to the expedience of alliance politics and the vagaries of his own bureaucracy.

The Question of Trusteeship

There can be no doubt about Roosevelt's anticolonial and anti-French sentiments, particularly with respect to Indochina. In his way

7. Samuel I. Rosenman, ed., *The Public Papers and Addresses of Franklin D. Roosevelt: Victory and the Threshold of Peace, 1944–45* (Harper, 1950), p. 562. Henry Wallace also related that he personally carried this offer to Chiang. See Henry A. Wallace, *Toward World Peace* (Reynal and Hitchcock, 1948), p. 97.

he maneuvered for an international trusteeship. But at Yalta in February 1945 Roosevelt accepted a trusteeship formula that could only be interpreted as leaving the fate of Indochina solely in French hands. Under this formula, Indochina could become a trusteeship only at the voluntary behest of France itself. Such a prospect had to be inconceivable to the Yalta participants.

Roosevelt compromised the principle of an international trusteeship under heavy pressure. De Gaulle was making promises of a better deal for the people of Indochina. Churchill, fearing the repercussion of a trusteeship on the British Empire, was vigorously protesting against any such idea. The leaders of the President's own bureaucracy were opposing him: the State Department, which favored both the return of the French to Indochina and eventual independence for the colonies;[8] and the War and Navy departments, which were concerned lest the principle of international trusteeship be so broad as to jeopardize eventual American possession of certain Japanese islands for future U.S. security purposes.[9]

While the President could not prevail over the objections of his allies and his bureaucracy in an explicit debate about the principle of international trusteeship, he could attempt a fait accompli by shifting the debate to one over military priorities. To this end Roosevelt used his military powers to restrict aid to French forces fighting in Indochina and to reject requests to transport French troops to Indochina. He could strengthen his position by arguing that anything more than a marginal allied effort in Indochina would detract from the main effort against Japan. Without allied support, French colonial authority was being supplanted by the Japanese, and de facto authority in the recesses of the country was being supplanted by the Vietminh.

In March 1945 during a discussion with Charles Taussig, adviser on Carribbean affairs, FDR shifted his position again. "If we can get the proper pledge from France to assume for herself the obligations of

8. Secretary of State Hull argued: "If France were prepared to restore her own popular institutions and to deal properly with the colonies, I favored the return of Indo-China, with France's pledge of eventual independence as soon as the colony became qualified for it, along the lines of our pledge to the Philippines." *Memoirs of Cordell Hull*, p. 1598.

9. See Henry L. Stimson and McGeorge Bundy, *On Active Service in Peace and War* (Harper, 1947), pp. 599–602; and Ruth B. Russell, assisted by Jeannette E. Muther, *A History of the United Nations Charter: The Role of the United States, 1940–1945* (Brookings Institution, 1958), pp. 343–44, 347.

a trustee, then I would agree to France retaining these colonies . . . with
the proviso that independence was the ultimate goal." Asked if he
would settle for self-government or dominion status, FDR said, "No—
it must be independence . . . that is to be the policy and you can quote
me in the State Department."[10]

President Roosevelt was trying to run down the middle between the
principle of anticolonialism and the pressures of alliance politics. He
would not choose principle, for that would alienate France and Great
Britain, the powers he counted on to rebuild the postwar world. He
would not endorse colonialism, for that meant abandoning a principle
that he considered a precondition for a better world. He sought to resolve this dilemma by proposing a French trusteeship, but the odds
were against this working. And of course in the midst of the complex
pressures of a world war, FDR was not always consciously calculating
or worrying about these trade-offs; Indochina was a peripheral concern
that he considered only sporadically and superficially.

Buying time and playing a longshot—that was what Roosevelt was
doing. Yalta, in effect, guaranteed France the right to hold Indochina
as a colony, and there could be no doubt that de Gaulle would assert
that right. At some point the French would return in force—unless decisive action were taken to keep them out, and that Roosevelt would
not do.

The Truman Administration

President Truman, largely guided by the compromise policy agreed
to within the State Department, persisted in the middle course of neither
opposing nor assisting the reestablishment of French control. In the
fall of 1945 the French returned only to find that Ho Chi Minh, the
leader of the Vietminh, had established the Democratic Republic of
Vietnam (DRV) with himself as President. This regime was well
ensconced in Tonkin and somewhat less so in Cochin China. A period of
negotiations between Ho and the French ensued until December 1946
when fighting broke out. In a matter of months the French plucked the
former Emperor Bao Dai of Vietnam from retirement in Hong Kong to
head a rival regime. All the while, the United States was declaring a

10. Quoted in Edward R. Drachman, *United States Policy Toward Vietnam,
1940–1945* (Fairleigh Dickinson University Press, 1970), pp. 54–55.

hands-off policy toward nationalist-Communist disputes. (In 1945, as World War II drew to a close, units of the Office of Strategic Services (OSS) had been in contact with Ho Chi Minh. OSS officers, in fact, accompanied the Vietminh on their march to Hanoi at the end of the war. Some of the Americans involved in these contacts were impressed with Ho and regarded his movement as worthy of support. In later years they seemed to consider this period a lost opportunity to generate cooperation between the United States and the Vietminh.)[11] The scene was remarkably similar to that in China at the same time—a tenuous truce between weak conservative nationalists and dynamic Communist nationalists, with the United States first seeking a compromise and ultimately siding with the non-Communists.

Patterns for Continued Conflict

Over the next two years a series of interlocking political patterns took root in Vietnam and between the Vietnamese and the French. These patterns diminished the possibilities for everything except continuing conflict. In slightly modified form they persisted beyond the French departure from Indochina in 1955 into the period of direct American involvement, or the second Indochina war.

First, there was the pattern of the French avoiding negotiations with the DRV. By failing in 1946 to agree on the relatively modest DRV demands for independence within the French Union, by establishing Cochin China as a separate state, and by seeking to deal with the DRV as only one of several representatives of the Vietnamese people, the French made serious negotiations with the DRV less and less likely. After mid-1946, the French would talk only with non-DRV representatives, even though the war was between them and the DRV. Constant war became inevitable as long as the French could not force a DRV surrender, and surrender was highly implausible because of a second pattern.

The second pattern developed because France was not simply fighting a DRV army but a movement that gained its real strength from its stronger claim of principle and nationalist legitimacy, and beyond that, from its ability to organize and motivate people. The modern military power of the French forces turned out to be of little avail in this guerrilla war fought, not by armies, but by small units. In this political struggle,

11. See R. Harris Smith, *OSS: The Secret History of America's First Central Intelligence Agency* (University of California Press, 1972), chap. 10.

it was the DRV leaders who stood fast against compromising Vietnamese independence; to a plurality of the Vietnamese, it seemed that only the DRV stood up unequivocally to the hated foreigners. And when compared with the French-puppet competition or the centrifugal and fractionated alternative centers of loyalty, such as the Hoa Hao or Cao Dai sects, the DRV grip on legitimacy and principle could only gain in luster.[12] Only the Communists' disciplined and centralized brand of nationalism could effectively transcend the diversity of Vietnamese society.

The Vietnamese competitors of the DRV suffered from a third pattern: the French would talk only to the weak and the weak could only compound their weakness by associating with the French. To bargain with the French was to make concessions, and to make concessions was to be discredited in the eyes of the Vietnamese. Bao Dai was discredited in this way. Perhaps the Bao Dai solution would have been tenable (that is, he would have had a political following in the country) if the French had been willing to make genuine concessions, but the French would not have launched Bao Dai in the first place if they had believed he would have compromised their dominion. Even if the French had granted independence to Bao Dai, however, the war would have persisted. The Vietminh were sufficiently strong to see to that.

Those Vietnamese who both refused to bargain with France and opposed the DRV suffered from a fourth pattern, that of being alternatives without a following. There were individuals who hoped to find a middle way. But the problem was precisely that they were only individuals, with weak particularistic constituencies and lacking firm support from large, reliable, and nationwide groups in the country. These individuals therefore were compelled to become fence sitters (*attentistes*) or to create their own support, which in turn meant courting the Army, the outsiders, or the religious sects. But the Army at this time was French-controlled, and the prospect of finding non-French outsiders who would help were slim. The United States was an "outside" possibility but not a very good one during the period. This left the religious sects and gangsters such as the Mafia-like Binh Xuyen. The sects and the gangsters were numerous, not without influence, and independent, but they were localized and not given to mutual coopera-

12. For a discussion of the concept of nationalist legitimacy in Vietnamese society, see John T. McAlister, Jr., and Paul Mus, *The Vietnamese and Their Revolution* (Harper Torchbooks, 1970), pp. 62–69.

tion. Under good circumstances, they would be difficult to mold into a constant base of political support. The odds were sharply against a non-Communist solution for all Vietnam.

But Vietnam had only a brief modern history as one country, and this allowed for a fifth pattern: the differences between northern Vietnam (Tonkin and most of Annam) and Cochin China and southern Annam. Originally the Vietnamese had lived only in the Red River Delta of Tonkin. After kicking out their Chinese rulers in the tenth century, the Vietnamese began their *nam tien,* or march to the South, finally occupying the area within Vietnam's present boundaries in the seventeenth century. The North had more of a Chinese cultural orientation, while the South had been subjected more to Khmer and Hindu influences. In the North the climate was harsher and the economy was primarily industrial, while the South was a rich rice basket. French colonial rule was always more intrusive in the South, where rice as well as rubber resources were exploited, than in the North. The Vietminh had been stronger in the North, and the DRV had had the opportunity to actually govern there for over a year. Vietminh rule in Cochin China ended soon after the British arrived to accept Japan's surrender. The sects were always stronger in the South. For these reasons the war was always to have a different flavor and a different course in the South.

Middle-Ground Policies and Growing Involvement

High-level officials back in Washington paid scant attention to these unfolding patterns. As the cold war bubbled up, Indochina was not on the roster of first-order crises. Events in Vietnam were being drowned out by a general foreign policy debate about U.S. policy toward Soviet communism; the beginning of the Marshall Plan and NATO; and the crises in Iran in 1946, Greece and Turkey in 1947, Czechoslavakia in 1948, and Palestine, China, and Berlin from 1947 to 1950. With occasional policy guidance from Secretary of State George C. Marshall and his successor Dean Acheson, American actions in the 1946–50 period were determined in the State Department by mid-level officials. But the department itself was torn between the Europeanists, devoted to France as a bulwark of stability in the New Europe and frightened by the electoral strength of the French Communist party, and the Asian specialists, who pleaded for the United States to swim with the anticolonialist tide and compromise with the forces of nationalism, whoever they might be. It was a split between those who saw France as a center-

piece in halting the advance of Soviet communism in Europe and those
who saw France as an obstacle to peace in an Asia that would have to
come to terms with an uncertain brand of communism—not unambigu-
ously Soviet, Chinese, or Titoist—but a nationalist communism nevertheless.

The compromise policy that evolved was more evenhanded than
hands-off. If anything, it was weighted slightly against declared French
interests on two grounds: in the long run, colonialism could not work,
and in the short run, French efforts in Indochina diverted resources
from French reconstruction at home. The lines of policy, then, ran in
somewhat crisscross patterns. Washington would continue to state its
general opposition to colonialism but would make no specific public
reference to French colonialism in Indochina. Washington would provide massive aid to metropolitan France but would make it clear that
this aid should not be used in Indochina. Washington would urge France
to settle differences with the Vietminh but would apply no pressure on
Paris to deliver. Finally, Washington, while staunchly anti-Communist
in public statements, would not slam the door on a settlement with the
Vietminh as late as the end of 1949, and neither would it endorse the
French–Bao Dai solution. This was before the Korean War reversed
Washington's plans for a limited defense perimeter in the Far East.
The State Department's ideal solution at this time was to promote a
non-Vietminh nationalist government that would voluntarily accept a
place within the French Union.[13]

The middle-ground position of letting the French and the Vietminh
work it out for themselves was bound to erode. With French intransi-
gence increasing, the battle in Vietnam building, and the pressures of
the cold war taking hold of the American political and strategic imagi-
nation, time was running out on the evenhanded approach. The tip-off
came in March 1949 when France signed the Elysée Agreements giving
nominal independence to Vietnam under the Bao Dai regime.[14] The
State Department informed its consul in Saigon on May 10 that the
United States desired the "Bao Dai experiment" to succeed, since there

13. See *The Pentagon Papers: The Defense Department History of United States
Decisionmaking on Vietnam*, Senator Gravel ed. (Beacon Press, 1971), vol. 1, pp.
31–32; and R. E. M. Irving, *The First Indochina War: French and American Policy,
1945–54* (London: Croom Helm, 1975), chaps. 1–6.

14. The agreements represented the culmination of negotiations between President Vincent Auriol of France and Bao Dai in the Elysée Palace on March 8, 1949.

apparently was no alternative.[15] In September the U.S. ambassador informed Paris that American aid for France in Indochina would be considered if "real progress" were made in reaching a "non-Communist solution . . . based on [the] cooperation of true nationalists" in Indochina.[16]

At this point all prior doubts within the State Department that Ho was a tool of the Kremlin withered away.[17] In the summer of 1949 a National Security Council (NSC) study reported: "It is now clear that southeast Asia is the target of a coordinated offensive directed by the Kremlin. . . . The extension of communist authority in China represents a grievous political defeat for us; if southeast Asia also is swept by communism we shall have suffered a major political rout the repercussions of which will be felt throughout the rest of the world, especially in the Middle East and in a then critically exposed Australia."[18] The blatant inconsistency between this analysis and previous analyses can only be explained by the impact that the fall of China to communism had on the American political and bureaucratic leadership.

By the summer of 1949 the Truman administration had become axiomatically anti-Communist, and the new middle position had to take this into account. Ho was ruled out as unacceptable, Bao Dai was ruled in as necessary, and the French were to be given direct support for the war. The State Department specialists saw the problems in this course but felt compelled to do something to stop the advance of communism. "Something," however, was not everything. The domestic repercussions and the perceived strategic implications of China's fall ensured that the United States would be *anti-Communist* in Vietnam; it did not compel President Truman to ensure a *non-Communist* Vietnam. Being anti-Communist meant that President Truman had to act—to declare himself against Ho and for the French. It also required aid to the French. Ensuring a non-Communist Vietnam meant doing everything the United

15. See *Pentagon Papers*, vol. 1, p. 33.

16. Ibid.

17. For example, a State Department cable to the U.S. ambassador in China in July 1948 had stated: "[Department] has no evidence of direct link between Ho and Moscow but assumes it exists, nor is it able to evaluate amount pressure or guidance Moscow exerting. We have impression Ho must be given or is retaining large degree latitude" (ibid., p. 34). See also the results of a survey conducted by the Office of Intelligence Research in the State Department in the fall of 1948 (ibid., p. 34).

18. Ibid., pp. 37–38.

States could do to prevent a Communist takeover in Vietnam. It required total U.S. commitment. At this stage the President maintained a sharp dividing line between helping the French substantially but indirectly and any direct U.S. commitment on military involvement. This distinction was dramatically underlined by Secretary Acheson's famous "perimeter" speech of early January 1950, in which he stated by omission that the United States would not ensure the security of either Korea or Indochina.[19]

But even this new consensus policy of being anti-Vietminh but not quite pro-French was destined for early oblivion. Writing at a later date, Dean Acheson explained the dilemma:

As we saw our role in Southeast Asia, it was to help toward solving the colonial-nationalist conflict in a way that would satisfy nationalist aims and minimize the strain on our Western European allies. This meant supporting the French "presence" in the area as a guide and help to the three states in moving toward genuine independence within (for the present, at least) the French Union. It was not an easy or a popular role. The French balked, with all the stubbornness that I was later to know so well, at moving swiftly where they could move, in transferring authority over internal affairs; and the Vietnamese pushed for control where they were least able to exercise it, in the conduct of their foreign relations. The Southeast Asian Office of the State Department doubted whether the Elysée Agreements would work as written; the Western European Office doubted that there was any chance that pressure would induce the French leaders to move further, and thought that it would only stiffen and antagonize them. The result was a decision to work with the British in getting Indian and Philippine help to push both French and Vietnamese toward further realistic steps.[20]

The United States never got around to pushing the French.

In early January 1950 Communist China and the Soviet Union granted recognition to the DRV. In the first American public statement linking Ho with international communism, Acheson announced that these acts of recognition "should remove any illusions as to the 'nationalist' nature of Ho Chi Minh's aims and reveals Ho in his true colors as the mortal enemy of native independence in Indochina."[21] On February

---

19. "Crisis in Asia—An Examination of U.S. Policy," Remarks by Secretary Acheson before the National Press Club, Washington, D.C., January 12, 1950, *Department of State Bulletin*, vol. 22 (January 23, 1950), pp. 115–16.

20. Dean Acheson, *Present at the Creation: My Years in the State Department* (Norton, 1969), pp. 671–72.

21. "Kremlin Recognizes Communist Movement in Indonesia," Statement by Secretary Acheson, February 1, 1950, *Department of State Bulletin*, vol. 22 (February 13, 1950), p. 244.

7 the United States announced its recognition of Vietnam, the Kingdom of Cambodia, and the Kingdom of Laos as independent states within the French Union. Negotiations immediately got under way between Paris and Washington for American aid, and in May a full-scale U.S. aid program was announced.

By these acts the U.S. leadership created a problem that was to haunt successor administrations. By blessing the French solution to the Indochina situation and by publicly linking Ho to the Kremlin, the United States had cashiered whatever opportunity it had for pressuring Paris into granting genuine Vietnamese independence. The French had been unsuccessfully pushing the anti-Communist crusade in Indochina on Washington for a long time. They could probably see that entangling the U.S. stake in a resuscitated France with the Indochina and anticommunism issues would put Washington in a bind. Anticommunism would make Indochina an American as well as a French struggle, forcing Washington to open its aid coffers virtually without limit. But as American aid and involvement increased, American leverage decreased. The French tail could wag the American dog. This problem in turn gave rise to a second: as U.S. leverage shrank, so too did the chance of inducing Paris to make the necessary reforms and compromises in Vietnam, and the more likely it became for the whole Vietnam enterprise to end in failure.

That the United States was trapping itself did not go unnoticed. Acheson repeatedly alluded to the double bind. In April 1950 the Joint Chiefs of Staff (JCS) recommended that "military aid not be granted unconditionally; rather that it be carefully controlled and . . . integrated with political and economic programs."[22] Edmund Gullion, then the American chargé d'affaires in Vietnam, said: "We obviously felt it [trying to achieve independence] was going to be a continuing process, and we hoped to be able to have some influence over it. But then we got involved in Korea, and since the French were in trouble in Indochina, we pulled our punches."[23]

In the space of four years U.S. policy toward the French effort went from hands-off to evenhanded to the laying on of hands. Yet by mutual agreement, the roles of France and the United States were made clearly distinct. The United States would provide the aid to prevent a Com-

22. *Pentagon Papers*, vol. 1, p. 66.
23. Quoted in Robert Shaplen, *The Lost Revolution: The U.S. in Vietnam, 1946–1966*, rev. ed. (Harper Colophon, 1966), p. 66.

munist takeover in Vietnam, but France still retained primary responsibility. It took the outbreak of the Korean War in June 1950 to fuzz the fast-disappearing limits on the American commitment.

Changing Rhetoric

When President Truman announced the American response in Korea and the extension of U.S. military protection to the Chiang Kai-shek regime on Formosa, he added this about Indochina: "I have similarly directed acceleration in the furnishing of military assistance to the forces of France and the Associated States in Indochina and the dispatch of a military mission to provide close working relations with those forces."[24] Publicly, U.S. official rhetoric on Indochina began to change, to escalate, and to suggest that Indochina was another potential Korea. The rhetoric took three new forms.

First, Indochina came to be seen as the cornerstone of Southeast Asian security. For example, a joint press release by the State Department and the Defense Department on September 23, 1951, stated that the participants of discussions between the French commander in chief and American officials "were in complete agreement that the successful defense of Indochina is of great importance to the defense of all Southeast Asia."[25]

Second, the rhetoric now depicted Southeast Asian security as vital to world peace and security because of the conviction that the advance of communism in this area was part of the Kremlin's plan for worldwide domination. In May 1951 President Truman spoke about the "Soviet design of world conquest" that "threatens to absorb the manpower and the vital resources of the East," and said that "the continued independence of these nations [Indochina, Burma, and the Philippines] is vital to the future of the free world."[26] And again on March 6, 1952, Truman declared:

Much of Asia at this moment is under communist attack. The free nations are holding the line against aggression in Korea and Indo-China, and are battling communist-inspired disorders in Burma, Malaya and the Philippines.

24. "U.S. Air and Sea Forces Ordered into Supporting Action," Statement by President Truman, *Department of State Bulletin*, vol. 23 (July 3, 1950), p. 5.

25. "Military Aid Program for Indochina Reexamined," ibid., vol. 25 (October 8, 1951), p. 570.

26. "Special Message to the Congress on the Mutual Security Program, May 24, 1951," *Public Papers of the Presidents of the United States: Harry S. Truman, 1951* (GPO, 1965), p. 309.

The loss of any of these countries would mean the loss of freedom for millions of people, the loss of vital raw materials, the loss of points of critical strategic importance to the free world.[27]

In addition to issuing such warnings, U.S. officials engineered a NATO resolution supporting French efforts in Indochina, which was no longer simply the scene of a backwater colonial war. It was now linked with the rest of the Free World in strategic importance to the United States.

The third and perhaps most significant change in public statements was that U.S. leaders no longer referred to Indochina as a French responsibility or even as primarily a French responsibility but only to the "primary role" of the French in Indochina. Indochina's security was now a Free World responsibility, meaning a U.S. obligation. France, in this view, had become a surrogate for the United States. Secretary Acheson, for one at least, was not unaware of this. In *Present at the Creation* he told of receiving a "perceptive warning" in the fall of 1950 from John Ohly, a State Department official, that the United States was "moving into a position in Indochina in which 'our responsibilities tend to supplant rather than complement those of the French.' We could, [Ohly] added, become a scapegoat for the French and be sucked into direct intervention. 'These situations have a way of snowballing,' he concluded." Acheson's response to this advice was revealing: "I decided, however, that having put our hand to the plough, we would not look back."[28]

From Korea on, the Truman administration was letting the public know officially what had been rumored in the press for over a year, namely, that U.S. security was vitally linked with the fate of Indochina. This had been the somewhat tentative position of the National Security Council since late 1949. But the public statement had the effect of reinforcing and sanctifying the private bureaucratic judgments. Thus by June 25, 1952, with the internal circulation of NSC 124/2, the U.S. objective had become "to prevent the countries of Southeast Asia from passing into the communist orbit." Moreover, the document stated that the United States should "continue to assure the French that the U.S. regards the French effort in Indochina as one of great strategic importance in the general international interest rather than in the purely

27. "Special Message to the Congress on the Mutual Security Program, March 6, 1952," ibid., *1952–53* (GPO, 1966), p. 186.
28. Acheson, *Present at the Creation*, p. 674.

French interest, and as essential to the security of the free world." It ended with a plan to increase American influence "on the policies and actions of the French and Indochinese authorities."[29]

NSC 124/2 also laid great stress on forming a military coalition to counter the possibility of Chinese intervention. Acheson already had been at work on this. While his conversations with British Foreign Minister Anthony Eden produced little on the joint handling of the China contingency, they were quite revealing on another account. According to Eden, Acheson said the U.S. government "considered that it would be disastrous to the position of the Western powers if South-East Asia were lost without a struggle," but that "on the other hand, the Americans were determined to do nothing in that area which would provoke a third world war."[30]

Aid Grows, Leverage Shrinks

The United States did not have to face this ultimate choice in Indochina and in Vietnam, however. The French were fighting in Vietnam, and the name of the game was to keep them fighting there. American aid to France was the way to meet this objective. Although the aid was never enough to satisfy the French, the amounts were substantial. In fiscal year 1951 economic and technical aid totaled at least $21.8 million, and military aid totaled at least $425.7 million. This amounted to 40 percent of the total cost of the war to France during that year. In fiscal 1952 economic and technical aid increased to $24.6 million, and military aid reached a new high of $520 million. This again constituted about 40 percent of the total cost of the war to the French. By 1953–54 it was 80 percent. Together with the other aid the French were receiving through the Marshall Plan and the Mutual Defense Assistance Plan, France was the single largest recipient of U.S. assistance.[31]

Secretary Acheson in retrospect maintained that despite this aid U.S. government officials generally agreed that "too little seemed to be happening in Vietnam in developing military power and local government responsibility and popular support," and that progress in this

29. *Pentagon Papers*, vol. 1, pp. 385, 387.

30. *Full Circle: The Memoirs of Anthony Eden* (Houghton Mifflin, 1960), p. 92.

31. For data on U.S. aid to France, see Allan B. Cole, ed., *Conflict in Indo-China and International Repercussions: A Documentary History, 1945–1955* (Cornell University Press, 1956), pp. 259–61. See also *Pentagon Papers*, vol. 1, pp. 184, 204.

direction was a prerequisite to winning the war.[32] And indeed it was plain that the United States, while urging reforms, was doing little to encourage them, and that the French still held onto the actual levers of power in Vietnam and refused to grant independence unequivocally.

Notwithstanding his feelings about the need for the French to offer reforms, Acheson believed the United States had no choice but to act as it had. "No one," he wrote later, "seriously advised that, with the Bonn agreements awaiting ratification by the Senate and the French National Assembly and the situation in Indochina in its usual critical state, it would be wise to end, or threaten to end, aid to Indochina unless an American plan of military and political reform was carried out."[33]

Given U.S. goals for a French role in stopping communism in Europe *and* in Indochina, Washington simply had little leverage on French policy, and not just because Paris had Washington over a barrel on German rearmament and the European Defense Community (EDC). These were added factors, but not the key ones. The United States would have supported France in Indochina regardless of these European considerations. French leaders, after all, were fighting a U.S. battle against communism in Indochina as well as fighting their own battle for a world role, for "honor" and domestic power. Given the U.S. desire for the French to continue fighting communism in Indochina, it was actually France that had the leverage, not the United States. Acheson saw this when he wrote that "withholding help to France would, at most, have removed the colonial power. It could not have made the resulting situation a beneficial one either for Indochina or for Southeast Asia, or in the more important effort of furthering the stability and defense of Europe."[34]

Stalemate

All the French efforts and all the American aid were not enough to put Vietnam back together again. In Vietnam there was a military stalemate, which changed in character from time to time. The year 1950 was a Vietminh year; 1951 was a French year. In 1952 the pendulum swung back to the Vietminh. While the French and South Vietnamese possessed numerical superiority, the French generals were always to lament that fewer troops were available to them for offensive action than to

32. Acheson, *Present at the Creation*, p. 675.
33. Ibid., p. 676.
34. Ibid., p. 673.

the Vietminh. By late 1951 the Vietminh, with a sanctuary in China, just about controlled the northern part of North Vietnam and the mountain chain reaching from there to Central Vietnam. They always retained the tactical initiative, the ability to choose when and where to fight.

The stalemate had its effect in France. Political opposition to the war mounted steadily, especially from the Left. But as opposition to the war in Indochina was growing in France, support for the war among the informed American public grew as well. In March 1952 Senator Mike Mansfield observed that it was "high time somebody said a good word for the French government in its efforts in Indochina."[35] On June 11, 1952, the *New York Times* editorialized Indochina as one of the "most crucial problems of the cold war." The French, the editorial went on, were defending an area of great strategic importance to the whole Free World. The *Times* insisted that although the President did not want to send U.S. troops to Indochina, this reluctance somehow had to be reconciled with the American desire to save Southeast Asia from communism.

The Truman Legacy

The Truman administration left a vast legacy for U.S. policy toward Vietnam consisting of the following:

A gap between what officials were telling the American people and what they really knew about the situation in Vietnam. Few official public statements were made about Indochina, but those that were issued referred to progress being made,[36] to the "Communist assault in Indochina [being] checked by the free people of Indochina with the help of the French,"[37] and to how "the French colonial regime [in Vietnam] ended with the signature of the so-called Pau accords on December 16."[38] (These accords followed negotiations in Pau, France, on handing over to the Vietnamese the control of immigration, trade, customs, and finance.) All these statements alluded to progress and never hinted what

35. *New York Times,* March 22, 1952.

36. "Crisis in Asia," p. 118.

37. "Address at a Dinner of the Civil Defense Conference, May 7, 1951," *Public Papers, Truman, 1951,* p. 267.

38. "Indochinese Resistance to Communist Domination," Statement by Donald Heath, Minister to the Associated States of Vietnam, Laos, and Cambodia, *Department of State Bulletin,* vol. 24 (February 12, 1951), p. 262; and *Pentagon Papers,* vol. 1, p. 60.

U.S. officials always believed—that Vietnam was in trouble. They knew the Vietminh had harnessed the forces of nationalism, that Bao Dai was ineffective and without a political following, and that at best the military situation was getting nowhere.

A substantial bureaucratic presence in Vietnam that wanted to improve the lot of the Vietnamese and to reform the Vietnamese army— to do the job of stopping communism. A U.S. military mission had moved in, economic and technical aid teams arrived, CIA operatives materialized, and embassy personnel flowered. American officials in Vietnam contributed little to decisions about Vietnam being made in Washington during this period. But the importance of these officials, their concerns, and the need for Washington to heed their concerns was to grow in the future.

A domestic mode of salesmanship that sought to justify all U.S. efforts abroad in the name of anticommunism. In the early years the leaders of the Truman administration had hoped to use the anti-Communist theme domestically and still be able to conduct a discriminating foreign policy. To a degree and for a time they succeeded, especially with respect to China policy. After the fall of China and the Korean War, however, discrimination became less and less possible, and the need to show consistency—that is, to oppose communism everywhere— became more and more enticing. The deepening U.S. involvement in and commitment to Vietnam stemmed in large part from domestic political pressures for consistency.

Strategic perceptions that the world was filled with dominoes. Given the assumption of a worldwide Communist conspiracy, the domino theory was a forceful and persuasive one. International security seemed fragile and the world full of weak links. The leaders of the Truman administration always hoped to keep the strategic linkage of the world in perspective and to maintain a set of priorities. The Western Hemisphere and Europe would come first; Asia would be a distant second. In an ultimate sense, they did stick to these priorities. The European priority was a key to limiting U.S. involvement in the Korean War. But the allure of seeing little problems as reflections of bigger problems could not be readily controlled. The growing importance of Vietnam derived in large measure from the logic of strategic linkage—to French politics, to China policy, to the Korean War, and to the global deterrence of Communist aggression.

The necessity of preventing a Communist takeover of Vietnam was

an American as well as a French responsibility. Certainly French prestige was more deeply committed than that of the United States, and it
was still a French fight, but U.S. public statements had gone far toward
committing American prestige to Vietnam as well. U.S. leaders did not
and would not contemplate the use of American ground forces in Vietnam, but they did not have to. American aid was sufficient for immediate purposes. President Truman and Secretary Acheson, however, did
contemplate using U.S. air and naval forces in the event of China's
intervention, despite objections from the American military. The point
was that in the last analysis the President was not prepared to lose in
Vietnam without a struggle.

The Eisenhower Administration

Throughout 1953 and the early months of 1954 the Eisenhower administration launched what had all the earmarks of a campaign of selling Indochina to the American public. Eisenhower, Secretary of State
John Foster Dulles, and other administration leaders spoke of the Indochina situation as a "cork in the bottle," as the beginning of a "chain
reaction," and finally in the President's own words at the height of the
Dien Bien Phu crisis, in terms of "falling dominoes."[39] Mirroring their
classified assessments, they publicly explained that Indochina was
Southeast Asia's rice bowl, the possessor of key resources such as rubber,
tin, and tungsten, and that along with Korea, it was a vital "flank" in the
worldwide struggle against communism. With the exception of certain
conservative newspapers, the press wholeheartedly joined in the education process. Although a few senators expressed a certain uneasiness
about the French and another Asian land war, Congress echoed the
administration's judgments.

The administration coupled these judgments with public warnings
to Moscow and Peking to stay out of Indochina. On April 16, 1953,
Eisenhower threatened the Soviet Union with "united action" if it persisted in direct or indirect aggression against Southeast Asia.[40] Then,
on September 2 Dulles dropped the blockbuster:

39. "The President's News Conference of April 7, 1954," *Public Papers of the
Presidents: Dwight D. Eisenhower, 1954* (GPO, 1960), p. 383.
40. "Address 'The Chance for Peace' Delivered before the American Society of
Newspaper Editors, April 16, 1953," ibid., 1953 (GPO, 1960), p. 183.

Communist China has been and now is training, equipping, and supplying the Communist forces in Indochina. There is the risk that, as in Korea, Red China might send its own army into Indochina. The Chinese Communist regime should realize that such a second aggression could not occur without grave consequences which might not be confined to Indochina.[41]

Meanwhile, on July 29, two days after the Korean armistice was signed, President Eisenhower's foreign aid program was promulgated, and it included $400 million for support of the fighting in Indochina. This was followed by an announcement on September 30 that France would receive an additional $385 million by the end of the calendar year for the express purpose of financing the Navarre Plan, which required supplying and equipping additional French and "native" forces.[42]

Administration officials accompanied their public warnings and aid announcements with claims that things were going well and that victory was assured—in contrast to classified assessments. Typical was Dulles's appearance on April 5, 1955, before the House Foreign Affairs Committee during which he took the opportunity to predict that current French efforts would "break the organized body of Communist aggression by the end of the 1955 fighting season and thereby reduce the fighting to guerrilla warfare which could, in 1956, be met for the most part by national forces of the three Associated States."[43] To the contrary, internal reports at the beginning of the year were premised on "continued stalemate" and later on deterioration.[44] Not until February 1954 did Eisenhower come forward with refreshing candor. In response to being

41. "Korean Problems," Address by Secretary Dulles before the American Legion in St. Louis, Mo., September 2, 1953, *Department of State Bulletin,* vol. 29 (September 14, 1953), p. 342.

42. The plan, "Principles for the Conduct of the War in Indochina," was presented to Lieutenant General J. W. O'Daniel, chief of the U.S. Military Mission in Indochina, by Lieutenant General Henri Navarre, the French commander. The Navarre Plan offered a strategy for victory without the direct involvement of U.S. forces. It proposed increasing French forces by 50,000 men, and native troops by 100,000. See *Pentagon Papers,* vol. 1, pp. 86, 410–11; and Melvin Gurtov, *The First Vietnam Crisis: Chinese Communist Strategy and United States Involvement, 1953–1954* (Columbia University Press, 1967), pp. 46–47.

43. " 'Not One of Us Alone': A Mutual Security Program for 1955," Statement by Secretary Dulles before the Foreign Affairs Committee of the House of Representatives, April 15, 1954, *Department of State Bulletin* (April 19, 1954), p. 582.

44. See William C. Foster, deputy secretary of defense, "Memorandum for the Joint Chiefs of Staff," January 19, 1953, *United States–Vietnam Relations, 1945–1967,* Study prepared by the Department of Defense for the House Committee on Armed Services, 92 Cong. 1 sess. (GPO, 1971), bk. 9, vol. 1, pt. V.B.3, p. 4. See also *Pentagon Papers,* vol. 1, pp. 391–92.

asked whether he considered the current situation in Vietnam critical, he answered: "Well, it's been critical for so long that it's difficult to just point out a period when it is more than normally critical. I think this is a fact: all of us have known . . . that the heart and soul of the population finally becomes the biggest factor of success or failure. . . . So, it is critical in the sense that we have had some evidence that there is a lack of enthusiasm we would like to have there."[45] In March Senator Mike Mansfield added: "We continue to receive optimistic reports from the administration about eventual victory in Indochina. I regret to say that reports from practically every other source indicate a stalemate of indefinite duration in that area."[46] This too was to become a recurrent pattern in the war.

During 1953 the French position in Indochina was shaky, with attendant consequences in Paris. On April 12 Vietminh forces invaded Laos— a move they would make again and again when stalled in Vietnam or when preparing a new offensive there. Paris in June found the new government of Joseph Laniel under pressure and vowing to "perfect" Indochina independence and bring peace. Laniel's diplomacy from late 1953 was directed toward convening a conference in Geneva to settle the war at the conference table.

What had been simmering throughout 1953 began to boil in the first months of 1954. In a speech on January 12 laying out the doctrine of massive retaliation and pointedly warning China, Dulles declared: "The way to deter aggression is for the free community to be willing and able to respond vigorously at places and with means of its own choosing."[47] Sketchy news reports over the next few weeks confirmed a sharp increase in the Indochina fighting. At the end of January the President's Special Committee on Indochina decided to augment the U.S. Military Mission in Indochina by 200 men, technicians and airplane mechanics, and to send twenty-two B-26 medium bombers to the French.[48]

This set off a senatorial debate that had a surprisingly critical tone. Eisenhower moved to take the sting out of the debate on February 10: "I say that I cannot conceive of a greater tragedy for America than to

45. "The President's News Conference of February 3, 1954," *Public Papers, Eisenhower, 1954,* pp. 226–27.

46. *Congressional Record,* vol. 100, pt. 3, 83 Cong. 2 sess. (1954), p. 3612.

47. "The Evolution of Foreign Policy," Address by Secretary Dulles before the Council on Foreign Relations, New York, January 12, 1954, *Department of State Bulletin,* vol. 30 (January 25, 1954), p. 108.

48. *Pentagon Papers,* vol. 1, p. 445.

get heavily involved now in an all-out war in any of those regions."[49] At a news conference on March 10, right at the beginning of the Dien Bien Phu siege, the President was asked if there was any danger of U.S. involvement. He answered: "There is going to be no involvement . . . unless it is a result of the constitutional process that is placed upon Congress to declare it."[50]

Dien Bien Phu was pushing the crisis to a denouement. Vietminh General Vo Nguyen Giap halted the drive into Laos. On March 13 he suddenly swung his forces around and began the investment of the fortress at Dien Bien Phu. Although no more than 18,000 French Union forces were defending this garrison, the battle quickly assumed the proportion of a Waterloo.

Mounting Pressures

As the Dien Bien Phu crunch and the Geneva Conference approached, the Eisenhower administration was beset by a number of contradictions and dilemmas, any one of which was sufficient to cause policy to founder.

First was the contradiction of stakes between the United States and France. While Washington was seeking to stop communism, Paris was striving to save the French empire. Put another way, whereas Washington was propping up a domino, Paris was trying to keep its key to the Great Power washroom. The United States viewed Indochina as a general security matter. France saw Indochina as an issue of international prestige. If Indochina went Communist, Washington foresaw the security of the whole Free World coming into jeopardy. If Indochina fell to the Vietminh, France would be finished in Asia and French authority in North Africa would undoubtedly be challenged by North African nationalists taking encouragement from a French colonial defeat. In one sense the potential French loss was more tangible and real than that foreseen by the Americans, but in no sense was it perceived by Frenchmen as a matter of Western survival.

A second contradiction was the clash over priorities between France and the United States. Washington wanted France both to keep fighting in Indochina and to join the EDC, but since France did not have the resources for both enterprises, Washington ran the risk of getting it to do neither. In the eyes of the Laniel government, France could not both

49. *Public Papers, Eisenhower, 1954*, p. 253.
50. Ibid., p. 306.

increase its military and financial efforts in Indochina and participate in the EDC. Even to consider the EDC, France had to have a dominant military position over West Germany, and to the extent that France did more in Indochina, it would have fewer resources on the European continent with which to counterbalance German forces. As Eisenhower asked French Foreign Minister Georges Bidault: "Just what nation does France now regard as a potential enemy, Germany or Russia?"[51] Washington was simply more interested in both the EDC and Indochina than Paris was.

The contradictions in stakes and priorities produced a clutch of dilemmas. First was the continuing dilemma of leverage. Despite French dependency on dollar aid and U.S. military equipment, the United States found itself trapped by its own interests, the lack of perceived alternatives, circumstances, and French promises and maneuvering. If France abandoned the EDC, the alternative would be a long-term massive American military presence in Europe. The French understood this and therefore were not panicked by Dulles's threat to undertake "an agonizing reappraisal" of U.S. interests in Europe.[52] If France stopped carrying the torch in Indochina, the United States might have to pick it up and do battle on its own. Knowing this, the French even threatened Washington with withdrawal if funds were not made available.[53] American priorities and alternatives, then, set overall limits on U.S. leverage. Within these limits, American leverage was further constrained by circumstances. One was that the State Department saw the Laniel government as the last hope of the United States for Indochina and the EDC; the left-of-center government waiting in the wings would be opposed to both. Another constraining circumstance was that while U.S. aid strengthened the hands of those Frenchmen who wanted to continue the war, these same Frenchmen would brook no American interference in the conduct of the war. At several points the French resisted American efforts to play a larger part in training and advising the Vietnamese army.[54]

51. Dwight D. Eisenhower, *The White House Years: Mandate for Change, 1953–1956* (Doubleday, 1963), p. 245.

52. For reference to Dulles's statement, see Robert Endicott Osgood, *NATO: The Entangling Alliance* (University of Chicago Press, 1962), pp. 94–95.

53. See cable, Douglas Dillon to secretary of state, July 29, 1953, *United States–Vietnam Relations*, bk. 9, pt. V.B.3, pp. 107–08.

54. See *Pentagon Papers*, vol. 1, pp. 405–07.

A second dilemma sprang from the independence issue—a particular target for American leverage. On the one hand, if the Laniel government granted independence to the Associated States, French support for continuing the war would be totally undermined; yet on the other hand, if Paris failed to grant independence, French efforts in Indochina would be doomed to failure. Eisenhower and Dulles attached special importance to the independence issue. True independence, in their opinion, would remove the taint of colonialism from the war and give the French some real indigenous nationalist support. The French saw it differently. Premier Laniel insisted that complete independence was impractical, since the Associated States could not defend themselves, and that if they were not a part of the French Union, France would have no obligation to defend them. Yet it was equally obvious that France had little indigenous support and either had to grant unequivocal sovereignty or forfeit any hopes of winning. By March 1954 this dilemma was already a thing of the past; it was too late for France to recoup support lost because numerous Vietnamese had gone over to the Vietminh and other nationalists wanted the French to go home.

Because the hour was late and the situation poor, a third dilemma arose with respect to negotiations. Washington did not want Paris to negotiate until the military situation improved yet anticipated only continued deterioration of this situation. From the Washington vantage point any foreseeable settlement would be tantamount to surrender—whether in the form of a cease-fire, a territorial partition, or a coalition government. All these were judged to lead to a Communist takeover. Washington's aim, therefore, was to try to keep France from the negotiating table. Just holding on seemed the only acceptable alternative, but the status quo, by Washington's own estimation, could not last. The Navarre Plan was not working out. When Bidault insisted on placing Indochina on the agenda of the Geneva Conference, Dulles had no choice but to accede. Since Washington contemplated neither fighting nor switching, negotiations became inevitable.

In late 1953 Eisenhower, in effect, kept putting one basic question to the bureaucracy: Since we all agreed in NSC 5405 of January 16 that we must "prevent the countries of Southeast Asia from passing into the communist orbit," how do we accomplish this in Indochina?[55] Given the agreed upon position that the loss of Indochina would have cata-

55. Ibid., p. 434.

strophic consequences for U.S. security, the answer should have been
that the United States must be prepared to take all action short of nuclear war with the Soviet Union to prevent defeat. But instead the twofold bureaucratic answer was (1) that U.S. military intervention would
be unnecessary if the French would only do what they were told; and
(2) that if China intervened, the United States should bomb China.
And yet, as the State Department and Defense Department knew, these
were not answers at all. It was late in the day militarily to worry about
French political reforms in Indochina, and Chinese intervention was
regarded as likely only in the event of U.S. intervention. But the failure
to answer was an answer in itself. The government was not prepared to
act on the implications of its own words. Another solution would have
to be found. In a speech on March 29 Dulles warned the public about
the Indochina crisis and called for "united action."[56] The United States
would not go it alone, but it was announcing its intention to go it with
others.

Unsuccessful Maneuvers for United Action

At this point, the chronology of events becomes important. The Dien
Bien Phu battle began on March 13, 1954, and the outpost surrendered
on May 8. The Geneva Conference started on April 26 and concluded
on July 21. Between March and July, the maneuvering of the Eisenhower administration can be characterized either as egregious bumbling
saved only by the unwillingness of allies to participate and the restraint
of enemies or as a dazzling display of neutralizing potential domestic
opposition and of deterring hostile states bent on total victory. Whichever it was, it held lessons that were to be remembered by the generation of political leaders to come.

On March 20 French Chief of Staff Paul Ely arrived in Washington.
He wanted a promise of American air support if China intervened by
air at Dien Bien Phu and more U.S. B-26s. He received no answer on
the former and a promise on the latter. But more was in store. Whether
by prearrangement or not, the JCS chairman, Admiral Arthur Radford,
informally proposed a one-time massive U.S. air strike against Vietminh
positions on the perimeter of Dien Bien Phu. As the admiral was later

56. "The Threat of Red Asia," Address by Secretary Dulles before the Overseas
Press Club of America, New York, March 29, 1954, *Department of State Bulletin,*
vol. 30 (April 12, 1954), pp. 539–42.

to admit, his real purpose was to provoke a military reaction from Peking, bringing the United States and China to war before China had a chance to become strong enough to threaten U.S. interests in the future.[57] The idea of such a provocation was not to escape later American leaders.

On April 3 Eisenhower arranged a meeting in the White House for Dulles and Radford to brief congressional leaders. Radford presented his plan. The reaction was predominantly negative. The congressmen asked Radford if any of the other chiefs supported his proposal, and the admiral had to admit that his colleagues did not all agree with him. (According to Chalmers Roberts's famous account, Radford was the only one of the JCS to support the air strike; according to Lieutenant General James Gavin, all supported it except Chief of Staff of the Army Matthew Ridgway.[58] According to later testimony of the JCS themselves, Air Force Chief of Staff Nathan Twining supported Radford, while Chief of Naval Operations Robert Carney and Marine Corps Commandant Lemuel Shepherd reluctantly supported Ridgway.)[59] Ridgway had weighed in hard against intervention. He maintained that victory could not be assured by air and naval power alone, that even using atomic weapons would not reduce requirements for ground forces, and that seven divisions with air support would be needed for victory without Chinese intervention and without French forces, and twelve if China intervened.[60] The legislators told Dulles to go hunting for allies.

Eisenhower accomplished three things by this meeting. First, he isolated Radford, Vice-President Richard Nixon, and other advocates of unilateral intervention. Although some, including the French, continued to push for it in the coming months, this idea was effectively buried. Second, the President co-opted the congressional leadership. In rejecting the go-it-alone approach, they had been cornered, thus achieving Eisenhower's third purpose of building domestic support for multilateral intervention, or united action.

57. Chalmers M. Roberts, *Washington Post*, October 24, 1971.

58. See Chalmers M. Roberts, "The Day We Didn't Go to War," in Marvin E. Gettleman, ed., *Vietnam: History, Documents, and Opinions in a World Crisis* (Fawcett, 1965), pp. 96–104; and James M. Gavin in collaboration with Arthur T. Hadley, *Crisis Now* (Random House, 1968), pp. 41–48.

59. See Richard K. Betts, *Soldiers, Statesmen, and Cold War Crises* (Harvard University Press, 1977), p. 21.

60. See *Pentagon Papers*, vol. 1, pp. 471–72.

The next day Eisenhower set his course. He would intervene with force if Congress approved, and congressional approval would be contingent on the following conditions:

(1) United States intervention must be part of a coalition to include the other free nations of Southeast Asia, the Philippines, and the British Commonwealth.

(2) The French must agree to accelerate their independence program for the Associated States so there could be no interpretation that United States assistance meant support of French colonialism.

(3) The French must agree not to pull their forces out of the war if we put our forces in.[61]

So far as the eye could see, Eisenhower and Dulles set out to deliver on these conditions. Obeying an iron law of politics, Eisenhower was not saying he would intervene or that he would not. He was saying "it depended."

The British held the key, and on April 4 Eisenhower sent a personal message to Prime Minister Winston Churchill. It read in part:

... our painstaking search for a way out of the impasse has reluctantly forced us to the conclusion that there is no negotiated solution of the Indochina problem which in its essence would not be either a face-saving device to cover a French surrender or a face-saving device to cover a Communist retirement. The first alternative is too serious in its broad strategic implications for us and for you to be acceptable....

Somehow we must contrive to bring about the second alternative. ...

If I may refer again to history; we failed to halt Hirohito, Mussolini and Hitler by not acting in unit and in time. That marked the beginning of many years of stark tragedy and desperate peril. May it not be that our nations have learned something from that lesson?[62]

The message could not have been more strongly put. Meantime, the U.S. ambassador in Paris, C. Douglas Dillon, was told by Foreign Minister Bidault that "immediate armed intervention of U.S. carrier aircraft at Dien Bien Phu," based on the Radford-Ely exchanges, was now "necessary to save the situation."[63] Dulles informed French Ambassador Henri Bonnet in Washington on April 5 that American force would have to be a part of a coalition.[64]

On April 6 a few senators held a lively debate. John F. Kennedy said

61. Eisenhower, *Mandate for Change*, p. 347.
62. *Pentagon Papers*, vol. 1, p. 99.
63. Ibid., p. 100; see also pp. 97–98.
64. See Robert F. Randle, *Geneva, 1954: The Settlement of the Indochina War* (Princeton University Press, 1969), p. 114.

"the United States and other nations may properly be called upon to play their fullest part" and called on the French to grant full independence. Everett Dirksen rejoined that if the United States applied too much pressure, the French might dump Indochina in the United Nations' lap. Warren Magnuson agreed. Kennedy responded that Washington should at least support French recognition of future independence. John Stennis supported united action. But the tenor of the speeches was distinct unhappiness about the use of any American troops.[65]

On April 7 the Eisenhower administration started a public campaign that was to last until the end of the month. That day, Eisenhower publicly presented the domino theory, and aid administrator Harold Stassen announced a $3.5 billion aid program, of which the principal item would be $1.13 billion for Indochina. On April 16 Nixon declared: "If to avoid further Communist expansion in Asia and Indochina, we must take the risk now by putting our boys in, I think the Executive has to take the politically unpopular decision and do it."[66] On April 26 the President evoked the "cork in the bottle" image.[67] Dulles tried to calm a Congress awakened by this speech by saying that it was unlikely that U.S. troops would actually have to be sent.

With all this as a backdrop, Dulles had set off to London and Paris to organize immediate united action. The reaction was negative in both capitals. The French were against internationalizing the war. That would take the war out of their hands, and their opposition was to be expected, although after considerable arm-twisting, Bidault told Dulles on April 22 that he now favored coalition action to save Dien Bien Phu.[68] But then came the crusher—on April 27 Churchill told the House of Commons that Britain "was not prepared to give any undertakings about United Kingdom military action in Indochina in advance of the results of Geneva."[69]

The plan had fallen apart. Although publicly there was still talk about united action and although Washington and Paris continued to debate a date for Indochina independence (with France still holding

65. *Congressional Record,* vol. 100, pt. 4, 83 Cong. 2 sess. (1954), pp. 4671–80 (quotation, p. 4674).

66. Quoted in Eisenhower, *Mandate for Change,* p. 353.

67. "Remarks at the 42nd Annual Meeting of the United States Chamber of Commerce, April 26, 1954," *Public Papers, Eisenhower, 1954,* p. 421.

68. *Pentagon Papers,* vol. 1, p. 104.

69. Ibid., p. 105.

out), this phase was over. Not until June 15 did Dulles tell the French that the time had run out. Meanwhile, in Washington agreements were being reached on political and military levels providing for a larger American role in the training of Vietnamese forces—a matter of far-reaching importance.[70] By the end of June U.S. diplomacy had visibly shifted to planning for a general regional defense organization to influence the Geneva settlement and to prepare for its aftermath.

The most striking point about this failure of American diplomacy was the ease with which it was explained away at home. One day the administration simply changed its tune. Asked at a press conference on April 29 what he meant when he had referred to the desirability of a modus vivendi in Indochina, Eisenhower replied: "You certainly cannot hope at the present state of our relations in the world for a completely satisfactory answer with the Communists. The most you can work out is a practical way of getting along."[71] In a public statement on May 3 Dulles even managed to present the Dien Bien Phu debacle as a victory of sorts:

The gallant defenders of Dien-Bien-Phu have. . . . taken a toll such that, from a military standpoint, the attackers already lost more than they could win. . . . The Communist rulers are learning again that the will of the free is not broken by violence or intimidation. . . . The violent battles now being waged in Viet-Nam and the aggressions against Laos and Cambodia are not creating any spirit of defeatism. On the contrary, they are rousing the free nations to measures which we hope will be sufficiently timely and vigorous to preserve these vital areas from Communist domination.[72]

One of the measures, SEATO, was designed to make the domino theory inoperative.

The switch was accomplished in one easy motion. A number of senators made speeches about the "terrible defeat," but no one broke stride. Even the military fell into line at the end of May. The JCS informed the secretary of defense that "from the point of view of the United States, with reference to the Far East as a whole, Indochina is devoid of decisive military objectives and the allocation of more than token U.S. armed forces to that area would be a serious diversion of limited U.S. capabilities."[73]

70. "U.S. and French on United Action, May–Mid-June 1954," *United States–Vietnam Relations,* bk. 1, pt. III.A.2, pp. 19–24.
71. "The President's News Conference of April 29, 1954," *Public Papers, Eisenhower, 1954,* p. 428.
72. *Pentagon Papers,* vol. 1, p. 599.
73. "U.S. and French on United Action," p. A-20.

The Geneva Accords

The door was now open for a Geneva settlement. In mid-June Pierre Mendès-France replaced Laniel as premier, pledging to end the war in one month. Jockeying continued among the conference participants, with the U.S. representative as an active observer. Then, suddenly in July the deadlocks began to break. The Vietminh, which had been bargaining to gain acceptance of its superior position in Vietnam, backed off and compromised under heavy pressure from Moscow and Peking. The first agreements, covering the cessation of hostilities, provided for a cease-fire; a temporary military demarcation line at the seventeenth parallel; regroupment of forces; and a ban on any additional military personnel, arms, bases, and alliances. Enforcement of these terms was to be overseen by the newly created three-power International Control Commission acting under the direction of the conference cochairmen, the USSR and Great Britain. The French and the Vietminh signed. The Final Declaration, which was not signed, included provisions for respect of "independence, unity, territorial integrity," general elections in July 1956, withdrawal of French forces, and no reprisals.[74] The Vietnam government, now under the leadership of Ngo Dinh Diem, condemned this declaration. Under Secretary of State Walter Bedell Smith, in a separate declaration, said that the United States would "refrain from the threat or the use of force to disturb" the agreements and "would view any renewal of the aggression in violation of the aforesaid agreements with grave concern and as seriously threatening international peace and security."[75]

The accords were flawed from the start. Ostensibly they fully presumed the near-term unification of North and South Vietnam, and the DRV had every right to expect unification to be under its leadership. The Diem government, however, had immediately announced its intention to resist, and the temporary demarcation line, which was the basis of the settlement, was bound to become the basis for future struggle. Most important, Eisenhower told the press on July 21 that the United States did not feel "bound" by the accords, which to him were simply the "best . . . under the circumstances."[76] In less than two months SEATO came into being. Composed of the United States, Britain,

74. See *Pentagon Papers*, vol. 1, pp. 270–82.
75. Ibid., p. 162.
76. Eisenhower, *Mandate for Change*, pp. 371, 374.

France, Australia, New Zealand, Pakistan, the Philippines, and Thailand, with South Vietnam, Laos, and Cambodia added as protocol nations, SEATO was to be the new shield against further Communist expansion.

Reform: A Lost Cause

On the surface it seemed that the United States was going to step right in where the French left off—but inside the executive branch a battle was about to rage over this issue. All considered the regime in South Vietnam to be shaky and likely to soon fall to the Communists. From August 1954 until June 1955 the Joint Chiefs of Staff and the State Department crossed swords.

The opening phase was highlighted by a chicken-egg dilemma that was to be repeated with even greater intensity during the Kennedy years. In response to a draft State Department cable the Joint Chiefs stated that Washington should not assume the burden of training the Vietnamese forces until "there be a reasonably strong, stable civil government in control."[77] Dulles replied that "one of the most efficient means of enabling the Vietnamese Government to become strong is to assist it in reorganizing the National Army and in training that army."[78] The JCS stuck to the substance of their position, but retorted that "if it is considered that political considerations are overriding," they would go along.[79] This phase ended with an Eisenhower letter to Diem released on October 25, saying U.S. aid would be forthcoming "provided that your Government is prepared to give assurances as to the standards of performance."[80] It appeared as though the Joint Chiefs had won, but they had not. The direct assistance program began and no reforms were forthcoming.

In a little over a month, however, the military were back on the attack, this time in the person of former Army Chief of Staff Lawton Collins who had been sent to Vietnam as the President's personal emis-

77. Memorandum for the secretary of defense, August 4, 1954, *United States–Vietnam Relations*, bk. 10, pt. V.B.3, p. 701. See also the memorandum for the secretary of defense, August 12, 1954, ibid., pp. 714–16.

78. Letter to Secretary of Defense Charles E. Wilson, August 18, 1954, ibid., p. 728. See also letter from Dulles to Wilson, October 11, 1954, ibid., pp. 768–69; and memorandum for the Joint Chiefs of Staff, October 14, 1954, ibid., p. 770.

79. Memorandum for the secretary of defense, October 19, 1954, ibid., pp. 773–74.

80. "Letter to the President of the Council of Ministers of Viet-Nam Regarding Assistance for That Country, October 25, 1954," *Public Papers, Eisenhower, 1954*, p. 949.

sary. Collins, like the French, thought Diem was hopeless. He reported from Saigon that gradual withdrawal from Vietnam was "least desirable," but that "in all honesty and in view of what I have observed here to date it is possible this may be the only sound solution."[81] The U.S. ambassador in Saigon, Donald Heath, disagreed. Heath acknowledged that "a fiscal commitment of $300 million plus our national prestige" might be "lost in a gamble on the retention of free Viet-Nam," but that withholding support would "have a far worse effect." As he understood it, Dulles's policy was a "time buying operation."[82] Dulles confirmed this, saying that the U.S. objective was to see to it that the Vietminh could "only take over by internal violence," that "we have no choice" but to support Diem "if only to buy time," but that the United States must be "flexible."[83] At year-end Dulles decided that the United States should "take the plunge" and begin aid and training.[84]

The dilemma of whether to assist the Diem government before it instituted reforms or to give aid in anticipation of reforms rested on two deeper dilemmas. First, the Diem group could not stabilize its rule without reforms, and yet it could not reform without undermining its own authority. Reforming meant sharing power and wealth, but to share some would be to jeopardize all. In the mandarin tradition, the Diem group intended to monopolize power in a centralized quasi-authoritarian administration.[85] Second, to precondition and delay aid would enhance the chances of warding off the North Vietnamese in the long run, while increasing the prospects for a Communist takeover in the short run. And so the American military advisers began to replace the French and a new massive aid program was initiated.

As 1955 wore on, with Diem still in the seat and with pressures building in Congress and the press to support him, these dilemmas were fast becoming moot. On June 13 Eisenhower approved NSC recommendations that smacked of those of pre–Geneva Conference days. One in effect was to back Diem's stand against holding Vietnam-

81. *Pentagon Papers*, vol. 1, p. 226.

82. Memorandum to Walter Robertson, assistant secretary of state for Far Eastern Affairs, December 17, 1954, *United States–Vietnam Relations*, bk. 10, pt. V.B.3, p. 825.

83. Cable to American embassies in Saigon and Paris, December 24, 1954, ibid., 853–54.

84. Memorandum for the record, December 29, 1954, ibid., p. 859.

85. See John T. McAlister, *Vietnam: The Origins of Revolution* (Knopf, 1969); Dennis J. Duncanson, *Government and Revolution in Vietnam* (New York: Oxford University Press, 1968); and McAlister and Mus, *The Vietnamese and Their Revolution*.

wide elections in July 1956.[86] Another was to "take necessary military
and any other action to assist any state or dependent territory in the
SEATO area willing to resist Communist resort to force."[87]

By 1956 the State Department could claim that the Diem Government was "appreciably stronger" than it had been six months or a year
earlier.[88] Diem had emerged as somewhat of a strong man. Rival military leaders, the armed religious sects, the Binh Xuyen gang—all had
come to a kind of quiet standstill. The North Vietnamese were busy
consolidating their territory and instituting far-reaching social and
economic changes. But it was a peace of the tired and the preoccupied.
Diem had problems: the taint of colonialism through past association
with Bao Dai and then ties to the Americans, his autocratic way of
governing, nepotism, and his Catholicism. His support derived pre-
eminently from the Catholics and the urban middle class, many of
whom had come South after Geneva, while the country he was trying
to rule was populated mostly by Buddhists, Confucianists, and rural
animists. In short order he was to alienate the bulk of the peasantry
and the non-Communist nationalist groups by abolishing village elections and instituting population relocation and censorship. Then, in
1957 the terrorizing and assassination of pro-Diem officials began. The
group responsible, called the Vietcong and composed of Communists,
former Vietminh, nationalists, and varieties of Diem opponents, appears to have been largely indigenous. There is no public evidence
that the DRV began to direct Vietcong activities in the South until
some time in 1960–61 with the creation of the National Liberation
Front (NLF). Throughout this period Diem had little trouble holding on to power. But while the very fact that he was lasting created a
favorable image of Diem in America, he was getting weaker in Vietnam all along.

Spotlight on Laos

It was to Laos that American policymakers and newsmakers were
turning their attention.[89] Events in Laos were to have an important

86. Memorandum for the National Security Council, June 13, 1955, *United
States–Vietnam Relations*, bk. 10, pt. V.B.3, p. 984.
87. "Statement of Policy by the National Security Council on Current U.S. Policy
in the Far East," December 22, 1954, ibid., p. 841.
88. "Intelligence Brief," February 7, 1956, ibid., p. 1048.
89. See Charles A. Stevenson, *The End of Nowhere: American Policy toward
Laos since 1954* (Beacon Press, 1972); Arthur J. Dommen, *Conflict in Laos: The*

bearing on how Hanoi was to view U.S. intentions in Indochina and on how Washington would come to feel the enhanced value of Vietnam.

Under the Geneva provisions the Laotian settlement followed the Vietnam pattern, but with two exceptions. There was no explicit territorial division (although the Communist Pathet Lao were to stay in the northern part of the country), and the French were to continue in a military advisory role. In effect the Vietminh had sold out the interests of their ally, the Pathet Lao, just as they had cashiered the dreams of the Free Khmer party in Cambodia. Vietnam would always come first. Nevertheless, Hanoi remained interested in preserving the viability of the Pathet Lao and in protecting that portion of Laos that abutted Vietnam. China's interest in Laos stemmed from a common border; the United States was interested because Laos lay between Vietnam and Thailand, and the USSR because everyone else was interested.

The Laotian intrigue, which was homegrown more than foreign-inspired, centered around three factions: a right-wing group led by General Phoumi Nosavan, the Pathet Lao led by Prince Souphanouvong, and a center, or neutralist, group led by Prince Souvanna Phouma. After three years of slipping and sliding, the three factions came to an intricate agreement and on November 19, 1957, a coalition government was dutifully formed. Washington fought this modus vivendi tooth and nail.[90] Laotian elections were held and the integration of the Pathet Lao forces began. All was seemingly going well until two things happened: the right-wing-controlled Royal Army instituted a program to combat communism, and Washington withheld aid payments on which the neutralist Souvanna Phouma government had become so dependent. Souvanna resigned, and with CIA backing, Phoumi took over, denouncing the Geneva accords and seeking unrestricted American military aid. Phoumi jailed Souphanouvong, and in May 1960 civil war erupted. Peking cried outrage, Moscow called for a

---

Politics of Neutralization, 3d ed. (Praeger, 1971); and Bernard B. Fall, Anatomy of a Crisis: The Laotian Crisis of 1960–1961 (Doubleday, 1969).

90. See, for example, the testimony of J. Graham Parsons, deputy assistant secretary of state for Far Eastern Affairs, in United States Operations in Laos, Hearings before a Subcommittee of the House Committee on Government Operations, 86 Cong. 1 sess. (GPO, 1959), p. 195. "I struggled for 16 months to prevent a coalition," Parsons said. Walter S. Robertson, assistant secretary of state for Far Eastern Affairs, said, "We did everything we could to keep it from happening" (ibid., p. 196).

reconvening of the Geneva powers, Washington refused, and Hanoi once again began direct aid to the Pathet Lao. The U.S. intelligence community summed up the situation as follows: "The Communist resumption of guerrilla warfare in Laos was primarily a reaction to a stronger anti-Communist posture by the Laotian Government and to recent US initiatives in support of Laos."[91] The chance of Communist success, in this view, was high, and the risks were low.

The fighting went on with increasing Pathet Lao success and with deepening outside involvement. Washington, in covert violation of the 1954 accords, had sent in a military training mission in civilian clothes (the Program Evaluation Office) in the late 1950s, assumed the total costs of the Royal Army, and established a special military task force to intervene if the need arose. Kong Le, commander of a Royal Lao paratroop battalion, staged a bloodless coup and brought back Souvanna Phouma. Washington continued direct but covert aid to Phoumi, and Souvanna countered by establishing diplomatic relations with Moscow. Soviet aid started to arrive in December 1960, and Kong Le joined forces with the Pathet Lao. The State Department issued public warnings and the Defense Department announced increased troop readiness to intervene if necessary. On January 11 Prince Norodom Sihanouk called for a fourteen-nation conference on Laos, but the United States rejected the proposal because it would only offer a forum for Communist propaganda.[92] The fighting went on.

The Eisenhower Legacy

During these years the public spotlight focused on Laos, not Vietnam. But back in South Vietnam, it was again a time of trouble. In August 1960 the intelligence community noted "adverse trends" that would lead to the collapse of Diem if they remained unchecked.[93] Diem faced dangers from the growing Vietcong insurgency in the countryside and from his own military leaders closer to Saigon. Ngo Dinh Nhu, Diem's notoriously ruthless, manipulative brother, made matters worse. In November a military faction staged a coup but failed. Diem still retained sufficient support from other military leaders to survive with his powers intact.

91. "The Situation in Laos," *United States–Vietnam Relations*, bk. 10, vol. 4, pt. V.B.3, p. 1242.

92. Stevenson, *The End of Nowhere*, pp. 122–23.

93. "Short-Term Trends in South Vietnam," *United States–Vietnam Relations*, bk. 10, pt. V.B.3, p. 1298.

This was the situation inherited by the new President, John F. Kennedy. But he had inherited more than an immediate crisis; the Eisenhower legacy was rich in rhetoric and momentum.

First, the Eisenhower administration had kept the flame burning under the anti-Communist rhetoric in general and the importance of Indochina in particular. The spark of a change that flickered in the rhetoric of May 1954 was quickly snuffed out. By 1956 one official after another rose to evoke the old domino images. Then on April 4, 1959, four years after the original domino speech, Eisenhower said: "The loss of South Viet-Nam would set in motion a crumbling process that could, as it progressed, have grave consequences for us and for freedom."[94] To be sure, in referring to consequences, he chose the word "could" rather than "would," and in his public letter to Diem in October of the following year he underlined the point that "the main responsibility for guarding [Vietnamese] independence will always, as it has in the past, belong to the Vietnamese people and their government."[95] Nevertheless, the effect as reflected in the news media and on Capitol Hill was to reinforce U.S. international and domestic political stakes in the future of Vietnam.

Second, it was Eisenhower along with Dulles who made the decision to substitute the American presence for the French presence in Vietnam. The small military mission that was there as the French began to leave was expanded into a Military Assistance Advisory Group of about 300 men and then expanded once more in 1960 by a subterfuge in violation of the Geneva accords. By 1958 the American economic aid mission in South Vietnam bulked larger than anywhere else in the world. But the fact of substitution was as important as the bureaucratic force that came into being.

Third, because of the magnitude of that presence the Saigon government was nearly totally dependent on Washington. American dollars underpinned the Saigon economy and underwrote most of the costs of the Saigon armed forces. American military men trained and accompanied those forces. That dependence, plain for all to see, served both to heighten the American responsibility and to fashion an American-Vietnamese tar baby.

94. "Address at the Gettysburg College Convocation: The Importance of Understanding, April 4, 1959," *Public Papers, Eisenhower, 1959*, p. 71.
95. "Message to President Diem on the Fifth Anniversary of the Independence of Viet-Nam, October 26, 1960," ibid., 1960 (GPO, 1961), p. 808.

Fourth, the Eisenhower administration constructed an international rubric for intervention—SEATO. American negotiators riddled SEATO with loopholes, but the facade was what mattered. Some SEATO allies could always be counted on to "internationalize" U.S. intervention. Future presidents would have to worry less about the appearance of going it alone. Of course, the prime purpose of SEATO was to deter aggression, but at the same time, it also enhanced the potential to involve.

Finally, the legacy was noteworthy as much for what Eisenhower did not do as for what he did. He did not intervene at the time of Dien Bien Phu. This was a model that others might have imitated. But he also did not use his prestige to accept the set backs and take the opportunity to disengage the United States from Indochina. The opportunity was there; his administration already had been chastened by the Geneva settlement, and the military favored disentanglement rather than limited involvement. But Eisenhower chose to take over directly from the French. He kept America out of war, and he kept America in Vietnam.

CHAPTER THREE

Picking up the Torch: The Kennedy Administration

On January 19, 1961, President-elect John Kennedy met with President Eisenhower, and chaos in Laos dominated their discussion of pressing world problems. The next day Kennedy inaugurated his administration by promising to "pay any price, bear any burden, . . . support any friend, oppose any foe to assure the survival and success of liberty."[1] Foreign policy was to be his first priority; he did not even mention domestic goals in his inaugural address.[2] From his very first days in office, Vietnam called him to the test.

Soon after the inauguration White House aide Walt Rostow insisted that Kennedy read a memo written by Brigadier General Edward Lansdale, who had just returned from a trip to Vietnam. When Kennedy finished reading Lansdale's alarming analysis of deterioration in the field, he looked at Rostow and said, "This is the worst one we've got, isn't it?" Less than a week before, the President had routinely approved a new Counterinsurgency Plan (CIP), which aimed to raise South Vietnamese forces by 20,000 men and increase training and equipment. Now he directed Rostow to turn his attention to Vietnam and get the President more material to read on guerrilla warfare.[3]

1. "Inaugural Address," January 20, 1961, *Public Papers of the Presidents of the United States: John F. Kennedy, 1961* (Government Printing Office, 1962), p. 1.

2. In his address Kennedy also said: "To those new states whom we welcome to the ranks of the free, we pledge our word that one form of colonial control shall not have passed away merely to be replaced by a far more iron tyrany." (Ibid.)

3. W. W. Rostow, *The Diffusion of Power: An Essay in Recent History* (Macmillan, 1972), p. 265. See also *The Pentagon Papers: The Defense Department History of United States Decisionmaking on Vietnam*, Senator Gravel ed. (Beacon Press, 1971), vol. 2, pp. 6, 27. At the time, Rostow wrote that the President said the Lansdale memorandum was the first indication he had had of the urgency of the

During Kennedy's first year Vietnam was only one of several problems. Despite the jolt of the Lansdale memo, other crises took most of the administration's attention, a situation that paradoxically was partly responsible for the increase in the U.S. commitment to Vietnam. Early decisions on Vietnam were boxed in between the fiasco at the Bay of Pigs, a compromise neutralist settlement in Laos, and rising tension in Berlin. In 1954, when Eisenhower had had to weigh intervention in Indochina, the administration had just scored foreign policy "victories" by toppling left-wing leaders in Iran and Guatemala. The Korean War was also less than a year behind. In that context the costs of inaction did not seem to outweigh the costs of intervention. But in 1961 Kennedy needed an arena in which he could demonstrate firmness. Since he did not yet know what would happen in Berlin, where nuclear war loomed as a real danger, and since he was planning to settle for half a loaf in Laos, Vietnam seemed like one good place to make a stand. Kennedy told Averell Harriman as much when the latter was preparing the negotiating position on Laos for Geneva.[4]

"Ironically, the collapse of the Dulles policy in Laos had created the possibility of a neutralist solution there," Arthur Schlesinger, Jr., recalled, "but the survival of that policy in South Vietnam, where the government was stronger and the army more willing to fight, left us in 1961 no alternative but to continue the effort of 1954."[5] After the June summit meeting with Khrushchev in Vienna, the President is reported to have told James Reston, "Now we have a problem in making our power credible, and Vietnam looks like the place."[6] The following month Robert Komer of the National Security Council staff recommended a vast increase in the momentum of U.S. involvement in Vietnam: "I believe it is very important that this government have a major anti-Communist victory to its credit in the six months before the Berlin crisis is likely to get really hot. . . . here [Vietnam] the odds are still in

---

Vietnam situation. See W. W. Rostow, memorandum for McGeorge Bundy, "Meeting Saturday Morning, January 28, in the President's Office, on Viet-Nam," January 30, 1961, in John F. Kennedy Library, National Security Files, Vietnam Country File (cited hereafter as JFKL/NSF-VNCF), 1/61–3/61.

4. See *Pentagon Papers*, vol. 2, p. 76.

5. Arthur M. Schlesinger, Jr., *A Thousand Days: John F. Kennedy in the White House* (Houghton Mifflin, 1965), p. 538.

6. Quoted in General William C. Westmoreland, *A Soldier Reports* (Doubleday, 1976), pp. 409–10.

our favor, which makes Vietnam a better place than Laos to achieve the desired result."[7]

Facing these multiple crises, Kennedy saw Vietnam not only as a relative problem but as a connected one. Khrushchev's speech on January 6 pledging Soviet support for wars of national liberation had impressed him, and at the end of the month Kennedy spoke of the "relentless pressures of the Chinese communists" in Southeast Asia.[8] Later in the spring he told a gathering of editors:

The message of Cuba, of Laos, of the rising din of Communist voices in Asia and Latin America—these messages are all the same. The complacent, the self-indulgent, the soft societies are about to be swept away. . . . No other challenge is more deserving of our every effort and energy . . . our security may be lost piece by piece, country by country. . . . We intend to reexamine and reorient our forces of all kinds . . . for a struggle in many ways more difficult than war. . . . For I am convinced that we in . . . the free world possess the necessary resource, and the skill. . . .[9]

Henry Fairlie observed that postmortems "criticize the Kennedy administration for consistently thinking in terms of a Communist bloc; but this was also the thinking, with few exceptions, of the spokesmen of informed opinion."[10]

Vietnam was a mess, but it was a piece of the cordon of containment. For the next three years Vietnam would pose several issues. The issue of goals would arise, though usually offhandedly, at the beginning and end of the administration. To what degree should the United States commit itself to save the South? How explicit should the commitment be? Should any conditions be placed on it? Were there any alternatives to commitment? The issue of *means,* however, would dominate discussion. Were the critical needs of the war military or political? What kind of leverage could be used on Diem? How could the population be rallied against the Communists? How should advisers be used? Should combat troops be sent? As U.S. involvement grew, so did disagreements within the government about these questions of means. But the prin-

7. R. W. Komer, memorandum for Rostow, "Are We Pushing Hard Enough in South Vietnam?" July 20, 1961, JFKL/NSF-VNCF, 7/14/61–7/21/61.

8. "Annual Message to Congress on the State of the Union, January 30, 1963," *Public Papers, Kennedy, 1961,* p. 23.

9. "Address Before the American Society of Newspaper Editors, April 20, 1961," ibid., p. 306.

10. Henry Fairlie, "We Knew What We Were Doing When We Went into Vietnam," *Washington Monthly,* vol. 5 (May 1973), p. 10.

cipal goal, prevention of Communist control of South Vietnam, remained virtually unquestioned.

Fastening the Commitment: 1961

Just as the Cuban exile invasion failed and the situation in Laos heated up, the President directed Deputy Secretary of Defense Roswell Gilpatric to prepare a program for saving South Vietnam, a souped up version of the CIP. On May 1, 1961, the Gilpatric Task Force completed its report, recommending a variety of military, economic, propaganda, and covert actions. More notably it advised making explicit a firm commitment to do whatever would be necessary to defend South Vietnam. Deputy Under Secretary of State George Ball took over the project, however, and produced a major redraft of the report that softened the statements of unqualified commitment and also eliminated the special role Lansdale was to have played in Saigon. These changes were designed in part to maintain American leverage against President Diem. Around the same time, Senator J. William Fulbright publicly opposed intervention in Laos but said he would support troop commitments to Thailand and Vietnam.[11]

The President quickly approved the revised report, in National Security Action Memorandum (NSAM) 52 of May 11. While the report had toned down the commitment, NSAM 52 nevertheless stated clearly the U.S. objective "to prevent Communist domination of South Vietnam," and authorized the various supporting actions.[12] The Joint Chiefs of Staff had provisionally recommended deploying U.S. troops to Vietnam, "assuming that the political decision is to hold Southeast Asia outside the Communist sphere"[13] but no one was yet recommending using American units in direct combat with the Vietcong. Kennedy did send 400 Special Forces for training purposes.[14] The essential significance of

11. For the action plans on Vietnam and Fulbright's reaction, see *Pentagon Papers*, vol. 2, pp. 35–47, 637–42.

12. Ibid., p. 51. Part of the reason for softening the commitment may have been uncertainty about the status of the Diem regime. The day before NSAM 52 was issued Rostow warned Kennedy of cable traffic suggesting that Diem might be overthrown. W. W. Rostow, memorandum to the President, "Viet-Nam NSC Paper," May 10, 1961, JFKL/NSF-VNCF, 5/8/61–5/19/61.

13. *Pentagon Papers*, vol. 2, p. 49.

14. Ibid., pp. 50–51.

NSAM 52 was to commit the United States but not unequivocally. The President was not going any further overboard than immediate circumstances required. And for the moment the State Department had topped the Pentagon in organizing and controlling the development of the U.S. effort.

Deterioration and Assessment

In mid-June a mission went to the field under Eugene Staley, president of the Stanford Research Institute, to study economic problems in the war effort. The Staley mission's report wound up focusing on the issue of what force levels of the Army of the Republic of [South] Vietnam (ARVN) the United States should support. Staley posed two alternatives—supporting an increase to either 200,000 or 270,000 men, depending on the level of Vietcong activity. Kennedy authorized the lower increase, since he could defer a decision on the larger number until the 200,000 level was reached, which would not be until late 1962. No significant conditions were imposed that Diem had to meet in order to get the additional aid, and in moderating the growth in involvement, the United States was not rocking Diem's boat.[15]

Means remained proportional to short-run threats but less than many officials believed long-run success would require. Vietnam policy debates from the beginning of the administration centered on how to save Vietnam, not whether to save it. Only the State Department, with its sensitivity to diplomatic flexibility and the desire to prompt Diem to produce in return for assistance, and the President, with his sensitivity to keeping options open and his desire to avoid getting painted into any unnecessary corners, did anything to keep the commitment rhetorically mild. But the end remained the same: to keep Communists from governing South Vietnam. (Reassessment of ends was more characteristic of the bureaucratic defections and postmortems of the late 1960s.)

It was in this spirit that the government faced the rapid deterioration in the field in the fall of 1961. When Kennedy dispatched Maxwell Taylor to survey the situation, he instructed the general to recommend measures to shore up the South. Taylor said that his directive "was drawn in strict consistence with the statement of U.S. policy set forth in the May NSAM" and that he "was not asked to review the objectives

15. For a discussion of the Staley mission and its recommendations, see ibid., pp. 62–65.

of this policy but the means being pursued for their attainment."[16] The only major official in the government at this time advocating anything like backing out of Vietnam was Under Secretary of State Chester Bowles, who proposed extending the Laos neutralization solution to the rest of Southeast Asia.[17] Indicatively, Bowles, who had always been too close to the liberal wing of the Democratic party for the administration's comfort, was removed from any position of influence shortly thereafter when he was replaced as under secretary in the "Thanksgiving Day Massacre" reorganization of the State Department.[18] The more immediately relevant contribution to policy from the State Department as concern mounted in the fall was a paper, "Concept of Intervention in Vietnam," prepared by Deputy Under Secretary U. Alexis Johnson, that endorsed a combination of separate proposals by Rostow and the JCS for sending 20,000–25,000 SEATO troops to Vietnam.[19]

Taylor took to the field in October with Walt Rostow as his deputy and a team of military and Foreign Service officers in train. On the way they stopped to see Admiral Harry Felt, Commander in Chief of the Pacific (CINCPAC) who confirmed the critical situation and urged prompt American aid. Felt recommended logistical help, especially engineer and helicopter units, but significantly, he recommended against committing combat troop units at the time.[20] This put him in opposition to the JCS and William Bundy, acting assistant secretary of defense in the Office of International Security Affairs. Bundy had just argued "that it *is* really now or never if we are to arrest the gains being made by the Viet Cong," and that an "early and hard-hitting operation has a good chance (70% would be my guess) of *arresting* things and giving Diem a chance to do better."[21]

In Vietnam the Taylor team surveyed the situation in a whirlwind tour of nearly two weeks. This was Taylor's second trip to Saigon. He had visited in 1955, when one of his predecessors as Army Chief of Staff,

16. Maxwell D. Taylor, General, U.S. Army (Ret.) *Swords and Plowshares* (Norton, 1972), p. 226.

17. Schlesinger, *A Thousand Days*, p. 545.

18. Roger Hilsman, *To Move a Nation: The Politics of Foreign Policy in the Administration of John F. Kennedy* (Doubleday, 1967), p. 50.

19. Rostow had proposed a 25,000-man SEATO force to guard border areas; the JCS rejected this option as infeasible and ineffective and recommended instead that a force be committed to the central highlands. *Pentagon Papers*, vol. 2, pp. 73–78.

20. Ibid., pp. 83–84; and Taylor, *Swords and Plowshares*, pp. 227–28.

21. *Pentagon Papers*, vol. 2, p. 79 (emphasis in the original).

J. Lawton Collins, had arrived as Eisenhower's special envoy to straighten out the tangled state of affairs that had followed the partition of Vietnam. Collins had gone from pessimism so deep as to prompt him to recommend replacement of Diem and U.S. withdrawal to less desperate and resigned acceptance of Diem and endorsement of continued aid. When Taylor's turn came, there was no question of either withdrawing or dumping Diem. Instead, Taylor concentrated on coaxing Diem to ask for what he needed—including U.S. troops—to get the Vietcong back under control.[22]

On the way home Taylor cabled his report from the Philippines. He proposed sending a logistical task force and elaborating and increasing the covert operations and assistance measures already under way, but his most crucial recommendation was to introduce a force of about 8,000 regular combat troops to provide base security. This was matched by a caveat in the cover letter that an air offensive against North Vietnam might have to be undertaken in the future. Appendixes to the final version of the report by subordinate members of the mission, such as William Jorden and Sterling Cotrell of the State Department, painted an even darker picture and were more scathingly critical of the corruption and instability of the Diem regime. These officials had nothing better to recommend than the leaders, though, and Cotrell agreed that if increased aid did not reverse the negative trend, the United States should move to attack the North.[23] The central statement in Taylor's own report was his contention that "the U.S. should become a *limited partner* in the war";[24] and he pointed out soberly, "If the first contingent is not enough to accomplish the necessary results, it will be difficult to resist the pressure to reinforce. If the ultimate result sought is the closing of the frontiers and the clean-up of the insurgents within SVN [South Vietnam], *there is no limit to our possible commitment* (unless we attack the source in Hanoi)."[25]

New Decisions

The mission was essentially saying that for the moment the United States could have its cake and eat it too—involvement with modera-

22. See Taylor, *Swords and Plowshares*, pp. 229–33; and *Pentagon Papers*, vol. 1, pp. 205–06, 226.

23. *Pentagon Papers*, vol. 2, pp. 84–96.

24. Ibid., p. 653 (emphasis added).

25. Ibid., p. 90 (emphasis added). See also Taylor, *Swords and Plowshares*, pp. 242–44.

tion—but that costs could grow. No one of consequence was yet seriously suggesting that the prospective costs of the means should challenge devotion to the ends. Policy reassessment remained a matter of "how," not "whether." "It was a yeasty time in Washington," as Kalb and Abel said. "Everyone seemed to have at least ten ideas a day."[26] So when the Taylor-Rostow proposals came before the inner circle, the consensus favored adopting them.[27] But there were equivocations on both sides. Secretary of Defense Robert McNamara, Deputy Secretary Roswell Gilpatric, and the Joint Chiefs of Staff believed 8,000 troops would not "tip the scales decisively" and would only tie the United States down "in an inconclusive struggle."[28] Six divisions might be needed. Forwarding these views to the President on November 8, McNamara focused on "the basic issue" in the Taylor report: whether to accept firmly the commitment to prevent Communist domination of South Vietnam and to face the likelihood of necessary military actions in the future. McNamara and the JCS explicitly opposed sending any major units such as Taylor proposed unless this resolution was undertaken explicitly.[29]

On the other side the President and the State Department remained more cautious about crossing any bridges before necessary. Three days after the McNamara memo, the secretary of defense mysteriously reversed his position and joined Rusk in a memo that approved increased assistance but tacitly opposed sending any combat units. More assistance was also to be conditional on government reforms by Diem. They did stipulate, though, that the United States should be prepared to introduce combat forces "if that should become necessary for success" and to attack North Vietnam.[30] Nevertheless, the President now had a paper that told him he could defer troop commitment for the moment. Some analysts have deduced that Kennedy himself asked McNamara to

26. Marvin Kalb and Elie Abel, *The Roots of Involvement: The U.S. in Asia, 1784–1971* (Norton, 1971), p. 127.

27. Theodore Sorensen, in *Kennedy* (Harper and Row, 1965), p. 653, said all the President's advisers favored Taylor's recommendations. Assistant Secretary of Defense Paul Nitze reportedly demurred, as he had on Rostow's earlier recommendations for troop deployments, because trying to keep a commitment on the ground limited would be like trying to stay "a little bit pregnant." See Stewart Alsop, *The Center: People and Power in Political Washington* (Harper and Row, 1968), pp. 162–63.

28. *Pentagon Papers*, vol. 2, p. 108.

29. Ibid., pp. 108–09.

30. Ibid., pp. 110–16.

revise his recommendation so that the President would not have to turn down Pentagon advice officially.[31]

Whatever prompted McNamara's change, the Rusk-McNamara memo still emphasized strenuously the need for unequivocal resolve: *"The United States should commit itself to the clear objective of preventing the fall of South Viet-Nam to Communism."* They warned that "the loss of South Viet-Nam . . . would not only destroy SEATO but would undermine the credibility of American commitments elsewhere. Further, loss of South Viet-Nam would stimulate bitter domestic controversies."[32] The President took advantage of the recommendations for lesser involvement, approving the memo almost verbatim in NSAM 111 in late November. Significantly, however, he made one deletion: the explicit reference to broad commitment. "Oddly, I do not recall that any particular importance was attached to the omission," Taylor wrote.[33] Perhaps this was because Kennedy made clear to his advisers that he was ready to go further, but only when the pinch came. Rostow recalled:

As Kennedy rose from the Cabinet table, having indicated the elements in the Taylor report he finally approved, he remarked: "If this doesn't work perhaps we'll have to try Walt's Plan Six"; that is, direct attack on North Vietnam. . . . He took the minimum steps he judged necessary to stabilize the situation, leaving its resolution for the longer future, but quite conscious that harder decisions might lie ahead.[34]

The President clearly understood the warnings of bigger things to come. Incrementalism would preserve flexibility; massive immediate involvement would yield more certainty but fewer choices.[35] The more

31. See Robert L. Gallucci, *Neither Peace nor Honor: The Politics of American Military Policy in Viet-Nam*, Washington Center of Foreign Policy Research, School of Advanced International Studies, Studies in International Affairs, 24 (Johns Hopkins University Press, 1975), p. 24.

32. *Pentagon Papers*, vol. 2, p. 111 (emphasis in original). See also ibid., p. 17.

33. Taylor, *Swords and Plowshares*, p. 248.

34. Rostow, *Diffusion of Power*, p. 278.

35. The President's natural desire to preserve as much flexibility as possible may have led some observers to believe he did not appreciate the implications of commitment. John McCloy, an eminent conservative member of the establishment, told Kennedy at this time that he should consider the commitment very carefully because, once in, it would be impossible to turn back. "Kennedy stated that he had very few, if any, options. . . . McCloy thought President Kennedy felt he could do this [increase U.S. involvement] without making an irretrievable commitment." See Endicott Peabody, memorandum to the President, "John McCloy on Vietnam and the Presidency," November 6, 1967, in Lyndon B. Johnson Library, National Security File, Vietnam Country File (cited hereafter as LBJL/NSF-VNCF), 7(C)1 (Past Presi-

forthcoming the United States, the less tractable Diem would be to demands for reform and the harder it would be to resist demands at home for greater success. He told Schlesinger at the time, "But it will be just like Berlin. The troops will march in; the bands will play; the crowds will cheer; and in four days everyone will have forgotten. Then we will be told we have to send in more troops. It's like taking a drink. The effect wears off, and you have to take another."[36] And although the measures he authorized in NSAM 111 stopped short of those Taylor had thought were the minimum needed for success, they were substantial. When the new helicopter companies arrived in Vietnam in early December, the International Control Commission caucused in emergency session to consider whether it should even continue operating in South Vietnam, since an aid increase of this size breached the Geneva accords.[37]

The Issue of Resolve

Why did the question of American *resolve* dominate so much of decisionmaking on Vietnam in 1961? Today the assumptions behind the discussions in 1961 can seem naive, U.S. actions can seem misdirected, and the drive by some constituencies in the bureaucracy to shore up Diem with American timber can seem recklessly abandoned. Why did the United States not try to exploit the Sino-Soviet split then instead of waiting a decade? Why did decisionmakers not agree that Diem was hopeless? Ironically, commitment in Vietnam was to become the child that devoured its parent. Spawned by containment, it discredited containment. By the 1970s a majority of the public in one opinion survey could not be found to support any U.S. military intervention abroad other than to resist an invasion of Canada.[38] But in 1961 this was all yet to come. At the time, containment of communism was a clear and universally accepted goal within the government. Vietnam was the linear

---

dential Statements of USG [U.S. government]), item 4b. This pairing of the belief that there were no present options with the determination not to foreclose future options seems paradoxical to the observer with hindsight but must have seemed prudent to the President at the time.

36. Quoted in Schlesinger, *A Thousand Days*, p. 547.

37. *Pentagon Papers*, vol. 2, pp. 126–27.

38. John E. Rielly, ed., *American Public Opinion and U.S. Foreign Policy, 1975* (Chicago Council on Foreign Relations, 1975), pp. 16–20. Indicators that the public mood began to swing back in the other direction by the mid-1970s can be found in William Watts and Lloyd A. Free, "Nationalism, Not Isolationism," *Foreign Policy*, no. 24 (Fall 1976), pp. 3–26.

descendant of Greece in 1947 and Korea in 1950—and perhaps of China in 1949, a potential that gnawed at the consciousness of decisionmakers.

Resolve to follow through in containment had palpable urgency in 1961. Kennedy had won the presidency by the skin of his teeth. Although he had campaigned hawkishly on some strategic issues, such as the phony missile gap, Nixon had attacked him for being soft on the defense of Quemoy and Matsu. The establishment of a Communist state in Cuba after 1959 had also been a rude shock to the United States and even many liberals had become disillusioned with left-wing revolutionary movements, which came to be equated with creeping international Communist aggression. The domino theory evoked no groans or amused chuckles among the establishment. Disaster at the Bay of Pigs and the other crises of 1961 only served to highlight the linkage of the issues of apparent communism-on-the-move and American resolution to resist. Right-wing critics were also waiting in the wings at home to argue that the party that had sold out the West at Yalta and in China would do the same thing in Southeast Asia. The year 1962 was to be the heyday of the John Birch Society.

For the overwhelming majority of policymakers the perceived costs of defeat in Vietnam would remain prohibitive well into the 1960s. Strategically, the prospective costs were erosion of containment and damage to American credibility; domestically, the backlash from the right was always lurking. The costs of raising the ante seemed clearly lower. Significantly, the issue that was *not* addressed was the point at which both cost curves could cross in the future. No evidence shows that the principals sat down and established any hypothetical limit to future U.S. involvement; a determination, for instance, that the United States could conceivably go to 100,000 troops (or 500,000, or a million), but no further. The debate always hinged on the issue of commitment, but in terms of the immediate price of maintaining the commitment, not the possible ultimate point at which the price of commitment might exceed the return.

Buildup and Breakdown

In moderating the recommendations of the Taylor mission, the President gambled and won. Taylor and Rostow's dire prediction turned out to be wrong. South Vietnam did not collapse without U.S. troop units. Actually, 1962 was a pretty good year in the field as far as leaders in Washington could see. The only crisis alarming enough to provoke the dispatch of regular troop units—5,000 men to Thailand—was in neighboring Laos, and that was defused; the troops went home after the neutralization settlement was reached in July. Although American advisers in Vietnam were being killed regularly by the end of the year, things in general seemed to be working satisfactorily. With no jarring bad news from the battlefield, there was little to catalyze serious debate at home. In fact, in July McNamara initiated planning for the phaseout of U.S. military involvement.[39]

This relative lack of debate reflects the significance of the decisions in 1961. Once the final determination had been made to exceed the Geneva limits on foreign advisers, subsequent decisions on the buildup appear to have been made with alacrity. With 3,200 American soldiers in Vietnam at the end of his first year in office (there were fewer than 700 when he began), Kennedy had almost quintupled American involvement. This number more than tripled again in 1962, with 11,300 of the U.S. military in Vietnam by the end of the year. These exponential increases were not matched again for over two years, until the massive escalation and ground combat unit commitments of 1965. Yet these decisions were made with negligible internal controversy. On other issues, if consensus was lacking even on small points, the whole debate over the larger framework would usually open up again.

The new year of involvement began with a conference in Honolulu, which led to the establishment of U.S. battalion advisory teams, province advisers, and more training for irregular South Vietnamese defense forces. In February the Military Assistance Advisory Group (MAAG) was replaced by a full military field command, designated the Military Assistance Command, Vietnam (MACV), and four-star General Paul Harkins took over from three-star General Lionel G. McGarr. Advisers and equipment continued to pour in. Plans were drawn up in abundance in the State and Defense departments to replace the old CIP—a National Campaign Plan, a Comprehensive Plan for South Vietnam, a Strategic Concept for South Vietnam. In Washington an elite interdepartmental consultation mechanism, the Special Group for Counterinsurgency, was established to coordinate unconventional containment efforts on a global scale.[40]

39. See *Pentagon Papers*, vol. 2, pp. 160, 165.

40. See ibid., pp. 175–80, 419, 660–61; and *Final Report, Foreign and Military Intelligence*, S. Rept. 755, 94 Cong. 2 sess. (GPO, 1976), p. 52.

Not until the end of the year did bad news begin to come in from the field and reinvigorate policy debates. The first dramatic indicator was the debacle in January 1963 at Ap Bac, where an ARVN division was badly mangled by a much inferior Vietcong force. Disturbing information began to slip into the press and the Washington grapevine from military advisers in the provinces, contradicting the rosy official reports from Harkins and the upper echelon of MACV. Political officers in the embassy began to dispute the optimism of their boss, Ambassador Frederick E. Nolting.[41]

A Military or Political War?

The hitherto latent split in American officials' perceptions of the war cracked wide open in 1963. Basically the difference was between those who saw the fundamental obstacles to success in military terms and those who saw them in political terms. It was a curious cleavage, a sort of two-dimensional hawks versus doves division. On one side were most of the State Department participants at the assistant secretary level and lower, and middle-level CIA personnel. This group was comparatively dovish in its views on increasing direct U.S. military involvement but hawkish in its recommendations for twisting Diem's arm and manipulating South Vietnamese political forces. On the other side were the higher levels of the professional military and the Defense Department secretariat and the top officials in the CIA. This group stressed focusing on the military prosecution of the war and resisted complicating or upsetting military operations by involvement in political intrigue and social reform. They were hawkish on the Vietcong and dovish on Diem.

In the area of military strategy the issue was not whether one was for or against force, but rather what *form* force should take. The split evolved around the relative merits of conventional military operations as opposed to police-style and unconventional paramilitary tactics. Roger Hilsman, director of the State Department Bureau of Intelligence and Research; Edward Lansdale; Michael Forrestal, National Security Council staffer for Far Eastern matters; and others pushed hard for a major role for U.S. Special Forces and variants of the police strategy recommended by the British Malaya hand and head of the British Advisory Mission in Vietnam, Brigadier Sir Robert Thompson. Their principal brainchild, which Diem and Nhu eventually messed up, was the

41. See Hilsman, *To Move a Nation*, pp. 447–49; and David Halberstam, *The Best and the Brightest* (Random House, 1972), pp. 200–06, 252.

Strategic Hamlet Program.[42] This view matched the enthusiasm of administration civilians—especially Rostow, Robert Kennedy, and the President himself—for the development of sophisticated counterinsurgency programs; counterinsurgency was designed to wage political war, to "win hearts and minds."[43] And winning hearts and minds seemed to be something the Diem government was less committed to with each passing day.

The U.S. military establishment, however, looked askance at unconventional forces and worried that emphasizing them would produce a weak and static defense posture, detracting from the first priority of developing a conventional South Vietnamese army capable of dynamic offensive operations. Crackerjack police and strategic hamlets were all well and good, but as General Earl G. Wheeler later said in criticizing the related enclave military strategy, "No one ever won a battle sitting on his ass."[44] Militarily, then, the strategy debate was a matter of emphasis. Critics who see the 1961–63 bureaucratic debate as a simple struggle between cautious diplomats and Pentagon adventurists are off the mark. Even Robert Gallucci, a critic of our interpretation, admitted, "It is not that State Department actors were 'doves,' for they issued prescriptions involving the use of American military troops, and they did not shrink from advocating violent means."[45] The greater difference was the emphasis the diplomats (though McNamara joined heartily on this point) put on the political basis of the war and on their belief that political improvement—increasing the administrative effectiveness of the South Vietnamese government and increasing popular support for the government—was a prerequisite to military progress. The key in this view was leverage.

Leverage: the old refrain. It was a recurrent theme from the early 1950s, when the French were the target, to the early 1970s, when the Thieu regime was the target. And it rarely seemed to work. How could the United States make its clients act like clients? The premise of the

42. See Hilsman, To Move a Nation, pp. 429–36. "The strategic hamlet program was, simply, a way of arming the villages of Vietnam so that they could defend themselves if they were attacked by a small band of marauding guerrillas and at least hold out until reinforcements came if they were attacked by a large band" (ibid., p. 431). See also Pentagon Papers, vol. 2, pp. 674–75, 720; and Gallucci, Neither Peace nor Honor, pp. 26–27.

43. See Pentagon Papers, vol. 2, pp. 650–51, 681–84.

44. Quoted in Henry F. Graff, The Tuesday Cabinet: Deliberation and Decision on Peace and War under Lyndon B. Johnson (Prentice-Hall, 1970), p. 128.

45. Gallucci, Neither Peace nor Honor, p. 31.

CIP of January 1961 was that planned increases in military support would be doled out as Diem came across with administrative reforms in Saigon. When Ball one-upped the Defense Department in revising the Gilpatric report in May, he changed the approach to put more conditions on aid. New programs authorized after the Taylor mission were also supposed to be contingent on reforms. But Diem masterfully temporized and obscured his noncompliance at each stage, issuing decrees but failing to follow them up. Then, as later, there was always a catch. Political instability made reforms imperative for the long run but also made it imperative not to throw the fragile government into chaos in the short run; leverage required knocking South Vietnamese heads, but if they were knocked hard enough to matter, the Communists would profit. When Robert Komer suggested that the way to get rid of an incompetent ARVN commander was simply to cut off his support, General William Westmoreland answered, "You cut off all support to the Eighteenth ARVN and the Viet Cong will know it as fast as General Giai. The next thing you know, here they come through Lam Dong!"[46]

The paradox came out in other ways. In 1965, for instance, some American officials wanted to maintain influence over the uses to which U.S. economic aid was put by keeping the authority to sign off on disbursements of the Agency for International Development, but the State Department objected because it would undermine efforts to develop greater South Vietnamese self-reliance and independent effectiveness.[47] In the Buddhist crisis of 1966 officials considered withholding U.S. aid to Thieu and Nguyen Cao Ky and withdrawing U.S. troops into base camps, but this seemed to make no sense since it would only increase Communist chances to take advantage of the situation.[48] U.S. advisers were also constrained in reporting corruption, according to Westmoreland, "lest they get a reputation as spies and *lose* their leverage with their counterparts."[49] How could the United States force the replacement of "bad" South Vietnamese officials with good ones, Allan Good-

46. Quoted in W. Scott Thompson and Donaldson D. Frizell, eds., *The Lessons of Vietnam* (Crane, Russak, 1977), p. 230.

47. *Pentagon Papers*, vol. 2, pp. 478–80.

48. Militant Buddhists and students found an opportunity to protest against the Saigon government by staging mass demonstrations when Thieu and Ky removed General Nguyen Chanh Thi from his command. See Westmoreland, *A Soldier Reports*, chap. 9.

49. Ibid., p. 244 (emphasis added). See also ibid., p. 212; and Frances Fitz-Gerald, *Fire in the Lake: The Vietnamese and the Americans in Vietnam* (Atlantic-Little, Brown, 1972), p. 366.

man, academic analyst of Vietnamese politics, asked, "if you can't 'take your marbles and go home?' . . . If you just simply can't say, 'The U.S. mission is leaving?' "[50] Who would pull the strings on whom? Vietnam seemed to end by showing, as Samuel Huntington, Harvard professor of government, put it, that "our leverage varies inversely with our commitments."[51]

The supreme irony was that leverage was designed to increase the political vitality and viability of the government so that it would be more effective in mobilizing the country against the Communists, but the government could not implement many of the reforms without cutting its own throat. American officials wanted Diem to consolidate his Byzantine military command structures and intelligence networks, eliminate administrative overlapping, and delegate more authority to subordinates. But in doing this Diem would be giving his political rivals the tools to make a coup against him. Moreover, any aid cuts that might have been substantial enough to induce Diem to do what the Americans wanted him to do would have been substantial enough to jeopardize the war effort. It was all déjà vu. Even in the darkest days of the Chinese civil war Chiang Kai-shek never allowed the United States to put any significant political conditions on the aid program. In both instances, it was often unclear who was the real patron and who the client.[52]

Edward Lansdale had agreed that the political component of the war was more important than the strictly military one. But he differed with the others who shared this view, in opposing the arm-twisting approach. The alternative he posed in 1961 was a strategy of political consultation

50. Quoted in Thompson and Frizell, *Lessons of Vietnam*, p. 229.

51. Quoted in Richard M. Pfeffer, ed., *No More Vietnams? The War and the Future of American Foreign Policy* (Harper and Row for the Adlai Stevenson Institute of International Affairs, 1968), p. 230.

52. For discussions of aid versus reforms, see Hilsman, *To Move a Nation*, p. 500; Tang Tsou, *America's Failure in China, 1941–50* (University of Chicago Press, 1963), p. 388; and Halberstam, *The Best and the Brightest*, p. 149. The client, paradoxically, could even ward off pressure by considering the rejection of aid, which from the patron's standpoint threatened to weaken the war effort. Shortly before the attacks on the Buddhists, which created a crisis in relations with the United States, Diem and Nhu reportedly planned to demand a reduction in the number of American personnel in South Vietnam because they were incensed about infringements on their sovereignty by the U.S. MAAG and Special Forces, which failed to coordinate their activities properly with the palace. See CIA, Telegram Information Report No. TDCSDB-3/654, 285, April 22, 1963, JFKL/NSF-VNCF, 8/24/63–8/31/63.

and the power of example, based on a small elite and autonomous American cadre that would stay in Vietnam for an extended time. This presidential task force would supposedly use trust, suasion, and example, rather than leverage, to lead the Diem government in the path of righteousness.[53] The State Department had successfully torpedoed this proposal (shortly thereafter Lansdale was eased out of work on Vietnam), in part because it was garishly unorthodox administratively (compromising the ambassador's control of the country team), in part from wariness of Lansdale's reputation for free-wheeling behavior and his personal connections with Diem, and probably in part because it seemed naively soft-nosed toward the South Vietnamese government.

Much as that may have been the case, it is not clear that the State Department officials who focused on the political war were all that more perceptive than either Lansdale or the military officials who focused narrowly on the military war. The civilian officials were right in that the fundamental problems in the South Vietnamese war effort were political and sociological. But until late 1963 they had as many illusions about the U.S. capacity to mold the situation politically as the military had about the U.S. capacity to produce a winning team on the battlefield. They recognized that the means to the end should be different, but few yet questioned that *any* means might be insufficient. And the strategies they chose to push, such as Thompson's, were not clearly the solution to political problems.

Thompson's view of counterrevolution was a rather mechanistic one, focusing on organizational and administrative efficiency rather than problems such as land reform, political parties, or popular ideology. In fact, given the turbulent revolutionary issues at stake in Vietnam, it was remarkable how politically sterile the Thompson doctrine was. Thompson abhorred the idea of partisan political intervention, but the administrative program he recommended presupposed a viable political system, which was just what was lacking.[54] (One of the initial ventures in the Strategic Hamlet Program—Operation SUNRISE, a forced resettlement of population in the spring of 1962—was an unpopular and awkward move of questionable success that should have signaled the prob-

53. See *Pentagon Papers*, vol. 2, pp. 442–43; Edward Geary Lansdale, Major General, U.S.A.F. (Ret.) *In the Midst of Wars: An American's Mission to Southeast Asia* (Harper and Row, 1972); and FitzGerald, *Fire in the Lake*, p. 269.

54. See Sir Robert Thompson, *Defeating Communist Insurgency: The Lessons of Malaya and Vietnam* (Praeger, 1966); and comments by Thompson and Huntington in Pfeffer, *No More Vietnams?* pp. 244–45.

lems that were to come in the first phase of pacification drives.) But most significant of all, the political war types, while more realistic in recognizing the political decay under Diem, were much less cautious than the military war types in resolving to have the United States try to set it straight.

Taking the Reins: 1963

The split between the political war and military war strategists widened in the political crisis of the summer of 1963, culminated in the autumn coup against Diem, and marked a middle watershed in U.S. policy between the commitments of 1961 and the massive military intervention of 1965. American analysts were disagreeing about progress on the battlefield (Harkins, Nolting, and the top echelons of MACV and the country team continued to spew optimism, while lieutenant colonels in the boondocks and second echelon Foreign Service officers in the embassy saw decline all around), but political chaos was there for all to see in lurid detail. Two years to the day after the Gilpatric report that led to NSAM 52, South Vietnamese troops fired on Buddhist protesters in Hue, killing nine and wounding numerous others. For the rest of May and into the summer Buddhist groups mobilized in demonstrations against the government, and monks began to immolate themselves. With no willingness on Diem's part to do anything meaningful to accommodate the Buddhists, and with Madame Nhu issuing acerbically cavalier taunts about "barbecued bonzes," Deputy Chief of Mission William Truehart warned Diem in June that the United States might have to disassociate itself from him if he were not more forthcoming. Little noticed in most commentaries on this period, Truehart's warning was the toughest posture toward Diem that a major U.S. official in the field had assumed since General Collins's early recommendations during his 1954–55 mission. (Nolting, on home leave at the time, was later embittered by Truehart's change of heart on Diem.)[55]

The End of American Patience

In Washington and Saigon the crisis threw the battle lines in the policy debate into high relief. Harkins; Nolting; CIA Station Chief John Richardson; McNamara; Taylor; the JCS Special Assistant for Counter-

55. For details of the crisis in 1963, see *Pentagon Papers*, vol. 2, pp. 207–08, 229–30; and Hilsman, *To Move a Nation*, p. 468.

insurgency and Special Activities (SACSA), Major General Victor Krulak; and Vice-President Johnson opposed dirtying American hands with intrigue against Diem and plumped for getting on with the war in the provinces. Henry Cabot Lodge; Ball; Harriman; Forrestal; Hilsman; Truehart; most of Richardson's staff; John Mendenhall, a senior Foreign Service officer; and Robert Kennedy resolved that something had to be done politically. At a minimum, Ngo Dinh Nhu, who had assumed the proportions of a Rasputin-like nemesis to both the Vietnamese public and the American reformers, had to go.[56] At a maximum, as the summer wore on this group believed the United States might have to support a military coup to put the government in more responsive hands. Ironically, as time ran out it was the American civilians who favored supporting the South Vietnamese military against their civilian government, while the American soldiers favored the South Vietnamese civilians against their military opponents.

The possibility of backing a coup was not altogether new, though it had never been seriously considered. In 1961, shortly after the Taylor mission, the President had asked Ambassador John Kenneth Galbraith to drop by Saigon and relay his suggestions. Galbraith's assessment, which seems curiously uncharacteristic of his later attitudes, had three basic points: no reform was possible unless the United States got rid of Diem; if it did so, the war would not be hard to win; and a military government would be a hopeful alternative to the American mandarin client. He advised: "Given even a moderately effective government . . . I can't help thinking the insurgency might very soon be settled." And later:

Washington is currently having an intellectual orgasm on the unbeatability of guerrilla war. . . . It is a cliché that there is no alternative to Diem's regime. . . . No one considered Truman an alternative to Roosevelt. . . . There was none I imagine for Rhee. . . . It is a better rule that nothing succeeds like successors.
We should not be alarmed by the Army as an alternative.[57]

56. See Hilsman, *To Move a Nation*, pp. 491–92, 497–99; Taylor, *Swords and Plowshares*, pp. 290–94; and *Pentagon Papers*, vol. 2, p. 204. Johnson's early devotion to Diem was a subtle indicator of the attitude of dogged perseverance he would later assume as President. When he visited Vietnam on a special mission in May 1961 he touted Diem as the Churchill of Southeast Asia and responded to a journalist's question about how closely the United States should tie itself to Diem by saying, "Shit, man, he's the only boy we got out there." Quoted in Halberstam, *The Best and the Brightest*, p. 135. See also Lyndon Baines Johnson, *The Vantage Point: Perspectives of the Presidency, 1963–1969* (Holt, Rinehart and Winston, 1971), p. 61.

57. *Pentagon Papers*, vol. 2, pp. 122–23, 124.

Lansdale agreed with Galbraith that Diem could not be pressured successfully, but he differed on the risks a coup would pose. He believed any successors to Diem would be no better and that the Vietcong would exploit the confusion following a coup.[58] By late 1963 the disagreement was still between those who believed that the bad situation could only get worse after Diem and those who believed it could only get better.

Henry Cabot Lodge, appointed ambassador as a gesture of bipartisanship, arrived in Saigon on August 22, one day after Nhu's police attacked pagodas throughout the country. He took charge immediately. On August 24 he cabled Washington, to blame Nhu. What followed later the same day was to be the most controversial communication in the history of the U.S. involvement. It was a weekend in Washington, and many of the principals were out of town. At the State Department, Harriman, Forrestal, and Hilsman drafted a reply to Lodge.

US government cannot tolerate situation in which power lies in Nhu's hands. Diem must be given chance to rid himself of Nhu. . . . If, in spite of all your efforts, Diem remains obdurate and refuses, then we must face the possibility that Diem himself cannot be preserved. . . . You may also tell appropriate military commanders we will give them direct support in any interim period of breakdown central government mechanism.[59]

The cable was cleared by Ball, on a golf course, and by the President, on the telephone, in Hyannisport. A Voice of America broadcast was initiated that exonerated ARVN from complicity in the pagoda raids, and CIA's Lieutenant Colonel Lucien Conein met with South Vietnamese generals to apprise them of the new U.S. policy.[60]

When pro-Diem partisans heard of the cable, they counterattacked and lambasted it as hastily adventurous. But the new policy was already rolling, and Lodge was in the forefront. He warned Washington on August 29: "We are launched on a course from which there is no respectable turning back: The overthrow of the Diem Government. . . . We should proceed to make all-out effort to get Generals to move promptly."[61]

When Rusk questioned him about whether a new approach to Diem

58. See ibid., pp. 25–26, 30.

59. Ibid., p. 734.

60. See ibid., pp. 735–36; and Hilsman, *To Move a Nation*, pp. 485–88. Hilsman said Taylor cleared the cable for the Defense Department, but Taylor denied this. His first reaction was that the anti-Diem people had taken advantage of the principals' absence to get the cable out (*Swords and Plowshares*, p. 292).

61. *Pentagon Papers*, vol. 2, p. 738.

—which the Harkins-McNamara group wanted—would be advisable, the ambassador emphatically said no, arguing that the best chance of resolving the crisis "is by the generals taking over the government lock, stock and barrel."[62] But the generals, after running into complications and retaining doubts about U.S. support, aborted their coup.

The End of Diem

Although Diem was reprieved, the cauldron continued to bubble into the fall. There were second and third thoughts within the National Security Council. Those opposed to involving the United States in intrigue recommended rapprochement with Diem. Roger Hilsman favored the "Pressures and Persuasion Track" rather than the "Reconciliation Track" because it would be possible to shift from the former to the latter at any time, but not vice versa.[63] The President apparently agreed, leaning toward pressuring Diem and toward dumping him if there were no new results. In a TV interview in early September he emphasized the need for greater popular support of the government in South Vietnam and mentioned pregnantly that this might require a change in "personnel." He also dispatched representatives of the warring U.S. factions—Mendenhall for the State Department, Krulak for the Defense Department —on a quick survey trip to the field.[64] When they returned and reported to the NSC, the glaring disparity in their assessments provoked Kennedy's famous quip, "You two did visit the same country, didn't you?"[65] Perhaps still uncertain, the President sent another high-level mission at the end of the month—McNamara and Taylor. In early October Kennedy authorized covert contacts with the dissident Vietnamese generals, not to encourage a coup actively, but to "build contacts with possible alternative leadership," as McNamara and Taylor had recommended.[66]

Washington was sliding fitfully toward a coup again, but Lodge was running confidently. He prompted less ambiguous encouragement to the generals and had CIA Station Chief Richardson—who was known to favor more conciliation toward Diem—recalled. On October 5 Kennedy instructed Lodge to avoid encouraging a coup; his cold feet were

62. Ibid., p. 239.
63. Roger Hilsman, memorandum to Rusk, "Viet-Nam," September 16, 1963, JFKL/NSF-VNCF, Action Plans 9/18/63–9/21/63.
64. *Pentagon Papers*, vol. 2, pp. 213–14.
65. Ibid., p. 244.
66. Ibid., p. 250; see also p. 217.

due to worries the United States might be tarred with involvement in a coup that might fail. Lodge pressed for more clearly benign neutrality that would give the generals a green light.

Kennedy, in effect, was throwing responsibility for American complicity in a coup back onto Lodge. The President had been disturbed by the different appraisals from Lodge and Harkins at the end of August, but Lodge had advised then that the United States was irrevocably committed to the generals. Washington authorized the ambassador to suspend aid at his discretion, and Lodge subsequently cut off payments to Colonel Le Quang Tung's Special Forces—Nhu's "palace guard"— on October 17. On October 30 Lodge cabled that there was little the United States could do to influence the Vietnamese generals' decision for or against a coup, and reassured Washington. The same day Bundy shot back that Washington regarded it as unacceptable that the United States could not influence the plot. Yet he relayed the President's decision to have Lodge try to restrain the coup leaders *only* if the plot did not seem sure of success.[67]

This period marked the beginning of strong initiative from the field —Harkins's dissent from the Lodge view notwithstanding (Harkins, in effect, was cut out of the decisionmaking in the final days before the coup). Up to the last minute, Washington agonized over implicating the United States in a failed coup, but Lodge persisted forcefully in preventing any discouragement of the generals. And when the coup finally broke on November 1, CIA officer Conein was on the scene quickly with $42,000 to pay the plotters' troops.[68]

Along with the beginning of initiative from the field, which would continue to be central in determining short-range strategy, the coup marked a renewed and deeper assumption of responsibility by the United States. In acquiescing to the overthrow the President set the stage for further Americanization of the war. He did not shrink from the responsibility, but it is not clear that he intended all the implications. It was hoped that dumping Diem would get the South Vietnamese in a

67. For information pertaining to Lodge's view and the administration's reaction to it, see ibid., pp. 212–20, 253–54, 257–62, 789–92. Lodge's breezy memoir disputes imputations in the Pentagon Papers that he promoted the coup but does not contradict the record of cable traffic. See Henry Cabot Lodge, *The Storm Has Many Eyes: A Personal Narrative* (Norton, 1973), pp. 208–12.

68. See Halberstam, *The Best and the Brightest,* p. 289; and *Interim Report, Alleged Assassination Plots Involving Foreign Leaders*, S. Rept. 465, 94 Cong. 1 sess. (GPO, 1975), p. 22.

position where they could pursue the war effectively. As Kennedy was fond of pointing out, the Lord helps those who help themselves, and "in the final analysis it is their war."[69] Ten days after that statement, however, he added: "What helps to win the war, we support; what interferes with the war effort [implicitly, Diem] we oppose. . . . *But we are not there to see a war lost.*"[70]

The hope that the coup would bring greater South Vietnamese self-reliance was in vain, however. A brief flurry of elation occurred in early November and prompted the rallying of the Cao Dai and Hoa Hao sects to the new regime. (Henry Cabot Lodge was even euphoric enough on the eve of the coup to envision that *North* Vietnam could be pushed toward neutralization.)[71] But the honeymoon was soon followed by bad news. New evidence became available of distortion in the optimistic military reporting of battlefield and strategic hamlet progress, and pessimism reigned again by the end of the year. McNamara noted the surprise that followed the coup by saying, "We did not know how deep the rot was."[72] Moreover, Diem's demise was the prelude to political chaos, not the finale. Coups and countercoups would plague Saigon for the next two years and would pose the primary impediment to American hopes for military progress.

The American pro-Diem faction may have been obtuse in failing to recognize his hopelessness and in failing to see how bad the military situation in the field had actually gotten by late 1963, but it may have been more sober than the anti-Diem faction in recognizing the implications of crossing the coup threshold. The military turned out to be right in their prediction that a coup would produce chaos and impair the

69. "Transcript of Broadcast with Walter Cronkite Inaugurating a CBS Television News Program, September 2, 1963," *Public Papers, Kennedy, 1963* (GPO, 1964), p. 652.

70. "The President's News Conference of September 12, 1963," ibid., p. 673 (emphasis added).

71. Henry Cabot Lodge, "Toward the Neutralization of North Viet-Nam," October 30, 1963, LBJL/NSF-VNCF, vol. 5, item 40.

72. Quoted in Graff, *Tuesday Cabinet*, p. 121. For a discussion of this period, see *Pentagon Papers*, vol. 2, p. 273; and vol. 3, pp. 2, 7, 22, 23. The Strategic Hamlet Program had been quite successful in some respects. The head of the National Liberation Front, Nguyen Huu Tho, confessed that the program had reduced Communist effectiveness to the point where the NFL had to reconsider its whole strategy of armed uprising. After the battle of Ap Bac, however, the Communists rebounded. (See Dennis J. Duncanson, *Government and Revolution in Vietnam* [New York: Oxford University Press, 1968], pp. 326–27.) It was *late* in 1963 that the Saigon government's war effort collapsed most clearly.

prosecution of the war. (A Special National Intelligence Estimate had predicted the same back in July.)[73] A case could even be made that the train of events made direct U.S. intervention inevitable. With Diem's blood at least partially on American hands, it would be even more difficult psychologically to resist further moves needed to shore up the South. Lyndon Johnson was later to characterize getting rid of Diem as "the worst mistake we ever made."[74]

Did the political war types fail to realize this? Yes and no. No naive ebullience about quick or easy military victory followed the passing of Diem, but there also was little serious consideration of alternatives to pressing on. Compromise with the Communists was not entertained. The United States had compromised in 1954, but the proviso then was that the half of Vietnam it had settled for should become an inviolable bastion (which is why the United States did nothing to prevent Diem's cancellation of the 1956 nationwide elections that negotiators in Geneva had agreed on). After the assassinations of Diem and Kennedy, Senator Mike Mansfield recommended a Laos solution—U.S. withdrawal and division of the country between the Saigon government and the Vietcong—but the proposal fell on deaf ears. Compromise never became an option of any popularity within the government until frustration welled up in the post–1965 escalation period, and even then the support for it did not surface volubly until the policy reassessment that followed the Tet offensive.

Rejecting the Chance to Withdraw

In late 1963 only two officials at the policy level mentioned even in passing the possibility of what today so clearly seems to have been opportune at the time: using the political crisis as a pretext for U.S. withdrawal. One, a highly influential adviser, was shortly to fall from grace as soon as Lyndon Johnson became President: Robert Kennedy. The other was a middle-echelon State Department member of the Vietnam working group: Paul Kattenburg. But at the meeting where Kattenburg ventured this possibility his superior, Dean Rusk, quickly countered it by demanding that the meeting proceed on the assumption the United States would *not* pull out. No one rose to Kattenburg's defense; "The Administration hewed to the belief that if the U.S. be but

73. See *Pentagon Papers*, vol. 2, p. 209.
74. Quoted in Graff, *Tuesday Cabinet*, p. 53.

willing to exercise its power, it could ultimately have its way in world affairs."[75]

Other doves believed that concessions should not go as far as acquiescing in Communist victory. In 1962 Galbraith had urged that the United States be receptive to a negotiated settlement but on the not unambitious basis of "any broadly based non-Communist government that is free from external interference."[76] Similarly, in 1964 George Ball, prescient in his recommendations against U.S. escalations, was still assuming a negotiated settlement could secure South Vietnamese autonomy and North Vietnamese cessation of support for the insurgency.[77] No one of consequence was taking seriously the choice of letting South Vietnam go—gradually or quickly—down the drain.

No one of consequence, perhaps, except the President. One slim shred of evidence suggests Kennedy was contemplating withdrawal as early as the spring of 1963. Kenneth O'Donnell testified that the President said he planned to get out but had to wait until after the 1964 election (Barry Goldwater was already a contender at that point) in order to avoid a McCarthyite Red scare.[78] But it is unlikely that this was more than a tentative, speculative, offhand remark. Aside from the callousness and self-serving political cynicism it implies, why did Kennedy entrust his intention to his appointment secretary rather than to his executive advisers? (He did mention the possibility to Senator Mansfield, but whether this was to allay the fears of one of the few congressional doves or really to chart a firm intention can still only be guessed.) Undoubtedly the possibility lingered in Kennedy's mind; it would have been consistent with the elbowroom on commitment he had sought in the 1961 decisions. But as an intention, it could hardly have been more than a contingency plan. If Kennedy had seriously meant to extricate the United States, the Diem coup would have been a perfect pretext. Yet none of the President's statements before, during, or after the coup hinted at a weakening of the American commitment to South Vietnamese independence. The only weakening was in the support for the

75. *Pentagon Papers*, vol. 2, p. 204. See also pp. 742, 743; and Hilsman, *To Move a Nation*, pp. 501, 504.

76. *Pentagon Papers*, vol. 2, pp. 670–71.

77. See George W. Ball, "A Light That Failed," *Atlantic Monthly*, July 1972, pp. 45 ff.

78. Kenneth P. O'Donnell and David F. Powers with Joe McCarthy, *"Johnny, We Hardly Knew Ye": Memories of John Fitzgerald Kennedy* (Little, Brown, 1972), p. 16.

Diem regime, which had come to be seen as an obstacle to success against the Communists. Diem had to go precisely so that the war could proceed.

Withdrawal was more likely expected to come from success, as Mc-Namara envisioned in his phaseout plan, which may have been a cosmetic exercise but was not finally abandoned until 1964. While Kennedy's attitudes to the Soviet Union were changing in 1963, after the reduction in tension following the Cuban missile crisis and when détente seemed possible, China was still assumed to be ravenous and intractable, the éminence grise pulling the strings in Vietnam, ever ready to pounce. Summary rejection is not too strong a term to describe the fate of any precipitate withdrawal suggestions in Kennedy's councils of war. For Kennedy, Vietnam policy had been a fight to keep the power of decision in his own hands. That was why he had bridled at McNamara's attempt on November 8, 1961, to get him to make a show of accepting an unconditional and open-ended commitment, which would have boxed him into accepting a priori all the future accoutrements— and lack of choice—that were implicit in such a declaration. That was why he had welcomed the softer options in the memo from Rusk and McNamara three days later. But these examples of maintaining presidential flexibility were not decommitting steps; Kennedy did not couple them with anything that would have given force to decommitment. It is notable, too, that all the questions about how the President felt were raised, not near the time of his death, but well into the Johnson administration. Theodore Sorensen's account, published in 1965, leaves no doubt of Kennedy's resolve.[79]

Kennedy's decisions over three years were, as Gallucci characterized them, "studied moderation," but not for the reasons Gallucci cited. Escalation came in 1965 not simply because the process of debate was constricted and Pentagon-dominated under Johnson, while it had been "open" and cushioned by the political orientation of the State Department until 1964;[80] rather, the sequence of cause and effect were reversed. The debate was more open at times during the earlier period (though probably no more open in autumn 1961 than after 1964) because choices had not been so narrowed by events. The objectives remained consistent from 1961 to 1965, but the tightening of the noose

79. Sorensen, *Kennedy.*
80. Gallucci, *Neither Peace nor Honor,* pp. 12, 14.

on the battlefield after Kennedy's death tightened the range of means that could be used to uphold the objectives. As Sorensen said, JFK's "essential contribution . . . was both to raise our commitment and to keep it limited."[81] For those three years, it was possible to do both. The developing crunch between commitment and limitation was to be the central problem faced by Lyndon B. Johnson in his first year in office.

81. Sorensen, *Kennedy,* p. 652.

CHAPTER FOUR

Intervention in Force: The Johnson Administration, I

Vietnam became the high drama of the Johnson administration. For previous presidents Southeast Asia had been an ongoing, ever-nagging problem, occasionally flaring into crisis but usually remaining a secondary issue in the mosaic of international and domestic politics. That the war should come to dominate all other issues in the second half of the 1960s was a bitter pill to Lyndon Johnson, who, unlike Kennedy, was much more interested in and adept at dealing with domestic problems. Vietnam would be Johnson's despair as he saw his first love, the Great Society—which he characterized as his "beautiful woman"[1] —upstaged and stunted by war expenditures and rising domestic controversy.

This chapter and the next outline the unfolding of the four acts of the high drama: hesitancy, planning, and coming up against hard choices in 1964; decisions on massive intervention and the development of basic strategy in Americanizing the war in 1965; committing increasing doses of force and groping for solutions during the time of gradual escalation from 1966 through 1967; and the final reckoning and redirecting of strategy toward disengagement in early 1968. Several intermingled strands of strategy and decision influenced policy-making in these years: the air war against North Vietnam, the ground war in South Vietnam, the "other war" of pacification and nation-building in South Vietnam, and the quest for negotiations with North Vietnam. Underlying the whole sequence of decisions were external and internal constraints: on the first count, the reactions of China and the Soviet Union to U.S. escalation, a concern that declined slightly

1. Doris Kearns, *Lyndon Johnson and the American Dream* (Harper and Row, 1976), p. 286.

over time; and on the second count, the erosion of domestic support for administration policy, a concern that increased substantially over time.

Preparing for Pressure: 1964

Vietnam did not dominate Johnson's consciousness in his initial year in office to the extent it would thereafter. During LBJ's first intelligence briefing the day after Kennedy's assassination, Director of Central Intelligence John McCone concentrated on the Soviet strategic nuclear threat, and the first NSC meeting on December 5 hardly touched on Vietnam. The President barely mentioned Southeast Asia in his first State of the Union Message, and his first major directive on Vietnam—NSAM 273—simply reaffirmed Kennedy's policy. Preoccupied with reelection and absorbed in Great Society legislation, Johnson left Vietnam to Defense Secretary Robert McNamara's watchful eye for much of 1964, except for the period of the Tonkin Gulf crisis in August.[2]

The President's most significant act before the August crisis was to approve NSAM 288 in March, following the return of McNamara and Maxwell Taylor from their most recent trip to the field (in 1963–64 the defense secretary and JCS chairman seemed to be on a perpetual shuttle between Washington and Saigon). This NSAM was "minimal in the scale of its recommendations at the same time that it stated U.S. objectives in the most sweeping terms used up to that time."[3] At no time during the strategy debates of 1964 was this commitment to the defense of Vietnam questioned. NSAM 288 also authorized planning studies for striking North Vietnam. The JCS saw this as the preparation of a program for implementation in the near future (in contrast to the planning group in the State Department and the Office of International Security Affairs (ISA) in the Defense Department that viewed it, as apparently the President did, as a contingency planning exer-

2. See Chester L. Cooper, *The Lost Crusade: America in Vietnam* (Dodd, Mead, 1970), pp. 221–22, 225–26; *The Pentagon Papers: The Defense Department History of United States Decisionmaking on Vietnam,* Senator Gravel ed. (Beacon Press, 1971), vol. 2, p. 170; and Rowland Evans and Robert Novak, *Lyndon B. Johnson: The Exercise of Power* (New American Library, 1966), p. 532.

3. *Pentagon Papers,* vol. 3, p. 3.

cise).[4] Moreover, the JCS saw NSAM 288 as a clear affirmation of U.S. commitment to defeating the Communist insurgency, and in the policy debates of the following years they would cite it frequently in dismissing suggestions for moderation or deescalation ventured by the small corps of quasi-doves within the government.

Changes of the Guard

As 1963 ended, the principals had continued to steer a middle course between reinforcing commitment and accelerating direct American involvement. Both the Harriman-Hilsman-Forrestal low-profile strategy and the military direct pressure strategy were rejected. But the balance was tilting progressively toward military war measures and against the strategy of those in the government who focused on the political aspects of the war. For one thing, political chaos in South Vietnam made the political war seem an intractable mess, not susceptible to easy U.S. control; for another, an increase in military pressure came to be seen as one way to help stabilize the South Vietnamese government.

As the trend became clear, the political war strategists began to melt away. "Harriman, Hilsman, Truehart, Forrestal and Kattenburg very quickly became nonplayers," as Halberstam said.[5] Hilsman resigned, emphasizing in his parting memo the need for an "oil-blot" pacification strategy, avoidance of large-scale operations, and rejection of redirecting the war effort toward North Vietnam.[6] Truehart was eased out, and Kattenburg bailed out, leaving the Interdepartmental Working Group on Vietnam for another job (before he left he said the war was lost and argued presciently that if the United States went in, it would lead to half a million troops and five or ten years of war).[7]

The forthright dominance of the State Department in the war councils, obvious in the spring of 1961, was now a thing of the past. Secretary of State Dean Rusk did not wish to challenge the military's assessments in the policymaking process, and criticism of some of the State Department's contributions led to a shift in the locus of planning to William Bundy's Far East bureau, to ISA in the Pentagon, and later to Walt Rostow's staff in the White House. Through the fall of 1964,

4. See ibid., pp. 9, 50, 106–08.
5. David Halberstam, *The Best and the Brightest* (Random House, 1972), p. 369.
6. *Pentagon Papers*, vol. 3, pp. 9, 43.
7. Halberstam, *The Best and the Brightest*, pp. 370–71.

nevertheless, the administration actually followed the courses of action recommended by the State Department more than it did those of the military.[8]

Political instability in Saigon remained the primary source of the principal decisionmakers' consternation and frustration. By February the Strategic Hamlet Program had come to a halt, "and there was an ubiquitous group of lean and hungry generals," as Chester Cooper noted, "waiting in the wings for a chance to get into the spotlight and into the treasury."[9] In the spring General Nguyen Khanh, leader of the junta, started circulating the idea of a "march North" against the DRV. McNamara and Taylor had to tighten his leash, admonishing him that the United States would support no ARVN moves across the seventeenth parallel. In his first report in August, after succeeding Henry Cabot Lodge as ambassador, Taylor was pessimistic about all aspects of the situation.[10] The political musical chairs game of government by coup, countercoup, and quasi-coup continued throughout the year; there were seven governments in Saigon in 1964, three between August 16 and September 3 alone.[11] "Khanh and [General Duong Van] Minh checked in and out of their offices in the Presidential Palace like traveling salesmen at a commercial hotel," as Cooper put it.[12] An attempt at civilian government (under Tran Van Huong) in the good old American sense was also abortive. The South Vietnamese military Young Turks dissolved the High National Council shortly before Christmas.[13] The situation at year-end, as Taylor described it, was a "three-cornered conflict, most of it unfortunately public: the Huong government versus the generals, the generals versus the American Ambassador, and the Buddhists versus the government and the Ambassador."[14]

In this context, hitting North Vietnam began to loom as the only alternative to fiasco. McNamara's planning for phased U.S. withdrawal was abandoned. Throughout most of Johnson's first year, however,

8. See Robert L. Gallucci, *Neither Peace nor Honor: The Politics of American Military Policy in Viet-Nam,* Washington Center of Foreign Policy Research, School of Advanced International Studies, Studies in International Affairs, 24 (John Hopkins University Press, 1975), pp. 32–34, 40; and *Pentagon Papers,* vol. 3, p. 204.

9. Cooper, *The Lost Crusade,* p. 227.

10. Ibid., p. 233; and *Pentagon Papers,* vol. 3, pp. 12, 64, 66.

11. Cooper, *The Lost Crusade,* p. 253.

12. Ibid., pp. 246–47.

13. Ibid., 249–51.

14. Maxwell D. Taylor, General, U.S. Army (Ret.), *Swords and Plowshares* (Norton, 1972), p. 331.

nearly all his advisers favored deferring the application of direct pressure against the North, although they dallied with strategies that came close to it.[15] Only the JCS, Lodge, and Rostow forthrightly promoted it. In March the Joint Chiefs recommended an air campaign, reiterating this advice throughout the year in a barrage of memos, usually couched in terms of implementing NSAM 288. August produced the "Rostow Thesis," a rationale for the need to strike at the "source" of the insurgency and subsequently criticized by ISA and the State Department's Policy Planning Council.[16] Lodge proposed his own "carrot and stick" approach. Mini-escalation was in fact undertaken in the spring in the extension of reconnaissance flights over Laos, with a consequent loss of U.S. aircraft. (The administration did not conceal these measures. William Bundy gave journalists full details on the operations.[17] Mike Mansfield warned Johnson that further reconnaissance in Laos would risk more plane losses and increase the danger of an action-reaction acceleration of American involvement.)[18] Throughout the year, though, the President held off on major measures, and "raised procrastination to the level of an art form."[19] One incident punctuated this year of hesitancy: the Tonkin Gulf crisis.

The Tonkin Gulf

On August 2, 1964, North Vietnamese torpedo boats pursued and attacked the U.S. destroyer *Maddox* in the Gulf of Tonkin. The destroyer registered no damage beyond a one-inch bullet hole, but the incident electrified Washington. The President gathered a group of admirals together for a tongue lashing. " 'You've got a whole fleet and all those airplanes,' he exploded, 'and you can't even sink three little old PT boats.' . . . The red-faced admirals explained that, by the peace-

15. McGeorge Bundy forwarded a memorandum to the President from Michael Forrestal (May 29, 1964), who said rather ambiguously: "What I think is needed fairly soon . . . is action by the United States in some part of Southeast Asia which gets across forcefully to the Vientnamese [sic] a sense that Communist insurgency can be contained and that we will do whatever is required to insure this." (LBJL/NSF-VNCF, vol. X, item 10.)

16. See *Pentagon Papers*, vol. 3, pp. 107–10, 120, 131–33, 144–48.

17. U.S. Department of State, "Transcript of Background Press and Radio News Briefing," June 17, 1964, LBJL/NSF-VNCF, vol. XII, item 34.

18. Memorandum to the President, June 9, 1964, LBJL/NSF-VNCF, vol. XI, item 3.

19. Joseph C. Goulden, *Truth is the First Casualty: The Gulf of Tonkin Affair—Illusion and Reality* (Rand McNally, 1969), p. 91.

time rules of engagement, naval forces were to shoot back if attacked, but they were not to pursue and destroy the attacker. The President soon fixed that."[20] U.S. forces in Southeast Asia went on the alert, and the *Maddox* continued to steam in the gulf, defiantly showing the flag, and was reinforced with a second destroyer, the *Turner Joy*. Two nights after the North Vietnamese attack nervous tension was running high on the American ships and visibility was poor when a confused incident occurred that the commanders took for a second North Vietnamese attack.

When word reached Washington the President and his lieutenants swung quickly into action. Johnson ordered retaliatory air strikes and went on television to announce the action, even before the planes reached their targets.[21] This strike, code-named PIERCE ARROW, was the first overt American punitive attack on North Vietnam. It hit ports and naval facilities and destroyed 10 percent of North Vietnam's petroleum stocks. It represented both a culmination and a prologue: PIERCE ARROW capped the period of strategy-making that focused on restricting American involvement in Indochina to aid, assistance, and covert pressure against the DRV, and it foreshadowed the final turning of strategy toward acceptance of the inevitability of more direct U.S. participation in the war. The confusion and misunderstanding of what had really happened to the U.S. destroyers at the time of the alleged second North Vietnamese attack (which would only be fully exposed years later), combined with the nearly unanimous certainty in Washington that a forceful demonstrative response was necessary, were symbolic of the thinking that characterized government planning for Vietnam throughout 1964. What was really significant about the August crisis was not what happened out in the Tonkin Gulf but what was going on in Washington.[22]

20. Eugene G. Windchy, *Tonkin Gulf* (Doubleday, 1971), p. 5.

21. Ibid., p. 225. This timing was a mistake; the intention had been to hold the announcement until the strikes had occurred.

22. Within two days after the retaliatory raids the director of the U.S. Information Agency (USIA) forwarded a summary of world press reaction to the President, assuring Johnson that "U.S. action is generally viewed as justified . . . generally reflects support." (Carl T. Rowan, memorandum for the President, "Reaction to Viet-Nam Situation," August 6, 1964, LBJL/NSF-VNCF, vol. XV, item 128.) Rowan assured Johnson six months later, at the time of the decision to begin bombing North Vietnam, that according to a USIA study, American withdrawal from Vietnam would produce "dismay in many parts of the world." (Rowan, memorandum to the President, February 8, 1965, ibid., vol. XXVII.)

Although PIERCE ARROW was the first overt use of American force against the DRV, it was not the first use of force per se. Covert operations authorized in NSAM 52 had been under way for three years. For the most part they had consisted of minor and mostly ill-fated attempts to infiltrate North Vietnam with U.S.-backed South Vietnamese commandos and reconnaissance teams. More ambitious courses, however, were developed in September 1963 in CINCPAC's operations plan—OPLAN 34-63—which was refined by MACV and Saigon's CIA station in OPLAN 34-A three months later. OPLAN 34-A envisioned a two-phase program of intelligence collection, psychological operations, and sub rosa escalating "destructive undertakings" against North Vietnam.[23] The President approved the plan and directed that the first phase begin in February. The rationale behind 34-A was to "convince the DRV leadership that they should cease to support insurgent activities in the RVN [Republic of (South) Vietnam] and Laos."[24]

Notably, there was no consensus that 34-A would achieve these goals. CINCPAC doubted that many of the actions in the program would have that effect and argued that only air attacks and other stronger operations were likely to accomplish the stated objectives. The Board of National Estimates reviewed a number of the proposed operations and concluded that even if they all succeeded, they would not convince the DRV to change its policy.[25] Nevertheless, 34-A was inaugurated, and after a late start the first phase was in full swing by summer. On August 7, 1964, in the heat of the Tonkin Gulf crisis, Congress resoundingly approved the Southeast Asia Resolution. Of the 535 members in both houses, only two—Senators Wayne Morse and Ernest Gruening—voted against it. Known as the Tonkin Gulf Resolution, it authorized the President to take vigorous measures to protect American forces and came to be regarded by the administration as the functional equivalent of a declaration of war (it was repealed in 1971). What Congress did not know when it passed the resolution was that 34-A operations were going on in the vicinity when the North Vietnamese attacked the *Maddox*.

The *Maddox* was also engaged in what some skeptics would have considered hanky-panky. The destroyer was on a DESOTO patrol, a mission to gather electronic, radar, and communications intelligence

23. *Pentagon Papers*, vol. 3, p. 150; see also p. 141.
24. Ibid., p. 151.
25. Ibid., pp. 151–52.

off the DRV coast. Although there were plans (never fully implemented) to coordinate the DESOTO mission with 34-A and separate the two so that the North Vietnamese would not confuse them,[26] it is not clear, despite the administration's contention, that the North Vietnamese did not consider the *Maddox* a part of the covert naval contingent that was bombarding parts of the North Vietnamese coast. Only Wayne Morse got inklings of the dimensions of what was going on in the gulf, through an anonymous Navy informant who urged him to get the logs of the *Maddox* (he was unable to do so).[27]

J. W. Fulbright, who would sour on the war within a year, rammed the Southeast Asia Resolution through the Senate, rebuffing an amendment by Gaylord Nelson that would have put the Senate on record against further extension of the conflict. The resolution remained so comprehensive that the administration claimed on several occasions in later years that it made any declaration of war superfluous. The administration's claim was not without grounds, given the legislative history of the resolution. During the debate the following exchange occurred between Republican Senator John Sherman Cooper and Fulbright, the bill's floor manager, who soon came to rue his role on the issue:

COOPER: In other words, we are now giving the President advance authority to take whatever action he may deem necessary? . . .

FULBRIGHT: I think that is correct.

COOPER: Then, looking ahead, if the President decided that it was necessary to use such force as could lead into war, we will give that authority by this resolution?

FULBRIGHT: That is the way I would interpret it.[28]

In subsequent years some disillusioned critics would cite Tonkin Gulf as a trumped-up crisis designed by the administration to provide a pretext for escalation. Suspicious evidence included the secret 34-A program, William Bundy's admission that contingent drafts for a con-

26. See Windchy, *Tonkin Gulf*, pp. 71, 83–84, 175; *The Gulf of Tonkin: The 1964 Incidents*, Hearing before the Senate Committee on Foreign Relations, 90 Cong. 2 sess. (Government Printing Office, 1968); Goulden, *Truth Is the First Casualty*, pp. 83–250; and Anthony Austin, *The President's War* (Lippincott, 1971).

27. Windchy, *Tonkin Gulf*, p. 151.

28. *Congressional Record*, vol. 110, pt. 14, 88 Cong. 2 sess. (1964), p. 18409. See also Windchy, *Tonkin Gulf*, pp. 18–23, 34–35; and Cooper, *The Lost Crusade*, p. 244.

gressional resolution had been prepared before the attacks,[29] and the fact that the massive naval and air deployments (OPLAN 37-64) to Southeast Asia at the time of the crisis were not called back but were kept in place after the crisis had passed. Most important, it became evident that the second attack, after all, had quite possibly been a figment of the jittery destroyer crews' imaginations. (In an unguarded moment the following year, LBJ said of the second incident, "For all I know, our Navy was shooting at whales out there.")[30] The government at the time also gave no inkling of the vigorous planning that went on throughout 1964 for further pressures on North Vietnam. Cynicism was fueled as well by the knowledge that as late as 1968 executive officials dissembled in congressional testimony about what kinds of specific recommendations for escalation had been given four years earlier.[31] In fact, the planning for increased pressures dominated the entire year, before and after the crisis.

29. Documents in White House files show that a draft resolution was written and apparently discussed in the NSC at least as early as almost two months before the crisis in the gulf, and a scenario for engineering a "general," or permissive, resolution was considered. Documents also show, however, that the desirability of such a resolution was not yet assumed. ("Alternative Public Positions for U.S. on Southeast Asia for the Period July–November 15," draft memorandum for discussion, June 10, 1964, and copy of draft resolution, LBJL/NSF-VNCF, vol. XI, items 18, 19; and "Elements of a Southeast Asian Policy that Does Not Include a Congressional Resolution," memorandum for meeting on June 15, 1964, ibid., vol. 12, item 40.)

30. Quoted in Goulden, *Truth Is the First Casualty*, p. 160. See also Windchy, *Tonkin Gulf*, pp. 51, 245–46; and *Pentagon Papers*, vol. 3, pp. 186–87.

31. In the 1968 hearings General Earle Wheeler testified that the JCS had made no recommendations for a bombing program before the crisis. (*Gulf of Tonkin, Hearing*, pp. 21–22.) Three years later the Pentagon Papers would reveal this as a bald untruth. This is one of the few incidents that give substance to the notion of the credibility gap. On indicators that the second attack in the gulf never occurred, see Windchy, *Tonkin Gulf*, pp. 195–219, 252–53, 258, 263–68, 280–81, 288; and Goulden, *Truth Is the First Casualty*, pp. 143–47, 151. A third incident of suspected attack on a DESOTO patrol occurred a month later, attended by many of the same uncertainties about the reality of the second attack on the *Maddox* and the *Turner Joy*. The official Navy investigative report concluded that the U.S. ships had encountered and engaged real targets but admitted that the ships had not received fire and that the only evidence of enemy craft presence came from radar sensors. See U.S. Navy COMDESDIV 52, "Incident in the Gulf of Tonkin on 18 September 1964 Involving USS Morton (DD 948) and USS Edwards (DD 950)," n.d., LBJL/NSF-VNCF, Tonkin Gulf folder for September 18, 1964, item 1. Doubts that either the second or third attack actually occurred derive from the unreliability of radar, which sometimes mistakes waves, fish, debris, or other phenomena for ships.

Weighing the Use of Force

But in mitigation of the view of the Tonkin Gulf crisis as an administration conspiracy to excuse escalation, the real and continuing hesitancy to embrace escalation at the time must also be considered. Shortly after the crisis in the gulf, the State Department directed the Saigon mission to avoid actions that might seem provocative, and both DESOTO patrols and 34-A operations were suspended. The week after PIERCE ARROW, William Bundy recommended consideration of surfacing the 34-A program (to raise South Vietnamese morale), beginning air attacks in the panhandle (southern North Vietnam), and other actions. "Probably the sequence should be played somewhat by ear," he wrote, "with the aim of producing a slightly increased tempo, but one that does not commit us prematurely to even stronger actions."[32] Maxwell Taylor favored going ahead with cross-border operations into the panhandle, but McNamara was strongly opposed. Taylor favored immediate resumption of DESOTO patrols, though most officials in Washington favored holding off for ten days to two weeks.[33]

The DESOTO missions were soon resumed and then suspended once again in September after the unconfirmed indication of a third North Vietnamese attack. Such caution and uncertainty reflected Washington's deferral of a decision to go to the mat. Months later, when the United States began bombing North Vietnam in retaliation for a Vietcong attack on American installations at Pleiku, McGeorge Bundy would acknowledge the extent to which the incident served as a pretext for escalation by saying, "Pleikus are streetcars"; such incidents could be relied on to happen regularly, offering opportunities to implement decisions already contemplated.[34] If the government was indeed firmly resolved on escalation in 1964, DESOTO could have served as such a streetcar.

Through 1964 the President kept clinging to the possibility that direct and sustained use of American force might be averted, but he did

32. William Bundy, "Next Course of Action in Southeast Asia," August 13, 1964, LBJL/NSF-VNCF, vol. XV, item 135a.

33. McGeorge Bundy, memorandum for the President, August 13, 1964, ibid.

34. Quoted in Townsend Hoopes, *The Limits of Intervention: An Inside Account of How the Johnson Policy of Escalation Was Reversed* (McKay, 1969), p. 30. See also *Pentagon Papers*, vol. 2, p. 329; and vol. 3, p. 298.

not equivocate on the goal behind U.S. policy. As ever, the credibility of American commitments was seen to be at stake. One reason the United States was in Vietnam was to convince allies of its dependability. Yet, annoyingly, support from allies was weak, and some became increasingly alienated by U.S. persistence over the years. Even Rusk, who invoked SEATO obligations so often in justifying U.S. policy, opposed using the SEATO framework to combat the Pathet Lao offensive in the spring of 1964 because some of the pact's members would have been obstructive. For all the rhetoric, SEATO as an entity would play a negligible role in Vietnam. The intelligence community also warned later that fall of the alienation of allies: "The US would probably find itself progressively isolated in the event the US sanctions did not soon achieve either a Communist reduction of pressures in South Vietnam or some progress toward meaningful negotiations."[35] So also did George Ball: "What we might gain by establishing the steadfastness of our commitments we could lose by an erosion of confidence in our judgment."[36]

Whether or not America's allies shared the sense of urgency, the top officials of the U.S. government still believed in the domino theory in one form or another. In the fall of 1964 a memo from the Board of National Estimates in answer to a request from the President had said that North Vietnamese control of South Vietnam and Laos would not necessarily mean the loss of Southeast Asia. Nevertheless, in a September strategy meeting Rusk, McCone, and Wheeler agreed that if the United States lost in Vietnam, it would "lose all of Southeast Asia."[37] China remained the ultimate problem. Rusk stated just before the escalation in 1965 that Peking's militant ideology reflected "appetites and ambitions that grow upon feeding." Just before Tet he still equated "the doctrine spewing out of Peking" with *Mein Kampf*.[38]

Rusk steadfastly rejected suggestions to reevaluate China policy.[39] The assumption of China's aggressive intent was fueled by the border

35. *Pentagon Papers*, vol. 3, p. 598; see also p. 174.

36. George W. Ball, "A Light that Failed," *Atlantic Monthly*, July 1972, p. 43. This article is a reprint of Ball's memorandum of October 5, 1964, to McNamara, Rusk, and McGeorge Bundy.

37. *Pentagon Papers*, vol. 3, p. 194. For Board of National Estimates memo, see ibid., p. 174.

38. Rusk quoted in ibid., vol. 3, p. 724; and in Henry F. Graff, *The Tuesday Cabinet* (Prentice-Hall, 1970), p. 135.

39. Halberstam, *The Best and the Brightest*, p. 345; see also pp. 102–03.

war with India in 1962. The view of China as instigator behind the scenes was reinforced most impressively in 1965 by Minister of National Defense Lin Piao's manifesto on wars of national liberation. The President himself saw Communist "pincers" at work in 1965, and his memoirs contain a remarkable description of what he called the "Djakarta-Hanoi-Peking-Pyongyang axis on the move."[40] (Some would perceive a conspirational linkage of Communist strategy again at the time of the Tet offensive. The coincidence of the *Pueblo* seizure, North Korean guerrilla attacks on South Korea, Soviet buzzing of West Berlin, and Pathet Lao capture of Nam Bac raised the specter to military leaders of a coordinated worldwide Communist thrust.)[41] At the time of the early escalation decisions, even those who were comparatively dovish saw China as expansionary. In an example of what James Thomson bemoaned as the "banishment of real expertise" on Asia,[42] Michael Forrestal wrote in a memo to William Bundy in November 1964:

... Communist China shares the same internal political necessity for ideological expansion today that the Soviet Union did during the time of the Comintern and the period just following the Second World War. . . . This will impel her . . . to achieve ideological successes abroad. . . . our objective should be to 'contain' China for the longest possible period. . . . and at the same time strengthen the political and economic structure of the bordering countries. . . . We should delay China's swallowing up Southeast Asia until (a) she develops better table manners and (b) the food is somewhat more indigestible.[43]

These perceptions of strategic necessity overshadowed whatever incentives there were for disentanglement. Chester Cooper reflected later that in December 1964, with the seventh government in Saigon "headed for the junk heap . . . the time was ripe for a serious reappraisal. . . . Never again in his [Johnson's] term of office would he have more political elbowroom to pick and choose among options."[44] But LBJ was not about to become the first President to lose a war. And the argument above would have been relevant only if the administration had not genuinely cared about the perceived strategic importance of Vietnam. Dean Rusk noted that the fallacy in all the hand-wringing

40. Lyndon Baines Johnson, *The Vantage Point: Perspectives of the Presidency, 1963–1969* (Holt, Rinehart and Winston, 1971), p. 606; see also pp. 134–36.

41. See Marvin Kalb and Elie Abel, *Roots of Involvement: The U.S. in Asia, 1784–1971* (Norton, 1971), p. 213.

42. James C. Thomson, Jr., "How Could Vietnam Happen? An Autopsy" *Atlantic Monthly*, April 1968, p. 49.

43. *Pentagon Papers*, vol. 3, p. 644.

44. Cooper, *The Lost Crusade*, p. 253.

about finding a dignified way to get out was a misunderstanding of administration aims: "We were not interested in saving face but in saving Vietnam."[45]

But even as late as the fall of 1964 the President was not sure that saving Vietnam (in the sense that was crucial to him—preventing Communist victory) required the sustained and direct use of American force. The one disservice of the *New York Times* in its original exposé of the Pentagon Papers was in implying that the decision to bomb North Vietnam was made in September 1964 and concealed to avoid jeopardizing Johnson's reelection.[46] Though the weight of opinion in the bureaucracy had indeed shifted clearly in this direction by September, the President had not made up his mind. In fact, a week after the White House strategy meeting that the *Times* identified as establishing the consensus for bombing, the President received a memorandum, apparently from McGeorge Bundy, that stated:

Now, as for ten years, there are three basic choices in Vietnam: (1) to move to a full-scale war like Korea; (2) to pull out; (3) to keep on, as we are going, with extensive but measured support for the Vietnamese in fighting their own battles.

You are fully committed to the *third* course, as Eisenhower was and Kennedy was.[47]

After the election Johnson initiated a month-long policy review that

45. Quoted in Graff, *The Tuesday Cabinet*, p. 88. Rusk's point may be one reason that nothing came of an informal (and tentative) Soviet initiative in May 1965, through Pierre Salinger, to facilitate reciprocal deescalation. The U.S. ambassador in Moscow, Foy Kohler, reported: "It was clear from their remarks that Soviets assume we would welcome some avenue of withdrawal so long as this would not involve loss of American prestige." ("Project MAYFLOWER—The First Bombing Pause," in U.S. Department of Defense, Office of the Secretary of Defense, Vietnam Task Force, "United States–Vietnam Relations, 1945–1967" [DOD, n.d.; processed], VI.C.1, pp. 123–24. Hereafter cited as USVNR, Negotiations Volumes. See bibliographical note, p. 375.) For a definitive analysis of the entire U.S. search for negotiated settlement, see Allan E. Goodman, *The Lost Peace: America's Search for a Negotiated Settlement of the Vietnam War* (Hoover Institute Press, 1977).

46. See Neil Sheehan, "The Consensus to Bomb North Vietnam: August, 1964–February, 1965," *The Pentagon Papers as Published by the New York Times* (Bantam, 1971), pp. 307–10.

47. "Background Comment on Vietnam for Coffee-Hour with the Press," memorandum for the President, September 14, 1964, LBJL/NSF-NSC Staff File, vol. 6, item 22 (emphasis in original). The memo is unsigned but appears to be from Bundy since it is on White House stationery. The fact that it concerned discussion with the press might appear to sustain the "conspiratorial" interpretation of the *Times*, but this would not be consistent with Johnson's subsequent direction of the month-long review of options.

culminated in a consensus for a two-phase expansion of the war. Phase I would intensify air strikes in Laos and covert actions against the DRV; Phase II would be a sustained, escalating air campaign against the North. (Johnson approved the first phase for December but only approved the second "in principle.") The two-phase plan had emerged from an NSC working group that had developed three options. Option A was a continuation of limited operations; Option B would augment the current policy with heavy and systematic pressures on the North; and Option C was a more modest campaign against the DRV. The Joint Chiefs favored B, although they disagreed on timing and intensity.[48]

In September only Air Force Chief Curtis LeMay and Marine Commandant Wallace M. Greene, Jr., favored immediate provocation of North Vietnam.[49] After November, though, there would be few differences among the Joint Chiefs. (Taylor opposed his military colleagues on most of the issues that arose in this period.) The State Department and the Office of the Secretary of Defense favored Option C. When the NSC principals met on November 24 they reached no clear consensus but in effect chose Option A together with "the lowest order of Option C actions . . . in a manner that would represent the least possible additional commitment."[50] There were two dissenters: Ball on one side, Wheeler on the other.[51] LBJ rather tentatively chose the compromise course. Even so, just before he decided to authorize the bombing, he would still tell one "skull session" at the White House, "I'm not going north with Curtis LeMay [who wanted to pulverize the DRV, not prod it], and I'm not going south with Wayne Morse."[52] Still steady on the middle, for the same reasons as ever. For Johnson the logic of the compromise course was both politically pragmatic (to avoid defections and minimize the intensity of dissent on either end by hedging in both directions) and intellectually pragmatic (to play safe, since he lacked personal expertise in foreign affairs and was confronted by disagreement among the experts).

Doubts about even this limited bombing option persisted. The ra-

48. See *Pentagon Papers*, vol. 3, pp. 5, 14, 111, 135, 202, 238–39, 246.

49. General Curtis E. LeMay with MacKinlay Kantor, *Mission with LeMay: My Story* (Doubleday, 1965), p. 564. See also Gallucci, *Neither Peace nor Honor*, p. 161, note 7.

50. *Pentagon Papers*, vol. 3, p. 246. For Taylor's views, see ibid., pp. 242–48.

51. Ibid., pp. 237–38.

52. Quoted in Charles Roberts, *LBJ's Inner Circle* (Delacorte, 1965), p. 23.

tionale behind it, curiously, was "the use of power to prevent using power."[53] The military were in the forefront of the hawks, but even they were not totally united until the end of the year. Army Chief of Staff Harold K. Johnson had nagging doubts, and in the Saigon Mission Council Westmoreland was dubious. But most interesting of all, the decisionmakers seemed strangely oblivious to the discouraging results of the Sigma II war games—in which many of them had participated—which projected that bombing would accomplish little.[54]

The NSC group that had produced the options also worked with an undercurrent of doubt about the efficacy of limited pressures. Its intelligence panel saw little chance of breaking Hanoi's will. This echoed the earlier warning in February of an interagency group under Robert Johnson of the Policy Planning Council.

Overt action against North Vietnam would be unlikely to produce reduction in Viet Cong activity sufficiently to make victory on the ground possible in South Vietnam unless accompanied by new U.S. bolstering actions. . . . The most to be expected would be reduction of North Vietnamese support of the Viet Cong for a while and, thus, the *gaining of some time* and opportunity by the government of South Vietnam to improve itself.[55]

The JCS representative, Vice Admiral Lloyd Mustin, also criticized the limited strategy, arguing that substantially destroying North Vietnamese capabilities, rather than massaging their intentions with limited strikes, would be necessary to achieve the objectives of NSAM 288. The final draft assessment of the November working group also, significantly, omitted an earlier draft's reference to potential costs and risks in pursuing current objectives and contained no suggestion of seeking alternatives to these objectives.[56]

With all these reservations, why did the principals and the President ultimately decide to go ahead? There are basically three reasons.

First and foremost, the possibility of accepting defeat, of pulling the plug on American commitment, was simply not considered. George Ball was a lonely devil's advocate and was tolerated because that was seen as a useful function. (Johnson himself, in fact, sometimes asked Ball to play that role.) There was also one critical weakness in Ball's position. In his forceful, clairvoyant warnings about the costs of escala-

53. Halberstam, *The Best and the Brightest*, p. 513.
54. See ibid., pp. 460–62, 485, 490, 503; Blair Clark, "Westmoreland Appraised," *Harper's*, November 1970, pp. 99–100; and Ball, "A Light that Failed," p. 39.
55. *Pentagon Papers*, vol. 3, p. 156 (emphasis added); see also pp. 141, 213.
56. Ibid., pp. 213, 219.

tion, he almost always stopped short of admitting frankly that the price of his own preferred alternative was acceptance of the defeat of South Vietnam by the Communists. Even in his most powerful and articulate memo against escalation in October 1964, Ball had held out the prospect of a negotiated settlement on relatively favorable terms. (Mike Mansfield's dissent suffered from a similar weakness.) Nevertheless, this last major brief of Ball's against escalation several months before the bombing began was remarkable in its prescience.

It is the nature of escalation that each move passes the option to the other side, while at the same time the party which seems to be losing will be tempted to keep raising the ante. *To the extent that the response to a move can be controlled, that move is probably ineffective.* If the move is effective, it may not be possible to control—or accurately anticipate—the response.

Once on the tiger's back we cannot be sure of picking the place to dismount.[57]

The second reason for escalation, which followed from the consensus for preventing a Communist victory, was that if disaster or stalemate threatened and withdrawal was precluded, there was no alternative but to turn up the spigot, forge ahead, and hope for the best. After all, it might not work, but then again it might. In this vein it is interesting to note that in the fall of 1964 intelligence estimates of the North Vietnamese response to more U.S. pressure seemed less pessimistic than they usually were.[58]

Finally, the third reason, whose chief proponent was Ambassador Lodge before he left Saigon, was that some bombing would be useful

57. Ball, "A Light that Failed," p. 41 (emphasis added). See also Graff, *The Tuesday Cabinet*, p. 71. At the end of 1963 and the beginning of 1964 Mansfield wrote to President Johnson, appending memos on Southeast Asia he had sent to Kennedy over the years. The senator emphasized the dangers and costs of getting into another Korea in Vietnam. But the alternative he posed was a relatively favorable diplomatic settlement: "A settlement might be on terms which reduced our influence (and costs) *provided* it also inhibited Chinese political domination [emphasis in original]." Neither in this memo nor in one to Kennedy in August 1963— which argued that American interests in Vietnam were peripheral and suggested numerous symbolic gestures to reduce tension—did Mansfield indicate that the United States should accept a Communist government in Saigon. (Memorandums to the President, December 7, 1963, and January 6, 1964, and "Observations on Viet Nam," August 19, 1963, LBJL/NSF-VNCF, vol. II, items 119, 125.) The exception to Ball's unwillingness to accept Communist victory was his stance just before the major escalation decision of July 1965. See his memo of June 29, 1965, in *Pentagon Papers*, vol. 4, pp. 609–10, and the reconstruction of NSC meetings that July in Jack Valenti, *A Very Human President* (Norton, 1975), chap. 4.

58. *Pentagon Papers*, vol. 3, p. 206.

more for its effect in bolstering the morale of the tipsy Saigon government than for its effect on the DRV.[59]

Alternatives to the Use of Force

There were only two alternatives to the direct application of force for those who still intended to save South Vietnam.

1. *Developing a stronger and more stable Saigon government, which thus would be more able to fend for itself.* The only way the United States could encourage this development, given the recalcitrant mischief of the various juntas of 1964, was through leverage. But in these early days before escalation, when the Saigon government's performance was the centerpiece of strategy, the administration usually found itself unable to follow through on leverage; and after escalation, leverage could achieve little that was not marginal to the total war effort. (Not until 1972, when Nixon had finally decided to reach a negotiated settlement even if it entailed substantial concessions, did the United States go to the mat and force Thieu to come to terms, and even then it did so by offering offsetting secret assurances, subsequently invalidated by legislation, that the United States would "respond with full force should the settlement be violated by North Vietnam.")[60]

Leverage in itself implied deeper involvement to produce the desired performance, and this blurred into the option of supplanting the recalcitrant natives rather than prodding them. Rusk cabled a litany of dilemmas to Lodge in May 1964 and said, "Somehow we must change the pace at which these people move and I suspect that this can only be done with a pervasive intrusion of Americans into their affairs." Only the day before he had cabled to express his anxiety about bureaucratic inadequacies of the Saigon government that

cause us to have great doubts that many of these benefits are actually reaching the hamlets and the villages. . . . It may be that in addition to force-feeding these materials into the Vietnamese distribution channels at Saigon, we will need more Americans at the rural end of the distribution system extracting the commodities themselves and placing them in the hands of Vietnamese officials to present to the peasants as benefits from the Khanh Government. . . . I know that this raises the risk of casualties. . . . On the

59. Ibid., p. 173.
60. See Tad Szulc, "Behind the Vietnam Cease-Fire Agreement: How Kissinger Did It," *Foreign Policy*, vol. 15 (Summer 1974), pp. 21–69; and text of Nixon's assurance in Bernard Gwertzman, "Thieu Aide Discloses Promises of Force by Nixon to Back Pact," *New York Times*, May 1, 1975.

other hand I can think of no other way to be sure that what we are trying to do is actually accomplished.[61]

As with the rest of Vietnam policy, the most relevant comparisons were with U.S. involvement in the Chinese Civil War and the Korean War. In China the American clients (Chiang Kai-shek's Nanking regime) were inept and corrupt, and the United States limited its commitment in defense of the nationalist government against the Communist Chinese. In Korea the American clients (Syngman Rhee's Seoul regime) were militarily competent and efficient, and the United States extended its commitment to defending against the Communist Korean and Chinese invaders. But in South Vietnam the United States had the worst of both worlds: inept clients and deepening commitment. Rusk's acceptance of this situation was no doubt affected by the results in the earlier two cases. As assistant secretary of state for the Far East in the early 1950s, Rusk had seen Truman's administration pilloried for "losing" China. And while there was also much public unhappiness with the war in Korea, the most forceful dissent came from those, such as General Douglas MacArthur's supporters in the Senate, who favored escalation.

In May 1964 Rusk met with Khanh to short-circuit the General's "march North" rhetoric and prompt more efforts to achieve stability in Saigon by warning that the United States would never again get involved in a conventional Asian land war.[62] But within less than a year the persisting incompetence of the government of South Vietnam drove the United States into just such a war. Maxwell Taylor lamented, "One of the facts of life about Vietnam was that it was never difficult to decide what should be done, but it was almost impossible to get it done."[63] The Saigon government's political problems continued through 1964, and leverage remained a focus of frustration in Washington discussions. In the fall the President decided to make the Phase II escalation planned by the NSC working group "contingent on GVN [Government of (South) Vietnam] reform and improvement," but the decision in February 1965 to proceed with Phase II was made "in spite [or possibly because?] of the failure of the South Vietnamese to have complied with our requirements." Johnson had asked in a strategy meet-

61. Cables 2022 and 2027, Rusk to ambassador, May 20 and May 21, 1964, LBJL/NSF-VNCF, vol. IX, item 69.

62. *Pentagon Papers*, vol. 2, p. 322.

63. Taylor, *Swords and Plowshares*, p. 311.

ing in September 1964, "Can we really strengthen the GVN?" But this issue, the real crux of later decisions, as the Pentagon Papers noted, had been "too long submerged by repeated assertions that it [the United States] *must* do so."[64]

2. *Diplomacy.* At this stage diplomacy was not much of an alternative to force. Lodge cabled Rusk on May 21, 1964: "It is vitally important to avoid Security Council action which in any way encourages convening of Geneva Conference. Such a conference would be a body blow to the will to win and would probably having [sic] catastrophic results."[65] The United States had secret contacts with North Vietnam beginning in June 1964, through an intermediary, J. Blair Seaborn, the Canadian delegate to the International Control Commission. Both sides sketched possible settlement terms, "but the main subject stressed repeatedly by each was its determination to do and endure whatever might be necessary to see the war to a conclusion satisfactory to it. . . . they were not inclined to compromise their way out." When Seaborn told Pham Van Dong that the American commitment had implications far beyond Southeast Asia, the North Vietnamese official appeared to confirm the domino theory: "Pham Van Dong laughed and said he did indeed appreciate the problem. A US defeat in SVN [South Vietnam] would in all probability start a chain reaction. . . . But the stakes were just as high for the NLF and its supporters."[66] The DRV position stiffened even further after the Tonkin Gulf retaliation.

In formulating instructions for Seaborn, Joseph Mendenhall of the State Department wrote that the Canadian should let the DRV know American policy "is to see to it that North Viet Nam contains itself and its ambitions within the territory allocated to its administration by the 1954 Geneva agreements. . . . policy in South Viet Nam is to preserve the integrity of that state's territory against guerrilla subversion." In exchange the United States offered assurance that it sought no bases in

64. Johnson's positions noted in *Pentagon Papers*, vol. 3, pp. 111, 113, 117; and vol. 2, p. 114. See also ibid., vol. 2, pp. 277–82, 414. LBJ also asked in September 1964 whether Vietnam was "worth all this effort" and was assured by the principals that it was. (Johnson, *The Vantage Point*, p. 120.)

65. LBJL/NSF-VNCF, vol. IX, item 73. On December 4, 1963, Lodge had similarly cabled Averell Harriman to oppose a proposed conference on Cambodian neutrality because it would appear that the Laos formula was being extended to Vietnam, a sort of creeping neutralization. (Ibid., vol. I, item 39.)

66. "Seaborn," USVNR, Negotiations Volumes, VI.C.1, Discussion, pp. 1–3.

the area, did not seek to overthrow the DRV, and was willing to offer trade and aid to the Hanoi regime.[67] The latter points could hardly be impressive to the North Vietnamese leaders, and the former were a blunt negation of their fundamental aims. It is notable, furthermore, that nothing in this secret initiative differed at all from the *public* stated position of the United States.

With the military situation at a low ebb and no stable coherent government in Saigon to pose a meaningful counterweight to the Communist National Liberation Front, American policymakers were basically disinterested in the possibilities of a diplomatic settlement. To William Bundy, diplomacy was futile as long as the DRV ignored previous agreements it had signed on Indochina in 1954 and 1962. Following the Tonkin Gulf crisis he wrote: "We must continue to oppose any Vietnam conference. . . . Negotiation without continued military action will not achieve our objectives in the foreseeable future."[68]

A policy planner in the State Department explained the attitude to journalists David Kraslow and Stuart Loory: "The moment we moved toward negotiations at that stage, it would have been an admission that the game was up."[69] In September 1964 UN Ambassador Adlai Stevenson relayed from Secretary General U Thant a report of a North Vietnamese feeler for "direct, secret, low-level exploratory talks."[70] But the report never even reached the President, apparently because his subordinates did not take it seriously and because they believed the military balance in the field would clearly have to be redressed— convincing Hanoi to moderate its aims—before useful talks could begin.[71] As Rusk said: "A negotiation aimed at the acceptance or the confirmation of aggression is not possible."[72] (Thant informed the DRV of Washington's rejection of talks on the day before the FLAMING DART reprisal raids began.) The White House learned at the end of the year that an unidentified Vietnamese had approached journalist

67. Ibid., pp. 5–8 (quotation, p. 6).

68. William Bundy, "Next Course of Action in Southeast Asia" (third draft), August 13, 1964, LBJL/NSF-VNCF, vol. XV, item 135a.

69. David Kraslow and Stuart H. Loory, *The Secret Search for Peace in Vietnam* (Vintage, 1968), p. 95.

70. Ibid., p. 99.

71. Philip Geyelin, *Lyndon B. Johnson and the World* (Praeger, 1966), pp. 202–06.

72. Quoted in Kraslow and Loory, *The Secret Search*, p. 102.

Felix Greene, claiming that Hanoi wanted to establish unofficial contact with the American government.[73] With attitudes as they were, obviously nothing came of this straw in the wind; U.S. leaders saw no alternatives to escalation.

Prelude to Escalation

The first step up the ladder was the initiation of BARREL ROLL, armed reconnaissance and bombing on the trails in Laos in December. (The rules of engagement were somewhat similar to those of the "protective reaction" policy under Nixon.) One State Department official said the President "was privately relieved that he could take such a momentous first step somewhere other than in Vietnam. . . . We had decided it would take some bullets and bombs. . . . Since they had to be fired, Johnson thought it best that it be off in the woods where it would escape notice."[74] But, ominously for the strategy of graduated response, the bombings did not deter the Pathet Lao or reduce North Vietnamese use of the Ho Chi Minh Trail. And the Vietcong attack on U.S. planes at the Bien Hoa airfield on November 1, which had led Ambassador Taylor to recommend retaliation (Johnson refused, possibly because the American presidential election was only two days away), was followed by the bombing of the Brink American officers' billet on Christmas eve. Taylor again recommended retaliation against North Vietnam, and the President again held off.[75] By the end of the year Taylor was extremely pessimistic about the trends in the war. Thus 1964 was Johnson's year of comprehension. The crunch was coming, and Johnson saw all too well that he had a tar baby on his hands. If the administration was not going to reconsider its commitment to saving South Vietnam, it might well have to take the next "streetcar."

Crossing the Rubicon: Early 1965

Right after the inauguration in January 1965 McNamara and Mc-George Bundy forwarded a memorandum to the President emphasizing

73. "Conversation between Felix Greene and Michael V. Forrestal," memorandum for the record, December 15, 1964, LBJL/NSF-VNCF, vol. XXIII, item 145.

74. Quoted in Goulden, *Truth Is the First Casualty,* p. 99. See also *Pentagon Papers,* vol. 3, p. 14.

75. *Pentagon Papers,* vol. 3, 262–63.

that hard decisions on boosting U.S. commitment could no longer be delayed. They noted that Rusk disagreed: "What he does say is that the consequences of both escalation and withdrawal are so bad that we simply must find a way of making our present policy work. This would be good if it was possible. Bob and I do not think it is."[76] Rusk, of course, was no closet dove; he simply perceived accurately the severity of the costs that lay ahead. "There was a consistency to Rusk," Halberstam observed. "He had been the least eager to get in because he had never seen the task as easy, and had few illusions about air power and the quick use of force. In fact, his positions from start to finish, right through to Tet, were remarkably similar to those of the Army generals. . . . if we went in we had to be prepared for a long haul."[77] The President valued Rusk's counsel and shared in spades his concern for costs; thus for the moment he continued to defer what McNamara and Bundy considered the undeferable decision.

The aid-and-advice support strategy for the war was bankrupt by 1965, but not for lack of trying. (Taylor noted wryly in a message to McGeorge Bundy that the U.S. Military Mission was charged with implementing a twenty-one-point military program, a forty-one-point nonmilitary program, a sixteen-point U.S. Information Service program, and a twelve-point CIA program—"as if we can win here somehow on a point score.")[78] Around this time the President also made a big to-do about the Southeast Asian economic revolution he had proposed in a speech at Johns Hopkins University, coercing Eugene Black to head the new Asian Development Bank and touting his plans to the press. LBJ still clutched at the possibility of winning his war by extending his Great Society to Vietnam. But this hope was ephemeral, overtaken by the escalation that was already beginning.[79]

Pleiku and the Decision to Bomb

On February 7 McGeorge Bundy's "streetcar" arrived. Major Vietcong attacks hit U.S. advisers' barracks at Pleiku and a helicopter base at Camp Holloway. Bundy was in South Vietnam at the time and had a deeply emotional reaction when he visited American casualties in

76. Quoted in Halberstam, *The Best and the Brightest*, p. 518.
77. Ibid., p. 621.
78. *Pentagon Papers*, vol. 3, p. 6.
79. See Eric F. Goldman, *The Tragedy of Lyndon Johnson* (Knopf, 1969), pp. 408–09; and Evans and Novak, *Lyndon B. Johnson*, pp. 542–44.

the hospital. He fired off a strong and articulate memo to the President immediately upon his return:

. . . without new U.S. action defeat seems inevitable—probably . . . within the next year or so. There is still time to turn it around, but not much.

The stakes in Vietnam are extremely high. The American investment is very large, and *American responsibility is a fact of life.* . . .

There is one grave weakness in our posture in Vietnam which is within our own power to fix—and that is a widespread belief that we do not have the will and force and patience and determination to take the necessary action and stay the course. . . .

At its very best the struggle in Vietnam will be long. It seems to us important that this fundamental fact be made clear. . . . Too often in the past we have conveyed the impression that we expect an early solution. . . . there is no shortcut to success. . . .[80]

Backed by the vast majority of his advisers, Lyndon Johnson authorized the bombing of North Vietnam. Ball, the official institutional dissenter, was heard but not heeded. The President reacted less charitably to the few major politicians who questioned the action. Mike Mansfield dissented, and Ambassador to Moscow Llewellyn Thompson was also wary. LBJ particularly resented Vice-President Hubert Humphrey's last-ditch try to stop escalation. One day before the scheduled start of the ROLLING THUNDER bombing campaign, Humphrey drafted a memorandum with Thomas Hughes of the State Department's Bureau of Intelligence and Research. In it he warned: "It is the first year when we can face the Vietnam problem without being preoccupied with the political repercussions from the Republican right. . . . Our political problems are likely to come from new and different sources (Democratic liberals, Independents, Labor). . . ."[81] Humphrey was banished from the war councils for months afterward (even George Ball did not want the vice-president involved in his internal resistance movement, because Humphrey had become a pariah to Johnson), until he resolved to jump back on the bandwagon.

The consensus now was that bombing—although its form and pace were still in dispute—was the only alternative; this despite the studies

80. *Pentagon Papers*, vol. 3, pp. 309, 311 (emphasis added). See also Halberstam, *The Best and the Brightest*, p. 521.

81. Quoted in Laurence Stern, "Early Humphrey Memo Urged LBJ Not to Escalate the War," *Boston Globe*, May 10, 1976. For discussions of reactions to Johnson's authorization of bombing, see also Halberstam, *The Best and the Brightest*, pp. 521–22, 534; and Hoopes, *The Limits of Intervention*, p. 31.

in 1964 that had predicted negligible results from a limited air campaign. As Bundy reasoned: "Measured against the costs of defeat in Vietnam this program seems cheap. And *even if it fails to turn the tide —as it may*—the value of the effort seems to us to exceed the cost." While he saw the odds of success as only between 25 percent and 75 percent, the campaign would at least "damp down the charges that we did not do all that we could have done."[82]

Bundy also argued that the South Vietnamese morale boost from bombing would enable the United States to press Saigon more effectively for reforms. Ambassadors Lodge and Taylor had used a similar rationale in June and December of the previous year. In this, though, they were caught in a blatant contradiction of their own logic, curiously unremarked by the Pentagon Papers analysts. Advisers had *opposed* bombing for the same reason, that is, the effect it would have on political stability in the South. In early autumn 1964 Taylor had warned: "We should not get involved militarily with North Vietnam and possibly with Red China if our base in South Viet Nam is insecure and Khanh's army is tied down." Yet very soon afterward he argued that it might be necessary to move the date closer for deliberate escalation against the North because the Saigon government might not be able to remain viable until January. In order "to avoid the probable consequences of a collapse of national morale," Taylor argued it would be necessary "to open the campaign against the DRV without delay."[83] Similarly, in 1966 the Office of the Secretary of Defense continued to rationalize the bombing as necessary to sustain South Vietnamese morale, while the President deferred McNamara's recommendation to strike POL (petroleum, oil, lubricants) targets because of the political turmoil in the South. Decisionmakers believed alternately that the United States had to bomb to shore up Saigon and that it could not bomb because Saigon was not shored up enough.[84]

This contradiction capsulizes much of the irony of Vietnam policy as a whole. In a comparable *Catch-22* situation, Khanh had agitated in the spring of 1964 for the march North, yet his government opposed extending the covert 34-A operations because they would expose South Vietnam's vulnerable political base to greater pressure from the enemy.

82. *Pentagon Papers*, vol. 3, pp. 312 (emphasis added), 314.
83. Taylor quoted in ibid., pp. 198, 199; see also pp. 14–15, 106.
84. See ibid., vol. 4, pp. 3–4, 79–80.

This bizarre sequence of reasoning reflected the underlying dilemma: regarding almost any alternative, the United States seemed damned if it did and damned if it didn't. Implicitly, bombing alone would just not be enough to do the job.

Ground Combat Deployments

In the spring of 1965 the debate was almost exclusively on bombing strategy, with very little discussion of troops. During the previous year even the JCS had been backing a strong air campaign in order to *avoid* the deployment of ground forces. But once planes from Da Nang began striking the North, Westmoreland felt an imperative need for some U.S. troops to provide security for the airbase against Viet- cong retaliation. Thus 3,500 U.S. Marines landed at Da Nang on March 8 (the JCS instructed CINCPAC that the Marines "will not, repeat will not, engage in day to day actions against the Viet Cong").[85] Taylor, who had great trepidation about Westmoreland's request, later wrote with a touch of rue: "It was curious how hard it had been to get authority for the initiation of the air campaign against the North and how relatively easy to get the marines ashore. Yet I thought the latter a much more difficult decision and concurred in it reluctantly."[86]

When Taylor returned for Washington conferences in March he proposed a wide-ranging set of nonmilitary measures: decentralization of Saigon's administration, rural development, land reform, support of youth groups, improvement of coastal transport, slum clearance, edu- cational assistance, increased intelligence and counterespionage, and establishment of a U.S. interagency group on pacification directed by a senior officer under the ambassador. This was the last instance of real focus on aid and assistance—in contrast to direct American inter- vention—as ways to affect the war in the South. The measures were ap- proved in NSAM 328 of April 1. But within two days Washington sent out messages that the top policymakers had decided to go beyond NSAM 328, and within two weeks the President approved additional military deployments. Taylor responded angrily to these moves: "I was not asked to concur in this massive visitation. For your information, I do not concur."[87] Later he wrote: "When I left the President in Wash-

85. *United States–Vietnam Relations, 1945–1967*, Study prepared by the De- partment of Defense for the House Committee on Armed Services, 92 Cong. 1 sess. (GPO, 1971), vol. 4, pt. IV.C.4, p. 1. See also *Pentagon Papers*, vol. 3, p. 236.

86. Taylor, *Swords and Plowshares*, p. 338.

87. *Pentagon Papers*, vol. 3, p. 103; see also pp. 97–100, 102.

ington, I had not realized that he had made up his mind on a number of important subjects. . . . arriving in Saigon, I soon sensed that, having crossed the Rubicon on February 7 [the Pleiku bombing decision] he was now off for Rome on the double."[88]

How did this happen? After so much agonizing hesitancy in approving the bombing, why were troops sent in with such confident dispatch and with more vigor than the supplicants in the field expected? The principal answer is simply that President Johnson had decided to bite the bullet and take command; he was the driving force in eliciting and approving the troop commitment. When he sent Harold Johnson (who, among all the military, was most reticent in moving for escalation) to the field early in March, he gave him a verbal dressing down, complaining, "You're not giving me any ideas and any solutions for this damn little pissant country. Now, I don't need ten generals to come in here ten times and tell me to bomb. I want some solutions. I want some answers."[89] It could surprise no one, then, when the Army chief returned in mid-month and recommended committing one U.S. division to South Vietnam. The day after General Johnson's return, President Johnson personally urged the JCS to propose measures to "kill more VC." Five days after that, on March 20, sure enough, the chiefs submitted their first recommendation for direct combat use of American troops. In mid-April two more Marine battalion landing teams waded ashore at Phu Bai and Da Nang.[90]

Off for Rome on the double? Almost, but not quite. On April 2 the JCS asked the secretary of defense to swing into wartime administration and to clear the decks of "all administrative impediments which hamper us in the prosecution of this war."[91] But there were still only a total of four battalions of U.S. combat troops in South Vietnam. How far troop involvement would go had not been finally determined. The nervous ambivalence about troop commitment was reflected in Assistant Secretary of Defense John McNaughton's distress when the Marines were first sent; he preferred sending the 173rd Airborne Brigade from Okinawa instead because it was less heavily encumbered with equipment and vehicles—less obtrusive than the Marines.[92] Some of the policy-

88. Taylor, Swords and Plowshares, p. 341.
89. Quoted in Halberstam, The Best and the Brightest, p. 564.
90. See Pentagon Papers, vol. 3, pp. 406, 408, 427–28.
91. Ibid., p. 407.
92. See ibid., p. 402.

makers apparently were still trying to intervene without the appearance of intervention. George Ball of course opposed the move,[93] but he was joined in April by a dissenter from the other side. John McCone, just leaving the government, opposed a U.S. ground role unless much stronger measures were undertaken against the North, and he considered the bombing program in progress far too feeble. Graduated air strikes, McCone argued, would play into Hanoi's hands by promoting graduated opposition within the United States. The troop decision was wrong if not accompanied by decisively punitive bombing because "we can expect requirements for an ever-increasing commitment of U.S. personnel without materially improving the chances of victory."[94] The momentum, though, was clearly in McCone's direction; it simply did not go all the way in that direction. And when General Johnson had reported after his March field trip, requesting a policy determination about "how much more the U.S. must contribute directly to the security of VN," McNamara had answered with the solid resolution still so characteristic of all the principals except Ball, "Policy is: Anything that will strengthen the position of the GVN will be sent."[95]

In Saigon Taylor's irritation persisted, and he more than any other major official opposed the April ground buildup. He had cabled even before the first deployment in March: "Once this policy is breached, it will be very difficult to hold line. . . . French tried to adapt their forces to this mission and failed; I doubt that US forces could do much better." The history of Taylor's views on troop commitment is another example of the acute ambivalence felt by so many officials throughout the first half of the 1960s in decisions on increasing U.S. involvement. He had favored troop deployments in November 1961 and August 1964 but

93. In an interview in 1977 George Ball asserted that in April 1965 McNamara, as well as his lieutenant, John McNaughton, had agreed privately with Ball that more strenuous military measures were not advisable. (See Thomas Warham Janes, "Rational Man—Irrational Policy: A Political Biography of John McNaughton's Involvement in the Vietnam War" [B.A. honors thesis, Harvard University, 1977], p. 79.) One way to square this recollection with the rest of the record is that defeat did not seem the price of restraint in April but did by July. The Pentagon Papers analysts noted that in June there was "hardly a trace in the files of the Secretary's opinion." In mid-July McNamara made a trip to the field and reported that the situation had deteriorated. (*Pentagon Papers*, vol. 3, p. 475.)

94. John McCone, memorandum to Rusk, McNamara, M. Bundy, and Taylor, April 2, 1965, LBJL/NSF-VNCF, 1965 Troop Decision folder, item 14b. See also *Pentagon Papers*, vol. 3, pp. 16, 100–101, 407.

95. *Pentagon Papers*, vol. 2, p. 356.

opposed them in March 1965. He would change his mind again four months later.[96]

On April 6 NSAM 328 authorized more active use of ground forces than had been allowed by the JCS instructions of the previous month. Yet as the Pentagon Papers analysts noted, "The whole tone of the NSAM is one of caution."[97] At the Honolulu conference two weeks later the President's major advisers agreed to recommend an increase in the American troop level to a total of 82,000, with the understanding that additional deployments would be considered later.[98] (The chronology of these early troop decisions that NSC staff members assembled for the President's reference at the time of the major decision on the escalation of troop levels in July—a document unavailable to the Defense Department team that compiled the Pentagon Papers and never before published—is interesting for what it shows about the White House perspective on these rapid developments. Its text appears in the appendix.)

In the spring of 1965 U.S. leaders were really still standing waist-deep in the middle of the Rubicon. The final push across came in the summer. In May and June South Vietnamese forces were severely battered in several battles. American troops were close to the scene in these instances but were not committed to save the ARVN units.[99] In late June Westmoreland asked for forty-four additional U.S. battalions, though he warned that there was no guarantee they could force the Vietcong to desist. But the decision to drastically raise the ante came in July. The catalysts for this almost panicky move were a striking series of Vietcong successes in taking over district headquarters; an apparent threat to take over the entire highlands area, cut the South in half, and establish a National Liberation Front government in the region they controlled; a Mission Intelligence Committee estimate that ARVN defeats raised the possibility of collapse; and evidence of infiltration of regimental-size North Vietnamese troop units.[100] Westmoreland saw that ARVN bat-

---

96. Taylor quoted in ibid., vol. 3, pp. 418–19. For further discussion of his views, see ibid., vol. 2, p. 292, and vol. 3, pp. 17, 281, 389–90, 400–401; Halberstam, *The Best and the Brightest*, pp. 486–87; and Taylor, *Swords and Plowshares*, p. 347.

97. *Pentagon Papers*, vol. 3, p. 475; see also pp. 702–03.

98. Robert McNamara, memorandum to the President, April 21, 1965, LBJL/NSF-VNCF, vol. 33, item 103a.

99. Herbert Y. Schandler, *The Unmaking of a President: Lyndon Johnson and Vietnam* (Princeton University Press, 1977), pp. 25–26.

100. *Pentagon Papers*, vol. 3, pp. 392, 413–15, 438. See also Johnson, *The Vantage Point*, p. 138.

talions were being destroyed faster than they could be replaced, and believed that the Vietcong were entering the third phase—large unit actions—of Mao's guerila war strategy. "I saw no solution," he wrote later, "... other than to put our own finger in the dike."[101]

Washington saw no other solution either. As Chester Cooper pointed out in a version of the "investment trap" explanation, the American troops in Vietnam at the time "were now a hostage. They represented too large a force to pull out without a tremendous loss of prestige, yet they were too small a combat force . . . to take over the burden of the fighting."[102] It may also not have been psychologically insignificant that the President had just finished intervening in the Dominican Republic, where U.S. troops seemed to accomplish their mission with a minimum of difficulty.

The Last Clear Chance

It was also clear that the bombing of the DRV, undertaken five months earlier with desperation about the present and hope for the future (a potent combination that fueled most of the critical escalation decisions throughout the war), had not succeeded in coercing the Communists either in the North or the South. Some analysts believe that this was no surprise, especially given the pessimism of 1964 projections on bombing effects, and even that the military services had expected it to fail—hoping that it would function to further commit the government to take more decisive action on the ground.[103] Whether or not decision-makers harbored such cynical stratagems, the decision to move toward a massive influx of American troops did not follow automatically and was not undertaken cavalierly. The President had apparently decided for the most part what he was going to have to do, but a final round of serious discussions on choices and commitments ensued nonetheless. July 1965, in fact, was one of the last instances of high-level considera-tion of U.S. objectives in depth, until the reassessment of policy in 1968 after the Tet offensive. On few occasions in the intervening three years

101. General William C. Westmoreland, *A Soldier Reports* (Doubleday, 1976), p. 126; see also p. 139.

102. Cooper, *The Lost Crusade,* p. 285.

103. Robert Gallucci asserted: "For those who had to concern themselves with the bounds of public opinion, the function of air power was to fail openly so that large scale losses of American lives on the ground in Asia could be justified." (*Neither Peace nor Honor,* p. 53.)

would the principals again focus intently on fundamentals rather than on the alternative means (the degree and pace of escalation) to the agreed upon ends.

The highlight of this consideration was the counterpoint of two State Department memos on July 1. One was from George Ball, who argued eloquently but ritually and in vain in favor of cutting American losses and disengaging before disaster overtook the United States and crippled its choices. *"This is our last clear chance,"* he pleaded, *"to make this decision."*[104] Rusk, Ball's boss, opposed this, reiterating the central goal of preventing a North Vietnamese takeover of the South and the need to defend South Vietnam to validate the reliability of American commitments, even to the point of risking war with the Soviet Union. "We must accomplish this objective," he intoned ominously, "without a general war *if possible.*"[105]

McNaughton reflected some lowering of sights by this time; he decided that the main objective of U.S. policy was no longer to "help a friend" but to avoid humiliation. (He did not yet buy Ball's prophetic warning that if the United States did escalate, *"humiliation would be more likely than the achievement of our objectives—even after we have paid terrible costs."*)[106] William Bundy and Clark Clifford took a position between Ball and Rusk, favoring the deployment of sufficient additional forces to prevent defeat coupled with attempts at a diplomatic solution. Of congressional leaders consulted, only Mansfield opposed additional commitment, warning, "We cannot expect our people to support a war for three-to-five years. . . . Remember, escalation begets escalation."[107]

The Defense Department also undertook an attempt to project whether the United States actually had the capacity to ultimately achieve the central objectives. This exercise was unique in the history of Vietnam decisionmaking, which in retrospect is shocking uniqueness, given the stakes in the issue throughout a quarter-century of Indochina policy. (This is one of the few points that effectively challenges our thesis that the system worked.) But the clarity and results of the exercise left much to be desired, and unfortunately for analysis, the documentary evidence on it is skimpy. In July McNamara directed JCS Chairman Earle Wheeler to assess "the assurance the U.S. can have of

104. *Pentagon Papers*, vol. 4, p. 22 (emphasis in original).
105. Ibid., p. 23 (emphasis in original).
106. Ibid., p. 22 (emphasis in original); see also p. 47.
107. Quoted in Schandler, *Unmaking of a President*, p. 30.

winning in South Vietnam if we do everything we can."[108] At the same time, Assistant Secretary of Defense McNaughton advised Wheeler's assistant, Lieutenant General Andrew Goodpaster: "With respect to the word 'win,' this I think means that we succeed in demonstrating to the VC that they cannot win."[109]

The catch in these ambiguous directives to the military leadership was McNamara's open-ended subordinate clause ("if we do everything we can") and the nature of McNaughton's criterion for victory (after all, as long as the United States was not defeated on the battlefield and pushed out, it would be demonstrating to the Vietcong that they could not win; and that is what happened until U.S. troops were withdrawn in the early 1970s). The full report of July 14 of the JCS study group is not in the Pentagon Papers, but an excerpt is. The group maintained: *"There appears to be no reason we cannot win if such is our will—and if that will is manifested in strategy and tactical operations."*[110] Here, as well, the kicker was in the unlimited options implied in the subordinate clause. In years to come the JCS would explain the failure to win by fulminating about the administration's refusal to authorize the necessary scale and types of operations—the decisions not to fulfill McNamara's qualifying condition, "if we do everything we can." The apparent failure of this estimating exercise itself to transcend the ambiguities of acceptable *ultimate* costs is an intriguing testament to lost opportunities to face up to the prospective upper limits of the American will to persevere.

These critical ambiguities were not sufficiently addressed or resolved in the July deliberations of the principals, but neither were they overlooked. They were simply submerged in the consensus that the United States had no choice other than to press on in preventing the Communist absorption of South Vietnam. When LBJ asked Wheeler, "Bus, what do you think it will take to do the job?" the General asked for a more precise definition of the job.[111] He warned that victory in the sense of driving the Communists from the field and thoroughly pacifying South Vietnam could take from 700,000 to a million men and seven years. To simply deny victory to the Communists—à la McNaughton's definition —lesser levels of force could be enough. No one except Clark Clifford,

108. *Pentagon Papers,* vol. 4, p. 290.
109. Ibid., p. 292.
110. Ibid., p. 291 (emphasis in original).
111. Quoted in Halberstam, *The Best and the Brightest,* p. 596. See also Valenti, *A Very Human President,* chap. 4.

and least of all the President, seemed to pay much attention to Wheeler's upper estimate, or to take it seriously. And if the President was indeed deciding to stave off defeat rather than to go for broke, the upper limits were not the central issue at the moment.

Clifford, a prestigious consultant who had the genuine respect of the President, agreed to the decision but with great reluctance and trepidation. Declassified White House files reveal that in May, in fact, he had written a short personal letter to Johnson, somberly stating his fears about the probable results of massive commitment. (The letter appears in the appendix.) The prevalent view that Clifford was a staunch hawk whose shift after the Tet offensive of 1968 was an unheralded reversal is an oversimplification. What Clifford's position in 1965 underlines is the dilemma of most of the leadership: the combination of great pessimism with the conviction that there was still no acceptable alternative to commitment. The same agonizing paradox emerges from a draft memorandum unearthed from John McNaughton's personal papers. On July 13 McNaughton recommended to McNamara that the United States deploy the forty-four battalions requested by Westmoreland and consider committing more forces later to seek a victory (which he had earlier defined as demonstrating to the Communists that they could not win). Assuming that force levels would evolve to between 200,000 and 400,000, McNaughton then estimated that the probability of success for the United States and Saigon in 1966 was only 20 percent, the probability of inconclusive results was 70 percent, and the odds for defeat were 10 percent. For 1967 the respective probabilities were 40, 45, and 15 percent; for 1968 they were 50, 30, and 20 percent. Thus McNamara's principal adviser on the war saw no more than a 50–50 chance of success—modestly defined—even after three years and also saw increased chances of collapse as time went on.[112] Nevertheless, McNaughton recommended the escalation.

The principals and their major subordinates were not deluded; they were simply still unwilling to see the costs of perseverance as a meaningful challenge to sticking with the basic objective. But this in itself did contribute to the nervously muddled quality of some of their thinking. McNaughton estimated that even with 200,000 to 400,000 U.S. troops, the chance for a win by 1968 was only 50–50; yet in his memo to Goodpaster he indicated that "assurance" of a win, for estimating pur-

112. Memorandum quoted in Janes, "Rational Man," pp. 92–93.

poses, should be defined as better than a 75 percent chance. He cap-
sulized the July crunch in a memo:

The dilemma. We are in a dilemma. . . . it may be that while going for victory
we have the strength for compromise, but if we go for compromise we have
the strength only for defeat—this because a revealed lowering of sights from
victory to compromise (a) will unhinge the GVN and (b) will give the DRV
the "smell of blood."[113]

The President's Choice and the Public's Reaction

A dilemma it was, and a dilemma it remained. The stakes always
seemed immense, and in the context of cold war assumptions, defini-
tions, and constraints the leaders' choices always seemed foreordained.
In June 1965 LBJ said there were only two alternatives to his policy;
the Barry Goldwater solution and the Wayne Morse solution.[114] A month
later McNamara saw three options: cut losses and withdraw, continue
at the current level (75,000 troops), or "expand promptly and substantially the U.S. military pressure."[115] Taylor always saw four alternatives:
"all-out, pull-out, pull-back, or *stick-it-out"* (to which the DRV had
comparable options: *"escalate, play dead, protract,* and *negotiate"*).[116]
The President posed five choices to the NSC at that time.

We can bring the enemy to his knees by using our Strategic Air Command. . . .
Another group thinks we ought to pack up and go home.
    Third, we could stay there as we are. . . . Then, we could go to Congress
and ask for great sums of money; we could call up the reserves and increase
the draft; go on a war footing; declare a state of emergency. . . . But if we go
into that kind of a land war, then North Vietnam would go to its friends,
China and Russia. . . .
    Finally, we can give our commanders in the field the men and supplies
they say they need.

He noted: "I had concluded the last course was the right one."[117]

But what would this middle course achieve? It would hurt the enemy
but not destroy him. As long as the United States could not cripple the
Vietcong and North Vietnamese capacity to put some level of forces in
the field, it could not end the war on American terms. There were three
overlapping results that strong but limited force might bring about, and
at certain stages did appear to bring about: a gradual, asymptotic with-
ering away of Communist military capabilities to the point that the

---

113. *Pentagon Papers*, vol. 4, p. 48; see also pp. 25, 292.
114. Graff, *The Tuesday Cabinet*, p. 53.
115. Johnson, *The Vantage Point*, p. 145.
116. Taylor, *Swords and Plowshares*, p. 379 (emphasis in the original).
117. Johnson, *The Vantage Point*, p. 149.

threat could be handled by the South Vietnamese; the buying of time to build up South Vietnamese forces to a higher level capable of waging the war with more independence; and convincing the North Vietnamese to negotiate.

On July 28, 1965, the President announced, "I have today ordered to Vietnam the Airmobile Division and certain other forces which will raise our fighting strength from 75,000 to 125,000 men almost immediately. Additional forces will be needed later, and they will be sent as requested."[118] By November 10 the package for the first phase of troop commitment was fixed at 219,000.[119] The entire escalation period of decisionmaking on Southeast Asia, for almost three years to come, would be one uncomplicated by competing foreign policy crises—unlike the Kennedy administration's experience. The Dominican intervention was past, the Mideast crisis of 1967 would be resolved unilaterally by the Israelis, and not until the seizure of the *Pueblo* in January 1968 would another crisis intrude—an intrusion that would be followed directly by the Tet offensive and the revision of Vietnam policy. From 1965 through 1967 Lyndon Johnson would be staring Ho Chi Minh straight in the face.

Nor were there many domestic constraints by 1965. The real implications of public opinion at that time are unclear and perhaps always will be. But as escalation began in the fall of 1965, 64 percent in a Gallup survey still viewed greater involvement as having been necessary rather than as a mistake. Yet at the same time, the public seemed hardly more duped about the likely outcome than did the administration. Thirty percent believed the war, like the Korean War, would end in a stalemate; only 29 percent believed there would be a U.S. victory; and 26 percent, perhaps as uncertain as a large number of the policymakers, made no prediction.[120]

The President and the principals were acutely conscious of these polls, while most of the active antiwar Democrats often were not. Citing 70 percent public support for government policy in June 1965, Rusk noted frankly, "We are not under pressure here to get out."[121] (One might have argued that by the same token the administration was not under pressure to get in. But here the problem was the *anticipated* pressure of backlash if the United States stayed out and the Communists

118. *Pentagon Papers*, vol. 3, p. 477.

119. Ibid., p. 478.

120. George H. Gallup, ed., *The Gallup Poll* (Random House, 1972), vol. 3, pp. 1971–72.

121. Quoted in Graff, *The Tuesday Cabinet*, pp. 43–44.

won.) Eight months later, with polls at his fingertips, the President cited figures: 10 percent "want to go hot-headed—Goldwater types," 10 percent "are ready to run," 20 percent favored more bombing, and 60 percent believed "we are doing right."[122] LBJ probably noted to himself that these figures, although showing a majority for support, indicated three times as much hawkish disagreement as dovish. The President's popularity often rose after escalation; it went up 14 percent, for example, after the Tonkin Gulf retaliation.[123] At the beginning of 1966, 61 percent favored escalation if the bombing pause failed to produce enemy response, and a year later 67 percent still supported ROLLING THUNDER.[124]

Setting the Pattern of Perseverance: Late 1965

The record of agonizing deliberations in late 1964 and early 1965 showed that policymakers knew what they might at worst be getting into, even if most of them chose not to dwell on the odds that the worst would come to pass. But were they deceived during the years of escalation about how well the war was progressing? Yes and no. They were deceived to the extent that they *hoped* for the best when faced with contradictory or ambiguous indicators, or to the extent that they listened intently to the optimistic assessments from the field while conveniently forgetting the qualifying conditions attached to these assessments or the pessimistic analyses from other sources.

But at best they were deceived indirectly or temporarily—or they deceived themselves. They never saw the light at the end of the tunnel for long, and the documentary record provides little to substantiate the "quagmire theory" view that each increment of additional troops or each notch of escalation in the air war were expected to bring victory. The human mind's capacity to perceive and balance evidence with perfect rationality is limited, and men are peculiarly able to combine pessimism and optimism, doubt and confidence, recognition of negative evidence and persistence in positive assumptions, all at the same time.[125]

122. Quoted in ibid., p. 103.
123. Windchy, *Tonkin Gulf*, p. 25.
124.Gallucci, *Neither Peace nor Honor*, p. 101.
125. See John D. Steinbruner, *The Cybernetic Theory of Decision: New Dimensions of Political Analysis* (Princeton University Press, 1974); Robert Jervis, "Hypotheses on Misperception," *World Politics*, vol. 20 (April 1968), pp. 454–79;

Did Advisers Deceive Decisionmakers?

Two arguments are often advanced to justify the proposition that top decisionmakers were fooled about what was happening or were tricked into additional escalation at each step along the way. One is that duplicitous military leaders deliberately avoided shocking civilian policymakers by making small requests for increases periodically, promising results with each step, and raising the ante almost imperceptibly over time, instead of demanding at the beginning the full extent of the military commitment they knew would ultimately be needed.[126] Another is that duplicitous military staffers in the field and accessories at the top of the CIA purposely understated enemy strength in order not to shock the civilians into reassessing commitment.[127] There is some evidence for both arguments but not enough to dispel the weightier evidence to the contrary, even if one goes back to the first days of direct intervention in 1965.

On the first count, Wheeler's unheeded caveat in July about the total troop requirements of an expansive conception of victory poses the most obvious rejoinder. And when at that time the President asked Westmoreland through the JCS if the forty-four battalions he was requesting would force the enemy to back down, the commander responded, "The direct answer to your basic question is 'No,' " and wrote to Washington, "Instinctively, we believe that there may be substantial additional U.S. force requirements."[128] In addition, the military made troop requests in gradual increments because of constraints beyond their control. In fact, in 1966 McNamara was pressing them to accelerate deployments

Jervis, *Perception and Misperception in International Politics* (Princeton University Press, 1976); and Joseph H. De Rivera, *The Psychological Dimension of Foreign Policy* (Charles Merrill, 1968).

126. See Arthur M. Schlesinger, Jr., *The Crisis of Confidence: Ideas, Power and Violence in America* (Houghton Mifflin, 1969), p. 172; and Kearns, *Lyndon Johnson*, p. 275.

127. See *U.S. Intelligence Agencies and Activities: The Performance of the Intelligence Community*, Proceedings of the House Select Committee on Intelligence, 94 Cong. 1 sess. (GPO, 1975), pp. 683–92; Sam Adams, "Vietnam Coverup: Playing War with Numbers," *Harper's*, May 1975, pp. 41–46; Martin Arnold, "Ellsberg Witness Asserts Military Falsified Reports," *New York Times*, March 7, 1973; Jack Anderson and Les Whitten, "Numbers Game on Tet Offensive," *Washington Post*, October 31, 1975; and John M. Crewdson, "False Troop Data in Vietnam Cited," *New York Times*, September 19, 1975.

128. Westmoreland, *A Soldier Reports*, p. 141.

faster than they were able to. The logistical support base in South Vietnam was inadequate in the first year of U.S. combat to absorb troop units at a rapid rate; moreover, because the President refused to mobilize reserves as the JCS recommended, the troops were simply not available—raising them through the draft and training them took time. As LBJ told Westmoreland in their first big head-to-head conference in Honolulu, "I will give you everything you want. . . . But I may have to give it to you a little slower than you want."[129] The President, however, never did give the commander everything he wanted. *Incrementalism did not follow from illusion about victory around each corner; it followed from the strategy of progressive pressure and the progressive failure of strategy.*

A document sometimes cited to show Westmoreland's excessive optimism in official councils was the three-phase campaign plan he developed in 1965 (his *public* optimism, encouraged by the President and many administration officials and expressed in a torrent of upbeat statements in the mid-1960s, was usually greater).[130] The Pentagon Papers analysts deduced a prognosis for victory by the end of 1967 in this plan. But the wording of the plan was imprecise about the terminal date of the second phase (to begin in 1966), from which the final phase was to take a year and a half, and Westmoreland maintained that he neither stated nor intended a prediction of victory for 1967. He also made no prediction about the total number of troops that might ultimately be needed.[131] In any case, if this was deception, it was not very inspired deception.

On the second count, the Saigon command may indeed have understated enemy capacity at many points along the way. According to Halberstam, for example, when Colonel William Crossen made a calculation at MACV in April 1965 of the North Vietnamese capacity to reinforce, which came out to an astoundingly high figure, the general on Westmoreland's staff he showed it to said, "Jesus, if we tell this to the

129. Quoted in Hugh Sidey, *A Very Personal Presidency* (Atheneum, 1968), p. 82. See also *Pentagon Papers*, vol. 4, pp. 279–80; and Westmoreland, *A Soldier Reports*, pp. 185–86.

130. When the Tet offensive began, for example, Wheeler instructed Westmoreland in a cable: "The President desires that you make a brief personal comment to the press at least once each day. . . . to convey to the American public your confidence in our ability to blunt these enemy moves, and to reassure the public here that you have the situation under control." (Quoted in Schandler, *Unmaking of a President*, p. 83.)

131. See *Pentagon Papers*, vol. 3, pp. 482–85; vol. 4, p. 296; and Westmoreland, *A Soldier Reports*, pp. 142–43.

people in Washington we'll be out of the war tomorrow. We'll have to revise it downward."[132] But in general it is more likely that subordinates in the field, faced with uncertain data that allowed a substantial range of possible interpretation, were most often translating the secret hopes of their superiors into their reports: when reality was unclear, hope for the best. Moreover, officials had a case of their own with which to refute the higher estimates used by mavericks such as CIA analyst Sam Adams.[133]

More to the point, however, MACV itself was *emphasizing* Communist strength and infiltration when making crucial troop requests. When Westmoreland estimated that the Vietcong and North Vietnamese Army buildup rate in the South was double that scheduled for the United States in his Phase II program, McNamara understood the implications perfectly. He decided at that time—the *fall* of 1965—to back a troop increase to 400,000 by the end of 1966, also recognizing the possible need for *another 200,000* in 1967. Eventually the secretary would backtrack on this total figure of 600,000, but obviously none of the military in the early period of troop commitment were fooling him into thinking the numbers could be kept low. And at this same time in 1965, when he was contemplating a number of troops that far exceeded the number actually reached—even at the apex in 1968—McNamara admitted to the President that even this "will not guarantee success." The secretary's somber but remarkably predictive warning went further: "US killed-in-action can be expected to reach 1000 a month, and the odds are even that we will be faced in early 1967 with a 'no-decision' at an even higher level."[134] This, to say the least, was no naive perception of light at the end of the tunnel.

Strategy on the Ground

The strategy for using American troops for offensive operations, rather than just for the base security mission that had prompted the

---

132. Halberstam, *The Best and the Brightest*, p. 545.

133. For criticisms of Adams's conclusions, see letters by Vice Admiral Rufus L. Taylor, USN (Ret.), and James C. Graham, in *Harper's*, July 1975, pp. 14, 16; *New York Times*, December 4, 1975; and Don Oberdorfer, "Intelligence in Tet Fight Held Success," *Washington Post*, December 4, 1975. On the tendency of ambiguity to reinforce wishful thinking, see Richard K. Betts, "Analysis, War, and Decision: Why Intelligence Failures Are Inevitable," *World Politics*, vol. 31 (October 1978).

134. *Pentagon Papers*, vol. 4, p. 623; and Westmoreland, *A Soldier Reports*, p. 154.

landing of the first Marine battalions, also evolved quickly and not imperceptibly. The original enclave strategy was backed at first by Taylor (who, ironically, would testify eloquently against it when his old Army colleague James Gavin proposed it in Fulbright's hearings on administration policy early in 1966), as well as by CINCPAC and the Marine Corps. The adoption of such a defensive enclave concept would have represented a last cleaving to the pacification-oriented counterinsurgency strategy that had been favored by Hilsman, Thompson, and Lansdale. (After 1968, General Creighton Abrams's tactics would resemble it to some degree.)[135]

But Westmoreland was adamant in pushing for the traditional attack mission of the infantry and against the passive beachhead tactics of the Marines (whose historic doctrine, curiously, was *least* inclined to static defense tactics). The commander of MACV feared that with limited U.S. manpower tied down in garrisoning only a portion of the population in villages, large enemy units would be free to roam at will, able to concentrate forces for attacks at points of their choosing. The enclave option remained viable only as long as the policymakers thought the bombing campaign might bring results by itself; since this hope was short-lived, so was the restriction on offensive operations. The security strategy gave way to the search and destroy strategy long before the new large increments of troops poured in late in 1965.[136]

135. See *Pentagon Papers*, vol. 2, pp. 533 ff.; vol. 3, pp. 6, 394, 397, 453, 468, 470–71, 478–81; and Westmoreland, *A Soldier Reports*, pp. 140–49, 381.

136. See Westmoreland, *A Soldier Reports*, pp. 164–65; and Gallucci, *Neither Peace nor Honor*, pp. 106–18. The Honolulu Conference of April 20, 1965, produced a determination "to break the will of the DRV/VC by denying them victory." (*Pentagon Papers*, vol. 3, p. 410.) Herbert Schandler interpreted the shift from the enclave strategy to search and destroy as a decisive choice to achieve victory. (*Unmaking of a President*, pp. 24, 31, 290–97.) But the evidence that either the President or the principals expected clear-cut victory in the classic sense is negligible, as our analysis shows. The working definition of "win" used by the Pentagon study group in July 1965, *after* search and destroy was inaugurated, was "succeed in demonstrating to the VC that they cannot win." (*Pentagon Papers*, vol. 4, p. 293.) A more accurate interpretation is that search and destroy was undertaken (1) to increase the costs to the Communists dramatically and, in conjunction with other measures, to increase their incentives to negotiate on terms favorable to the United States; (2) in the *hope* that it would cripple the Communists sufficiently to permit the South Vietnamese to ultimately handle the military challenge themselves; and (3) to reduce the time span within which either of the first two possibilities could occur. It was widely believed that the enclave strategy could perpetuate the relative advantages of the Communists in the balance of power within the South. In short, we view the difference between the two ground strategies, *in the view of civilian leaders*, as a continuum rather than a dichotomy.

A gratifying low ratio of American-to-enemy casualties in the first major ground engagements, particularly the battle of Ia Drang valley in November 1965, confirmed the viability of the attrition strategy to MACV. With this in view, the scant attention given in succeeding years to exactly how much was ultimately supposed to be accomplished by U.S. forces on the ground is still only slightly understandable. Westmoreland submitted yearly campaign plans to Washington in both 1966 and 1967. "It was a most important document," Taylor recalled, "because it provided the basis for troop requests. . . . Yet, so far as I could see, it was never carefully reviewed and formally approved, disapproved, or amended. . . . under the language of the document, General Westmoreland would be entirely justified to ask for troops to defend all Vietnam to its utmost frontiers."[137] The frustration that would follow in the next three years—with vast numbers of American troops in the yet more vast countryside and massive search and destroy operations usually failing to come to grips and hold contact with the Communist units they sought to trap and fight—was captured by Army Major Josiah Bunting in his bitter novel-cum-memoir, *The Lionheads*: "Think of Primo Carnera going after Willie Pep in a pigsty ten miles square."[138]

Strategy in the Air

Policymakers also were not deceived about the efficacy of the air war, although they were disappointed. *The military promised much if allowed to bomb heavily, quickly, and without restraint but promised little if bombing was to be slow, limited, and restricted.* The civilian leaders imposed such restraints from the beginning, and relaxed them only gradually and never completely. In contrast to the military, most of the civilian leaders favored a symbolic use of bombing to give the Communists an incentive to deescalate. Aside from increasing the danger of Chinese or Soviet intervention, it was feared that unlimited bombing would in effect kill the hostage. In early consideration of bombing options this rationale had been reflected in a curious cable from Lodge to the President on May 15, 1964: "If you lay the whole country waste, it is quite likely that you will induce a mood of fatalism in the Viet Cong. Also, there will be nobody left in North Viet Nam on

137. Taylor, *Swords and Plowshares*, p. 375.
138. Josiah Bunting, *The Lionheads* (Braziller, 1972), p. 71. For an interpretation of why the nature of Vietnamese society and the tactics of the Communists doomed the search and destroy strategy, see Jeffrey Race, *War Comes to Long An* (University of California Press, 1972), pp. 224–27 and passim.

whom to put pressure. . . . What we are interested in here is not destroying Ho Chi Minh (as his successor would probably be worse than he is), but getting him to change his behavior. That is what President Kennedy was trying to do in October with Diem and with considerable success [sic!]."[139]

There were three fundamental competing strategies in the bombing campaign against North Vietnam: (1) the graduated response-slow squeeze-reprisal concept designed to prod Hanoi to accommodation, favored by the State Department and ISA in 1964; (2) the massive all-out assault designed to smash Hanoi's military, economic, and industrial capabilities, favored by the Air Force throughout the war; and (3) the interdiction strategy designed to cut lines of communication and logistical systems and to intercept supplies destined for Communist forces in the South, favored to varying degrees by all policymakers after 1965. Only this third concept was ever fully implemented. The first was tried very briefly in the FLAMING DART reprisal raids after Pleiku but quickly merged into Admiral U. S. G. Sharp's "graduated pressures" concept (a compromise between the State Department–ISA and Air Force positions) in the ROLLING THUNDER program.[140] The second approach was never fully or consciously implemented. The *rate* of escalation the Air Force favored—rapid and immediate, in order to destroy Hanoi's assets before they could be dispersed and before effective air defenses could be constructed—was explicitly rejected, although most of the targets in General McConnell's "94-Target Plan" were gradually authorized over the course of three years.

Whichever variant of bombing strategy was pursued, it never produced the results government leaders hoped for, and progressive failure encouraged progressive escalation. As that old guerilla war theorist and critic of top-heavy American military tactics Sir Robert Thompson remarked, "A failure of strategy in applying the means to achieve the aim, will frequently lead to a policy of increasing the means."[141] But while the means were increased, they were increased slowly and fitfully because nonmilitary constituencies in Washington war councils worried that precipitate escalation (1) would risk prompting Soviet or Chinese

139. "Seaborn," USVNR, Negotiations Volumes, VI.C.1, p. 2.
140. See *Pentagon Papers*, vol. 3, pp. 271–73, 318, 340 ff., 359–60.
141. Quoted in Richard M. Pfeffer, ed., *No More Vietnams? The War and the Future of American Foreign Policy* (Harper and Row, for the Adlai Stevenson Institute of International Affairs, 1968), p. 171.

intervention; (2) would impede chances for negotiations; and (3) would be cost-ineffective. Disagreement over bombing objectives and costs would pit government civilians, especially in the Péntagon, against their military colleagues in a continuing dispute that grew in acrimony over the course of the preparation and implementation of the air war. Debates would center on the alternative merits of (1) the graduated response goal (using bombing for political signaling) as a prod to Hanoi's intentions, and (2) the 94-Target Plan, whose goal was to use bombing to achieve victory by destroying Hanoi's capability to wage war.[142]

Why did the civilians argue so vigorously against the military for the reprisal concept in the 1964 planning, and why was it then abandoned so quickly in the new year?

Many of the civilians agreed with a Special National Intelligence Estimate in May 1964 that graduated pressure might only affect Hanoi's will and could not affect enemy capabilities because "major sources of communist strength in SVN are indigenous."[143] Bundy's rationale for bombing in his Pleiku memo was that "the object would not be to 'win' an air war against Hanoi, but rather to influence the course of the struggle in the South."[144] To Lyndon Johnson, "limited bombing was seduction, not rape, and seduction was controllable, even reversible."[145]

Johnson's distrust of the military ("The generals . . . know only two words—spend and bomb," he said in 1965)[146] also led him instinctively to hew to a limited course and to retain tight control of air strikes. For most of the war, targets were doled out abstemiously and with detailed personal attention in the Tuesday Luncheons (to which no military officer was regularly invited until late 1967). LBJ and McNamara also regulated the pace of escalation personally by minimizing autonomy in the field, discouraging the development of comprehensive campaign plans, and refusing to accept bombing proposals in more than weekly target packages. Predictably this caused intense resentment among the professional soldiers.[147]

142. See *Pentagon Papers*, vol. 3, pp. 132, 145, 271, 312–21, 628–30; and Goulden, *Truth Is the First Casualty*, pp. 88–91.

143. *Pentagon Papers*, vol. 3, pp. 124–25.

144. Ibid., p. 313.

145. Kearns, *Lyndon Johnson*, p. 264.

146. Quoted in Evans and Novak, *Lyndon B. Johnson*, p. 539.

147. See *Pentagon Papers*, vol. 3, p. 344; vol. 4, p. 19; and Gallucci, *Neither*

In the initial FLAMING DART raids, targets in North Vietnam were matched in tit-for-tat fashion against Vietcong "provocation" attacks in the South. If the graduated response theory was to work, "compellence"—the mirror image of deterrence, the coaxing of an enemy to back down in the face of prospective destruction by giving him a little taste of what could come—would take effect, and Communist attacks in the South would decline in intensity.[148] But the Vietcong were not compelled, and the North Vietnamese did not respond as the Russians had responded in Berlin or Cuba. Sustained bombing superseded FLAMING DART reprisals, but civilians did not abandon hope that Hanoi might respond to limited coercion by limiting its own effort. In early April reconnaissance revealed Soviet surface-to-air missiles (SAM-2s) under construction in the North.[149] Washington refused permission to strike the sites. In Saigon, McNaughton denigrated their significance. As the furious Westmoreland recounted:

"You don't think the North Vietnamese are going to use them!" he [McNaughton] scoffed to General [Joseph H.] Moore. "Putting them in is just a political ploy by the Russians to appease Hanoi."

It was all a matter of signals, said the clever civilian theorists in Washington. We won't bomb the SAM sites, which signals the North Vietnamese not to use them.[150]

McNaughton turned out to be wrong. The DRV was soon using its SAMs to knock down large numbers of U.S. warplanes.

There was an essential fallacy in the graduated response strategy.

Peace nor Honor, pp. 91–92. An anonymous general had a disgruntled ditty:

> I am not allowed to run the train
>   The whistle I can't blow.
> I am not allowed to say how fast
>   The railroad trains can go.
> I am not allowed to shoot off steam
>   Nor even clang the bell.
> But let it jump the goddam tracks
>   And see who catches hell!

(Quoted in Richard J. Stillman, "The Pentagon's Whiz Kids," *U.S. Naval Institute Proceedings*, vol. 92 [April 1966], p. 57.)

148. See *Pentagon Papers*, vol. 3, pp. 271, 312–18; and Admiral U. S. G. Sharp, USN, Commander in Chief, Pacific, and General William C. Westmoreland, USA, Commander, Military Assistance Command, Vietnam, *Report on the War in Vietnam (as of June 30, 1968)* (GPO, 1968), p. 15. The "compellence" theory is elaborated in Thomas C. Schelling, *Arms and Influence* (Yale University Press, 1966).

149. *Pentagon Papers*, vol. 3, pp. 365–66.

150. Westmoreland, *A Soldier Reports*, p. 120.

"The trouble with our policy in Vietnam," said Assistant Secretary of Defense Paul Warnke as he left office in 1969, "has been that we guessed wrong with respect to what the North Vietnamese reaction would be. We anticipated that they would respond like reasonable people."[151] The rationale imputed to the North Vietnamese an economic motivation, a mechanistic calculation of costs and benefits, a logical willingness to lower demand as price rose. It was as if General Giap would manage a revolution the way McNamara managed the Pentagon. It implicitly assumed that Vietnamese reunification was a relative value to Hanoi that could be relinquished as the pain threshold rose, rather than the absolute value it was. The American military, even if they did not recognize this fallacy, advised as though they did. As the civilians came to doubt the logic of reprisals, the bombing shifted to an ongoing program of escalating pressure. But each step of gradual escalation failed to produce what leaders hoped for. As George Ball had anticipated in October 1964, "To the extent that the response to a move can be controlled, that move is probably ineffective."

But even as the failure of graduated response was implicitly acknowledged—though it was never completely abandoned in civilian minds—and the rationale of the bombing shifted to the crimp it could put in the DRV's capabilities to support the war in the South, Pentagon civilians began to perceive the failure of the new rationale. Henceforth their logic of bombing would rest on a combination of coercion and interdiction. McNamara's concern over the cost-ineffectiveness of the resulting destruction began immediately, just as FLAMING DART gave way to ROLLING THUNDER in February 1965. The following July he recommended limiting the bombing so that it would emphasize threat, minimize DRV loss of face, optimize interdiction versus political costs, coordinate with other influences on the DRV, and avoid undue risks and costs.[152]

Bombing and Negotiation

What interest there was in diplomacy was intimately tied to the bombing program. Graduated response, after all, and the limitations on targeting were supposed to elicit from Hanoi some form of reciprocity and interest in accommodation. The intersection of these concerns with the concern for military progress occurred in the debates on bombing

151. Paul C. Warnke, Oral History Interview, in Lyndon B. Johnson Library.
152. Pentagon Papers, vol. 4, pp. 28–29; see also vol. 3, pp. 332–33.

pauses. Johnson listed sixteen bombing pauses and seventy-two peace initiatives in his memoirs, but only a few of the pauses were complete, and only a few of the initiatives had much significance.

In roughly general terms, the Office of the Secretary of Defense, with occasional support from the State Department, lobbied for bombing pauses in order to get the DRV to the negotiating table, and MACV, CINCPAC, and the JCS, with occasional support from the State Department, opposed bombing pauses in order not to give the Communists a free ride to the battlefield. The first pause, Project MAYFLOWER, was in May 1965, three months after ROLLING THUNDER began. In late April the director of intelligence and research in the State Department had written to the White House staffer detailed to keep track of peace possibilities that Hanoi's position on negotiations had hardened after the retaliatory raids of February gave way to sustained air war, and that this position was unlikely to become more flexible unless the attacks stopped.[153] In considering a pause in the bombing the U.S. mission in Saigon hoped "to link the intensity of U.S. bombing after the resumption closely to the level of VC activity during the pause. The purpose would be to make it clear to Hanoi that. . . . a downward trend in VC activities would be 'rewarded' in a similar manner by decreasing U.S. bombing."[154] This reasoning was clearly the extension of the tit-for-tat signaling rationale of the old reprisal concept of bombing. Not surprisingly, its success was no greater than it had been before FLAMING DART was supplanted by ROLLING THUNDER. The MAYFLOWER pause lasted five days with no result. Rusk gave Ambassador Foy Kohler in Moscow a message, suggesting a reciprocation by Hanoi, to deliver to North Vietnamese diplomats. The note was returned the next day without comment.[155]

Just after the bombing was resumed on May 18, the head of the North Vietnamese Economic Delegation in Paris, Mai Van Bo, approached French intermediaries with what they initially saw as an offer to soften the DRV position. But on further investigation American officials concluded the initiative had no new substance.[156] The North Vietnamese

153. Thomas L. Hughes, "Negotiating under Pressure—Hanoi's Position," memorandum for Chester Cooper, April 23, 1965, LBJL/NSF-VNCF, Southeast Asia Special Intelligence Material, vol. V, item 3a.

154. "MAYFLOWER," USVNR, Negotiations Volumes, VI.C.1, Text, p. 122.

155. See Pentagon Papers, vol. 3, pp. 282–83, 362–79; and Kraslow and Loory, The Secret Search, pp. 121–23.

156. "MAYFLOWER," Text, pp. 128–30.

used the same technique (delaying their response to a U.S. halt in bombing until a few hours after it resumed) again on January 31, 1966, after a thirty-seven-day suspension (see below). According to the Pentagon Papers analysts, "The DRV probably used this gap for two purposes: propaganda and bargaining. The propaganda value was potentially high—couldn't the U.S. wait a few hours before plunging back to the attack? More importantly it was a way of cancelling out the U.S. negotiating blue chip."[157]

Between the two bombing pauses of 1965 another set of contacts with Hanoi began in August: the "XYZ" affair. Retired Ambassador Edmund Gullion and another former Foreign Service officer were dispatched to several meetings with Mai Van Bo. The Pentagon Papers analysts termed these meetings "the most serious mutual effort to resolve matters of substance between the U.S. and the DRV before and since."[158] Yet no progress resulted. The emptiness of the XYZ episode is indicative of the comparative lack of seriousness of the other contacts before 1968.

The most energetic and ambitious American initiative was the thirty-seven-day bombing pause beginning Christmas Eve, 1965, and known as the peace offensive. Ambassador Henry A. Byroade in Rangoon was given a message to deliver to the North Vietnamese consulate, and other countries received dramatic visits from U.S. representatives seeking help in reaching the North Vietnamese. Harriman flew on a ten-nation trip, beginning in Warsaw; McGeorge Bundy went to Ottawa; Assistant Secretary of State Thomas Mann went to Mexico City; Arthur Goldberg wended to the Vatican, the Italian government in Rome, and Paris; Hubert Humphrey flew to Tokyo; G. Mennen Williams took a whirlwind tour to fourteen African countries. The White House promulgated a fourteen-point U.S. peace program (an ironic reflection, almost certainly unconscious, of the Wilsonian underpinnings of the philosophy of some of the central policymakers, especially Rusk), of which he said, "We have put everything into the basket of peace except the surrender of South Vietnam."[159] The North Vietnamese response was an article in a

157. "XYZ," USVNR, Negotiations Volumes, VI.C.1, Summary, p. 1; see also "PINTA: RANGOON," ibid., Text, pp. 1–3.

158. "XYZ," ibid., Summary, p. 2; see also pp. 3–4, 6–8, and Text, pp. 8–9, 12–15, 18–19, 21–22. "Bo (R) and Gullion (X) had four meetings. . . . Bo did not show up for an arranged fifth meeting. . . . Y, another ex-FSO [Foreign Service officer], saw Bo only once and nothing was said, and Z never existed. It is obvious that XYZ should be renamed X." (Ibid., Summary, p. 2.)

159. Kraslow and Loory, *The Secret Search*, p. 141.

Hanoi journal entitled, "Johnson Puts Everything in the Basket of Peace except Peace."[160]

As ambitious as the peace offensive was—"fandangle diplomacy" in Kraslow and Loory's words—its significance was mitigated on the battle-field, perhaps owing to organizational processes and preplanned deployment schedules, rather than to specific intent. In January, just as tentative evidence showed that the pause was getting some tacit reciprocity (military contacts with the North Vietnamese Army dropped sharply), the United States went ahead and reinforced its troops by 6 percent. Eleven thousand additional American soldiers landed in the country between late December and mid-January, and a large ground offensive was mounted in the Iron Triangle, the Communist stronghold near Saigon. Ho Chi Minh noted this when he publicly denigrated the peace offensive on January 28.[161] Whether intentionally or not—and there is some evidence that U.S. leaders indeed knew what they were doing[162]—the deployment hinted at a tendency that would arise again, to develop second thoughts and back off from an initiative. (In planning the bombing limitation in 1968 Johnson was more careful. JCS Chairman Wheeler cabled Westmoreland that the President pointed out at a meeting the day before his television speech at the end of March that "we had often been accused in the past of accompanying peace initiatives with increased military operations." So Westmoreland was directed to conduct operations during this period in a low key, "as being merely in the usual run of offensive operations.")[163]

The pattern of the Americanized war was set in 1965. The basic decision on overt intervention was made; the fundamental strategies for war on the ground and in the air were set and would change only mar-

160. "PINTA: RANGOON," Text, p. 15.

161. Kraslow and Loory, *The Secret Search*, pp. 145, 147–51.

162. On December 17, 1965, William Bundy sent a note to Rusk, "Last Thoughts on the Pause Proposal." He mentioned having lunch with a Soviet diplomat during which he inferred that Hanoi would denounce the bombing pause "unless we do something major with respect to the South—which I take to imply the *suspension of reinforcements. This I most emphatically do not feel we should do.*" ("PINTA: RANGOON," Text, p. 1a [emphasis added].) It should also be noted that some in the administration had expected the pause would fail but saw it as a necessary last-chance offer before undertaking planned escalation. See *Pentagon Papers*, vol. 4, pp. 303, 623.

163. Quoted in Schandler, *Unmaking of a President*, p. 280.

ginally before 1968; and attempts to secure the elusive and secondary prize of negotiations were begun and would continue, ambivalently and occasionally blunderingly, over the next several years. The United States had galloped beyond the Rubicon, to use Taylor's metaphor, but the road to Rome for the next two years was really a dark and unending tunnel.

CHAPTER FIVE

Coming Home to Roost:
The Johnson Administration, II

Commentaries about the making of U.S. Vietnam policy generally focus on the dramatic decisions—those of November 1961, the Diem coup of 1963, the Tonkin Gulf retaliation in 1964, the inauguration of bombing and ground combat in 1965, and the reassessment following Tet in 1968. Few words are expended on the three-year period of gradual escalation after the United States intervened in force. Yet this period is important —historically, of course, because it was when the American blood and treasure invested in Southeast Asia grew astronomically, provoking domestic convulsions at the end—but also intellectually because it raises an obvious issue that requires explanation. Why did the United States continue to escalate, to pour money and lives into South Vietnam, and to devastate North Vietnam after 1965, when escalation failed to bring the Communists to terms? Why was involvement capped only in 1968 rather than the year before or the year before that? Conventional wisdom has it that expectations of success at each step along the way kept leaders chained to the escalator. This explanation is wrong for both the escalation period and the pre-1965 decisions. George Ball had warned before the decisions in 1965: "Once on the tiger's back we cannot be sure of picking the place to dismount."[1] The reasons that American leaders did not dismount for so long, however, were no different from the ones that impelled them to get on. Thus the decisions of 1966–68 were always tactical rather than strategic. The "policy" alternatives considered were alternative numbers of ground troops or alternative

1. George Ball, "A Light that Failed," *Atlantic Monthly*, July 1972, p. 41.

bombing programs.[2] This is surprising from the perspective of hindsight but predictable from the perspective of the previous decisions.

On the Tiger's Back: 1966–67

The basic trends apparent by late 1965 continued throughout 1966, although slight variations emerged in the attitudes of policymakers. Decisions were dominated by the issues of troop levels and bombing targets, but other aspects of the war also drew attention, especially among the quasi-doves in the government. One issue was pacification. The HOP TAC pacification program—the successor to strategic hamlets—had flopped in 1965. The country team pursued new programs energetically, but they were plagued by dispersion of authority and lack of coordination. Another situation, the political stability of the GVN, so long the prime source of frustration for Americans, actually improved. Musical chairs government came to an end after the Ky coup in June 1965. Except for the interlude of the Buddhist "Struggle Movement" in the spring of 1966, when General Nguyen Chanh Thi defied Saigon and the GVN verged on a civil war within a civil war, GVN political crises would cease to be a central problem. (At the end of the crisis in 1966 the ambassador indulged in a pathetic search for a silver lining. According to Westmoreland, Lodge "likened Vietnam to a man critically ill, yet so irascible that he throws pitchers of water at his doctor. That at least shows, Lodge continued, that he is getting better.")[3]

But leverage issues continued to bubble up in late 1966, especially that of GVN corruption. Variants of the old paradox remained: the United States could not twist the arms of the South Vietnamese too hard because that would make them look like U.S. puppets, a situation that would detract from the political development that leverage aimed to achieve. Moreover, as the war became Americanized, leverage opportunities dropped by the wayside. U.S. advisers' roles diminished in importance as combat command slots in American units took priority. Proposals for the encadrement of U.S. and Vietnamese personnel were vetoed. Ideas for a combined U.S.-ARVN command and joint coordinat-

2. Herbert Y. Schandler, *The Unmaking of a President: Lyndon Johnson and Vietnam* (Princeton University Press, 1977), p. 335.
3. General William C. Westmoreland, *A Soldier Reports* (Doubleday, 1976), p. 176.

ing staff were dropped. Washington had leverage on the brain more than the mission in the field did, and by late 1966 leverage was reduced to coaxing at two removes ("Komer, in Washington, continued to *prod* the Mission to *goad* GVN").[4]

Hope, Resignation, and Malaise

Trepidation continued hand in hand with hope and persistence. In April 1966 another intragovernmental policy review perceived an evolution "from hesitancy to perplexity." As ever, a trinity of options emerged. Option A, advocated particularly by George Carver of the CIA, was the perseverance option. Option B had two variants: an optimistic version developed by Deputy Assistant Secretary of State Leonard Unger, aimed at finding a good way out through favorable negotiations, and a pessimistic version by Assistant Secretary of Defense John McNaughton, recommending acceptance of less than Unger's conditions. Option C was George Ball's ritual urging to cut U.S. losses. In Saigon, meanwhile, the U.S. mission was trying to balance the military need for more American troops against constraints posed by the economic chaos of inflation in South Vietnam caused by the introduction of additional forces. According to the Pentagon Papers analysts, "In essence, what Ambassador Lodge seemed to be looking for was a solution which would balance the conflicting inexorables [sic] . . . those of battle and inflation. He ended up by straddling the fence."[5] "Conflicting inexorables" indeed were, had been, and would continue to be the essence of the American problem in Vietnam.

Of those that bothered Lodge, the military one weighed heaviest. When the President badgered Westmoreland at a Honolulu conference in February to predict how long the war would last, the commander refused to give an answer any more precise than "several years."[6] But clinging to hope like the successful veteran political gambler that he was, LBJ gamely told an interviewer in that same month, "After the Alamo, no one thought Sam Houston would wind it up so quick." And when the same interviewer asked McNamara how large a commitment the United States was prepared to make, the secretary responded, "I

---

4. *The Pentagon Papers: The Defense Department History of Decisionmaking on Vietnam,* Senator Gravel ed. (Beacon Press, 1971), vol. 2, p. 392 (emphasis added); see also pp. 279, 355, 413, 475–79, 499.

5. Ibid., vol. 4, p. 343; see also pp. 81–93, 338–43.

6. Westmoreland, *A Soldier Reports,* pp. 159–60.

can't answer that," altering his answer hastily to "I *don't* answer that."[7] Even earlier, in January 1966, McNaughton saw clearly how long the tunnel might be. Addressing the issue of the ultimate U.S. troop level he wrote that "depending on a number of factors, it could reach 1,000,000."[8]

By the latter part of the year, McNamara was more frank to the President himself. In October he recommended (1) stabilizing force levels at 470,000; (2) stabilizing the bombing program; (3) constructing an electronic barrier along the DMZ and Laotian border; (4) vigorously pursuing pacification; and (5)—the most significant—letting Hanoi know the limits of effort and setting in for a long haul. In December he wrote to Johnson.

I see no reasonable way to bring the war to an end soon. . . . we must continue to press the enemy militarily. . . . we must improve our position by getting ourselves into a military posture that we credibly would maintain indefinitely. . . . The prognosis is bad that the war can be brought to a satisfactory conclusion within the next two years. The large-unit operations probably will not do it. . . . The solution lies in girding, openly, for a longer war.[9]

The defense secretary did not agree with the professional military view that success would come from ending the restraints on action. He was especially critical of the results of the air war. His advocacy of this leveling-off strategy indicated his increasing disillusionment with Westmoreland and Sharp's strategies and the dovishness that came to characterize his views in his last year in office. His position would evolve from being one of the more aggressive in the early 1960s, to that of holding the line after the first year of escalation, to that of one of the most ardent internal doves by the time he left the Defense Department.

As for the air war, a study on ROLLING THUNDER done in the summer of 1966 by the JASON division of the Institute for Defense Analyses concluded devastatingly that the bombing "had no measurable direct effect,"[10] and this in turn had a profound effect on McNamara.

7. Johnson and McNamara quoted in Henry F. Graff, *The Tuesday Cabinet* (Prentice-Hall, 1970), pp. 81, 104 (emphasis added).

8. From McNaughton personal papers, quoted in Thomas Warham Janes, "Rational Man—Irrational Policy: A Political Biography of John McNaughton's Involvement in the Vietnam War" (B.A. honors thesis, Harvard University, 1977), p. 112.

9. *Pentagon Papers*, vol. 4, pp. 348, 349, 353 (emphasis in the original). See also ibid., vol. 2, pp. 594–95; and David Halberstam, *The Best and the Brightest* (Random House, 1972), pp. 630–32.

10. *Pentagon Papers*, vol. 4, p. 116; see also pp. 74–81, 107, 110–12, 116–23.

This assessment followed the failure of the last major escalation Mc-Namara ever endorsed: attacks on the POL resources of the DRV. The secretary had reluctantly recommended the POL strikes after a long debate. Opponents had feared these were the first of the "vital" targets and that bombing them might cause Hanoi to ask its allies to come into the war—the equivalent of MacArthur's march to the Yalu in Korea. (Here again, though, was the central contradiction in the "carrot and stick" limited-pressure strategy that Ball had foreseen. Pressure was designed to coax North Vietnam to come to terms, but the amount of pressure that might hurt enough to bring Hanoi to that point was more than the amount that risked widening the war.) The opponents had seized on the POL issue as the last chance to establish a "firebreak" against boosting the bombing to the point where it would prompt Soviet or Chinese intervention. As it was, the POL strikes did enable Hanoi to extract more aid from its friends.

From then on, the battle on bombing within the Pentagon was fought on cost-effectiveness grounds (while in other quarters of the government, such as Averell Harriman and Chester Cooper's "peace" shop, the negotiations problem was stressed). In October 1966 the Defense Department's Systems Analysis Office produced "issue papers" that challenged the military benefits of ROLLING THUNDER as being too few considering their economic costs, a challenge vehemently rejected by the JCS. The CIA also presented a computation of ROLLING THUNDER results, showing that the United States spent $9.60 to inflict each dollar's worth of damage on the DRV in 1966—more even than the 6.6-to-1 ratio of the previous year.[11]

Within the Office of the Secretary of Defense (OSD) at least, dovish attitudes were beginning to well up. It was a hard-nosed dovishness, in contrast to the moralistic tone of the developing antiwar movement outside the administration, and was based on a pragmatic criticism of the inadequacy of means more than on a challenge to ends. It was a subtle, hardly vocal dovishness. Until well beyond the escalation in 1965 these internal doves seemed to be an eccentric splinter group. Serious disaffection did not emerge until escalation led only to stalemate. This is often not appreciated in retrospect. Ian Maitland demonstrated convincingly, with quotations, that perseverance was grudgingly accepted into 1965, not only by most of the attentive foreign policy public, but

11. See ibid., pp. 132, 136.

as well by even those members of the press corps, such as Neil Sheehan and David Halberstam, who would later point their fingers most stridently at the insanity of the administration.[12] Alain Enthoven, whose Systems Analysis Office together with McNaughton's ISA would lead the fight within the Pentagon against escalation, confessed, "I fell off the boat when the troop level reached 170,000"—but not before.[13] McNaughton's disillusionment also did not thoroughly crystallize until after 1965. After Tonkin Gulf he joined the JCS in urging actions to provoke the DRV, since this would "provide good grounds for us to escalate if we wished."[14] McNaughton's dovishness was not excessively different from the President's; he pushed, not for withdrawal, but for minimizing escalation. In January 1966 his memos suggested that the United States should accept a compromise—a coalition government, neutralization, or even an anti-American regime in Saigon—but he did not suggest that the Americans should accept a Communist victory.[15]

Roger Hilsman, whose departure from government in 1964 is usually touted as dovish protest, left a parting memo to Rusk that included some remarkably strong recommendations for perseverance.[16] At this same time Michael Forrestal, also portrayed by Halberstam as a closet dove,

12. See Ian Maitland, "Only the Best and the Brightest?" *Asian Affairs,* vol. 3 (March-April 1976), pp. 263–72. Henry Fairlie observed that "too many Americans, especially American journalists, who now perceive that their judgment failed at the time, are today anxious to exonerate themselves by pretending that the necessary information was not available." ("We Knew What We Were Doing When We Went into Vietnam," *Washington Monthly,* May 1973, p. 7.)

13. Quoted in Townsend Hoopes, *The Limits of Intervention: An Inside Account of How the Johnson Policy of Escalation Was Reversed* (McKay, 1969), p. 146.

14. *Pentagon Papers,* vol. 3, p. 193.

15. From McNaughton personal papers, cited in Janes, "Rational Man," pp. 111–12.

16. "The alacrity with which the Communists fell into line after we introduced troops into Thailand following the fall of Nam Tha illustrates the effectiveness of such moves," Hilsman wrote to his chief on March 14, 1964. Noting Asian doubts about American resolve he continued, "DeGaulle, Lippmann, and Mansfield have set the neutralist hares running with self-fulfilling prophecies that dishearten those who wish to fight. . . . But what gives these lofty, unrealistic thoughts of a peaceful neutralist Asia their credibility is, again, fundamental doubts about our ultimate intentions." As for the Communists: "We must give them reason to assume that *we are prepared to go as far as necessary to defeat their plans and achieve our objectives*" (emphasis added). Hilsman did warn against overmilitarizing the war, but he recommended a buildup of the U.S. military posture in Southeast Asia. McGeorge Bundy, who apparently obtained the memo from either Hilsman or Rusk, forwarded it to the President with his approval. (LBJL/NSF-VNCF, vol. V, item 98b.)

wrote confidentially to McGeorge Bundy, "Actually, I am somewhat more worried by those who argue for a bugout in Southeast Asia than I am by the adherents of Rostow."[17] Richard Goodwin, who publicly attacked administration policy in 1966 and later, had drafted LBJ's 1965 Johns Hopkins speech, which was sprinkled with ringing affirmations of U.S. commitment.[18] Before 1966 there were ambivalent or uncertain doves, but very few—Paul Kattenburg and James Thomson were among them—whose opposition was firm and whose negative views on escalation overrode their willingness to support it.

Aborted Negotiations

Doves outside the Pentagon, particularly those in the State Department, continued to pin their hopes on a diplomatic breakthrough. However, as a result of two visits to Peking and Hanoi in 1966 by a Canadian, Chester Ronning, American leaders concluded that there was no "real 'give' in Hanoi's position."[19] The administration's quest for negotiations was not insincere, it was simply conditional. The DRV was expected to give reciprocity—termination of infiltration—for an end to American bombing. The purest exposition of the reciprocity principle that looked beyond bombing and negotiations was the Declaration of Peace at the Manila Conference in 1966. Johnson pledged to withdraw all U.S. troops from South Vietnam within six months after Hanoi took its forces out of the South.[20] Negotiation was desirable only from strength, because the United States still wanted to achieve its objectives, and tolerable only from a position of equivalent concessions. But the North Vietnamese had precisely the same conditional motives. Leonard Unger captured the problem in a memorandum in April 1966: "There is no assurance that a negotiated settlement can pass successfully between the upper millstone

17. "Vietnam," memorandum, March 18, 1964, ibid., item 59. Forrestal's views seem more equivocal six weeks later in a memo to McNaughton. (Ibid., vol. VIII, item 133.)

18. See Harry McPherson, *A Political Education: A Journal of Life with Senators, Generals, Cabinet Members and Presidents* (Little, Brown, 1972), p. 391.

19. Memorandum, William P. Bundy to the government of Canada, April 26, 1966, "Ronning," USVNR, Negotiations Volumes, VI.C.1, Chronology, pp. 17, 34–35. For the comprehensive *public* record of diplomacy, see *United States–Vietnam Relations, 1945–1967*, Study prepared by the Department of Defense for the House Committee on Armed Services, 92 Cong. 1 sess. (Government Printing Office, 1971), vol. 12, pts. VI.A, VI.B.

20. For an account of the Manila Conference, see Chester L. Cooper, *The Lost Crusade: America in Vietnam* (Dodd, Mead, 1970), pp. 310–20. (There was some semantic equivocation in the final communiqué.)

of extensively dangerous concessions . . . and the nether millstone of terms insufficiently attractive."[21] The ambivalence about negotiations (a charitable interpretation), or the disinterest in them (a cynical interpretation), was apparent when Johnson appointed Averell Harriman to be "in charge of peace" in the summer of 1966 but did not invite him to the Tuesday Lunches where, among other matters, bombing target packages were approved. The result was that peace initiatives were sometimes out of phase with military strategy.[22]

The American military were never very interested in peace offensives. Taylor regarded bombing as a "blue chip" to be exchanged for something concrete *at* the bargaining table, not something to be squandered to *get* negotiations. He warned of the danger of repeating the Korean negotiating experience, which had been that discussants temporized interminably at the table while the war went on. (The United States did repeat that experience after all.) The professional soldiers accepted bombing pauses with incredulity and lessening tolerance. In mitigation it should be noted that in order to maintain the security of clandestine contacts, these soldiers were not always kept fully informed about the diplomatic moves connected with imposed bombing restrictions.[23] This fact is related to the abortion of one of the few promising negotiating initiatives: Operation MARIGOLD.

MARIGOLD was an attempt to develop a channel to Hanoi through intermediaries. The process began in June 1966 when Janusz Lewandowski, a Polish member of the International Control Commission, approached first the Italian ambassador in Saigon, Giovanni d'Orlandi, and then Lodge. Lewandowski indicated that Ho Chi Minh would enter into serious discussions with the United States if bombing was suspended and that the DRV position was very flexible: Hanoi would not demand either the establishment of a Socialist regime or neutralization in the South, would not interfere with the Saigon government, and would consider a "reasonable calendar" for U.S. withdrawal.[24] U.S. officials were suspicious about this initiative, and many subsequent

21. *Pentagon Papers*, vol. 4, p. 83.

22. See Cooper, *The Lost Crusade*, p. 309.

23. See *Pentagon Papers*, vol. 3, pp. 203–04; vol. 4, pp. 95, 97, 207; USVNR, Negotiations Volumes, VI.C.2., Chronology, pp. 102–03; and Taylor, *Swords and Plowshares*, p. 394.

24. USVNR, Negotiations Volumes, VI.C.2., Discussion, p. 13, and Chronology, pp. 2–3, 23. See also Henry Cabot Lodge, *As It was: An Inside View of Politics and Power in the '50s and '60s* (Norton, 1976), pp. 171–73. Lodge's account of MARIGOLD is unfortunately brief and chatty.

problems were attributable to the ambiguous role of the intermediaries. The Poles acted as brokers, partial to Hanoi, rather than as neutral interlocutors, and occasionally blundered as go-betweens.[25]

The critical point was the month of December 1966. While the U.S. Ambassador to Poland, John Gronouski, was preparing for a particularly sensitive meeting with the Poles, American bombers struck particularly sensitive targets in the Hanoi area on December 2–4. The target package had been authorized on November 10, but bad weather delayed the strikes.[26] Many observers have concluded that policymakers at the top simply forgot, and those working on MARIGOLD at the lower levels did not know. These raids, and strikes again on December 13–14, were not canceled, and as a result, contacts with the North Vietnamese were. One official working on MARIGOLD saw the bombing reported in the newspaper and muttered, "Oh my God. We lost control."[27]

In reality this was not strictly so. On December 10 Nicholas Katzenbach, acting for Rusk, informed the embassies in Warsaw and Saigon that Washington had decided not to change the bombing schedule. He warned Gronouski: "This may well involve some targets which [Polish Foreign Minister Adam] Rapacki will insist represent further escalation. . . . we do not wish to withdraw the authorization at this time."[28] After MARIGOLD's collapse Gronouski cabled the State Department that the Poles claimed they had managed to get the North Vietnamese to keep the possibility of Warsaw talks open after the bombings at the beginning of December, but that Hanoi had recoiled and canceled any such possibility after the bombings of December 13 and 14.[29]

According to the Pentagon Papers analysts, after the DRV canceled

25. USVNR, Negotiations Volumes, VI.C.2, Discussion, pp. 1–3, and Chronology, pp. 4–7.

26. Ibid., Discussion, p. 16.

27. Quoted in David Kraslow and Stuart H. Loory, *The Secret Search for Peace in Vietnam* (Vintage, 1968), p. 5. Lodge agreed that the bombing was not sufficiently controlled (*As It Was*, p. 179).

28. Quoted in USVNR, Negotiations Volumes, VI.C.2., Chronology, p. 60; see also Discussion, p. 17. Benjamin Read, executive secretary of the State Department and primary monitor of the MARIGOLD operation, affirmed the accuracy of Kraslow and Loory's account in *The Secret Search*, except for the contention that the military and political tracks were separated. (Benjamin H. Read, Oral History Interview, Lyndon B. Johnson Library.)

29. See USVNR, Negotiations Volumes, VI.C.2, Chronology, p. 85.

the meeting, following the mid-month bombings, the United States responded first by suspending the bombing of Hanoi targets, "offering to halt all strikes within a ten-mile radius of the center of Hanoi in exchange for a similar show of restraint by the VC around Saigon, and finally putting the Hanoi sanctuary into effect unilaterally—when the prospects of getting explicit reciprocity seemed too faint. Thus in order to revive MARIGOLD, we offered formal assurances of restraint . . . that went well beyond those the Poles had urged us to accept informally after the strikes of December 2 and 4."[30] On January 20 Lodge cabled Rusk that there might be "some diminution" of Vietcong activity around Saigon; Rusk cabled back the next day that he did not read the evidence that way. Lodge reiterated his view on January 29, but major military incidents within ten miles of Saigon in mid-February led the ambassador to give up hope of Communist reciprocity, and he recommended rescinding the ten-mile sanctuary around Hanoi.[31] Meanwhile Foreign Minister Nguyen Duy Trinh had announced on January 28 the stiffening of Hanoi's position and had demanded an "unconditional cessation of US bombing and all other acts of war against the DRV" as the precondition for negotiation.[32] MARIGOLD was dead. Peace feelers, John McNaughton told a journalist on January 13, were "like making smoke-signals in a high wind."[33]

The bombing program was supposed to be a subtle diplomatic orchestration of signals and incentives, an exercise in carrots and sticks —to the civilians at least; the military would have preferred freedom to wield the stick with full force and let the carrot take care of itself. But in the case of MARIGOLD the program was not doing what either side of the tactical debate wanted. Given Rusk's ironclad insistence on full and explicit reciprocity and Hanoi's apparent rage at U.S. unwillingness to stop the mid-December bombings while the groping toward a Warsaw meeting took place, the symbolic and incentive rationale for bombing backfired. The carrots and sticks were not coordinated, at least not in a way that the North Vietnamese would respond to. *ROLLING THUNDER was succeeding neither in signaling nor in smashing.*

There were other instances after 1966 when bombing and diplo-

---

30. Ibid., Discussion, p. 13.
31. See ibid., Chronology, pp. 102–03, 105–06, 121–22.
32. Quoted in ibid., VI.C.3, Discussion, p. 2.
33. Quoted in Henry Brandon, *Anatomy of Error: The Inside Story of the Asian War on the Potomac, 1954–1969* (Gambit, 1969), p. 68.

macy seemed disjoined. One was when Alexsei Kosygin's visit to the United Nations in June 1967 coincided with a U.S. raid on Haiphong that damaged the Soviet ship *Turkestan*.[34] Another was just before that, in April, when an initiative was under way to demilitarize the DMZ again and expand it. Chester Cooper learned that a raid was scheduled against Haiphong power plants, but he could not get it canceled because Rusk was out of town, "and no one else in the State Department hierarchy was ready to face up to the . . . chore of confronting the President." The raids were thus neither a signal nor a conscious sabotage of the initiative. As Cooper noted, "There was just no interest or effort expended in orchestrating military and diplomatic moves; everyone was doing his own thing."[35]

Another Escalatory Compromise

Withal, there was no serious disaffection in the administration in 1966 and into 1967, only disillusionment with the prospects for the ongoing strategy. Internal doves did not yet balk at the war per se; they pursued perseverance with a different emphasis from that of the hawks. With much encouragement from the U.S. civilians, the GVN went through a major exercise in constitution-writing and "nation-building," electing a constituent assembly and finally holding presidential elections in 1967. Those Americans who doubted the efficacy and relevance of large-scale U.S. operations continued to lobby for more and better pacification. Later, "pacification" would become "revolutionary development"—a French moniker was discarded for the Communist one. When MACV took pacification over from the civilians in 1967 to make it work better, the move reflected the inexorable militarization of strategy that was the cause of the doves' despair. Gadflies such as John Paul Vann, a former Army lieutenant colonel who had left the service to become a civilian adviser, continued to push pacification, plying the provinces and nettling military commanders, but the bosses in Washington focused most of their attention on bombing, troops, and military statistics.

By the end of 1966, however, McNamara had clearly parted company with the professional military, seeking to level off the curve of commitment. In March 1967 Westmoreland made his next set of alter-

---

34. Kraslow and Loory, *The Secret Search,* pp. 85–86.
35. Cooper, *The Lost Crusade,* pp. 373–74.

native proposals for force increases: his "minimum essential force" would have added two and one-third divisions to bring troop levels to 565,000; his "optimum force" proposal would bring the number up to 670,000.[36] At the Guam Conference to review Vietnam developments, held March 20–21, he told the party from Washington that unless the Vietcong infrastructure disintegrated, which was unlikely, and unless infiltration could be capped, the war could continue indefinitely. The visitors, he wrote, were stunned; "John McNaughton, in particular, wore an air of disbelief."[37] And McNaughton, who had gradually become an in-house nemesis to the generals, would shortly wind up leading those in the Pentagon who opposed Westmoreland's requests, along with Alain Enthoven's irritatingly skeptical Systems Analysis Office.[38]

The OSD skeptics had a bit of subtle, indirect, and probably unintended support from a source closer to the action in the field—a reflective lieutenant general, Fred Weyand, one of Westmoreland's field force commanders. Later he would distinguish himself by anticipating the Tet offensive, participating as military adviser in the initial Paris negotiations, becoming the last commander in chief of the U.S. Military Assistance Command (COMUSMACV) before total U.S. withdrawal, and finally serving as Army Chief of Staff for two years in the mid-1970s. White House assistant Harry McPherson visited him in the field during a mission for LBJ and later described the meeting.

Fred Weyand . . . turned a drink in his hand. "Before I came out here a year ago, I thought we were at zero. I was wrong; we were at minus fifty. Now we are at zero. We've created a vacuum. . . . Now the question is, who's going to fill the vacuum?" It could be us, he thought, with another 200,000 troops. But the more we took responsibility, the more remote the day would become when the ARVN was ready to take our place.[39]

Pressed on battlefields both abroad and at home, the President brought Westmoreland back to the States to talk up the war before Congress and the press. The more private serious business of the trip was a conference on Westmoreland's requests. Westmoreland and Wheeler both presented Johnson a dreary picture of what lay ahead. Under the existing limit of 470,000 men, Westmoreland said the war

36. *Pentagon Papers*, vol. 2, p. 511. See also Westmoreland, *A Soldier Reports*, p. 227.
37. Westmoreland, *A Soldier Reports*, p. 214.
38. *Pentagon Papers*, vol. 4, pp. 456–67. See also Westmoreland, *A Soldier Reports*, p. 230.
39. McPherson, *A Political Education*, pp. 407–08.

would be a " 'meat-grinder' where we would kill large numbers of the enemy but in the end do little better than hold our own." He estimated that "with a force level of *565,000 men, the war could well go on for three years. With a second increment . . . leading to a total of 665,000 men, it could go on for two years.*"[40] When Johnson asked what would happen with no additions, Wheeler said that "momentum would die" and the enemy would recapture the initiative in some places; "we wouldn't lose the war but it would be a longer one."[41] In the end McNamara and the President put another notch in the tradition of compromise and authorized an increase to 525,000 men—above the "meatgrinder" level but below the minimum of Westmoreland's requests.[42]

Debate, Diplomacy, and Disillusionment

Internal opposition continued to build, though imperceptibly and with no visible consequence. Presidential aide Bill Moyers had grown dovish and left the White House in 1966. By 1967 the CIA was split between optimistic top analyst George Carver and pessimistic subordinates; disagreements about options at the working levels of the bureaucracy and among the principals were rife.[43] The most notable change was in the secretary of defense. Having been disappointed with the results of the war effort, he had dug in his heels against further escalation by late 1966. In 1967 his frustration with the bombing program intensified, and by the end of the year he favored an end to ROLLING THUNDER.

But at the top, until McNamara's defection, there was little wavering. Johnson's mission to Southeast Asia in 1961 had instilled a tenacious conviction in him that Vietnam was the frontier of freedom. Administration leaders in the darkest days of the mid-1960s would cite Eisenhower's letter of October 1, 1954, in which he pledged assistance to Diem; as McNamara said, the requirements of completing the mission as Eisenhower had defined it had been rising, but "the mission itself remains unchanged."[44] Rusk would testily counter congressional criti-

---

40. *Pentagon Papers*, vol. 4, p. 442 (emphasis in original).
41. Ibid., p. 443.
42. See ibid., p. 527.
43. Halberstam, *The Best and the Brightest*, p. 638.
44. Quoted in Graff, *The Tuesday Cabinet*, pp. 32–33.

cism and James Reston's contention that the secretary of state had pronounced a "Rusk Doctrine" committing the United States to the defense
of forty countries by saying, "I didn't vote for a single one of those
[treaty] commitments. Those guys [the senators] did. . . . When you
go into an alliance you have to mean it." Just before Tet the secretary
would assert that "the alternative to meeting one's commitments is
isolation. They cannot be met selectively. . . . The issue being tested
in Vietnam is credibility."[45]

Hawks, Doves, and the President

By the end of the year McNamara was in full disillusioned retreat.[46]
Why didn't the other skeptics break more forcefully with the President,
and why were their doubts not fully apparent to him until after Tet?
One problem was the President's obsession with consensus and the
consequent reluctance of junior-level personnel to challenge him. In
any meeting on a critical decision he was notorious for browbeating
his lieutenants into assent, going around the table and solemnly poll-
ing each one. Chester Cooper remembers fantasizing that when his
turn came he would jolt Johnson by dissenting. "But I was removed
from my trance," he said "when I heard the President's voice saying,
'Mr. Cooper, do you agree?' And out would come a 'Yes, Mr. President,
I agree.'"[47] Henry Graff, a historian who had long conversations with
the principals at the time, explained the problem in this way:

The advisers draw from their Chief the inspiration and prestige they require
to be of help to him, and the more visible and powerful they grow the less
useful they become. They find it harder and harder to say no to him, let alone
break with him over policy when he and it are under attack. As time passes,
an adviser's value to the President depreciates remarkably, but in the inner
circle nobody notices the change because the personal ties have been annealed
in the intense fires the President and his aides have endured together.[48]

Yet Johnson did not feel free to unleash the military without restraint. The President chose not to go all the way on the hawkish line

45. Quoted in ibid., pp. 83, 135–36.
46. See Phil G. Goulding, *Confirm or Deny: Informing the People on National
Security* (Harper and Row, 1970), chap. 6; Halberstam, *The Best and the Brightest*,
pp. 632–33; and Hoopes, *The Limits of Intervention*, pp. 83–91.
47. Cooper, *The Lost Crusade*, p. 223. See also *Pentagon Papers*, vol. 4, pp.
187–88; Halberstam, *The Best and the Brightest*, pp. 539, 599–600; Graff, *The
Tuesday Cabinet*, p. 164; and George Christian, *The President Steps Down: A Personal Memoir of the Transfer of Power* (Macmillan, 1970), pp. 87–88.
48. Graff, *The Tuesday Cabinet*, p. 24.

for two basic reasons: fear of provoking Hanoi's allies (he worried about "secret treaties" that might be triggered by a massive American escalation) and fear of provoking domestic doves. When military analysts presented an impressive quantitative study purporting to demonstrate how bombing and blockading Hanoi and Haiphong would shorten the war, Johnson shot back sarcastically, "I have one more problem for your computer—will you feed into it how long it will take five hundred thousand angry Americans to climb that White House wall out there and lynch their President if he does something like that?"[49] (In 1972 Nixon took the move and weathered the storm.) But Johnson also had to fend off hawks outside the executive branch. For one domestic pressure there was always a countervailing one; for a J. W. Fulbright there was a John Stennis, for a James Gavin there was a Curtis LeMay, for a Bobby Kennedy and a Eugene McCarthy there were a Barry Goldwater and a George Wallace.

In Congress the President was beset from both sides, particularly in the Senate. The dovish opposition centered in the Foreign Relations Committee and was dramatized in highly publicized and occasionally televised hearings, especially in early 1966 and early 1968. The irritated President sometimes took to calling the committee chairman "Senator Halfbright." The hawkish opposition centered in the Armed Services Committee and came to the fore most threateningly in Stennis's air war hearings of August 1967. Of the two sets of critics, the congressional hawks struck more fear in Johnson's heart, until the 1968 reassessment. Perhaps he recalled his own tenure on the Armed Services Committee during the MacArthur hearings in 1951 in which Republicans lambasted Truman for timidity in Korea and traumatized his administration.

Some Senate hawks actually offered a way out. Although Richard Russell joined Republicans such as Melvin Laird in tilting for escalation most of the time after 1965 (as secretary of defense years later, ironically, Laird lobbied for faster withdrawal than Nixon or Kissinger wanted), he warned Johnson in *early* 1965 against jumping further into the Southeast Asian imbroglio. But the President wrote this off at the time as conservative isolationism, and he may have rationalized,

49. Quoted in Halberstam, *The Best and the Brightest*, p. 641. See also Lyndon Baines Johnson, *The Vantage Point: Perspectives of the Presidency, 1963–1969* (Holt, Rinehart and Winston, 1971), pp. 119, 131, 149, 370; and Doris Kearns, *Lyndon Johnson and the American Dream* (Harper and Row, 1976), pp. 264–65, 270.

as Halberstam said, "that Russell, like Fulbright, did not care about colored people."[50] But then again, Russell suggested in April 1966 that a public opinion poll should be taken in Vietnamese cities on whether U.S. help was wanted, and if the results were negative, the United States should pull out.[51]

In any case the doves and hawks were both minorities. All in all, when the sound and the fury were penetrated it was actually clear that the dominant attitude in Congress was permissive and not all that different from the apprehensive but resigned persistence that characterized the President. The hawks never got a hawkish resolution through the floor, and antiwar votes got a majority in the Senate only after Nixon took office; in the House, they *never* got a majority in all the time that American combat units were stationed in Vietnam.[52]

All this reinforced the middle course, which was derived as well from Lyndon Johnson's aversion to fighting a war, much less declaring one. The military command structure was left unchanged (with no Southeast Asia command established, responsibility for the air and ground wars remained divided between CINCPAC and COMUS-MACV). Throughout the war no high command was established in Washington to coordinate all the dispersed military, economic, intelligence, and political programs.[53] The only centralization of strategy was in the Tuesday Lunches of the overburdened principals.

Johnson refused to put the economy on a war footing (from which followed inflation) or to mobilize the reserves to provide forces faster. In July 1965 he even scheduled his televised announcement of massive ground intervention for midday, rather than evening when the audience would have been larger, perhaps purposely soft-pedaling an opportunity to jolt and mobilize the public will. Johnson's private rea-

50. Halberstam, *The Best and the Brightest*, p. 528. See also, "Weekly Report," *Congressional Quarterly*, vol. 23 (December 24, 1965), p. 2496, and vol. 24 (March 25, 1966), p. 651; and Theodore Draper, *The Abuse of Power* (Viking, 1966), pp. 153-55.

51. *Pentagon Papers*, vol. 4, p. 98.

52. From 1964 through 1971 there were at least six votes in each house by which antiwar sentiment could be registered. The first successful antiwar measure was the Cooper-Church amendment, passed in the Senate on June 30, 1970, barring funds for U.S. military operations in Cambodia after July 1, 1970. The highest number of votes for an antiwar measure in the House during this period, however, was 175, or 40 percent of the chamber. See the data in Jack McWethy and others, *The Power of the Pentagon* (Congressional Quarterly, 1972), pp. 112-13.

53. See Cooper, *The Lost Crusade*, p. 413.

sons for not telling the nation to be prepared for a long haul, according to a confidante, were fear of provoking a "right-wing stampede," and fear of losing his Great Society programs. As one of the most successful political wheeler-dealers in recent Senate history, Johnson thought he could find a way to eat his cake and have it too. To those who argued that the Great Society required disengagement to free resources for domestic needs, he responded that pulling out of Vietnam would only generate more dissension and opposition at home rather than less. "I was determined to be a leader of war *and* a leader of peace," he told Doris Kearns. "I wanted both, I believed in both, and I believed America had the resources to provide for both."[54]

The rise of intense feeling against the war among elite groups in the public in 1966 and 1967 did not force the President's hand either. In fact, right up to the reassessment following Tet the trend of public opinion as a whole was remarkably consistent with the trend of opinion within the executive branch, despite the dramatic and forceful posture developed by the vocal left-wing opposition in the late 1960s. Not until the Nixon administration did executive policy fall clearly behind dovish public opposition. Only in the Tet offensive period did the curve of opposition, *in terms of regarding involvement as a mistake,* rise above 50 percent and exceed the curve of support (see figure 1). (Support for the war at the time of Tet, however, actually *climbed* slightly.) Johnson's popularity declined steadily after the 1964 election (with intermittent temporary rebounds), but through 1967 over half of the public favored *increasing* the strength of attacks on North Vietnam, while as late as October 1967 less than a third favored beginning withdrawal (table 1). And as figure 2 shows, despite the locus of vocal opposition and antiwar candidacies in the Democratic party, Democrats, and independents to a lesser degree, remained more supportive of the war than Republicans, with nearly perfect consistency until Nixon took office.[55]

Diplomatic activity continued, though in low gear compared with the military war. Washington, having touted multilateral solutions for

54. Quoted in Kearns, *Lyndon Johnson,* pp. 282–83. See also Johnson, *The Vantage Point,* p. 422; Halberstam, *The Best and the Brightest,* pp. 603 ff.; and Rowland Evans and Robert Novak, *Lyndon B. Johnson: The Exercise of Power* (New American Library, 1966), pp. 550–51.

55. Public opinion data from John E. Mueller, *War, Presidents and Public Opinion* (Wiley, 1973), pp. 56, 107; and W. W. Rostow, *The Diffusion of Power: An Essay in Recent History* (Macmillan, 1972), p. 479.

Figure 1. *Trends in Support for the War in Vietnam, 1965–71*

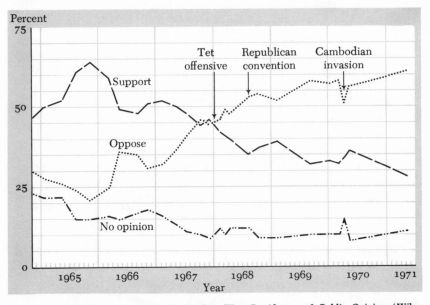

Source: Reproduced from John E. Mueller, *War, Presidents and Public Opinion* (Wiley, 1973), p. 56, with the permission of John Wiley and Sons, Inc.

Indochina in decades past, was now going it largely alone. The bilateralism of American–South Vietnamese war policy contrasted with Eisenhower's emphasis on united action in the 1954 crisis, and Dulles's "pactomania." The "More Flags" campaign that Johnson kicked off in the 1960s was sluggish. While the administration pointed proudly to vast numbers of nations giving assistance to South Vietnam, almost all of them made no more than token gestures: a medical team here, engineers there, a few hospitals and police advisers, a shipment of blankets, and so on. South Korea got into the war in a big way, with two divisions, but that was a wash item: the United States had two of its own divisions stationed back in South Korea. Moreover, the United States financed the Korean troops in Vietnam. Only Australia sent a large number of troops and paid for them. But despite its closer geographical proximity to what was supposed to be the Communist threat to its security, and its lack of commitments elsewhere (for example, to NATO), Australia's contribution remained smaller in relation to population size than that of the United States. It was on a trip to Asian capitals to drum up more help in the summer of 1967 that Clark Clifford was impressed by the

Table 1. *Proportion of the Public Favoring Various U.S. Vietnam Policies, 1966, 1967*

	Percent in favor of policy		Percent difference, 1966–67
Policy	November 1966	October 1967	
The United States should begin to withdraw its troops	18	31	13
The United States should carry on the present level of fighting	18	10	−8
The United States should increase the strength of its attacks against North Vietnam	55	53	−2
No opinion	9	6	−3

Source: W. W. Rostow, *The Diffusion of Power: An Essay in Recent History* (Macmillan, 1972), p. 480.

laggardness of the Asian allies, who, as Townsend Hoopes quipped, "apparently . . . had not been reading Rostow"; this lack of cooperation helped sow the seeds of the disillusionment Clifford experienced half a year later.[56]

More Initiatives for Negotiation

Hesitant moves for negotiations continued. Johnson groped toward contacts along several tracks. He tried to enlist the USSR's help in conferences with Soviet leaders at Indian Prime Minister Lal Bahadur Shastri's funeral and the Glassboro summit meeting of 1967. Some initiatives were direct, such as the talks U.S. chargé d'affaires John C. Guthrie had with North Vietnamese chargé d'affaires Le Trang in Moscow. Some contacts were made through nonofficial "volunteers" such as Italian professor Giorgio La Pira and American peace activist Peter Weiss in 1965 and American professor Henry Kissinger, Frenchmen Herbert Marcovich and Raymond Aubrac, American writers Harry Ashmore and William Baggs, and three pacifist clerics in 1967.[57] There were five main channels of diplomatic initiatives, each blessed with codewords giving them the significance of "genuine" activity, from 1967 to Johnson's abdication speech in March 1968: through Rumania

56. Hoopes, *The Limits of Intervention*, p. 171.
57. See Kraslow and Loory, *The Secret Search*, pp. 126 ff., 161–63, 166 ff.; Harry S. Ashmore and William C. Baggs, *Mission to Hanoi* (Putnam's, 1968); and USVNR, Negotiations Volumes, VI.C.2., Chronology, pp. 106–09. For Johnson's catalog of initiatives, see *The Vantage Point*, pp. 579–96.

Figure 2. *Trends in Support for the War in Vietnam, by Partisanship, 1965–71*

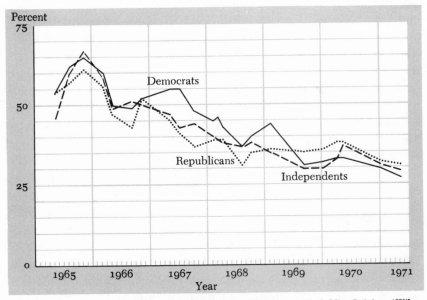

Source: Reproduced from John E. Mueller, *War, Presidents and Public Opinion* (Wiley, 1973), p. 119, with the permission of John Wiley and Sons, Inc.

from October 1966 to February 1968 (PACKERS); through Sweden from November 1966 to February 1968 (ASPEN); through Norway from June 1967 to March 1968 (OHIO); Kissinger's discussions with Mai Van Bo in Paris in September and October 1967 (PENNSYL-VANIA); and through Italy from February to March 1968 (KILLY).[58] The results of all these efforts were negligible.

Apart from Operation MARIGOLD, one major project produced brief hope (at a rung below the top of the U.S. hierarchy more than at the top itself) that North Vietnam might respond. This was SUN-FLOWER. On January 10, 1967, the United States passed a message to the DRV embassy in Moscow proposing direct talks, fully secret and secure. (The North Vietnamese were obsessed with secrecy because of Peking's opposition to negotiations—what the Pentagon Papers analysts called "the Chicom [Chinese Communist] pistol in their back.")[59]

58. See USVNR, Negotiations Volumes, VI.C.4.
59. Ibid., Chronology, p. 8. See also ibid., pp. 5–6, and Discussion, p. 22; and Donald S. Zagoria, *Vietnam Triangle: Moscow, Peking, Hanoi* (Pegasus, 1967), chaps. 1 and 4.

Five days later a memorandum to the President, apparently from either Rusk or William Bundy, conveyed the impressions of journalist Harrison Salisbury, who had returned from an unsanctioned visit to Hanoi and who believed that the North Vietnamese would be flexible after a halt in American air attacks. The memorandum concluded that Pham Van Dong's responses to Salisbury's questions were "interesting mood music but do not get us very far," and that Salisbury's report revealed "a deep conviction in Hanoi that our resolve will falter because of the cost of the struggle."[60] The interpretations in this memorandum give a clue to the combined pessimism and rigidity that were to characterize the American posture in the next serious SUNFLOWER initiative.

This initiative was a six-day bombing pause in February 1967, coupled with a two-phase plan communicated through two intermediaries. Phase A was the bombing halt, to be followed by Phase B, a reciprocal stop to augmentation in the South—the United States would not reinforce its troops and Hanoi would cease infiltration.[61] Chester Cooper gave the plan to Harold Wilson, who gave it to Aleksei Kosygin in London. The American position on DRV reciprocity was firm. As the deadline for the end of Phase A neared, Rusk's instructions to the U.S. team in London emphasized, "When we say 'stop infiltration' we mean 'stop infiltration.' We cannot trade a horse for a rabbit."[62] But within a day after the pause in bombing had begun evidence piled up from reconnaissance that the North Vietnamese were taking advantage of the opportunity to pour supplies into the South.[63] In the view of some participants this panicked Washington into hardening the U.S. posi-

60. USVNR, Negotiations Volumes, VI.C.3, Chronology, p. 7. The source of the memorandum is not specified, but the text describes Salisbury's report "to the Secretary." McNamara, the only other secretary working on the war, was not involved in the negotiations business, and the tone of the memorandum is identical to that in other communications from Rusk and Assistant Secretary Bundy.

61. Ibid., VI.C.3, Chronology, pp. 29–31, 45–46.

62. Quoted in ibid., p. 51. Ambassador Lodge in Saigon lobbied for a softer position—trading a bomb halt for cessation of Vietcong assassinations and kidnapping. (Ibid., p. 67.)

63. See Kraslow and Loory, *The Secret Search*, p. 191; and USVNR, Negotiations Volumes, VI.C.3, Discussion, pp. 12–13, and Chronology, p. 77. In cables to London Rusk and Rostow were especially concerned about the North Vietnamese massing three to four divisions just above the DMZ and insisted that these could not be moved into the South just before Phase B took effect. (See ibid., Chronology, pp. 52, 56.) This probably accounts for Washington's unwillingness to extend the time period within which Phase B could begin. (See Kraslow and Loory, *The Secret Search*, pp. 188, 194–95.)

tion on the timing and definition of Phase B. Before resuming the bombing Washington then refused to allow the amount of time that realistically would have been necessary to get a North Vietnamese response.[64]

More significant than SUNFLOWER was the San Antonio Formula (so called because Johnson presented it in that city in a speech before the National Legislative Conference in September 1967). The formula was an offer to stop bombing "when this will lead promptly to productive discussions. We, of course, assume that . . . North Vietnam would not take advantage of the bombing cessation or limitation."[65] In December of that year the President also considered direct contacts between the GVN and the National Liberation Front (a move that might have done some good four years earlier in the immediate wake of Diem's death, since it is not inconceivable that the NLF might have been split at that point).

North Vietnam brushed the San Antonio Formula aside. "Hanoi is in no mood for concessions or bargaining," wrote Wilfred Burchett, the Australian Communist journalist and confidant of the DRV politburo. "There is an absolute refusal to offer anything except talks for a cessation of the bombardment. The word stressed is 'talks,' not negotiations." DRV Foreign Minister Trinh, reported Burchett, was still saying talks *could* start if the bombing halted.[66] In January, however, Trinh announced that after an unconditional bombing halt "the DRV *will* hold talks," using a more encouraging tense than before.[67] Subsequently, in Senate testimony that he apparently did not clear fully with Johnson, Clark Clifford gave a very loose and relatively permissive interpretation of what would constitute the DRV's "not taking advantage" of a halt. He stipulated that normal resupply of troops in the South would be acceptable.[68] This dance of tacit diplomacy, however, was overtaken immediately by the Tet offensive.

If decisionmakers had put everything in perspective, they should not have been surprised—as the hawks were not—that negotiations

64. See Cooper, *The Lost Crusade*, pp. 353–62, 366–67; and Kraslow and Loory, *The Secret Search*, pp. 191–96. The President did allow a six-hour extension of the truce. (See USVNR, Negotiations Volumes, VI.C.3, pp. 62–63.)

65. Johnson, *The Vantage Point*, p. 267.

66. Quoted in Cooper, *The Lost Crusade*, p. 381.

67. Quoted in ibid., p. 384.

68. *Pentagon Papers*, vol. 4, p. 234. See also Hoopes, *The Limits of Intervention*, p. 124.

were difficult to get and that when gotten, they bore no fruit for four years. Critics often chided the administration for not recognizing that Vietnam was a revolution and a civil war. But these critics themselves should have realized that revolutions and civil wars are the conflicts least susceptible to resolution by negotiation because the essential stake in such conflicts is indivisible: who will govern the country? Genuine coalition governments are possible only between parties whose differences are not fundamental and bitter enough to have put them at each other's throats in the first place. None of the major revolutionary civil wars of this century were resolved by negotiation. Either the Left and the Marxists or the Right and the liberals *won*. Negotiation played no meaningful role in China's revolution (the United States could have taken a cue from the failure of Marshall's mission in 1945), or Cuba's, or the counterrevolutions in Spain, Greece, Malaya, and the Philippines. To the extent that negotiations do occur in civil wars, they are usually pro forma ratifications or impositions of decisions reached on the battlefield. Those Vietnam hands who asked "What is there to negotiate about?" were not being flippant.

Doves understandably clutched at the vision of diplomacy as a way out. It would have been if the only object had been a cosmetic excuse to give up without appearing to give up. But diplomacy may have been no more realistic a way to affirmatively safeguard U.S. objectives than was another project pushed by the OSD doves—the electronic counter-infiltration barrier along South Vietnam's borders (or "the McNamara Line," as military critics called it in a parody of the Maginot Line). Often, like their military opposites, pronegotiation doves could not see the forest for the trees, but for different reasons. Some would spend hours agonizing like lawyers and grammarians over nuances in the choice of words or translation of enemy statements, trying to find some hidden hint of flexibility.[69]

Those convinced that U.S. insensitivity prevented a breakthrough will always be able to cite the many ambiguities in the record of contacts. But the overriding fact that transcended the ambiguities and quasi-equivocations was the incompatibility of the minimum objectives of both sides. When caught in a stalemate, who wants to admit that *both* sides intend to negotiate from strength, to use negotiations to achieve their own mutually contradictory goals, to achieve their

69. See Cooper, *The Lost Crusade*, pp. 351, 353; and Kraslow and Loory, *The Secret Search*, p. 152.

military aims at the table rather than, or as well as, in the field? In revolutions, to reverse Clausewitz, politics can be the pursuit of war by other means.

From the beginning, as in LBJ's Johns Hopkins speech, Washington had sought *unconditional* discussions or *reciprocal* tactical concessions (what was there to lose?), and Hanoi, except for some uncertain evidence of flexibility during the MARIGOLD maneuvers, demanded an unconditional bombing halt before discussions (otherwise, what was there to gain?). "The object is not *talks*," an American official pointed out. "The object is settling the war."[70] Kraslow and Loory observed that "to distinguish between the two possibilities—talks or a settlement—was, in a sense, to reveal the United States' reliance on the battlefield option."[71] They might as well have said the same of the North Vietnamese. Not until the Tet offensive failed militarily for the Communists, setting back their battlefield option, and not until the offensive succeeded politically, crystallizing the war weariness in Washington, did negotiations become a genuinely desired option for both sides.

The Fight over Bombing

In the course of this whole period in 1967 the militarization of the war effort went on apace with COMUSMACV champing at the bit. The military command took over the pacification program from the State Department, and Westmoreland turned his attention to agitating for permission to strike into neighboring sanctuaries. The biggest job Ambassador William Sullivan had in Vientiane, according to one official, "was to keep Westmoreland's paws off Laos."[72]

Meanwhile, uneasiness about ROLLING THUNDER continued to build in the civilian reaches of the bureaucracy. An intelligence memorandum in May 1967 claimed that bombing had not eroded the DRV's morale, degraded its capability to support the war in the South, or significantly eroded its industrial-military base. Nevertheless, when there was a strategy review of the bombing in mid-1967, little changed. The perennial three options appeared. McNamara, his Deputy Cyrus

70. Quoted in Kraslow and Loory, *The Secret Search*, p. 88. See also Johnson, *The Vantage Point*, pp. 132–34; and USVNR, Negotiations Volumes, VI.C.2, Discussion, p. 18, and Chronology, pp. 56, 58–59, 79, 95.

71. Kraslow and Loory, *The Secret Search*, p. 91.

72. Quoted in Charles A. Stevenson, *The End of Nowhere: American Policy toward Laos since 1954* (Beacon Press, 1972), p. 217. See also *Pentagon Papers*, vol. 4, pp. 332 ff.

Vance, Navy Secretary Paul Nitze, and Walt Rostow proposed reorienting ROLLING THUNDER to concentrate on interdiction in the lower half of North Vietnam—the "funnel." In the next two weeks, according to the Pentagon Papers, "the Washington papermill must have broken all previous production records."[73] The outraged JCS and CINCPAC, together with William Bundy, opposed the change. The chiefs wanted more intensive attacks at the top of the funnel, in the Hanoi-Haiphong area. Secretary of the Air Force Harold Brown favored extending the current program, rather than shifting strategy in either of the two directions proposed. The director of central intelligence made no recommendations, because the CIA judged none of the alternatives capable of changing Hanoi's will and ability to persist. Disarray now reigned in bombing strategy, and the President, true to form, noted, "I decided to steer a course midway."[74] Brown's choice—persistence in the same program—prevailed.

Two more studies at the end of 1967, the ISA–Joint Staff SEACABIN contract and a second JASON study, were as shocking as the earlier OSD and CIA analyses. The JASON group concluded not only that ROLLING THUNDER did not work but that no alternative strategy would work: *"We are unable to devise a bombing campaign in the North to reduce the flow of infiltrating personnel into SVN."*[75] A complementary Systems Analysis study maintained that the bombing had paradoxically increased the North Vietnamese supply of labor (releasing underemployed agricultural workers) at the same time it increased the demand. Paul Warnke, the new assistant secretary for ISA, combined these studies at the end of the year to pull together a Defense Department position for halting the bombing. The entire effort to analyze the bombing—complete with the unaltered positions of the JCS on the one hand and those of other agencies on the other hand—would be repeated again in a National Security Study Memorandum, the NSSM-1 Vietnam policy review at the beginning of the Nixon administration.[76] The dismal decision in the spring to increase forces was

73. *Pentagon Papers,* vol. 4, p. 177.

74. Johnson, *The Vantage Point,* p. 368. See also *Pentagon Papers,* vol. 4, pp. 11–12, 160–66, 177–78, 189–96.

75. *Pentagon Papers,* vol. 4, pp. 224–25 (emphasis in the original).

76. Democratic Congressman Ronald V. Dellums of California entered the text of NSSM-1 in the *Congressional Record,* vol. 118, pt. 13, 92 Cong. 2 sess. (1972), pp. 16749–836. For further discussion of the 1967 studies, see *Pentagon Papers,* vol. 4, pp. 217 ff., 222–28.

followed, however, by a portentous memo from McGeorge Bundy (who had left the government). It resonated with the frustration, doubt, and skepticism that had begun to ooze from the OSD, and foreshadowed the decisions that would come less than a year later. Quite simply, Bundy recommended putting a ceiling on the U.S. effort.[77] The stage was being set for the post-Tet retrenchment of policy on the ground war, even if this was not fully recognized at the time.

Lavish support within the Senate Armed Services Committee for the disgruntled military commanders, however, had gotten LBJ jittery, and he moved more toward the hawks after Stennis's air war hearings in August.[78] In October the military presented one last major argument before Tet for more intensity in the war. Ironically, their recommendation to remove restrictions on operations, to mine ports and waterways, and to increase interdiction was based on a certain degree of agreement with the pessimistic OSD doves about the efficacy of the current policy. They remonstrated about the restraining tactical guidelines: "At our present pace, termination of NVN's [North Vietnam's] military effort is not expected to occur in the near future."[79] McNamara, however, had become not only thoroughly disenchanted but disgusted and ridden with anxiety. Harry McPherson recalled a State Department luncheon a few days before McNamara left office:

McNamara, obviously on edge, condemned the bombing. . . . He recited the comparative figures; so many tons dropped on Germany and Japan and North Korea, so many more on Vietnam. "It's not just that it isn't preventing

77. See *Pentagon Papers*, vol. 4, pp. 157–60.

78. See ibid., pp. 199–207; and *Air War against North Vietnam*, Hearings before the Preparedness Investigating Subcommittee of the Senate Committee on Armed Services, 90 Cong. 1 sess. (GPO, 1967). With all the notorious data on how many more tons of bombs were dropped on Southeast Asia than in all of World War II, most observers find it hard to comprehend how military leaders could keep straight faces in ascribing their failure to administration restraints. It is worth noting, though, that *less than one-tenth* (about 9.5 percent as of the end of 1971) of all the tonnage dropped in Southeast Asia was dropped on North Vietnam. Most ordnance—3.9 million tons out of a cumulative total of 6.3 million—was dropped in South Vietnam, in close-support missions for ground combat and B-52 ARC LIGHT missions. Even in 1967, the peak year of ROLLING THUNDER, bombing in the South was three times that of the North. Almost three times as much tonnage ultimately went into the Ho Chi Minh Trail areas of Laos as into the DRV. See Ralph Littauer and Norman Uphoff, eds., *The Air War in Indochina*, Air War Study Group, Cornell University, rev. ed. (Beacon Press, 1972), chap. 1. For more personal and graphic views of the bombing from the American perspective, see Frank Harvey, *Air War— Vietnam* (Bantam, 1967); and Jack Broughton, *Thud Ridge* (Lippincott, 1969).

79. *Pentagon Papers*, vol. 4, p. 211.

the supplies from getting down the trail. It's destroying the countryside in the South. It's making lasting enemies. And still the damned Air Force wants more." Rusk stared at his drink; Clifford looked searchingly at McNamara, but said nothing.[80]

In November McNamara advised stabilizing military operations in the South and stopping all bombing in the North by the end of the year. Having become one of the most blatant of doves by administration standards, his usefulness to Johnson the brakeman had ended. Clark Clifford opposed McNamara's deescalation plan at this time.[81] The President decided shortly afterward to put him in McNamara's place, little knowing the role that Clifford would play in the next two months.

Off the Tiger's Back: The Reckoning of 1968

"Westmoreland Requests 206,000 More Men, Stirring Debate in Administration," blared a *New York Times* headline on March 10, 1968. That such a request would lead to a shocked reassessment and turn-around in American policy might normally have seemed curious to those in the know, except for the events that lay behind it. After all, it would only have exceeded Westmoreland's last optimum force level request (665,000–670,000) by 10 percent, and it would only have reached the 732,000 level, which was no higher than figures the military had been bandying as early as 1965. As it was, the request had resulted from a ploy by the JCS chairman, with the innocent cooperation of COMUSMACV, to take advantage of a crisis and acquire the forces needed to do what the military had wanted to do all along. The ploy backfired, ironically, and led to the decision for disengagement—hesitant, tortuous, and drawn-out disengagement, but withdrawal nonetheless. After March 1968 American policy on Vietnam was all a retrograde operation, to use the military euphemism for retreat, punctuated only by Nixon's temporary reescalations in 1970 and 1972.

The Tet Offensive and Declining Confidence

This dénouement was triggered by the most dramatic battlefield crisis of the war, the countrywide Communist offensive that began on January 30, 1968, during the Tet holiday truce. For a while the offensive,

80. McPherson, *A Political Education,* pp. 430–31.
81. See Johnson, *The Vantage Point,* pp. 370–75.

stunningly more impressive than anything it had been thought the Communists were capable of mounting, rocked South Vietnam back on its heels, though it failed to achieve the objective of a mass uprising and ultimately led to a weakening of Communist military strength in the South for several years. Westmoreland had assumed that America's Dien Bien Phu was at the encircled Marine garrison of Khe Sanh but that the United States could win the battle there (which it did later that year through the crushing use of air support). But the real Dien Bien Phu turned out to be Tet. As in the Tonkin Gulf case, what happened in Washington was actually more important than what was happening at the scene of crisis in the field. The crucial difference was that in the Tonkin Gulf case the administration used the crisis to jump on one of Bundy's Pleiku-like streetcars; in the case of Tet the crisis served to push the administration off the streetcar.

In the summer and fall of 1967 the North Vietnamese appeared to shift from a protracted war strategy to a general offensive. Their tactics were to draw American forces toward the frontiers, away from populous areas. The major development was the siege of Khe Sanh, which the President followed so closely that he had a terrain model of the battle area constructed in the White House Situation Room. Some advance warning of the Tet offensive was available, but its scope and intensity were not anticipated.[82]

Scenes on TV of chaos, destruction, and American casualties en masse, following relatively optimistic administration pronouncements on progress in the war, flooded American living rooms in February. The American public saw the South Vietnamese national police chief summarily execute a Vietcong agent in one of the most wrenching pieces of film footage of the war. They also heard an American major say of combat action in the village of Ben Tre, "It became necessary to destroy the town to save it"—a bitter irony that seemed to many to capsulize the whole dilemma of Vietnam.[83] Viewership of network

82. See Schandler, *Unmaking of a President,* chaps. 3 and 4. Schandler's is the most thorough account of the Tet-period decisions—particularly of the role of the Clifford task force, in which he participated—and was enriched by General Westmoreland's provision of back-channel cables between the JCS and MACV—material that was never available to the compilers of the Pentagon Papers. See also Goulding, *Confirm or Deny,* chap. 10; and Westmoreland, *A Soldier Reports,* chaps. 17 and 18.

83. Quoted in Don Oberdorfer, *Tet!* (Doubleday, 1971), p. 185; see also pp. 161, 164–66.

news programs approached the peak record in this period. (Dean Rusk, agitated by what he saw as the subversive effect of sensationalized press coverage, snarled at a group of newsmen, "Whose side are you on?")[84] Eugene McCarthy won a plurality in the New Hampshire primary. (This was determined only after absentee ballots were counted. The President, who was not listed on the ballot, also had to depend entirely on write-in votes.) After a fruitless attempt to exchange noncandidacy for the establishment of a special presidential commission to review war policy, Robert Kennedy entered the race.[85] Like the aftermath of the Diem coup, Tet exposed the extreme vulnerability of the GVN that lay beneath the veneer of military progress, but it also exposed the vulnerability of administration policy at home.

By 1968 a five-to-three majority of the American public saw the original decision to go to war as a mistake, but simultaneously the number of those who wanted to end the war by escalating, even to the point of invading the DRV, exceeded the number favoring complete withdrawal by a comparable margin. Support for the war, according to polls, exceeded confidence in the President's handling of it, and that confidence was declining.[86] This accounted for the astonishing and rarely recognized phenomenon that Eugene McCarthy's total in New Hampshire contained three *hawkish* antiadministration votes for every two prowithdrawal votes; "of those who favored McCarthy before the Democratic Convention but who switched to some other candidate by November, a plurality had switched to *Wallace*."[87]

As an old Texas politician, Johnson was understandably sensitive to the difference between mass opinion and "attentive" public opinion, the reality of public feeling as a whole underlying the passionate and effectively mobilized minority dissent of the left wing and the elite. As early as 1966 a sample of elite opinion drawn from *Who's Who* showed 35 percent for deescalation, although 27 percent favored a step-up. Vocal opposition to the Vietnam War was much greater than it had been during the Korean War, but it neither influenced nor reflected a difference in popular support. "It appears," as John Mueller said, "that

84. Ibid., p. 170.

85. See ibid., pp. 240, 275–77, 294.

86. Schandler, *Unmaking of a President*, pp. 220–21.

87. Milton J. Rosenberg, Sidney Verba, and Philip E. Converse, *Vietnam and the Silent Majority: The Dove's Guide* (Harper and Row, 1970), p. 49 (emphasis added); see also pp. 33, 37.

political life can be carried on at several levels rather independently."[88] The shock of Tet, coinciding with the decline of public support below 50 percent, showed Johnson that he could no longer tread the middle course, no longer defer a decisive tilt to end the war one way or another. After considering the choices of trying to end the war through either massive escalation or moderate deescalation, LBJ finally chose the latter, then waffled on his choice until the end of his term of office. Even this half-hearted shift required a major jolt for Johnson.

Reinforcement Requests and the Reassessment

In the month after the offensive began, Westmoreland requested a moderate reinforcement of 10,500 men, and the participating principals all approved it, except for the Joint Chiefs, who considered it irresponsible in the absence of reserve mobilization. But the real debate was yet to come. Johnson cast around for solutions. He asked retired Army Chief of Staff Ridgway (who had been instrumental in preventing U.S. intervention in Indochina in 1954 and had opposed escalation in 1966) about an invasion of North Vietnam. The general scotched that idea quickly, noting that aside from whether or not it was desirable, forces were not available to do it. The same problem—the depletion of the U.S. strategic reserve—also dominated the concerns of the JCS. Even more vehemently than on the emergency augmentation issues, they opposed sending additional troops to Vietnam unless standby reserve units were mobilized.[89]

The JCS, Westmoreland, and CINCPAC Sharp, however, saw the offensive as an opportunity, believing that Johnson was now ready to move in the direction of decisive escalation that they had been pushing for years. Wheeler went to Saigon, and coaxed—conned, Westmoreland would later say privately—COMUSMACV into making an ambitious additional force request. Though Westmoreland was really not worried by the military threat in the Communist offensive itself, he put his mind to what he could do if he seized the initiative on the battlefield and was authorized to move into Laos and Cambodia. He came up with the figure of 206,000 men. Actually, however, Wheeler planned

88. Mueller, *War, Presidents and Public Opinion*, p. 266. See also George H. Gallup, ed., *The Gallup Poll* (Random House, 1972), vol. 3, pp. 2025–26.

89. See Oberdorfer, *Tet!* pp. 172–73; Johnson, *The Vantage Point*, pp. 386, 389; *Pentagon Papers*, vol. 4, p. 542; John B. Henry II, "February 1968," *Foreign Policy*, vol. 4 (Fall 1971), p. 9; and Schandler, *Unmaking of a President*, pp. 99–103, 109.

to use only about half that number immediately in Vietnam and to use the remainder to reconstitute the central reserve in the United States so that more forces would be available to respond to contingencies that were bubbling up elsewhere—in Korea, for example. When he returned to Washington, though, Wheeler lobbied for these forces as required to meet pressing needs in the field in Vietnam. Johnson, shaken by the Tet setback, soon decided to replace Westmoreland as commander with Creighton Abrams, and Westmoreland was shocked and bitter when he later discovered that Wheeler had portrayed his request to policymakers in terms of such baleful urgency.[90]

Faced with a stomach-churning number like 206,000, the President ordered what turned into an "A to Z" reassessment of policy. The central dramatis personae were at three levels, with consensus on commitment less certain at each step down in the hierarchy. First were the principals, most of whom started by being sympathetic to some force increase, though not the total in Westmoreland's request. Second was a group of eminent in-and-outers and recent administration veterans who had first met in November 1967—the "Wise Men," or officially, the Senior Informal Advisory Group on Vietnam. These included Dean Acheson, George Ball, McGeorge Bundy, Douglas Dillon, Cyrus Vance, Arthur Dean, John McCloy, Robert Murphy, Arthur Goldberg, Henry Cabot Lodge, Abe Fortas, and Generals Omar Bradley, Matthew Ridgway, and Maxwell Taylor. This group was divided, the majority initially tilting toward perseverance and finally tilting to deescalation. Third was the subcabinet and working level of the bureaucracy, who entered the debate through the study group that Johnson directed his new Secretary of Defense, Clark Clifford, to establish. Crucial in this last group were Paul Warnke and his personnel in ISA, who leaned most vigorously toward reorienting policy in the direction of disengagement.[91]

Tet had served to expose the Defense Department doves to each

90. Henry, "February 1968," pp. 8, 13, 16–21.
91. See *Pentagon Papers*, vol. 4, pp. 250, 266 ff., 549; and General Maxwell D. Taylor, USA (Ret.), *Swords and Plowshares* (Norton, 1972), p. 377. Johnson directed Clifford, "Give me the lesser of evils. Give me your recommendations." (Johnson, *Vantage Point*, p. 393.) Clifford, however, had the impression that his task force was only supposed to develop alternative ways to implement Westmoreland's request, and that the more far-reaching options his group eventually developed were really a venture beyond their mandate. (Schandler, *Unmaking of a President*, pp. 134–37.)

other and to bond them. The senior member of the disillusioned was Deputy Secretary Paul Nitze, who decided that meeting the request for 206,000 would simply be "reinforcing weakness." He refused to testify in Clifford's place before the Senate Foreign Relations Committee because he did not feel capable of defending administration policy, and he planned to offer LBJ his resignation if this was desired. (In Katzenbach's office at the State Department sentiment also arose for toughness in reviving the old idea of leverage: an "Operation Shock" proposal was floated that would have given the GVN an ultimatum to reform within three months or risk U.S. reevaluation of its commitment. Rusk quickly capped this leverage-with-a-vengeance plan.) Alain Enthoven's Office of Systems Analysis fed a number of papers into the ISA group. Among them was a searing draft that noted the stated U.S. objective since 1965 had been to maximize the costs and difficulties of North Vietnam, and went on: "Our strategy of attrition has not worked. Adding 206,000 more US men to a force of 525,000, gaining only 27 additional maneuver battalions and 270 tactical fighters at an added cost to the US of $10 billion per year raises the question of who is making it costly [for] whom."[92] The ISA group developed a plan to redefine the MACV mission as "a demographic strategy of population security"—a return to the enclave strategy abandoned three years earlier—on the grounds that no additional U.S. forces could achieve an end to the war. The security strategy would buy time for Vietnamization, behind an American screen. The JCS attacked this heretical challenge to the search and destroy strategy, and the final memorandum that went to the President on March 4 was a compromise.[93]

The memorandum that was discussed on March 4, however, did recommend changing strategy. The President decided to defer guidance pending a comprehensive reassessment of policy. By this time Clifford had become thoroughly disillusioned and felt discouraged because he lacked allies outside the Pentagon's civilian secretariat. He used sympathetic White House staffer Harry McPherson to get a sense

92. *Pentagon Papers*, vol. 4, p. 557. See also Hoopes, *The Limits of Intervention*, pp. 145–46; Marvin Kalb and Elie Able, *The Roots of Involvement: The U.S. in Asia, 1784–1971* (Norton, 1971), pp. 231–32; and Oberdorfer, *Tet!* p. 182.

93. See Robert Gallucci, *Neither Peace nor Honor: The Politics of American Military Policy in Viet-Nam*, Washington Center of Foreign Policy Research, School of Advanced International Studies, Studies in International Affairs, 24 (Johns Hopkins University Press, 1975), pp. 123–24; *Pentagon Papers*, vol. 4, pp. 561–68, 583; and Schandler, *Unmaking of a President*, chap. 7.

of Johnson's feelings and decided he "needed some stiff medicine" to bring home to the President what was happening in the country.[94] So Clifford proposed that the President consult the Wise Men before making a final decision. Then LBJ was hit with a one-two punch of defections by old respected hawks. First, Acheson shocked him by saying baldly that the Joint Chiefs did not know what they were talking about. Then Johnson saw that Clifford had jumped off the perseverance bandwagon. Clifford's conversion was largely due to the fact that he too had been unsettled by the JCS. When he came into office he asked the generals whether the 206,000 additional men would do the job; the answer was that there was no assurance they would and that it was uncertain how many would be needed or when. The secretary asked what the plan for victory was. The generals said there was no plan because the tactical restrictions imposed by the President precluded victory. They also said bombing could not win the war by itself, and there was no agreement on how long the war would last. Clifford told an interviewer years later, "I couldn't get hold of a plan to end the war, there was no plan for winning the war. It was like quicksilver to me."[95] As Halberstam put it, "Clifford forced Johnson to turn and look honestly at the war; it was an act of friendship for which Johnson could never forgive him."[96]

The Wise Men jolted Johnson when it became clear that a majority favored deescalation. Shocked, Johnson said that "somebody had poisoned the well."[97] This rejection of the old course of meeting the Communist ante whenever it was raised was matched by resistance to new troop commitments among the most dependable of Senate hard-liners —Richard Russell, John Stennis, and Henry Jackson.[98] The opposition of the Senate establishment had deeply affected Clifford as well. "If we wouldn't support it, who would?" Jackson later recalled. "Clifford was dismayed."[99]

94. Quoted in Schandler, *Unmaking of a President*, p. 255; see also pp. 175, 247, 254.

95. Quoted in ibid., p. 162. See also Hoopes, *The Limits of Intervention*, p. 204; and Kalb and Abel, *Roots of Involvement*, p. 233.

96. Halberstam, *The Best and the Brightest*, p. 653.

97. Quoted in Schandler, *Unmaking of a President*, p. 264.

98. See Oberdorfer, *Tet!* pp. 289–90.

99. Quoted in Schandler, *Unmaking of a President*, p. 211. Senator Margaret Chase Smith believed Clifford and the President were hoping that key members of Congress would share the responsibility for an escalation decision. Fulbright's de-

Johnson was crushed by defections within the government and the awesome costs that meeting MACV's request would pose. He had decided in 1965 not to put the country on a "real" wartime footing by mobilizing reserves or instituting economic controls and heavy taxes. It was no longer possible to avoid these measures and still follow the course of escalation. Treasury Secretary Henry H. Fowler warned that the price of the Westmoreland request would be cuts in domestic programs, other defense expenditures, and possibly foreign aid. Even then the dollar would suffer significantly. An international financial crisis was in the wind. House Ways and Means Committee Chairman Wilbur Mills demanded cuts in Great Society expenditures in return for a tax increase.[100] Military leaders were adamant on the necessity of calling up the reserves to support any troop commitment. (Throughout the war, as Schandler pointed out, "when the President began to search for the elusive point at which the costs of Vietnam would become unacceptable to the American people, he always settled upon mobilization.")[101] On April 4 Southeast Asia Deployment Program Number 6 was approved, formalizing the emergency augmentation and support forces committed after Tet and establishing a final ceiling of 549,500 for U.S. troops in South Vietnam.[102]

With the policy of persistence now ashes in his mouth, the President ordered a limitation of bombing, withdrew from the election race, and invited North Vietnam to negotiate. Johnson did not regard these decisions as irreversible at the time, but they rapidly came to be seen that way, and no serious consideration was given during the remainder of the administration to raising the troop level or renewing full-scale

---

mand in March for Clifford's testimony before the Senate Committee on Foreign Relations in hearings relating to the Foreign Assistance Act of 1968 also was a powerful catalyst for the solidification of the secretary's doubts. (Ibid., pp. 212–15.)

100. See ibid., pp. 139, 226–28.

101. Ibid., p. 56. LBJ had decided at a meeting on March 13 to deploy 30,000 more troops, but the deployments were not carried out, because an additional 13,500 men were needed as support troops for the earlier emergency augmentation force. (Johnson did have to mobilize a few reserve units to accomplish this.) When he received good reports of operational success from Westmoreland a week later, the President decided to restrict additional deployments to the 13,500 support troops. (Ibid., pp. 231–32.)

102. Pentagon Papers, vol. 4, p. 602. This ceiling was never actually reached. The highest total of troops in Vietnam, reached early in 1969, was 543,400.

bombing.[103] After much haggling and diplomatic maneuvering, followed by hollow and inconsequential wranglings over procedures for the talks in Paris and a total bombing halt in November, negotiations began at the end of the year. The negotiations would achieve little until the war heated up again in 1972. The initial talks may have been unproductive, but they were symbolic. The U.S. effort had finally leveled off and begun to decline. The long, stumbling ascent from purgatory was under way.

103. Clifford was energetic in fostering the "air of finality." See Schandler, *Unmaking of a President*, pp. 301–04, 313, 316–17.

PART TWO

Goals: The Imperative Not to Lose

CHAPTER SIX

National Security Goals and Stakes

The strength of a political philosophy lies in the questions it does not have to answer. A nation's foreign policy, like its political philosophy, rests on faith and on assumptions—beliefs about the world, about the intentions of others, and about power and security—that are no more demonstrable than any other set of beliefs. One may attack the policy or argue its implausibilities, but as long as its proponents can hold the faith of the flock, the ideas remain unassailable. Once the keepers of the gate feel compelled to answer challenges, the days of the policy's eminence are numbered.

Thus runs the story of the containment doctrine, unassailable from 1947 to 1968, then suddenly vulnerable and on the defensive. But how and when did this doctrine of the indivisibility of peace and the willingness to threaten and use force to stop the advance of communism embrace Vietnam? Truman cast the net of his doctrine worldwide but pulled it tightly only around Europe. Europe, not Asia, was the clear priority. Greece and Turkey were the original dominoes (if they fell, this could produce confusion and disorder in the Middle East and have a profound effect on Europe), not China or South Korea or Vietnam. Representing a consensus throughout the executive branch, Acheson put it this way:

Since our resources are limited, the weight of our effort must be brought to bear in these European countries which are most vital to our national security where the threat of aggression is most immediate, where our aid will be most effective, and where the ability of the economy to stand the financial strain of military expenditure is the least.[1]

1. "Statement by Secretary Acheson," before the House Foreign Affairs Committee, July 28, 1949, *Department of State Bulletin*, vol. 21 (August 8, 1949), p. 191.

Acheson reaffirmed this in his "perimeter" speech of January 12, 1950. Proclaiming that Washington would stay out of the civil war in China, Acheson revealed that vital U.S. military interests in Asia were restricted to a chain of Pacific islands running along the Aleutians to Japan and then to the Philippines.[2]

The Cautious Route to Commitment

Six months later these priorities lay shattered after the North Koreans struck across the thirty-eighth parallel, a move that came as a total surprise and was a profound psychological shock. The full weight of Mao's takeover in China began to be felt. Senator Joseph McCarthy was reaching the height of his powers. Republicans had been warning for years that Asia would be the real battleground between the United States and communism. It had become a world full of dominoes, and Vietnam was now one of them.

Inside the Truman administration the National Security Council provided a fascinating record of these changing perspectives. NSC 64 of February 27, 1950, called for the United States to take "all practicable measures . . . to prevent further communist expansion in Southeast Asia." Thailand and Burma "could be expected to fall," and the rest of Southeast Asia "would then be in grave hazard" if Indochina were controlled by the Communists. NSC 48/5 of May 17, 1951, referred to eliminating Communist influence in the area, but "without relieving the French authorities of their basic military responsibilities or committing United States armed forces." NSC 124/2 of June 25, 1952, discarded all qualifications, calling Indochina "of great strategic importance in the general international interest rather than in the purely French interest, and as essential to the security of the free world, not only in the Far East but in the Middle East and Europe as well." The objective followed with unrelenting logic: "To prevent the countries of Southeast Asia from passing into the communist orbit. . . ."[3] Weeks

2. "Crisis in Asia—An Examination of U.S. Policy," Remarks by Secretary Acheson before the National Press Club, Washington, D.C., January 12, 1950, ibid., vol. 22 (January 23, 1950), pp. 115–16.

3. For quotations from the three NSC documents, see *United States–Vietnam Relations, 1945–1967*, Study prepared by the Department of Defense for the House Committee on Armed Services, 92 Cong. 1 sess. (Government Printing Office, 1971), bk. 8, pt. V.B.2, pp. 283, 436, 522, 528.

before this document was even approved, a State Department communiqué publicly stated that Indochina was "an integral part of the world-wide resistance by the Free Nations to Communist attempts at conquest and subversion."[4]

The basic American commitment to Vietnam was set, internally and publicly. Over the years the precise rationale was to take some interesting twists and turns, and the military was to jump off the bandwagon for a while, but the top political leadership of the executive branch never wavered from the objective of preventing a Communist takeover.

The Eisenhower administration variations are perhaps the most interesting, for they seem at once to extend and to limit the commitment to a non-Communist Vietnam. NSC 5405 of January 16, 1954, was the basic document the leadership played with before Geneva. This document gave further detail to the central objective by vetoing a coalition government that would include the Communists and by urging American intervention to save Indochina should China first intervene. But contrary to the spirit of these undertakings, it warned: "U.S. support will continue so long as France continues to carry out its primary responsibility."[5] Paradoxically, Indochina was worth the risk of war with China but not worth trying to save without the French.

The Geneva settlement resolved this paradox but created a new one. NSC 5429/5 of December 22, 1954, stated the U.S. objective as follows: "Make every possible effort, not openly inconsistent with the U.S. position as to the armistice agreement, to defeat Communist subversion and influence, to maintain and support friendly non-Communist governments in Cambodia and Laos, to maintain a friendly non-Communist South Vietnam, and to prevent a Communist victory through all-Vietnam elections."[6] And yet in contrast to the prompting to "make every possible effort" the authors of this document moderated the consequences of losing Indochina. Gone were the expressed fears of the chain reaction reaching the Middle East and Europe. In their stead were fears for Asia in its own right. NSC 5612/1 of September 5, 1956, extended this line of reasoning. Communist control of "any single free country" in Southeast Asia "would encourage tendencies toward accommodation by the rest," and would set in motion severe economic and political

---

4. "Communiqué," June 18, 1952, *Department of State Bulletin*, vol. 25 (June 30, 1952), p. 1010.

5. See *United States–Vietnam Relations*, bk. 9, pt. V.B.3, pp. 217–38.

6. Ibid., bk. 10, pt. V.B.3, p. 851.

pressures, extending as far as India and Japan.[7] Asia was placed on a par with Europe. But a more profound change was that China had replaced the Soviet Union as the number one enemy in Asia. The Soviet threat was hardly mentioned in the Asian context. China was pictured as relentless, fanatical, and irrational. The authors of these NSC documents no longer labored under the notion of a Communist monolith, but saw a Sino-Soviet alliance with the potential for fraternal conflict.

These rather sophisticated themes were carried forward into NSC 6012 of July 25, 1960—and carried further into a more elementary paradox. On the one hand, this document continued to allude to the importance of Indochina to U.S. security: the United States "should not forgo necessary [military] action" in the area even without the United Nations and SEATO allies. On the other hand, it laid out the very sensible dictum that the fate of the nations concerned ultimately depended on their own will to resist aggression and to satisfy the aspirations of their people: "The United States should accordingly support and assist [these nations] so long as they remain determined to preserve their own independence and are actively pursuing policies to this end."[8]

Eisenhower gave voice to these somewhat schizophrenic discussions of objectives in a major speech on April 4, 1959, and in his public greetings to Diem on October 26, 1960. In the former he spoke of the "crumbling process" that would follow the loss of South Vietnam but concluded merely that "our own national interests demand some help from us." In the latter, he struck that note a bit harder, promising to continue aid as long as it would be "useful."[9]

While these cautionary statements about the U.S. commitment to South Vietnam may well have reflected the President's actual thinking at that time and while these statements certainly downplayed the importance of Vietnam in the public mind, one only had to note what was being said about Laos to be shaken. Throughout 1959 and 1960 the administration issued public declarations of "full support" to the right-wing Lao leaders and public threats to Moscow. Eisenhower privately told his chief advisers: "We cannot let Laos fall to the Communists even

7. Ibid., p. 1083.
8. Ibid., pp. 1285, 1286.
9. "Address at the Gettysburg College Convocation: The Importance of Understanding, April 4, 1959," *Public Papers of the Presidents of the United States, Dwight D. Eisenhower, 1959* (GPO, 1960), p. 313. See also "Message to President Diem on the Fifth Anniversary of the Independence of Viet-Nam, October 26, 1960," ibid., *1960* (GPO, 1961), pp. 337–38.

if we have to fight, with our allies or without them."[10] The words to the American people were not so blunt, but there was no mistaking the message—Indochina was vital to U.S. security.

The public and classified statements of the Kennedy administration crisscrossed like Eisenhower's but seem to have ended up in the same place. From the beginning great stress was placed on defeating "wars of national liberation," especially in Southeast Asia. On March 23, 1961, the new President began a news conference with a statement about Laos in which he warned: "My fellow Americans, Laos is far away from America, but the world is small. . . . Its own safety runs with the safety of us all."[11] Weeks later Kennedy approved NSAM 52, which bluntly stated the goal for Vietnam: "To prevent Communist domination of South Vietnam."[12]

But the matter was far from settled inside the executive branch. Days after the Taylor-Rostow report (see chapter 3), Rusk and McNamara sent the President a memo that began with a ringing declaration: the loss of South Vietnam would lead to "the near certainty that the remainder of Southeast Asia and Indonesia would move to a complete accommodation with Communism, if not formal incorporation within the Communist bloc." Its loss, the memo continued, "would not only destroy SEATO but would undermine the credibility of American commitments elsewhere. . . . [It] would stimulate bitter domestic controversies in the United States and would be seized upon by extreme elements to divide the country and harass the Administration." Then, the key point came: *"The United States should commit itself to the clear objective of preventing the fall of South Viet-Nam to Communism."*[13]

Kennedy rejected this recommendation in NSAM 111 of November 22, 1961. But if he was really resetting his sights, it did not accord with the rest of his behavior. He could have used this opportunity to redefine the American objective but did not. He could have slowed down the pace of American involvement but did not. Indeed in this very

10. Dwight D. Eisenhower, *The White House Years: Waging Peace, 1956–1961* (Doubleday, 1965), p. 610.

11. "The President's News Conference of March 23, 1961," *Public Papers of the Presidents, John F. Kennedy, 1961* (GPO, 1962), p. 214.

12. *The Pentagon Papers: The Defense Department History of United States Decisionmaking on Vietnam,* Senator Gravel ed. (Beacon Press, 1971), vol. 2, p. 642.

13. Ibid., p. 111 (emphasis in original).

same NSAM Kennedy went on to approve every other recommendation of the Rusk-McNamara memo. The President's rejection of the
key recommendation probably had more to do with tactics than with
the basic judgments about Vietnam's importance. At the end of the
year Kennedy sent a message to Diem that in effect affirmed American
support as long as North Vietnam aggressed, adding ominously: "We
shall seek to persuade the Communists to give up their attempts of
force and subversion."[14] For the next year and a half the President and
other senior officials repeatedly offered public explanations of why
Vietnam was "vital." At the same time, however, the President alluded
to the "primary responsibility" of the South Vietnamese.

This "their war–our war" dualism persisted down to Kennedy's last
days, but it had the effect of making the thrust of the American commitment more apparent, not less. The President told Walter Cronkite
that "in the final analysis it is the people and the Government itself
who have to win or lose this struggle. All we can do is help, and we are
making it very clear." He immediately added: "But I don't agree with
those who say we should withdraw. That would be a great mistake. . . .
I know people don't like Americans to be engaged in this kind of an
effort. Forty-seven Americans have been killed in combat with the
enemy, but this is a very important struggle even though it is far
away."[15] One week later in an interview with Chet Huntley and David
Brinkley, Kennedy likened the Vietnam situation to China in 1949, arguing that a reduction of U.S. aid to Diem would not be helpful right
then. Asked if he believed the domino theory, he said, "I believe it.
I believe it. . . . China is so large . . . [Vietnam's fall] would also give
the impression that the wave of the future in Southeast Asia was China
and the Communists. So I believe it." Driving the point home: "What
I am concerned about is that Americans will get impatient and say . . .
we should withdraw. That only makes it easy for the Communists. I
think we should stay. We should use our influence in as effective a way
as we can, but we should not withdraw."[16]

On November 26, 1963, just four days after the assassination of
President Kennedy, President Johnson approved NSAM 273. This docu-

14. "Exchange of Messages with the President of the Republic of Viet-Nam,
December 15, 1961," Public Papers, Kennedy, 1961, p. 801.
15. "Transcript of Broadcast with Walter Cronkite Inaugurating a CBS Television News Program, September 2, 1963," ibid., 1963 (GPO, 1964), p. 652.
16. "Transcript of Broadcast on NBC's 'Huntley-Brinkley Report,' September
9, 1963," ibid., pp. 659, 660.

ment perpetuated the language about assisting the South Vietnamese but for the first time introduced the word "win" into the U.S. objective. On March 17, 1964, however, all the gears of the past meshed in NSAM 288.

We seek an independent non-Communist South Vietnam. We do not require that it serve as a Western base or as a member of a Western alliance. South Vietnam must be free, however, to accept outside assistance as required to maintain its security. This assistance should be able to take the form not only of economic and social measures but also police and military help to root out and control insurgent elements.

Unless we can achieve this objective in South Vietnam, almost all of Southeast Asia will probably fall under Communist dominance (all of Vietnam, Laos, and Cambodia), accommodate to Communism so as to remove effective U.S. and anti-Communist influence (Burma), or fall under domination of forces not now explicitly Communist but likely then to become so (Indonesia taking over Malaysia). Thailand might hold for a period without help, but would be under grave pressure. Even the Philippines would become shaky, and the threat to India on the West, Australia and New Zealand to the South, and Taiwan, Korea, and Japan to the North and East would be greatly increased.

All of these consequences would probably have been true even if the U.S. had not since 1954, and especially since 1961, become so heavily engaged in South Vietnam. However, that fact accentuates the impact of a Communist South Vietnam not only in Asia but in the rest of the world, where the South Vietnam conflict is regarded as a test case of U.S. capacity to help a nation to meet the Communist "war of liberation."

Thus, purely in terms of foreign policy, the stakes are high. . . .[17]

The NSAM, authored in large measure by McNamara and other high-ranking officials, did insist that "the South Vietnamese must win their own fight" but hastened to make the point that "it is vital that we continue to take every reasonable measure to assure success."[18] No subsequent document superseded this one as a statement of American aims. Proponents of both escalation and deescalation tried after 1965 but failed to achieve a new consensus.

When the President does not want to engage his bureacracy for fear of leaks or when the prospect of bureaucratic agreement is unlikely, he and his cabinet and subcabinet advisers often turn to public speeches. These speeches do not usually go through the internal clearance process, thus giving wider rein to the political leadership. This is what occurred during the Johnson administration. For five years the public

17. *Pentagon Papers,* vol. 3, pp. 50–51 (emphasis added).
18. Ibid., p. 51.

witnessed a quest for new justifications and for a more palatable objective than simply preventing defeat. The themes were:

America keeps its word. Our purpose is peace. We are keeping a commitment made by Eisenhower. We have a commitment to SEATO countries. We merely want to return to the principles of the 1954 Geneva accords. In February 1966 Johnson said, "Our purpose . . . is, simply put, just to prevent the forceful conquest of South Viet-Nam by North Viet-Nam." In January 1967 he proclaimed: "We have chosen to fight a limited war . . . in an attempt to prevent a larger war—a war almost certain to follow . . . if the Communists succeed in . . . taking over South Viet-Nam . . . by force. . . . if they are not checked now the world can expect to pay a greater price to check them later." In May 1967 William Bundy reiterated, "We are acting to preserve South Viet-Nam's right to work out its own future without external interference."[19]

For the better part of twenty years the highest administration officials gave public and classified testimony to a simple syllogism.

First, there was a threat to Indochina and later specifically to South Vietnam. But who did U.S. leaders think was doing the threatening? In the late 1940s the assumption was that Moscow controlled all Communist advances. And yet the intelligence community did not characterize Ho Chi Minh as a puppet. He was seen as being able to act relatively independently of Moscow.[20] After Korea, China was seen as the principal opponent in Asia. This perception stuck through 1968. (An exception was the period of the Laotian crises and Khrushchev's rhetoric about wars of national liberation, from 1960 to 1962, when the Soviet Union emerged once again as the key source of trouble.) Washington paradoxically looked to Moscow for help on the Indochina question in 1954 and after 1965. The reasoning was that the Russians might want to avoid a direct confrontation as much as the Americans did and that Moscow also had an interest in curtailing Chinese influence in Southeast Asia. Although the Russians seemed less intractable than the Chinese, however, they were still a part of the problem. From 1964,

19. Johnson quoted in ibid., vol. 4, pp. 644, 662; Bundy quoted in ibid., p. 668.
20. See, for example, the cable sent by Secretary of State George C. Marshall to the American Embassy in Nanking, July 2, 1948, and the dispatch of the American consul general in Saigon, George M. Abbott, to the secretary of state, November 5, 1948, in *United States–Vietnam Relations*, bk. 8, pt. V.B.2, pp. 127, 151.

high officials could not be sure who was calling the shots in South Vietnam—Moscow or Peking or Hanoi itself.[21] Which Communist nation was doing the threatening was ultimately less important than that communism might triumph.

Second, if Vietnam fell to communism, other countries would soon follow. But which countries and how? Again the answers lacked precision and changed over time. Officials in 1952 saw the ripples going beyond Asia to the Middle East and Europe. No one directly expressed a clear sense of how this would happen, but fears of outright conventional attack were quite high. Eisenhower's concern was for Southeast Asia itself and for the hold of this region on Japan's future. Capitulation to communism would occur through internal accommodation and external pressures, out of fear but mainly through Communist control of the economic resources of the area. Under Kennedy the concerns began with Southeast Asia, Japan, and India but broadened out to the worldwide credibility of American commitments. The rather vague anxiety seemed to be that wars of national liberation would catch on in other underdeveloped countries and that the principal Communist powers would read the outcome in Vietnam as a test of the American will. Under Johnson it became an even more generalized fear about the consequences of not keeping the American word. Allies, perhaps more than adversaries, would begin to question their ties to the United States and to turn away from America, thus increasing their vulnerability.

Third, once this process of alliance unraveling began, U.S. security would be gravely impaired. No one tried to suggest that Russians and Chinese would be landing on American shores. That was not the point. What seemed to haunt U.S. leaders was the notion that if such a process began, it could not be controlled and there could be no telling where it would end. Through miscalculation at some stage, the United States and the Soviet Union might find themselves teetering on the brink of nuclear war. Only once did American leaders break out of this pattern of thought. That was in the late spring of 1954 when the odds were great that the Vietminh would definitely gain a territorial foothold in Vietnam. Facing this near certainty, Eisenhower and Dulles patched SEATO together to prevent further Communist advances.

21. See *Pentagon Papers,* vol. 3, pp. 50–56.

Otherwise, no administration ever showed any disposition to plan compensatory action in other nations to enhance the chances of their surviving a Vietnam defeat.

This syllogistic catechism was inviolate. The challenges were few and far between. General Matthew Ridgway as chief of staff of the Army in 1954 questioned whether Vietnam would be worth the potential costs and dangers of trying to save it. His opposition helped to blunt the proposed U.S. military intervention, although Eisenhower decided against intervention mainly because he lacked allied support. In 1956 General Lawton Collins, the President's special envoy to Vietnam, backed by the Joint Chiefs, proposed giving Vietnam low priority. Dulles and Eisenhower overruled him. Under Secretary of State George Ball raised the issue of international priorities and poked holes in the domino theory from the fall of 1964 through the summer of 1965. His arguments never made a dent. Clark Clifford as secretary of defense in 1968 openly challenged the possibility of winning the war, questioned Vietnam's strategic significance, and warned of catastrophic domestic repercussions that would attend continuation of the war. He helped to put a lid on the war but did not succeed in altering the basic commitment. No comprehensive and systematic examination of Vietnam's importance to the United States was ever undertaken within the executive branch. Debates revolved around how to do things better and whether they could be done, not whether they were worth doing.

Exploring the Security Issue

But this still leaves the central question unanswered: did the presidents and their key advisers *actually believe* that for reasons of American security they could not afford to lose Vietnam to communism? Realistically, this is a moot question; its answer is ultimately unknowable, but it must be asked nevertheless in any attempt to get at the roots of American involvement. Verbal and written commitments are neither absolutely binding nor do they necessarily reveal underlying motives. But whatever American leaders actually thought and expressed guardedly and privately to close associates, their public utterances, classified documents, aid programs, and advisers and troops had the effect of substantiating the American stakes in Vietnam.

Even so, the question is still worth probing, for despite the surface

trap these leaders had set for themselves, they still had their inner beliefs and possessed choice in the matter. In part what they were saying
about Vietnam until 1965 was nothing more than the typical rhetoric
used to justify security aid programs. Official rhetoric, classified and
public, was not known for its discriminating qualities. "Vital's" and
"great importance's" cluttered the run of speeches and documents,
especially after Acheson's perimeter speech, in which he failed to indulge in such clutter, was often blamed for the Korean War. Using
words for the purposes of deterrence, bolstering allies, and appeasing
the domestic audience was routine.

There was much to suggest that Vietnam was special, however. Heavy
U.S. strategic investment in the country highlighted this, though it did
not cause it. U.S. actions betokened more than the mere granting of
aid to another country in distress. The record of U.S. military and
economic assistance to fight communism in Indochina, detailed in chapter 2, tells this story quite clearly. The investment was made heavily and
steadily. From 1945 to 1951 U.S. aid to France totaled over $3.5 billion.
From 1955 to 1961 U.S. military aid of all kinds averaged about $200
million a year. This made South Vietnam the second largest recipient
of such aid, topped only by Korea. By 1963 South Vietnam ranked
first among recipients of military assistance. In economic assistance it
followed only India and Pakistan. On a per capita basis Vietnam ranked
behind only Laos throughout this period.[22]

In late 1953 Indochina was granted the highest military aid priority,
giving it precedence for equipment over every allied nation and the
U.S. armed forces as well.[23] It did not possess the largest Military Assistance Advisory Group, because of Geneva restrictions, but it had the
only MAAG headed by a lieutenant general. By 1958 South Vietnam
housed the largest U.S. overseas economic aid mission anywhere. These
little touches underscored the more essential fact that South Vietnam,
if not an American creation, was certainly a total dependent. It would
neither have come into being nor survived without massive U.S. support. Saigon's rulers had nowhere else to turn, and everyone knew it.

22. See Leslie H. Gelb, "Vietnam: The System Worked," *Foreign Policy*, vol. 3
(Summer 1971), pp. 140–67.

23. See Joint Subsidiary Plans, Division Memorandum, May 5, 1954, *United
States–Vietnam Relations*, bk. 9, V.B.3, p. 421, which states that "on 14 December,
1953, the Secretary of Defense informed the Chief, MAAG, Indochina, that Indochina has the highest MDAP [Mutual Defense Assistance Program] priority."

Perhaps Vietnam was special because of these sunk costs—the investment trap. In this popular view, Vietnam's importance derived from the cumulative effect of involvement. Leaders might have been inclined to give last year and the years before that, more than a particular calculation of Vietnam's actual importance, as justification for persistence at a particular time. It is, of course, impossible to separate the two concerns. Both calculations did play a part. But two points are striking. First, the investment argument, although a legitimate and persuasive one, was rarely employed either publicly or internally. Second, the *aims* of each succeeding administration held constant; they did not grow. Involvement grew because Vietcong power grew, raising the cost of pursuing the same aims.

Nor did Vietnam's vitalness rest on the related argument that American leaders expected success at low cost or in the near term. As indicated in earlier chapters, this was not the case at all. American leaders held to the assumption that the United States could not afford to lose Vietnam, not because they were promised victory or because they anticipated defeat, but because they believed they had to. They saw no acceptable alternative.

Evidence from memoirs supports this view and gives some indication of how far presidents were prepared to go to save Vietnam. The place to start is with the Roosevelt administration, for to a greater degree than any of its successors, except the Johnson administration, it had to act on its words about Southeast Asia. In the summer of 1941, months before the Pearl Harbor attack, the State Department issued the following statement:

> In the light of previous developments, steps such as are now being taken by the Government of Japan endanger the peaceful use by peaceful nations of the Pacific. They tend to jeopardize the procurement by the United States of essential materials such as tin and rubber which are necessary for the normal economy of this country and the consummation of our defense program. . . . The steps which the Japanese Government has taken also endanger the safety of other areas of the Pacific, including the Philippine Islands.[24]

But in war planning before the war and during its actual conduct the United States accorded the Southeast Asian theater the lowest priority. In practice this meant both that the area would be lightly defended and that little effort would be expended to recapture it. As an up-and-

24. "Japanese Military Démarche in Indochina," Statement by Acting Secretary of State Sumner Welles, July 24, 1941, *Department of State Bulletin*, vol. 5 (July 26, 1941), pp. 71–72.

coming general named Dwight Eisenhower reported to his superiors in 1942, the United States had to "differentiate sharply and definitely" between what was *"necessary"* and what was "merely *desirable."* Southeast Asia, he continued, was "not immediately vital to the successful outcome of the war."[25] The Roosevelt administration was in a resources bind, and it had to be tough with itself in deciding what was important. It had to establish priorities. In doing so, it threw into sharp relief the contrast between its words and deeds.

The Truman administration, although not involved in a world war, was in a somewhat similar situation. In the summer of 1952 Acheson met with the French and British foreign ministers to discuss joint action in the event of Chinese intervention in Indochina. Acheson said that in such an eventuality the American input to the defense of Indochina could not go beyond air and naval power. As Anthony Eden recalled, Acheson went on to say that it would be "disastrous" to lose Southeast Asia "without a struggle," but that allied actions to prevent this should "not provoke a third world war".[26] These two phrases used by Secretary Acheson are interesting because they seem to track President Truman's thinking on the limits of the U.S. commitment in the Korean War and thus might provide some indication of how far the President was prepared to go to prevent a Communist victory in Indochina.

President Truman did not want to lose the Korean War but was prepared to do so. In the fall of 1950 after the successful Chinese intervention in Korea, Truman approved a joint memo of the State Department and the Defense Department that said if the Chinese rejected a ceasefire and continued their offensive, the UN forces might be compelled to evacuate Korea. "The consequences of a voluntary abandonment of our Korean allies," the memo read, "would be such that any United Nations evacuation must be clearly the result of military necessity only." Truman did not want to "back out"; "if we got out," he said, "someone would have to force us out." The President reiterated this position in a message to General MacArthur on January 13, 1951. "In the worst case [continued Chinese military successes], it would be important that, if we must withdraw from Korea, it be clear to the world that that course is forced upon us by military necessity." The Joint Chiefs of Staff

25. Quoted in Maurice Matloff and Edwin M. Snell, *United States Army in World War II: The War Department Strategic Planning for Coalition Warfare, 1941–42* (U.S. Department of the Army, 1953), p. 157.

26. *Full Circle: The Memoirs of Anthony Eden* (Doubleday, 1956), p. 92.

and General MacArthur in particular wanted to go even further and suggested, as Truman later recalled, that "we might consider ways to withdraw from Korea 'with honor' in order to protect Japan," which, with few American troops stationed there, was vulnerable.[27]

The State Department, however, supported the President's position and, according to Truman, insisted that the United States "could not retreat from Korea unless . . . forced out."[28] This kind of ultimate contingency planning ceased in the spring of 1951, once the Chinese forces had been driven back to the thirty-eighth parallel and the battle line had been stabilized. For those moments of truth in the winter of 1950 and 1951, however, the leaders of the United States were prepared to set a limit on the U.S. commitment to the Korean War, even if that limit meant losing the war.

This limit was set for several reasons. First, the United States did not have the military resources available at that time to send further reinforcements to Korea. Second, the new forces that were being generated in the general U.S. defense buildup were earmarked for the European theater; for as Defense Secretary George Marshall had emphasized at an NSC meeting, the entire international position of the United States depended on keeping Western Europe strong. Third, the President and many others deeply believed that Korea was merely a Kremlin feint, and that the real attack would come shortly in Europe. According to Truman, "Europe was the most important target for world Communism's attack."[29] If these reasons for limiting the U.S. commitment applied to Korea where U.S. forces and prestige were directly engaged, they certainly applied to Indochina as well.

But what stands out is Acheson's remark about not losing "without a struggle." It shows limits to the centrality of Indochina and gives a sense of other affairs being more important. Beyond that, however, it did demonstrate a willingness to fight. Even at this early stage the United States was disposed toward using force to defend Indochina. That force was to be restricted to air and sea power, but it meant fighting nonetheless.

President Eisenhower's thinking about Indochina seems to be a puz-

27. The quotations in this paragraph appear in Harry S. Truman, *Memoirs,* vol. 2: *Years of Trial and Hope* (Doubleday, 1956), on pp. 400, 401, 436, and 432, respectively.

28. Ibid., p. 432.

29. Ibid., p. 380; see also p. 419.

zle. On the one hand, he talked about the loss of Indochina resulting in falling dominoes around the world, and on the other hand, he failed to "save" Indochina by intervening for the French at Dien Bien Phu. Sherman Adams, Eisenhower's assistant, provided an answer to the puzzle.

If the Communists had pushed on with an aggressive offensive after the fall of Dienbienphu, instead of stopping and agreeing to stay out of Southern Vietnam, Laos and Cambodia, there was a strong possibility that the United States would have moved against them. A complete Communist conquest of Indo-China would have had far graver consequence for the West than a Red victory in Korea.[30]

No one was in a better position to know Eisenhower's mind than Adams. And what Adams was saying was this: Eisenhower was prepared to lose Vietnam above the seventeenth parallel but was deadly serious about stopping the Vietminh advance at that point.

For a period after the Geneva Conference, Eisenhower can be said to have been uncertain about Vietnam. But by 1960, when the Laotian crisis was in full swing, Eisenhower had no doubts. What he would do for Laos, it can be presumed, he was even more likely to do in behalf of the still greater American stake in South Vietnam.

Memoir reports of President Kennedy's most private thinking veer in different directions: the Arthur Schlesinger–Kenneth O'Donnell school and the Theodore Sorensen–Robert Kennedy school. According to Schlesinger, Kennedy drew a hard line between aid and advisers and the direct involvement of regular combat units. Vietnam was worth the former but not the latter.[31] This was a reasonably clear dividing line in principle, although individual U.S. military personnel were already engaged in combat in 1962 and 1963, as ARVN unit advisers. O'Donnell has written that in the "spring of 1963 . . . the President told Mansfield that he had been having serious second thoughts about Mansfield's arguments and that he now agreed with the senator's thinking on the need for a complete military withdrawal from Vietnam. 'But I can't do it until 1965—after I'm reelected,' Kennedy told Mansfield."[32] Mansfield has confirmed this story, and yet it remains puzzling, not simply because of its obvious callousness, but because it is in sharp variance

30. Sherman Adams, *Firsthand Report: The Story of the Eisenhower Administration* (Harper, 1961), p. 120.

31. See Arthur M. Schlesinger, Jr., *A Thousand Days: John F. Kennedy in the White House* (Houghton Mifflin, 1965), chap. 20.

32. Kenneth O'Donnell, "LBJ and the Kennedys," *Life*, August 7, 1970, p. 51.

with the accounts of others who were far closer to Kennedy's inner feelings about Vietnam than either Schlesinger or O'Donnell. Sorensen wrote that Kennedy, "skeptical of the extent of our involvement but unwilling to abandon his predecessor's pledge or permit a Communist conquest, would not turn back from that commitment." And then Sorensen recorded that in November 1963 Kennedy "was simply going to weather it out, a nasty, untidy mess to which there was no other acceptable solution."[33] Robert Kennedy's well-known enthusiasm for counterinsurgency warfare and his later self-blame for his early attitudes toward Vietnam support Sorensen's accounts. This is not to imply that President Kennedy would have pursued the same course as Johnson. It is merely to affirm that Kennedy took the problem with great seriousness and that days before his death he saw "no other acceptable solution."

Three facts conspired to make it easier for Johnson to take the plunge on the assumed importance of Vietnam than for his predecessors. First, the world was a safer place to live in and Vietnam was the only continuing crisis. Europe was secure. NATO troubles were relatively minor. The Sino-Soviet split had deepened. Mutual nuclear deterrence existed between the two superpowers. Second, the situation in Vietnam was more desperate than it ever had been. If the United States had not intervened in 1965, South Vietnam would have been conquered by the Communists. Third, after years of effort the U.S. conventional military forces were big enough and prepared enough to intervene. Unlike his predecessors, Johnson had the ready military capability to back up his words.

Lyndon Johnson described his own thinking in his memoirs.

I knew our people well enough to realize that if we walked away from Vietnam and let Southeast Asia fall, there would follow a divisive and destructive debate in our country. . . . A divisive debate about "who lost Vietnam" would be, in my judgment, even more destructive to our national life than the argument over China had been. . . . Our allies . . . throughout the world would conclude that our word was worth little or nothing. . . . [Moscow and Peking] could not resist the opportunity to expand their control into the vacuum of power. . . . With Moscow and Peking . . . moving forward, we would return to a world role to prevent their full takeover of Europe, Asia, and the Middle East—*after* they had committed themselves.[34]

    33. Theodore C. Sorensen, *Kennedy* (Harper and Row, 1965), pp. 639, 661.
    34. Lyndon Baines Johnson, *The Vantage Point: Perspectives of the Presidency, 1963–1969* (Holt, Rinehart and Winston, 1971), pp. 151–52.

Johnson was the true believer who had to pay the full price for his thinking. Unlike his predecessors, he was confronted with the ultimate logic of U.S. objectives in Vietnam.

The Domino Theory

What the foregoing indicates is that the presidents and their principal advisers saw genuine national security merits in their belief that they could not afford to lose Vietnam to communism. The domino theory was at the heart of the matter. Its central tenets that security was indivisible and that weakness in one place would only invite aggression in other places held sway over U.S. strategic thinking for twenty years.

The persuasiveness of the domino theory rested on three analogies: historical, current, and psychological-legal. The lessons of each of these analogies reinforced the effect of the others.

First, two generations of presidents and high officials had lived through or were reared on the dominoes of the 1930s. Whatever their exact historical circumstances and consequences, these cases came to possess a simple and compelling message: if aggression is tolerated in small, out-of-the-way places, aggressors will be emboldened to attack larger, more vital places. U.S. leaders saw a straight line from the Japanese takeover in Manchuria in 1931 to the invasion of China to the invasion of Indochina to the attack on Pearl Harbor. They saw the same straight line from Italy's attack on Ethiopia in 1935 to German reoccupation of the Rhineland to the anschluss of Austria to the rape of Czechoslovakia at Munich to general war in Europe. The League of Nations, Great Britain, France, and Russia stood by and either invoked only token sanctions or actually cooperated with the aggressors. The United States stuck its head in the sand and merely refused to recognize the conquests. Manchuria, Ethiopia, Czechoslovakia, the great powers reasoned, were too insignificant to cause World War II. But world war was precisely what they invited and got.

The leaders in Paris, London, and Washington felt they could not get their peoples' backing for threats or fighting in such obscure places. Taking strong action would jeopardize their political power at home. Peace at any price seemed to guide their thoughts—always hoping for some other nation to do the job, for the appetites of the aggressors to be sated, for peace now and someone who would pick up the tab later. It was appeasement. And appeasement became the most odious word in the American diplomatic vocabulary.

It would have been surprising had American leaders drawn any other conclusion from the experience of the 1930s; and Vietnam in the post-war period seemed to have all the markings of another Manchuria or Ethiopia, especially after concessions on Vietnam in 1954 and on Laos in 1962. Well, there was some question about whether Ho Chi Minh was the instrument of Moscow or Peking or his own man. But no matter; he was a Communist and that was the important thing. There was some doubt whether Vietnam was a war of external aggression or a civil war growing out of a colonial past. But no matter; it was an effort to change the status quo by force, and that alone had to be resisted.

Second, current analogies tended to mold Vietnam into the shape and pattern of whatever else of major importance was going on in the world. At various times different dominant events or issues seemed to control perspectives on Vietnam. In the early Truman period, the parallels between America's China and Indochina policy are striking. From 1945 until 1947 Truman and Marshall actively sought to promote a coalition government in China between the Nationalists and Communists. The State Department followed suit in Vietnam. After the failure of the coalition approach in China, Truman did what was possible to keep open the option of a Nationalist-Communist compromise government. At the same time, despite French rigidity, the State Department remained open to a French-Vietminh settlement. Even after Chiang's forces were driven from the mainland and the war in Indochina increased in tempo, Truman pointedly kept hands off of both conflicts. Korea definitely changed the relatively laissez-faire attitude toward Indochina. Korea made Indochina appear as another front in an Asia-wide Communist assault—an assault that could spread to Europe. And Europe throughout the Truman administration was considered the keystone of American security, Franco-American relations and a strong France-in-Europe being the backbone of a resurgent Europe. France, then, had to be helped in Indochina in order not to be weakened in Europe.

These same considerations persisted into the Eisenhower administration. Indeed the linkages to French policy and anti-China policy became even stronger, until the French said "no more" at Geneva. Then, the dominating factor became the need for alliances—pactomania, the critics called it—to prevent any further Communist inroads. Vietnam was a SEATO protocol state. The image of the China menace loomed ominously over the quiet terminal years of the 1950s in Indochina.

For Kennedy, Vietnam came wrapped up in a bundle of problems. One more pressing than the next, they ranged from Cuba to Berlin to Laos to Khrushchev's speech on wars of national liberation. Vietnam seemed to be the test case for the new Communist challenge to the underdeveloped world—the gray, obscure areas. And then for Johnson, Vietnam itself emerged as the dominant event and issue, coloring American relations with the rest of the world.

Finally, the persuasiveness of the domino theory with respect to Vietnam resulted from thinking along the lines of some simple, albeit appealing, psychological and legal analogies. If you let your daughter come home late from a date without punishment, the next thing you know she will be pregnant. If you let a crime go unpunished, you invite more crime. Once the principle has been undermined, there is no stopping place. These analogies are straight-line projections into the future based on precedent. They have at least a measure of relevance to such diplomatic concepts as balance of power, credibility, honor, and commitment. U.S. action in one area does produce reaction in another. Foreign leaders, friendly and hostile, were watching what the United States was doing in Vietnam. Of course, it could be disputed whether they were all watching in the same way, especially when so few American allies were willing to help, when those that did help worked for cash and then only reluctantly, and when other world leaders almost unanimously condemned the American role. But the Americans' answer to such condemnation would be "That's what they say now; wait and see what they'll say if we withdraw."

These were not simplistic analogies, not mechanical formulae. It is in the nature of power to want to keep things from getting out of control, and control in diplomacy operates on the margins. The fear was not really focused on the Sino-Soviet monolith or on Russian and Chinese hordes streaming across borders. It was infinitely more subtle. One kind of fear was that if America bungled in Vietnam, allied leaders friendly toward Washington might lose some influence relative to their internal opponents who were less friendly to Washington or might slowly become more susceptible to Communist diplomatic pressures or saber rattling. Another fear was that rulers in the Kremlin or Peking, more adventurous than some of their colleagues, might be tempted to push harder or gamble. Taken to extremes, such analogies break down. Used cautiously as operating principles of politics, they are sound. It should not be forgotten that the domino principle was easy to understand and to explain to the American people. It was a vivid way of bringing the security issue home to America. The analogical force of historical, current, and psychological-legal dominoes blotted out— more, made irrelevant—the peculiarities of Vietnam.

If there was to be a reassessment of the reasoned faith in the importance of not losing Vietnam, it could not come from a foreign policy review within the upper echelons of the executive branch. These men were locked into their perspectives. It could come only from the outside, from the intrusion of the domestic political process.

CHAPTER SEVEN

Domestic Political Stakes

In March 1947 the White House called in congressional leaders for
a prepublic briefing on President Truman's Greek-Turkish aid program,
soon to be anointed the Truman, or Containment, Doctrine. Secretary
of State George C. Marshall led off with a justification of the program
on grounds of humanitarianism and loyalty to Great Britain. Under
Secretary of State Dean Acheson felt the briefing was not going over
and later recorded how he stepped in.

In the past eighteen months, I said, Soviet pressure on the Straits, on Iran,
and on northern Greece had brought the Balkans to the point where a highly
possible Soviet breakthrough might open three continents to Soviet penetra-
tion. Like apples in a barrel infected by one rotten one, the corruption of
Greece would infect Iran and all to the east. It would also carry infection to
Africa through Asia Minor and Egypt, and to Europe through Italy and
France, already threatened by the strongest domestic Communist parties in
Western Europe. . . .

A long silence followed. Then Arthur Vandenberg said solemnly, "Mr.
President, if you will say that to the Congress and the country, I will support
you and I believe that most of its members will do the same."[1]

Truman took the anti-Communist bit in his mouth and ran with it. It
was an effective sales pitch. For the next twenty years, one administration after another sold it as a national security policy to Congress, the
press, and the public; an approach based on power politics alone
probably would have failed.

If anything, Truman was slightly behind the times in seeing this.
Key legislators and influential journalists, like some of Truman's own
more suspicious advisers, had come to this conclusion sooner. They

1. Dean Acheson, *Present at the Creation: My Years in the State Department*
(Norton, 1969), p. 219.

already had grown impatient with the doctrine of "patience and firmness" that characterized the early postwar years. In the face of what they saw as Soviet challenges in Europe, they wanted a stronger American stand. Any and all opposition to communism became good politics.

But while Truman administration leaders were selling strenuous anticommunism to the public, they were not about to buy that brand for themselves unreservedly. The Asian mainland in general and China in particular would be the exception, they thought. Chiang Kai-shek's regime, corrupt and ineffectual, seemed hopeless against the discipline and dedication of Mao Tse-tung's Communists. Hundreds of millions of dollars in U.S. aid and equipment had not prevented the steady erosion of Chiang's position. By 1949 Truman had had enough and wanted to end the aid program. But Senator Arthur Vandenberg, Truman's Republican foreign policy mainstay on the Hill, objected, refusing to accept responsibility for the last push that would make a Communist victory possible. Truman continued a modest aid program, but within months Chiang's regime was driven to the island of Formosa. Acheson's China white paper, designed to explain that "China's fall" was beyond American control, found a hostile reception in Washington.[2]

With the outbreak of the Korean War some months later, the chain reaction—from hints of Communist subversion to Red-baiting to treason—had been triggered. Senator Joseph McCarthy, Republican of Wisconsin, embodied it all. Communism cannot vanquish Americanism, he preached, without complicity from the enemy within and without and the support of others who were soft on communism. The spy trials of Judith Copeland, Klaus Fuchs, Julius and Ethel Rosenberg, and none other than Acheson's close friend, Alger Hiss, fed a climate that was nothing short of hysterical. For three years until McCarthy's censure in mid-1954, McCarthyism gripped American life with fear. An accusation was enough to destroy a career. Eisenhower dismissed over 2,000 civil servants on security grounds. Although McCarthy's career ended with his censure, the Red scare he helped to create did not. No one, particularly liberals and civil servants, could forget. What had been the psychology of strategic anticommunism had become the pathology of domestic anticommunism.

Acheson's remark to Anthony Eden in 1952 that Indochina should

2. See Acheson's testimony in *Military Situation in the Far East,* Hearings before the Senate Committee on Armed Services and Committee on Foreign Relations, 82 Cong. 1 sess. (Government Printing Office, 1951), pt. 3, pp. 1667–2291.

not be lost "without a struggle" brought back shades of Vandenberg's "last push."[3] After China, who would end an aid program to a beleaguered country or propose a coalition government with Communists? Who would do less than whatever was necessary to prevent defeat? Who would take the responsibility of letting Indochina become another China? This was not the kind of political context that would encourage, condone, or even permit the rethinking of American strategic stakes in Vietnam. From 1950 on, there was no perceived conflict between the requirements of international and domestic politics. The political imperatives of both required a non-Communist Vietnam.

But American politics are curious. The imperative that the United States could not afford to lose all of Vietnam to communism by force did not come as neatly packaged as in an executive branch policy paper. Senators, congressmen, journalists, scholars, and pollsters—all would have their own audiences and political bases and their own way of expressing that goal.

The Two Phases of American Policy on Vietnam

The politics concerning the American stakes in Vietnam passed through two phases. Phase I began in 1950 with the start of the U.S. aid program to Indochina and ended in the summer of 1965 with massive American involvement on the way. Phase II went from the beginning of this escalatory process through the stalemated war, Johnson's political withdrawal, and the start of the Paris peace talks.

In Phase I the issue of the U.S. stakes in Vietnam/Indochina arose mostly indirectly in debates about economic and military aid programs and about limited war. Indochina became a specific target of public debate on only four occasions: at the times of Dien Bien Phu, the Laotian crisis, the Diem coup, and the Tonkin Gulf incident. The dominant, or consensus, group during this period was composed of most of the liberal Democrats and internationalist Republicans in Congress, the establishment press (most notably the *New York Times, Washington Post, Time,* and *Newsweek*), policy-oriented academicians, and researchers from think tanks such as RAND. Their support for U.S. aims in Vietnam was in a sense incidental to their larger concerns about

3. Acheson quoted in *Full Circle: The Memoirs of Anthony Eden* (Houghton Mifflin, 1960), p. 92.

aid and limited war. They were the ones who for years had carried the burden of justifying the military and economic assistance programs as a way of promoting economic development and stable democracies and as a substitute for direct American military involvement. They were also the ones, however, who argued that if these programs were threatened or jeopardized by Communist aggression or Communist-inspired insurgency, there was virtue in fighting a limited war to avoid fighting a wider war later or in having credible alternatives to thermonuclear retaliation. From time to time they did criticize corruption, waste, bureaucratic red tape, and the lack of support from allies, but all these ills, so they argued, were to be expected and forgiven in pursuit of the main objective. To them, Vietnam was a test case of their beliefs.

The bulk of the opposition to these goals and objectives during this first phase was centered in a small but influential band of southern Democrats and midwestern Republicans in Congress (especially Senator Robert Taft) and in conservative journals such as the *Chicago Tribune*. This combined group, of course, never advocated turning Vietnam over to the Communists. Quite the contrary, no other group surpassed them in devotion to the anti-Communist cause. But the catch was that they did not think that aid would pave the way to stability in the underdeveloped world. To them, aid was a handout, a waste. Similarly, they felt that limited war was a waste of American military technological superiority, a squandering of resources, and a misguided effort to fight the Communists at times and places of Communist choosing. Their way to stop the advance of communism was to threaten the "sources" of aggression in Moscow and Peking. The Communists, to this group's way of thinking, were fundamentally bullies and cowards, and if the United States would only show determination and willingness to wield its nuclear superiority, the Communists would back down. The members of this group did not offer any alternative solution for the Indochina problem, but neither would they take it as a challenge. Unlike the liberals, however, they did not make a major political battle on the Indochina issue. In 1961 they were joined in their opposition by a handful of renegade Democrats who believed the American position in Indochina to be hopeless, if not immoral.

In Phase II, liberals and conservatives began switching sides, and Vietnam itself became the central issue of political debate, leading in time to a general questioning of American cold war foreign policies. The dominant group in this phase consisted of conservatives who felt they had to support the flag, once committed; center Democrats who still held to the containment consensus and wanted to support the President; and others who did not develop their beliefs but simply averred that America had "to stick it out." The small but growing opposition to policy came from the ranks of former war aim supporters, liberal Democrats and Republicans, who in varying degrees now urged deescalation and negotiations but not explicit abandonment of the commitment. By 1967 they were joined by some conservatives who wanted to get out of Vietnam if Washington was not prepared to win the war. Indeed these conservatives went further than the liberal war opponents by actually advocating American withdrawal.

The following two sections are intended primarily to give a flavor of the various positions taken on U.S. policy toward Vietnam by the press, Congress, and the general public during the period 1950–68.

Phase I, 1950–65: The Moderate-Liberal Consensus Backs the Administration

During Phase I the establishment press rarely broke stride with the administration. A *New York Times* editorial on May 9, 1950, held that "Indochina occupies a critically strategic position—if it falls to the Communist advance the whole of Southeast Asia will be in mortal peril." The *Times* from then on would support both the domino theory and the importance of U.S. aid to France in the common struggle. Articles in *Time* magazine were written on the assumption of Indochina's importance, and *Newsweek* was quite explicit about the raw materials of the area being "essential to Western industrial civilization."[4] According to all three publications, it was vital not to "lose" Vietnam to communism, and to this end they all seemed favorably disposed toward intervention in 1953–54. The *Washington Post* went so far as to editorialize unfavorably on Eisenhower's statement that he believed it was necessary for him to gain congressional approval before going to war.[5] The conservative *Chicago Tribune*, on the other hand, editorialized against American involvement, charging on September 1, 1953, that the administration was duping the American people by claiming that "in opposing the native rebellion, it is fighting Communism."

Senators and congressmen were also beginning to carve out positions

4. "The Decisive Moment," *Newsweek*, April 12, 1954, p. 30.
5. *Washington Post*, March 12, 1954.

for themselves in Indochina. On the conservative side, Democratic Senator Edwin C. Johnson of Colorado intoned in early 1954 that "this present crusade to send troops to Indochina, with its uncalculated cost for an uncalculated result, is the most foolhardy venture in all American history. . . . To drift, drift, drift, drift closer and ever closer to this flaming candle, like some silly enchanted moth, is almost too fantastic for human minds to contemplate." And at the same time, the young Democratic Senator from Massachusetts, John F. Kennedy, agreed with Senator John Stennis's position that "the security of French Indochina is vital to the security of all Southeast Asia," and said "the war should be continued and brought to a successful conclusion."[6]

Later, at the start of the Dien Bien Phu crisis, Senator Kennedy would say: "I am frankly of the belief that no amount of American military assistance in Indochina can conquer an enemy which is everywhere and at the same time nowhere, 'an enemy of the people' which has the sympathy and covert support of the people." Kennedy saw the same difficulties if American troops took over from the French. These later remarks were greeted with approbation by the Republican Majority Leader, Senator William Knowland of California, and by Republican Senator Everett Dirksen of Illinois, both of whom took the opportunity to warn against another Korea.[7] The whole thrust of the debate in the Senate was critical of the "Indochina mess," but very few spoke out against military intervention. As the situation evolved, most senators and congressmen marched to the tune of "united action."

In the aftermath of the Geneva Conference, charges of an administration sellout became the vogue. In his *Newsweek* column, "Washington Tides," Ernest K. Lindley said "the partition of Indo-China may be a Munich."[8] While the *Times* and the *Post* considered the accords the best Washington could get under the circumstances, they called on the administration to take immediate steps through the proposed collective security organization to save the rest of Asia, including especially South Vietnam.[9] The *Tribune*, on the other hand, editorialized

6. Senators Johnson and Kennedy are quoted in *Congressional Record*, vol. 100, pt. 4, 83 Cong. 2 sess. (1954), p. 5477; and pt. 3, p. 2904.

7. For Kennedy, Knowland, and Dirksen statements, see ibid., pt. 4, pp. 4673, 4675, 4679.

8. Ernest K. Lindley, "Washington Tides: A Breathing Spell," *Newsweek*, August 2, 1954, p. 20.

9. See *New York Times*, July 22 and 23, 1954; and *Washington Post*, July 23, 1954.

that the proposed SEATO Pact would soon get the United States into trouble.[10]

Democratic Senator Mike Mansfield of Montana called Geneva "profoundly humiliating."[11] Most senators believed the United States should remain in Indochina to prevent further Communist gains there, and they generally supported the creation of a regional defense organization for Southeast Asia. A number of conservatives in the Senate, however, saw it otherwise. Speaking for them in proposing an aid cut to the Mutual Security Act, Democratic Senator Russell Long of Louisiana argued that there was "no longer a war going on in Indochina," which by "all indications" would "go Communist," and that therefore the aid was a waste.[12]

While the period of confusion that followed Geneva was reflected in the public debate, the thrust of where different groups wanted the United States to go remained clear. On May 15, 1955, the *Times* told its readers that the United States had no alternative to supporting Diem in Vietnam, and into 1956 *Time* and *Newsweek* rode the bandwagon. Diem, they said or implied, was a "strong man" and a "miracle worker." The *Post* even insisted that North Vietnamese violations of the Geneva agreements gave Diem grounds for not holding the 1956 elections throughout Vietnam.[13] Only the *Chicago Tribune* espoused an anti-administration position, charging on May 3, 1955, that U.S. aid was being wasted in Vietnam.

As for Congress, in early 1955 two senators, Mike Mansfield and Hubert Humphrey, along with prominent public personages such as Francis Cardinal Spellman, initiated a save-South-Vietnam drive by supporting the Diem campaign. Mansfield said the United States had no choice but to support Diem. Humphrey accused U.S. policymakers of "wavering," saying that this was no time for "weakness," and that the fall of the South would threaten the rest of Asia.[14]

No legislator and none of the elite press raised one word in protest when the July 1956 date for holding these elections passed. The backing for the anti-Communist Saigon regime even seemed to convert such former skeptics as Senator Knowland, who now urged support of Diem

10. *Chicago Tribune*, July 23, 1954.

11. *Congressional Record*, vol. 100, pt. 8, 83 Cong. 2 sess. (1954), p. 9998.

12. Ibid., pt. 11, pp. 14514–15.

13. *Washington Post*, May 11, 1955.

14. For Mansfield and Humphrey statements, see *Congressional Record*, vol. 101, pt. 4, 84 Cong. 1 sess. (1955), p. 5291; and pt. 5, pp. 6101–04.

to avoid a "continental Dien Bien Phu."[15] And into 1959, as conservatives began to charge misuse and waste of American funds by the Diem government, Senator J. William Fulbright rose to the defense, saying that although the aid may have been misused, it was still vital to continue in the long-term interests of the Free World.[16]

It was the burgeoning crisis in Laos in 1959, however, that once again brought the American stakes in Indochina into full scope. Since early 1958 the elite press had been building up the Laos story, portraying Laos as the victim of Communist violations of the Geneva accords of 1954. In an editorial on May 10, 1961, the *New York Times* called it a "stepping-stone" for a Communist takeover and added in an editorial on May 12 that the situation "involved not merely Laos and South Vietnam, but the danger that all Southeast Asia will fall to the Communists and that general war will be ignited." After the signing of the Declaration on the Neutrality of Laos on July 23, 1962, in Geneva, the establishment press closed ranks behind the President's settlement but with no expressions of congratulations. The position of the elite press and the liberal senators, similar to that of many conservatives, was that a coalition government and neutralization meant losing. And when the Laotian accords quickly broke down and fighting resumed, the air was filled with "I told you so's." But as the *Washington Post* editorialized on April 15, 1963: "Is Laos worth the risk or the cost of a Viet-Nam?"

Congressional comment about the situation shifted from the serious questioning of 1954 to mildly questioning acceptance of the U.S. involvement. On September 4, 1959, Mansfield lamented that Laos was teetering on the brink of collapse and asked "What is the answer?" The administration's answer was more of the same, for these countries had to be saved from Communist control. The next day Democratic Senator Thomas Dodd of Connecticut went further: "We will do whatever becomes necessary to defend Laos, including armed intervention." On September 7 Mansfield asked the questions about Laos that were soon to become popular with respect to Vietnam as well. Who is running American policy in Laos? Have the Defense Department and the CIA been given too much responsibility? Where are the President and the State Department? The conservatives, again, were not interested in these questions. Democratic Senator Olin Johnston of South Carolina

15. Ibid., vol. 102, pt. 8, 84 Cong. 2 sess. (1956), p. 11215.
16. Ibid., vol. 105, pt. 11, 86 Cong. 1 sess. (1959), pp. 13983–84.

said: "Laos is incapable of defending itself . . . and I presume we will wind up sending Marines and other men and equipment to save Laos. It will be the stark tragedy of Korea all over again." Senator Allen Ellender called further aid to Laos an "utter waste."[17] The initial consensus on commitment was indeed equivocal, but the equivocations eroded quickly as the commitment became established.

Throughout 1960 and 1961 men such as the influential Republican congressmen Walter Judd of Minnesota and Paul Findlay of Illinois stressed the theme that the fall of Laos to communism meant the collapse of the rest of Southeast Asia.[18] They joined two liberal Republican senators, Kenneth Keating and Thomas Kuchel, who urged that in Laos there was a Communist threat to the whole world and that the United States should not let itself be pushed around there.[19] In 1961, as the prospect of settling the crisis through a coalition government was being booted about, Republican Senator Styles Bridges of New Hampshire said: "I very sincerely hope that the U.S. position, as it develops, will be that we will . . . see to it that avowed Communists are not taken into any free neutral government in Laos."[20] This had been the conservative Republican line since the China debate in the 1940s, but this time such men as Dodd and Keating joined in. Their refrain was that a coalition government in Laos would inevitably turn Communist. The negative reaction toward a coalition government was coupled with a similar reaction to the neutrality of Laos. Allen Ellender supported the proposal for Laotian neutrality in 1962; senators Hugh Scott, Frank Lausche, and Strom Thurmond opposed it.[21]

While the focus was on Laos, three important forces were shaping the domestic political debate on Vietnam during the 1961–63 period. The first was the buildup of Vietnam's importance in the elite press. Typical *New York Times* editorials stated that the United States could not shirk the struggle in Vietnam. An editorial on March 12, 1963, de-

17. For the stands taken by the administration and the various senators mentioned in this paragraph, see ibid., pt. 14, pp. 18042, 18204, 18307, 18387; and pt. 15, p. 19338.

18. Ibid., vol. 106, pt. 7, 86 Cong. 2 sess. (1960), p. 8389; and vol. 107, pt. 7, 87 Cong. 1 sess. (1961), p. 8587.

19. Ibid., vol. 107, pt. 4, pp. 4706–08.

20. Ibid., p. 5115.

21. Ibid., vol. 108, pt. 1, 87 Cong. 2 sess. (1962), p. 1249; and pt. 2, pp. 1633, 2751.

clared: "The cost [of saving Vietnam] is large, but the cost of Southeast Asia coming under the domination of Russia and Communist China would be still larger." On August 31 of the same year the *Times* opposed a neutralist solution in South Vietnam as leading to Communist domination.

The *Washington Post* followed a similar path. On April 7, 1961, the *Post* editorialized: "The United States has a major interest in the defense of Viet Nam, not only because of the vast amounts of economic and military aid . . . but also because American prestige is very much involved in the effort to protect the Vietnamese people from Communist absorption." *Post* editorials in 1962 and 1963 began to ask "What is the United States really doing in Vietnam?" On August 4, 1963, the *Post* gave its own answer. In reaction to a White House prediction that U.S. military personnel would be out of Vietnam by 1965, the *Post* attacked the White House for its "low estimation of the political maturity of the American people." It added: "If the survival of an independent South Viet-Nam is important to the Free World and to the United States, the American people are equal to the sacrifices its defense will require."

Time and *Newsweek*, while less evocatory than the *Times* and the *Post*, also ran articles that assumed that the United States must get more involved in order to save South Vietnam from communism. Even that bastion of leftist ideology, the *New Republic*, while calling for a reexamination of the U.S. commitment to Vietnam and for efforts to achieve the neutralization of that country, could still editorialize in 1962: "Instead of letting the situation in Saigon 'segashuate' to the advantage of the Communist-led National Liberation Front, the President should in our view act decisively now to regroup non-Communist political forces while time remains." And it could even carry on in 1963 with its version of the domino theory: "Neither the US nor its allies can take a military defeat on the Southeast Asian mainland without imperiling the fragile edifices of non-Communist states there and dangerously jeopardizing the major prize in Asia, or perhaps in the world: India." To the *New Republic*, the U.S. *intent* in Vietnam was defensible; what was not defensible was America's continued support of Diem.[22]

A second force shaping the domestic political debate from 1961 to

22. See the comments of the editors in "Lost Ground in Laos," *New Republic*, May 21, 1962, p. 4; and "Dispensable Diem," ibid., April 20, 1963, pp. 3–4.

1963, and one equally important, especially for the practitioners of foreign policy, was the outpouring of books and articles in popular and scholarly journals by academicians and think tank researchers extolling the virtues and necessity of fighting guerrilla wars.[23] These defense intellectuals, as they were called, argued that limited wars could be fought and controlled without escalation to a wider war. Indeed, they argued, the only way to avoid a wider war through miscalculation in a nuclear age was to fight limited wars. This would demonstrate U.S. determination and will to the adversary, while at the same time reducing the risks. When Hubert Humphrey rose on the Senate floor on October 10, 1962, to say that the United States must learn to conduct guerrilla war, he spoke for the overwhelming majority of the Congress.[24]

The third of these forces was the liberal Democratic cry for reforms in South Vietnam. It became routine in 1962 and 1963 for liberals to attack the Diem-Nhu regime. The grounds for attack were easy to find—corruption, misuse of aid, religious persecution—all reaching a crescendo when pictures of Buddhist monks going through the rite of self-immolation appeared on TV and the front pages of newspapers. The liberals' solution, as it had been in China during General Joseph Stilwell's mission in World War II, was to make future American aid conditional on reforms. While the ranks of liberal critics in Congress swelled on this issue, only a handful of senators—Wayne Morse, George McGovern, and Ernest Gruening—questioned the basic American commitment to South Vietnam. On September 26, 1963, McGovern said: "The U.S. position in Vietnam has deteriorated so drastically that it is in our national interest to withdraw from that country our forces and our aid."[25] When Diem was finally overthrown, the liberals' expressions of sorrow for his murder could not hide their sense of relief. While conservatives worried aloud about future Saigon stability, most legislators and the elite press felt that the change offered "new hope."

The year 1963 also marked the beginning of any significant public

---

23. See, for example, D. M. Condit, *A Counterinsurgency Bibliography* (Department of the Army, Special Operations Research Office, 1963); Franklin Mark Osanka, ed., *Modern Guerrilla Warfare: Fighting Communist Guerrilla Movements, 1941–1961* (Free Press, 1962); and Lieutenant Colonel T. N. Greene, USMC, ed., *The Guerrilla and How to Fight Him* (Praeger, 1962). President Kennedy contributed a foreword to the latter volume.

24. *Congressional Record*, vol. 108, pt. 17, 87 Cong. 2 sess. (1962), pp. 22957–59.

25. Ibid., vol. 109, pt. 13, 88 Cong. 1 sess. (1963), p. 18205.

concern about the situation in Vietnam. At first the basic trend was toward public support of increased military measures to escalate the war, as demonstrated by jumps in the positive ratings given to the Kennedy and Johnson administrations on their handling of the war after specific, highly publicized events. After the Diem coup the ratings went from 38 percent in September 1963 to 57 percent in November. The retaliatory bombing of North Vietnam after the Tonkin Gulf incident was followed by a jump of 30 percentage points, from 42 percent in July 1964 to 72 percent in August.[26]

Much of the political debate in 1964 was skewed by the forthcoming presidential contest between Barry Goldwater and Lyndon Johnson. The debate did not turn on the issue of the American commitment to Vietnam but on whether Goldwater was likely to turn guerrilla war into nuclear war. Editorials in the elite press for the most part supported the administration and were still cautiously optimistic. To the *New York Times,* even though the situation in Vietnam was deteriorating, the United States could yet salvage something from it. According to an editorial on May 21: "Total victory is beyond our grasp; but it is within our capability to deny victory to the Communists—and increase their costs and difficulties. If we demonstrate that we will make whatever military and political effort that requires, the Communists sooner or later will also recognize reality." And the *Washington Post* editorialized on June 1 that the United States must continue to show in Vietnam that "persistence in aggression is fruitless and possibly deadly."

Even Senator Fulbright, in his famous "old myths and new realities" speech of March 1964, maintained that the United States had "no choice" but to continue resisting Communist aggression in Vietnam.[27] Although this speech was roundly attacked by many of Fulbright's colleagues, they did not challenge his discussion of the Vietnam situation. Similarly, the debate over the Tonkin Gulf Resolution in August found senators Morse and Gruening totally alone in asserting that whatever the rights and wrongs of this particular incident, the United States had gone too far in Vietnam. In that debate Fulbright not only told Senator Gaylord Nelson that Johnson had no intention of escalating the war but also told Senator John Sherman Cooper that the resolu-

26. Albert H. Cantril, *The American People, Viet-Nam, and the Presidency* (Princeton University Press, 1970), pp. 2–3.

27. *Congressional Record,* vol. 110, pt. 5, 88 Cong. 2 sess. (1964), p. 6232.

tion was in effect a blank check for the President to do whatever was necessary.[28]

Up to this point, then, the dominant moderate-liberal consensus had been large enough to include just about everyone. U.S. policy toward Vietnam was in fact discussed in a manner that could virtually be called a nondebate. The main theme, that the United States could not afford to lose, was being echoed over and over again by Congress, the press, and, later, the man on the street. Only the fringes of opinion were challenging the administration, and most of those who disagreed based their arguments on different assumptions. So there was never any real debate, any meeting of the minds, any searching analysis of the reasons *behind* U.S. involvement, any posing of the really vital questions that could ignite a meaningful debate. On the conservative side, those who opposed U.S. involvement in Vietnam based their arguments mainly on financial and strategic grounds: the United States was overextending its commitments abroad, draining its resources, dangerously weakening itself militarily—and for what? At the other end of the political spectrum, but representing an even smaller segment of public opinion, some groups, mostly Marxist-oriented (such journals as the *Monthly Review,* for example), also opposed U.S. involvement, mainly on moral and ideological grounds. But to most people in the dominant consensus, there was no need to answer these kinds of arguments. They could be easily ignored or glossed over because they represented the views of such a small minority. There was no need to doubt the importance of the United States preventing the forced Communist domination of Vietnam. It was self-evident. As long as the containment doctrine reigned as the premise of policy, a strong incentive for opposing commitment in Indochina was lacking, except for the issue of *costs,* which never became immense until after 1965, and by then additional costs were measured against sunk costs. The investment trap did not cause, nor does it fully explain, American perseverance, but it did condition the margins of tolerance.

By 1965, however, observers began to witness a breakdown of the political lines about war aims in Vietnam that had held for fifteen years. The margins of tolerance were shifting. Liberals were moving into opposition and conservatives were turning into supporters (though

28. For the opinions of the senators during this period, see ibid., pt. 14, pp. 18350, 18398–410, 18416–30, 18442–71.

their support, it should be noted, usually took the form of pressures for further escalation). The political picture became confused and the changes halting, with congressmen and journalists often jumping back and forth across the lines in response to presidential initiatives.

Phase II, 1965–68: Liberals Challenge the Administration; Conservatives Rally Round the Flag

Signs of this change had begun to appear in the more liberal press as far back as 1963. The *New Republic* was in the vanguard, making the point as early as September 1963 that since Diem would most likely never change, and that since Ho Chi Minh was the stronger of the two leaders and could probably better prevent Chinese expansionism into Vietnam, it seemed "increasingly possible that Ho is America's best bet." While continuing to oppose unilateral U.S. disengagement from Southeast Asia in 1964, the editors of the *New Republic* argued strongly for the convening of an international conference to reach a settlement. But by early 1965 a tone of frustration and anger had replaced the cautious support of the earlier years. The editors sharply criticized the administration for persistently deluding itself about the nature of the civil war in Vietnam and about the strength and staying power of the Vietcong. They called for deescalating the conflict and holding negotiations.[29]

Then the united front of the more centrist establishment press began to crumble. The *New York Times*, in contrast to its own previous clarity about war aims, started asking the administration to clarify *its* war aims. Later, in early 1966, without having officially altered its own position, the *Times* initiated the theme that "the U.S. should not be the party to this conflict that leaves any stone unturned in an honorable effort to achieve negotiations."[30] In addition, the *Times* gave no further support to escalation of the war. *Newsweek* found its commentators split down the middle, with outside columnists such as Emmet John Hughes and Walter Lippmann maintaining that Washington had no vital stakes in Vietnam and its own editors continuing to call the struggle vital to

29. See "Reunifying Vietnam," *New Republic*, September 14, 1963, p. 5; "Vietnam—A Way Out," ibid., October 3, 1964, p. 5; "Vietnam—What Now?" ibid., December 5, 1964, pp. 3–4; "The White Paper," ibid., March 13, 1965, pp. 5–7; and "Talking of Peace," ibid., April 17, 1965, pp. 5–6.

30. *New York Times*, March 6, 1966.

American security.[31] A *Time* essay on May 14, 1965, read: "Despite all its excruciating difficulties, the Vietnamese struggle is absolutely inescapable for the U.S. in the mid-6os—and in that sense, it is the right war in the right place at the right time."[32] *Time* went on in subsequent years to raise questions about the level of American involvement and about Lyndon Johnson's credibility but basically remained sympathetic to Johnson's plight throughout. Not until December 22, 1967, did another *Time* essay urge the President to "consider a peace that would arrest Communism instead of smashing it."[33]

The *Washington Post* seemed to stay by the administration's side longer and more steadfastly than the others. Following the administration's line, an editorial on December 16, 1965, charged that the problem was that "North Vietnam will not leave the South alone," and that "this is the root of the trouble." Again following administration arguments, on February 16, 1966, a *Post* editorial charged that the senators who had given the go-ahead in Vietnam with the Tonkin Resolution "are not right to attack the Government for abandoning that policy." If the senators wanted to change it, the editorial concluded, they could vote to do so. Other editorials praised Johnson and insisted that the American people would support him. But by the summer of 1967 the *Post* had taken a new middle-ground position of questioning both the escalation of the war and the critics who did not seem to care about defeat. In the words of an editorial on November 14, 1967: "It is too late for the President to expect silence as the necessary ingredient of his strategy. That he now needs a minimum of dissent and all the cooperation he can get is obvious. He is not likely to get it by denigrating or disdaining those whose questions are relevant and whose anguish is real."

What of the more conservative journals? Although the *U.S. News and World Report*, for one, had been editorializing vigorously in the

---

31. See, for example, Walter Lippmann, "War in Asia," *Newsweek*, March 14, 1966, p. 23; Kenneth Crawford, "C'est la Guerre," ibid., April 18, 1966, p. 53; Lippmann, "Turning Point in Vietnam," ibid., April 25, 1966, p. 17; Crawford, "The Political War," ibid., p. 30; Lippmann, "The Other Trouble," ibid., May 9, 1966, p. 23; Emmet John Hughes, "A View of Vietnam," ibid., May 30, 1966, pp. 22–23; Lippmann, "The Misconceived War," ibid., June 6, 1966, p. 19; and Arnaud de Borchgrave, "A Dissent from the Dissenters," ibid., pp. 32–33.

32. "Viet Nam: The Right War at the Right Time," *Time*, May 14, 1965, p. 30.

33. "What Negotiations in Viet Nam Might Mean," ibid., December 22, 1967, p. 22.

early 1960s against the "wave of defeatism" in U.S. policy vis-à-vis the
Communists and against the U.S. tendency to let the Soviet Union
"push us around," it had made few specific editorial references to Vietnam. Beginning in 1966 it came down hard on the side of victory in
Vietnam and urged the administration to do more: "What the U.S. is
doing in Vietnam is the most significant example of philanthropy . . . in
our times . . . for if imperialism becomes dominant, the right of peoples
everywhere to determine their own form of government will be for-
feited."[34]

If there was a dividing line in Congress, it came in the summer of
1965. On June 15 Senator Fulbright blasted the administration's policy,
saying that it was clear that "a complete military victory in Vietnam
. . . can in fact be attained only at a cost far exceeding the requirements
of our interests and our honor" and "that the unconditional withdrawal
of American support . . . would have disastrous consequences." U.S.
policy, Fulbright said, should be "one of determination to end the war
at the earliest possible time by a negotiated settlement involving major
concessions by both sides."[35] Senator Richard Russell, whose stand reflected the investment trap–sunk costs rationale, had told the Georgia
Association of Broadcasters on June 13:

It was a mistake to get involved there in the first place; I have never been
able to see any strategic, political, or economic advantage to be gained by
our involvement. Most of the military leaders whose knowledge and advice
I most respect have warned repeatedly that it would be an incalculable mistake for the United States to engage in a full-scale land war on the Asian
mainland. . . . Whether or not the initial decision was a mistake is now moot.
The United States does have a commitment in South Vietnam. The flag is
there. U.S. honor and prestige are there. And, most important of all, U.S.
soldiers are there.[36]

From that point Democratic liberals moved to the attack and conservatives and Republicans generally moved to support the President.
It was a confusing and curious phenomenon—a Democratic President's
most ardent foreign policy supporters being his chief critics on domestic affairs. Charges and countercharges ensued. The President's sup-

34. See the editorial opinions of David Lawrence in "The Wave of Defeatism,"
U.S. News and World Report, May 16, 1960; "The 'Cold War' Is a War," ibid., November 25, 1963; and "Vietnam—Our Great Philanthropy," February 21, 1966,
p. 112.
35. *Congressional Record*, vol. 111, pt. 10, 89 Cong. 1 sess. (1965), p. 13656.
36. Ibid., p. 13677.

porters labeled the liberals "isolationists" and "appeasers." The liberals labeled the supporters of the President "cold warriors." The Vietnam debate was opening up a wider debate on the fundamental principles of U.S. foreign policy, on the consensus that had governed since 1947.

Except for occasional questions posed by members of Congress, the press, and the universities, the debate for the most part had *still* not focused on the fundamental aims of U.S. policy in Vietnam or challenged the basic assumption that the United States could not afford to lose in Vietnam. It was a debate about strategy and tactics, with the liberals calling for deescalation and negotiations and the conservatives calling for escalation and victory. Those in the middle who essentially went along with the President's policy did not receive much of a hearing as the press concentrated its reports on the extremes. And when Democratic senators Eugene McCarthy and Robert Kennedy went on the attack against the President's policies in 1967 and 1968 and started to challenge Johnson in the Democratic presidential primaries, and when such Republicans as the influential congressman from Wisconsin, Melvin Laird, withdrew their support from the President's policies, debate over Vietnam policy became indistinguishable from the contest for political power.

The liberals called for a negotiated settlement, for cease-fires, for UN intervention, for Asian conferences, for dealing with the Vietcong, for truly free elections, and for a coalition government. All these proposals sidestepped the fundamental issue of whether the war should be ended by a total American withdrawal—that is, with what would appear to be an American defeat. With the exception of observers such as George Kennan and Hans Morgenthau and a growing number of formerly obscure academicians, this was true of the Fulbright Foreign Relations Committee hearings of 1966 and 1967 and of the televised teach-ins.

Liberal opponents of the war seemed to assume that Hanoi would negotiate on these terms if only Johnson would offer them. Reading through the lines of the liberal critique, however, it could be argued that they were saying that the United States should lose at the negotiating table, not on the battlefield—though they did not say this explicitly. Two leading war opponents, Richard Goodwin and Arthur Schlesinger, Jr., both put the arguments in that vein. In their books of this period they took as a given that the United States should not be driven from the battlefield but could negotiate a peace if the President only tried.[37] The conservatives, on the other hand, kept up the call for less restraint in the use of military force.

This shift in domestic political attitudes on the war was reflected to a lesser extent in public opinion polls. In February 1965, 67 percent of the American people approved the broader air strikes begun in that month. In May 59 percent felt the United States should continue the bombing of the North (21 percent said the bombing should be stopped; 20 percent were undecided). In July of the following year 70 percent approved the bombing of oil storage dumps in Haiphong and Hanoi (with only 11 percent opposed). Yet only a minority favored extending the ground war into North Vietnam or widening the war with the possible use of nuclear weapons.[38] That the pro-administration stance of the public was eroding, however, became evident in the increasing percentages of Americans who felt that "the U.S. had made a mistake sending troops to fight in Vietnam":[39]

	Percent
August 1965	24
March 1966	25
November 1966	31
February 1967	32
July 1967	42
October 1967	46

The shock of the Communist Tet offensive in February and March 1968 had a profound effect on domestic political debate on Vietnam. A *New York Times* editorial on February 25 said that the time had come for the United States to realize that escalation is illogical and urged a halt in the bombing. A *Time* article, referring to the increasing sentiment for withdrawal in the United States, said that this "indicates that for the U.S., 1968 has brought home the awareness that victory in Viet Nam—or even a favorable settlement—may simply be beyond the grasp of the world's greatest power." A *Time* essay five months later

37. See Richard N. Goodwin, *Triumph or Tragedy: Reflections on Vietnam* (Vintage Books, 1966); and Arthur M. Schlesinger, Jr., *The Bitter Heritage: Vietnam and American Democracy, 1941–1966* (Houghton Mifflin, 1967).

38. Cantril, *The American People*, p. 3. In January 1965 a Harris poll showed that less than one-fourth of the public favored extending the ground war with the North. In December 1965 another Harris poll found that two-thirds of the public believed that President Johnson was right in not going all out in winning a military victory in Vietnam and using atomic weapons.

39. Ibid., p. 4.

suggested a compromise solution: "The Vietcong might lay down their arms, for example, compete with ballots rather than bullets, and eventually take over South Viet Nam by democratic means. The U.S. would not like that, but it could live with it because it would not represent a defeat for the U.S. stand against armed aggression or a victory for the Maoist doctrine of wars of liberation."[40] The editors of the *New Republic* put it more bluntly: "The US will have to face frankly the prospect that Vietnam will be reunited, though not soon, and will then profess one or another of the fairly numerous brands of communism on the market."[41] On the other hand, the editor of *U.S. News and World Report* wrote: "Firmness is . . . more than ever necessary. The American Government has made a pledge to the people of South Vietnam which it cannot forsake." The magazine also continued the line that "if we fail in the Vietnam war, this can only open the way for the Communists to infiltrate and subvert the governments of small nations."[42]

Congress reflected the lingering ambiguity of the establishment press in its desire to somehow achieve U.S. goals in Vietnam but end the war as soon as possible. Senator Mike Mansfield said on March 26, 1968, that no additional troops should be sent to Vietnam above the 525,000-man ceiling already announced by President Johnson; he called for "the adoption of a patient strategy . . . to hold a strong and tenable position at no more than the present level of American involvement, for purposes of negotiating a decent and honorable settlement of the conflict."[43] Even this oldest of Senate liberal doves on Vietnam, in simply opposing troop *increases,* was in one sense endorsing the status quo. Most members of Congress welcomed the news of the forthcoming peace talks; House Speaker John W. McCormack said on April 3, for example: "It represents a step forward." However, that there was still a strong conservative sentiment to prosecute the war more vigorously was shown in the speeches on the same day by Democratic Senator Mike Monroney of Oklahoma and Republican Senator Strom Thurmond of South Carolina. Monroney suggested: "It is possible that Hanoi is using this as a propaganda ploy while continuing or stepping

40. "The War: Debate in a Vacuum," *Time,* March 15, 1968, p. 14; and "How the War in Viet Nam Might End," ibid., August 9, 1968, p. 22.

41. "Talks in Paris," *New Republic,* May 18, 1968, p. 7.

42. See the editorial opinions of David Lawrence in "The 'Doves' Cry Peace, Prolong the War," *U.S. News and World Report,* February 5, 1968, p. 92; and "The Curse of Defeatism," ibid., March 25, 1968, p. 100.

43. *Congressional Record,* vol. 114, pt. 6, 90 Cong. 1 sess. (1968), p. 7661.

up military activities." Thurmond urged: "We should continue preparations to prosecute the war at an increased rate so that the enemy will know swift retribution will follow any default."[44]

At the time of the Tet offensive, public opinion in Washington was in a fluid state. Positions on the war were drifting toward either the dovish or hawkish ends of the spectrum. Tet caused the drifts to jell, to set at once harder and more confused lines of debate. An American Institute of Public Opinion poll conducted in February 1968 found that 31 percent of the respondents wanted to end the war "even though it might sooner or later allow the Vietnamese Communists to take over," and 62 percent felt that the United States should "fight on until a settlement can be reached which will insure that the Communists do not get control of South Vietnam." A Harris poll conducted in December 1968 confirmed these results but in posing another question caught some of the growing ambivalence. Asked to choose between ending the fighting or pursuing a "satisfactory political settlement," 43 percent favored the former, 30 percent the latter, and 21 percent thought both were "equally important."[45]

The days of only modest opposition to U.S. war aims were over. But it was of major significance—particularly to U.S. policymakers, even as late as the end of 1968—that the bulk of the American people still wanted to avoid losing in Vietnam.

Practical Political Considerations

As has been shown, with the exception of a growing body of liberals who thought Washington could negotiate a Communist takeover without the appearance of losing and a small group of conservatives who always wanted to fight a different kind of war, the dominant American political belief about Vietnam until at least 1968 was that the U.S. objective of preventing a Communist victory was the right one. Four presidents were the main propagators of this view. They used the "bully pulpit" to educate Americans about Vietnam's importance. Most of the available evidence indicates that these presidents believed in the goal, but in the event that any began to doubt it, a host of other

44. For the reactions of the speaker and the senators, see *Congressional Quarterly: Weekly Report*, vol. 26 (April 5, 1968), p. 716.

45. Results of the polls are in Cantril, *The American People*, p. 13.

very practical considerations would have served to keep their feet to the fire.

Domestic politics is a dirty phrase in the inner sanctums of foreign policymaking. Officials involved in such policymaking rarely write memos with any explicit reference to domestic affairs and seldom even talk about them except to friends and newspapermen off the record. There is an American myth that politics stops at the water's edge, that the normal play of partisan competition and dissent gives way to unity in matters of foreign policy. This myth is unfounded but nevertheless potent. It creates great pressure to keep one's mouth shut, to think and speak of foreign affairs as if they are something above mere politics, something sacred. After all, so the myth runs, foreign policy deals with the security of the nation and is no subject to use for narrow political advantage. Therefore, the storehouse of booty on postwar foreign policymaking, the Pentagon Papers, possesses only a handful of memorandums on how Vietnam strategy was related to American politics. What few there are (some to the President and some from assistant secretaries to their bosses) deal with the matter in only the most glancing way. They make such points as (1) a bombing halt is necessary at this time to lay the basis for a future buildup of ground forces, or (2) escalation of the bombing without a peace overture would strain public support for the war. Such assertions without elaboration, scanty memoir material, and dubious interviews are all that is left to scholars seeking to analyze those political imperatives.

Imperatives against Losing

But substantial inferential evidence shows that the practical political imperatives against losing, as well as the shared foreign policy beliefs against losing, were very much on every president's mind.

First, presidents were worried that losing would open the floodgates of domestic criticism and that they would be attacked for being "soft on communism" or just plain soft. Sensitivity on this issue was widespread among politicians, journalists, and civilian defense intellectuals. But the presidents and those who served in the executive branch of government suffered particularly acute feelings of uneasiness. Only Eisenhower seemed to have and to feel relative immunity from these charges, except to the degree that he felt the need to placate the Taft wing of his party in his first years in office. But even he paid a certain price for this self-confidence by purging civil servants of "questionable" loyalty, by his silence in the face of McCarthyism, and by his ringing anti-Communist rhetoric. Dulles's preoccupation with right-wing attacks was legendary. One of Eisenhower's speechwriters reported that the President said about Dulles: "Well, I know how he feels, but sometimes Foster is just too worried about being accused of sounding like Truman and Acheson. I think he worries too much about it."[46] The irony was that in terms of public rhetoric it would have been a difficult task to surpass the anticommunism of Truman and Acheson. This fact in turn pointed to another realization. No amount of subsequent purity on the anticommunism issue could wash away earlier "slips." Once tagged the "Red Dean," always the Red Dean.

No one sensed his personal vulnerability on this matter more than Kennedy. During the Laotian crisis in 1961, as Arthur Schlesinger has written, "Kennedy told Rostow that Eisenhower could stand the political consequences of Dien Bien Phu and the expulsion of the west from Vietnam in 1954 because the blame fell on the French; 'I can't take a 1954 defeat today.' "[47] The Kennedy team simply did not want to be charged with being soft. Toughness was the image on which men such as Robert McNamara and McGeorge Bundy prided themselves. It would have been difficult to reconcile this pride with any show of weakness in foreign affairs.

Johnson, ever mindful of Truman's plight after the loss of China, wanted to avoid a similar fate. But Johnson's anxiety on this score probably went beyond looking over his right shoulder and may well have extended to looking right in front of him at the Kennedy team he had inherited and kept. As Tom Wicker wrote:

> Johnson had inherited those men with the war. Their reputations were, in many ways, staked on its success, and they were both personally, and in principle, committed to its continuance and even more to its intrinsic rightness. The war could hardly be liquidated or compromised without a corresponding repudiation of at least some of these men . . . , none of whom showed any inclination whatever to declare the war a lost cause, or one not worth the cost and effort.[48]

Members of the Kennedy team, in this view, would be in the front line in charging Johnson with being soft.

46. Quoted in Emmet John Hughes, *The Ordeal of Power: A Political Memoir of the Eisenhower Years* (Atheneum, 1963), p. 112.

47. Arthur M. Schlesinger, Jr., *A Thousand Days: John F. Kennedy in the White House* (Houghton Mifflin, 1965), p. 339.

48. Tom Wicker, *JFK and LBJ: The Influence of Personality upon Politics* (William Morrow, 1968), p. 249.

Second, the presidents were concerned that their influence would be dissipated by having to answer these charges. Past experience with domestic reaction to anything that resembled a gain for communism showed what could be expected. Congress and the press would not talk about anything else. The "loss" would be the number one news story for months at the least. The administration would have to try to show that the loss was not a defeat. Almost invariably it would not be successful in this line—especially in a situation such as Korea, where the truce did not bring an end to tension, and in Laos, where the neutral coalition government quickly broke down. The administration would consume invaluable time and energy in its own defense. That was the key point. The President would be on the defensive, making him look vulnerable to attack on other issues as well.

Third, the charges and the political vulnerability would in turn endanger the President's legislative program, especially by alienating the conservative leadership in Congress. Truman's domestic legislation, like Kennedy's, foundered from 1950 to 1952 largely because of the foreign difficulties of these administrations. The President's general weakness put the conservatives, who were opposed to most of these domestic programs anyway, in a stronger position to stonewall. And as Lyndon Johnson never tired of telling his circle of intimates, the conservatives held the reins of power in congressional committees. The liberal doves, he believed, would not be a problem. They would vote for his Great Society program regardless of their opposition to the war. But the conservatives would grasp any opportunity to defeat that program. Johnson's tack was astute, but it did not work either. While he did not lose the war in Vietnam, he did lose the battles for adequate funding of his Great Society.

Fourth, losing meant jeopardizing election prospects for the President and his party. It meant losing power. Academicians and public opinion experts have helped in a way to perpetuate the view that national security affairs are not significant in elections. They have demonstrated through careful interviewing and statistical analyses that foreign policy simply is not a salient issue to the voter and that whatever the President says and does goes. Presidents have known better. They could recall the prominence of the Korean War issue in the 1952 campaign; the issues of the missile gap, Cuba, Quemoy and Matsu, and U.S. influence abroad in 1960; and the effect of Goldwater's hard-line views on his 1964 candidacy. They knew that elites, people who pack influence in all walks of life, pay attention to foreign affairs. They have seen themselves as being attacked and supported at home for what they are doing abroad. Being professional politicians, the presidents have known or sensed that votes rest on a tapestry of feelings of which war and peace issues are an important part. Citizens may not single out national security affairs as the basis for their votes, but such affairs are inevitably an important part of their overall impression of how the President is doing his job. Moreover, media leaders make up their minds about the President by taking account of national security, and the overall mood they convey to the public affects public appraisals of the man in the White House.

Truman's popularity had plummeted to a 20 percent approval rating in 1952, largely over China and Korea. Kennedy's remarks to Mansfield and O'Donnell about his waiting for the right time after the 1964 campaign before withdrawing from Vietnam at least showed his awareness of the effect the loss of Vietnam would have on his candidacy. Johnson's popularity rating, which had gone below 35 percent in 1968, even threatened his renomination by the Democratic party, let alone his chances of being reelected. But since this election factor is often exaggerated, it should be remembered that neither Eisenhower in his second term nor Johnson after his 1964 landslide used the strength of electoral successes to ease the United States out of Indochina.

Fifth, the presidents were also concerned that backing away from Vietnam would undercut domestic support for a responsible U.S. world role. Presidents and their advisers often advanced the argument that fighting limited wars was a test of the ability of American democracy to carry out an effective foreign policy. Did the American people have the stuff to bear the burdens and frustrations of fighting a complex limited war? Did they understand that fighting a limited war would reduce the chances of a wider war or a nuclear war later? Could they see that the notion of victory in the nuclear age was both illusory and dangerous? Truman was the first to make this case during the Korean War. Kennedy repeatedly included this theme in his speeches, specifically with regard to Vietnam, wondering whether the American people could fathom the threat—"It was much easier when people could see the enemy from the walls," he said—and have the patience.[49] Would the people in their frustration and impatience turn back to pre–World War II isolationism? That was the underlying and driving concern. Allies

49. Quoted in Theodore C. Sorensen, *Kennedy* (Harper and Row, 1965), p. 510.

and adversaries would come to believe that the United States was once again withdrawing from the world. They would miscalculate the ultimate willingness of the American people to prevent aggression. The risks of direct superpower confrontation and world war would be increased.

From the vantage point of the 1970s, this sounds melodramatic, if not macabre. But it was the accepted wisdom in the 1950s and 1960s. Whether public opinion would have swung so dramatically from acceptance of internationalism back to isolationism now seems improbable. To those who were weaned on the origins of both world wars, the nightmare did not seem so remote.

Behind all these concerns was the fear of igniting a right-wing reaction—the nightmare of a McCarthyite garrison state. This haunted the liberal presidents and their supporters. Although the number of liberals holding public office in Washington and throughout the land at least equaled the number of conservatives, liberals nevertheless assumed that the country was fundamentally conservative. Scratch beneath the surface, they believed, as elitist progressives have in the past, and it will reveal ugliness, intolerance, and disregard for basic freedoms. In time the liberals hoped to lead the people back to grace. But in the meantime, they opined, liberal power rested on a fragile base of economic self-interest that could be readily washed away by appeals to baser emotions like extremist patriotism.

Thus liberals were always running scared when it came to national security. But were they right? Was the country fundamentally conservative?

The evidence is mixed. The following facts support the assumption that U.S. politics were essentially conservative: professional politicians widely held this view, the influence of conservatives in Congress was disproportionate to their numbers, President Truman did suffer because of China and Korea, and public opinion polls from 1954 until well after Tet did show that a majority of Americans were against losing South Vietnam to communism. Other facts, however, provide contrary evidence: the alternatives in the Vietnam polls (unilateral withdrawal or annihilation of the enemy) gave the respondent little choice; other polls showed a majority against losing to communism but also showed a majority against using U.S. forces to accomplish this; polls on foreign affairs usually follow the presidential lead; the President's overall popularity was dropping in the polls; and the majority of Americans eventually did turn against the war, or at least against fighting at any sizable costs in lives and dollars, with a majority in 1971 finally also saying that the war was "immoral." Perhaps the answer is that the presidents and the liberals were right about the conservative thrust of American politics until March 1968, and that it took the experience of the Vietnam War to change public tolerance of losing countries to communism. But more important, the presidents did nothing to try to change these realities. On the contrary, they pandered to them.

CHAPTER EIGHT

The Bureaucracy and the Inner Circle

With few exceptions, the presidents and their senior civilian advisers acted as if it were vital not to lose Vietnam to communism. With few exceptions, legislators, journalists, academicians, and other opinion leaders behaved the same way. And then there was the bureaucracy—the analysts and the operators in the CIA, the military, the Office of the Secretary of Defense, and the Foreign Service officers. What was their role in framing American stakes in Vietnam? The CIA, allegedly out to foil the worldwide Communist plot; the military, purportedly itching to do battle; and the Foreign Service officers, supposedly attaching undue importance to everything happening abroad—were they the motor force behind the basic U.S. commitment? Did they succeed in capturing and converting their bosses, the cabinet and subcabinet officials, and staffers in the White House to the faith, or was it the other way around?

Career Services and U.S. Stakes in Vietnam

To separate the beliefs of the professionals in the national security bureaucracy from their political bosses (the leaders and appointees down to the assistant secretary level) is not an easy chore. Memorandums signed by the bosses are often written by members of the staff. Sometimes the boss tells the staff man what to write and sometimes he does not. The problem of differentiation is particularly acute in the State Department or in the civilian sector of the Defense Department where political appointees directly supervise the work of the professionals. Nevertheless, planning papers do occasionally appear that bear the name and imprint of an individual Foreign Service officer and his colleagues. Speculation can proceed on that basis. The task is more manageable with respect to the CIA where the superiors usually are former professionals. The views of professional military men on policy matters, however, are quite distinguishable from the views of their political superiors. The latter often dictate what the military should do but are loath to dictate what the military should recommend. The military have a strong record of insisting on stating their views in untarnished form. This in turn makes it relatively easier to generalize about military positions. The policymaking side of the military is more of an institution with interchangeable parts than is the Foreign Service, which can be more affected by the accident of a specific person holding a specific job. The reader of formal military position papers (the Joint Chiefs of Staff memorandums) cannot help but be struck by the remarkable similarity of their wording over a long stretch of time.

Looking at the career professionals as distinct from the political leadership opens some interesting avenues of analysis. While the picture that emerges is not black and white, it does puncture several myths.

The CIA

There are two CIAs—the operational side and the analysts. From the end of 1954 on, the operators' mission was to create a viable South Vietnam to resist communism. With seemingly limitless funds and unaccountable vouchers, they sought and never stopped seeking that goal. The analysts, or the paper-writing estimators, were in another world, the Washington policy world, and it is this CIA that is of concern in this chapter. (There are actually third and fourth branches of the CIA—directorates of administration and of science and technology—but the clandestine and analytical branches are those that engage most attention.)

The CIA analysts make only rare appearances as a separately identifiable organization in the classified documents that establish U.S. stakes in Vietnam. The agency, along with other elements of the intelligence community, was a party to all those National Security Council papers in the 1950s that laid out the domino theory. Presumably the CIA analysts in the working groups either actively propagated the domino theory or posed no objections to it. These NSC papers stressed domino effects in Asia but mentioned repercussions elsewhere as well.

In 1961 the National Intelligence Estimate (NIE) of August 15 stated that nations such as Thailand, Cambodia, Burma, Indonesia, the Philippines, and Nationalist China had "to some extent" watched events in Laos "as a gauge of US willingness and ability to help an anti-Communist Asian government stand against a Communist 'national liberation' campaign." The NIE continued:

They will almost certainly look upon the struggle for Vietnam as a critical test of such US willingness and ability. All of them, including the neutrals, would probably suffer demoralization and loss of confidence in their prospects for maintaining their independence if the Communists were to gain control of South Vietnam. This loss of confidence might even extend to India.[1]

The NIE, unlike earlier policy papers, did not go on to mention any repercussions in the Middle East or Europe or with respect to Soviet-American relations.

In 1964, however, the intelligence community came close to actually negating the domino theory. President Johnson asked: "Would the rest of Southeast Asia necessarily fall if Laos and South Vietnam came under North Vietnamese control?" On June 9 the Board of National Estimates, dominated by the CIA, answered.

With the possible exception of Cambodia, it is likely that no nation in the area would quickly succumb to communism. . . . Furthermore, a continuation of the spread of communism in the area would not be inexorable, and any spread which did occur would take time—time in which the total situation might change in any number of ways unfavorable to the communist cause.

The estimate granted that the loss of South Vietnam and Laos "would be profoundly damaging to the U.S. position in the Far East" in terms of U.S. prestige and credibility in meeting other commitments. It also granted that Peking's prestige would be on the rise at the expense of the more moderate Soviet Union. But these admissions held less significance than the two basic caveats of the estimate. One was that the prognosis above was a "worst case," that is, outright Communist victory and the virtual elimination of the U.S. presence in Indochina; a fuzzier, or neutralist, case would not be as severe. A second caveat reminded the President that even in the worst case "the extent to which individual countries would move away from the U.S. towards the Com-

1. *The Pentagon Papers: The Defense Department History of United States Decisionmaking on Vietnam,* Senator Gravel ed. (Beacon Press, 1971), vol. 2, p. 72.

munists would be significantly affected by the substance and manner of U.S. policy in the period following the loss of Laos and South Vietnam."[2] To state the obvious, Washington would still retain leverage in Southeast Asia as well as in the rest of the world.

President Johnson never again asked for the CIA's opinion. It was generally known, however, that most CIA analysts held to this view even after the U.S. force buildup in 1965. Indeed while these analysts continued to grant the likelihood of adverse reactions in Asia to an American defeat in Vietnam, they also tended to delimit any significant aftereffects to Laos and Cambodia.

What explains the change in the CIA position before and after 1964? One possible explanation for the earlier position is the force, character, and control of the director of central intelligence, Allen Dulles. Like his brother, Allen Dulles was avidly anti-Communist, an exponent of the domino theory, and not hesitant about impressing his views on his staff. There is no specific evidence, however, that Dulles did so with respect to Vietnam. A second explanation is that in 1964 the agency's analysts saw a different world—an internally weak and divided China, unlikely to risk military ventures, and an ever-deepening split between Moscow and Peking. The first explanation, though only a hypothesis, probably has some validity and the second almost certainly does.

The Military

The U.S. military also altered its position but in the opposite direction from the CIA. From before World War II the dominant wing of the military emphasized Europe and relegated Asia to secondary status in American national interests. Opposition to land warfare in Asia was widespread among military professionals, especially after Korea and especially in the Army. Those military men anxious to use force envisioned air and naval action as the only logical action against Asian communism. The Joint Chiefs of Staff affirmed these priorities in the late 1940s, ending up by proposing a defense perimeter identical to that proposed in the Acheson "perimeter" speech in January 1950, and the Army resisted military involvement vigorously in 1954–55 in both Indochina and the Taiwan Strait.

The JCS seemed to break stride on only one occasion in early 1950. Asked for a strategic assessment of Southeast Asia, the chiefs replied

2. Quotations in this paragraph can be found in ibid., vol. 3, pp. 178–79.

in a memorandum to the secretary of defense on April 10 that the mainland states of that area "are at present of critical strategic importance to the United States" because of the requirement to stockpile strategic materials acquired there, as well as the need to defend the "line of containment."[3] This assessment can be explained, however, as a throwaway. The chiefs were merely asked if Indochina was important, not if it was worth fighting for.

Once the military had to confront the probability of actually fighting in Indochina, they reverted to form. Admiral Arthur Radford, chairman of the Joint Chiefs of Staff, and Air Force Chief of Staff Nathan Twining proposed intervention by air but were not supported by the other three members of the JCS. General Matthew Ridgway of the Army, in particular, rose in opposition, emphasizing the enormous costs and the uncertainty of the result. When the intervention issue again peaked in May of that year, the chiefs handed down a formal position in their memorandum to the secretary. *"Indochina is devoid of decisive military objectives and the allocation of more than token U.S. armed forces in Indochina would be a serious diversion* of limited U.S. capabilities."[4] After the Geneva Conference when the French began pulling out, the chiefs resisted a U.S. takeover of responsibility. "U.S. military support to that area," they said, "including the training and equipping of forces, should be accomplished at low priority and not at the expense of other U.S. military programs."[5]

But by 1961, if not sometime before, the chiefs did an apparent somersault. In the fall of 1961 they supported General Maxwell Taylor's troop requests but *only* if the United States became firmly committed to the defense of Indochina. By the following January it was a new ball game with the old domino theory. The JCS memorandum read in part:

The immediate strategic importance of Southeast Asia lies in the political value that can accrue to the Free World through a successful stand in that area. Of equal importance is the psychological impact that a firm position by the United States will have on the countries of the world—both free and

3. Ibid., vol. 1, p. 364.
4. Ibid., p. 511 (emphasis in original).
5. "Retention and Development of Forces in Indochina," Memorandum for the Secretary of Defense, September 22, 1964, *United States–Vietnam Relations, 1945–1967*, Study prepared by the Department of Defense for the House Committee on Armed Services, 92 Cong. 1 sess. (Government Printing Office, 1971), bk. 10, pt. V.B.3, p. 758.

communist. On the negative side, a United States political and/or military withdrawal . . . would have an adverse psychological impact of even greater proportion, and one from which recovery would be both difficult and costly.[6] They recommended that the United States "take expeditiously all actions necessary to defeat communist aggression in South Vietnam."

Two questions arise. If the chiefs believed that Indochina was "devoid of decisive military objectives" in the earlier period, why did they agree to, or at least raise no objections about, the NSC documents written in the 1950s that came to precisely the opposite conclusion? And why did the chiefs alter their position from low priority to high priority by 1961?

The answer to the first question comes from understanding the difference in the chiefs' mode of operation during the 1950s and during the 1960s. In the earlier decade, and particularly in the Eisenhower years, the JCS did not take formal stands on political issues. If the White House or the State Department pronounced an area vital on political grounds, the chiefs would salute and be quiet. They would only pose objections if asked for their military judgment. This was precisely what happened in October 1954 when the military and Secretary of State Dulles disputed the issue of taking over the training of Vietnamese forces from the French. The chiefs finally relented in this tug-of-war and agreed to send a training mission to Vietnam if "political considerations are overriding."[7] In the 1960s the chiefs were directed by Presidents Kennedy and Johnson to express their views on the political aspects of strategic problems as well as the strictly military ones.[8]

As to the change in the military position, it was real but equivocal. What the chiefs actually had been arguing in the 1950s was that the United States should not squander its resources, particularly manpower, in peripheral and limited wars on the rimland of China. These were the "wrong wars." To some, such as Radford, the right war would be against China and with no restrictions on weapons. To others, such as Ridgway, conflict with China was to be avoided as a draining distrac-

6. "The Strategic Importance of Southeast Asia Mainland," Memorandum for the Secretary of Defense, January 13, 1962, ibid., bk. 12, pt. VI.A, p. 448.

7. "Development and Training of Indigenous Forces in Indochina," Memorandum for the Secretary of Defense, October 19, 1954, ibid., bk. 10, pt. V.B.3, pp. 773–74.

8. The original directive was in NSAM 55, extracts of which are quoted in Maxwell D. Taylor, "Military Advice: Its Uses in Government," Vital Speeches, vol. 30 (March 15, 1964).

tion from the central confrontation with the Soviet Union in Europe. As long as China, which the JCS considered the source of aggression, remained untouched, war in Asia was bound to be both diversionary and inconclusive. Thus in 1952 the chiefs both reaffirmed their position against the use of U.S. ground forces in Indochina and opposed "acceptance of all of the military commitments . . . without a clear understanding that the United States must be accorded freedom of action . . . in the undertaking of appropriate military action to include action against Communist China itself."[9] This was again the chiefs' majority position in May 1954 when they argued that if the United States were to intervene, it "should adopt the concept of offensive actions against the 'military power of the aggressor,' in this instance Communist China, rather than the concept of 'reaction locally at the point of attack.' "[10]

By 1961 the chiefs were willing to fight the "wrong war" for complex reasons. General Lyman Lemnitzer, chairman of the JCS, and Army Chief of Staff General George H. Decker were not reincarnations of Ridgway. Reverses in Cuba, tension in Berlin, and retreat in Laos made Vietnam seem more important as a cold war testing ground to civilian leaders, and the JCS agreed. Insurgencies also looked more manageable by the use of limited resources, and Kennedy and Taylor's enthusiasm for fighting counterinsurgency wars had been successfully communicated, if not force-fed, to the ranks. Furthermore, by this time it was the U.S. military, not the French forces, that were in Vietnam. It was by then an American show, and the U.S. military had an established stake in it. Finally, the U.S. military were typically military in being cautious about initial involvement; but once in, their axiomatic goal was to do everything they could to win.

Foreign Service Officers

The position of the Foreign Service officers is by far the most difficult to encapsulate. More so than the CIA or the military, the views of Foreign Service officers on American stakes in Vietnam were fragmented and varied. In the period before the fall of China and before the Korean War, there was a clear split between Foreign Service officers with European careers and those with Asian careers. The former felt that

9. "United States Objectives and Courses of Action with Respect to Communist Aggression in Southeast Asia," Memorandum for the Secretary of Defense, March 3, 1952, ibid., bk. 8, pt. V.B.2, p. 489.

10. *Pentagon Papers*, vol. 1, p. 510.

Indochina was important to Washington because it was important to Paris. The Asian specialists, on the other hand, believed that the main American interests in Asia lay in propagating nationalism and in opposing colonialism. The Asian specialist's position on Indochina in most cases was the same as his position on China—promote compromise between the Communists and other nationalists and stay out militarily.

What happened after 1950 is well known. The old Asia hands were purged in the fury of McCarthyism. The new Asia hands, properly cowed and submissive, not only toed the anti-Communist line but were second to none in proposing the use of American force to oppose the advancement of communism. This all reached its peak during the Dien Bien Phu crisis when many Foreign Service officers were urging American intervention, while many military officers were rejecting it.

By 1961 the flavor began to change somewhat. Sterling Cottrell, chairman of the State Department's Vietnam Task Force, who accompanied Taylor and Rostow in their mission in the fall of 1961, raised some serious doubts about the American commitment. In remarks appended to the Taylor report, Cottrell wrote: "Since it is an open question whether the GVN can succeed even with U.S. assistance, it would be a mistake for the U.S. to commit itself irrevocably to the defeat of the communists in SVN." Cottrell argued that "the Communist operation starts from the lowest social level. . . . Foreign military forces cannot themselves win the battle at the village level. Therefore, the primary responsibility for saving the country must rest with the GVN." Cottrell concluded that "the U.S. should assist the GVN. This rules out any treaty or pact which either shifts ultimate responsibility to the U.S. or engages any full U.S. commitment to eliminate the Viet Cong threat."[11] His objections notwithstanding, Cottrell supported the Taylor-Rostow recommendations.

Another Foreign Service officer, Paul Kattenburg, made similar arguments in August 1963 in NSC discussions about the possible removal of Diem. When no one else dared to raise the question of American withdrawal from Vietnam, Kattenburg did. According to the minutes of the meeting, Kattenburg said the situation was tumbling irretrievably downhill and that "it would be better for us to make the decision to get out honorably."[12] He was vigorously opposed in this by another career

11. Ibid., vol. 2, p. 96.
12. Ibid., p. 742.

Foreign Service officer, Ambassador Frederick E. Nolting. Although Kattenburg was a veteran of ten years' service in Vietnam, his career, like his assessment of the war, was downhill from then on.

Less dramatically but in the same vein, another group of Foreign Service officers began to raise questions and suggest alternatives in the fall of 1964. Their input was to an NSC working group charged with reviewing next courses of action in South Vietnam. Early in the group's deliberations a State Department draft paper set the tone: "We must consider realistically what our over-all objectives and stakes are, not just what degree of risk and loss we should be prepared to make to hold South Vietnam." The group went on to suggest that South Vietnam and Laos in 1954 never "acquired the international standing of such former targets of Communist aggression as Greece, Iran and South Korea" and that Indochina was unique in having a "bad colonial heritage." Strikingly, it added:

The basic point, of course, is that we never thought we could defend a government or a people that had ceased to care strongly about defending themselves. . . . And the overwhelming world impression is that these are lacking elements in South Viet-Nam.[13]

In a later State Department paper the same working group worried about domestic reaction to the loss of Southeast Asia leading to "a wave of 'isolationism.' " But the group challenged the idea that this loss would adversely affect the U.S. position in other areas of the world where "either the nature of the Communist threat or the degree of U.S. commitment or both are so radically different than in Southeast Asia that it is difficult to assess the impact." Like the CIA estimate that appeared at the same time, the State Department paper said that the repercussions of the loss of Vietnam obviously depended on what else Washington was prepared to do in other countries. The domino theory, it concluded, would apply "if, but only if, Communist China . . . entered Southeast Asia in force and/or the United States was forced out of South Vietnam, in circumstances of military defeat."[14]

How typical these State Department papers of November 1964 were of the general Foreign Service officer view of Vietnam can only be guessed. It seems there was a high-low split in the department. High-ranking Foreign Service officers generally placed a high value on Viet-

13. Ibid., vol. 3, p. 217.
14. Ibid., pp. 219–20.

nam, while mid-ranking staff officers seemed skeptical, in effect opposing all they felt they could, given the feelings of their superiors. These
mid-career Foreign Service officers found support from a new group
of China experts who viewed Chinese ambitions more modestly than
the China hands of the fifties.

Once the American military effort got rolling in 1965, the hesitations
and doubts of these Foreign Service officers appeared to evaporate.
The stakes were not there from the start, they argued, but were there
now—assumptions that Foreign Service officers accepted and did not
question. Like the military, they felt it was now time to get on with the
job of managing the problem.

Pressure from the Top and from the Bottom

The account above is not intended to give a picture of the bureaucracy up in arms against high American stakes in Vietnam. Many, if not
most, of the career professionals probably both shared and prompted
the beliefs of their political leaders about the serious repercussions of
losing Vietnam. But whatever thoughtful and steady questioning of
stakes occurred either in the executive branch or outside did come from
the bureaucracy: from Asian specialists in the State Department up to
1950, from the military up to 1961, from sundry Foreign Service officers
in the 1961–65 period, and from CIA analysts beginning in 1964.

Those professionals who were doing the questioning did it through
the back door. They were not saying that the loss of Vietnam would not
hurt but were raising doubts about the feasibility of accomplishing U.S.
objectives. Thus in the early 1950s the military were arguing that the
costs of American intervention would be almost prohibitively high, the
well of demands almost bottomless, and the ultimate results uncertain.
In the early 1960s a few Foreign Service officers wondered aloud
whether Diem or any pro-American regime was salvageable no matter
what the U.S. level of effort. At times some professionals even went so
far as to suggest that there might be other lines of defense after the
fall of Vietnam. What they were suggesting in effect was that a Communist victory in Vietnam would make a difference in other countries,
but it would be a difference without an operational consequence. The
Thais, for example, would be more inclined to accommodate with
China, but given the Thai leaders' self-interests, their drift from the

United States had to be limited. When it came to protecting their regime, they would still have to turn to Washington.

Skeptics Lacked Influence

While parts of the bureaucracy expressed these doubts and alternatives, they did not press them. Like some of the comparably skeptical conservative senators, the dissenting bureaucrats would state their opinions but not make a fight. The CIA analysts saw themselves as evaluators, not as a pressure group. The military did not feel that establishing political goals was their business. After the fall of China, Foreign Service officers knew that they were not supposed to challenge shared images about stopping communism and that they were not supposed to argue with their bosses. These particular "don'ts" held for every career service but were particularly true in the Foreign Service. Paradoxically, precisely because the military is a highly disciplined organization, dissent on policy is somewhat tolerated. It is tolerated because loyalty is assumed once the order is given. In the Foreign Service, however, the dissenter's judgment, if not loyalty, can come into question. In addition, the axiomatic need to demonstrate strength stood in the way of vigorous opposition. No one wanted to appear weak. Everyone had to show he was prepared to use force.

Yet it is doubtful that the skeptical professional would have been influential had he pressed his views. In large part this was because the shared images were too strong. In part, too, it was because professional opinions varied at any one time, and superiors could pick and choose. Naturally, they would choose those views that confirmed their own judgments. Superiors also found it relatively easy to ignore or manage bureaucratic dissenters on policy matters. For example, William Sullivan, a high career official in the State Department, wrote a memorandum in 1964 to William Bundy about a public statement the former had prepared that expressed the importance of Indochina in stopping an aggressive China. "It is a first draft," Sullivan wrote, "and contains a number of statements which would probably give trouble to our 'specialists' but which ought to be able to be said, with some editing, as a political document."[15]

But there were other more revealing reasons for the doubters' lack of influence. One was that bureaucratic dissents missed the point. Al-

15. Ibid., p. 594.

though the judgment of the military that Indochina was devoid of strategic importance may have been accepted as right, the political leadership worried, not about Chinese hordes spilling across Asia, but about the diplomatic and internal political fallouts in other countries. And although skeptical Foreign Service officers may have been seen as right about being able to handle the fallout in these other countries in the early 1960s, the political leadership had to worry about the fallout at home in the United States. The bureaucrats' concerns lacked the breadth of those of their political leaders. A second reason was that bureaucrats calculated risks differently from their superiors; the expert may be right or he may be wrong, but the risks of being wrong loom much larger at the top than at the bottom. Bureaucrats could talk all they wanted about taking risks and managing the consequences of defeat; political leaders had to take the risks and suffer the consequences.

Accordingly U.S. stakes in Vietnam were determined from the top down, not the bottom up. The top—the inner circle of President, White House staff, and cabinet-level appointees—remains the only place where military, diplomatic, and domestic political imperatives are brought together, and this is what made the stakes in Vietnam so high. Thus Truman and Acheson in 1950 settled the split between the European-oriented and the Asian-oriented State Department specialists in favor of backing France to the hilt. Thus Eisenhower and Dulles pursued their preconditions for American intervention in 1954 despite the obvious reluctance of most of the Joint Chiefs. Thus President Kennedy, Maxwell Taylor, and Robert Kennedy geared up the bureaucracy to tackle wars of national liberation, instituting counterinsurgency seminars for State Department personnel, glorifying the Green Berets, and otherwise making fashionable what they regarded as a necessity. Thus in the 1964 policy review all the principal cabinet and subcabinet officials except George Ball decided in favor of the military, who called the Vietnam struggle vital, and against those Foreign Service officers who questioned the American stakes, and directed that the paper on U.S. objectives be rewritten to accord with the Joint Chiefs' views. Administration leaders thereafter neither condoned nor encouraged such policy reviews for fear of leaks to the press. The bureaucracy gave these decisions generalized support. More important, most bureaucrats did not oppose them.

Bureaucratic Reinforcement of Aims

Basically the bureaucracy reinforced given stakes in two ways. First, it was charged with and faithfully carried out the task of developing and rationalizing the imperatives against losing Vietnam. Second, it was asked to develop and did develop "viable solutions" to the problems of its leaders. These solutions or plans made the objectives of the leaders look realizable.

After the American presence in Vietnam was increased and the programs enlarged, however, the bureaucracy became like a cement block in the trunk of a car—it added tremendous momentum. Cautious, sometimes resistant, in the earlier years, each bureaucratic organization then had its own stakes. The military had to prove that American arms and advice could succeed. The Foreign Service had to prove that it could bring about political stability in Saigon and build a nation. The CIA had to prove, especially after the Bay of Pigs fiasco, that it could handle covert action and covert paramilitary operations lest.it chance having its operational missions in general questioned. The Agency for International Development (AID), like the State Department and the military, had to prove that pacification could work and that advice and millions of dollars in assistance could bring political returns. While this momentum effect took hold of the military earlier than the rest of the bureaucracy, by 1965 almost all career professionals became holier than the Pope on the subject of U.S. interests in Vietnam. This sounds like the investment trap, but it was a trap that affected the bureaucrats *implementing* policy much more than it affected the leaders who were *making* it.

Of equal importance, the bureaucracy set the subobjectives and made the plans and strategies for the war. The one exception was the strategy for bombing North Vietnam. This remained in the hands of the political leadership. Otherwise the bureaucracy, particularly in the field, found itself relatively free to construct its own programs and shape the war. Thus Westmoreland and the Joint Chiefs essentially made the decision to fight the big-unit war with multibattalion sweeps into enemy base areas, with free fire artillery zones, with widespread tactical bombing, and with high civilian and military casualties. Military, State Department, AID, and CIA professionals decided how to run the pacification, refugee, counterintelligence, and other programs.

Foreign Service officers and military men could establish the tone for relations between Washington and Saigon—to decide whether to pressure for reforms or merely to get along.

Like the Frankenstein monster, the bureaucracy, once created, became uncontrollable. It played only a subsidiary role in setting the basic American commitment in Vietnam but a central role in shaping the war itself.

Concluding Observations about the Imperative Not to Lose

Those who led the United States into Vietnam did so with their eyes open, knowing why and believing they had the will to achieve their objective of not losing Vietnam to communism. The deepening involvement was not inadvertent but mainly deductive. It flowed with sureness from the perceived stakes and attendant high objectives. U.S. policy displayed remarkable continuity of objectives.

Each postwar President inherited previous commitments, and each extended the commitments somewhat and enlarged direct American involvement in the war. Each administration from 1950 to 1969 believed that it was necessary to prevent the loss of Vietnam (and after 1954, South Vietnam) by force to communism. The reason for this varied from person to person, from bureaucracy to bureaucracy, over time and in emphasis. A few men argued that Vietnam had intrinsic strategic military and economic importance, but this view never prevailed or was overridden by psychological criteria or the Munich analogy. The reasons rested on broader international, domestic, and bureaucratic considerations.

The notion of arrogance of power played its part as well. Leaders of the world's first superpower were bound to have a sense of being Prometheus unchained, able to do anything—or at least to have the right to try to do anything and to meddle. But U.S. leaders went beyond this. They had convinced themselves that meddling was their obligation and responsibility. They seemed to think they would be held responsible at home and abroad for anything that went wrong in the world.

Writers will continue to look for the single cause or even the single most important cause of the U.S. commitment. Some will continue to argue that it was really all domestic politics, that the strategic justifications amounted to little more than rationalizations for the fear of losing domestic power at the next election. Others will say it was really the bureaucracy's fault—machismo getting out of hand. Still others will say it was really the military-industrial complex, the vested economic interests, out to gain a dollar at public expense. None of these explanations can be substantiated. More important, they miss the point. Obviously all the pressures mentioned were present. The point is that they were all pushing in the same direction, reinforcing each other: (1) strategically, the belief that the world was filled with dominoes leading ultimately back home—the psychology of strategic linkage, which also linked realpolitik with the liberal humanitarian impulse to save other people from tyranny; (2) domestically, the belief that one could not hold power or do anything constructive with his power or maintain political stability or retain support for a U.S. world role if he were to be held responsible for losing a country to communism—the pathological form of anticommunism; and (3) bureaucratically, the tendency to go along, adding momentum by proving that the organization could get the job done.

Almost all U.S. leaders—in the executive branch, in Congress, journalists, scholars, think-tankers, businessmen, and labor leaders—shared the psychology of strategic linkage and the pathology of anticommunism. Only a few voices in the wilderness were raised in opposition. Even as late as mid-1967 most critics were arguing that the United States could not afford to lose or be "driven from the field," that the real problem was the bombing of North Vietnam, and that this had to be stopped in order to bring about a negotiated settlement. Fewer still were urging that such a settlement should involve a coalition government with the Communists. Hardly anyone in the mainstream of American politics was saying that the outcome did not matter.

And the political trapping process kept almost everyone in line. Public doubters would be pounced on by the press. Bureaucratic skeptics would risk their careers. Various public figures vied with each other to explain the importance of Vietnam to the American people. And the people seemed to be believers too.

At the top of this process stood the presidents. Presidents could not treat Vietnam as if it were vital without creating high stakes internationally, domestically, and within their own bureaucracies. Their rhetoric could not be mistaken:

—It was a signal to the Communists that their actions would be met by counteractions.

—It set the American people's belief that the President would ensure that the threatened nation did not fall into Communist hands, although before 1965 this was emphasized without the anticipation of sacrificing large numbers of American lives.

—To Congress, it marked the President's responsibility to ensure that Vietnam did not go Communist and maximized incentives for legislators to support him or at least to remain silent.

—After 1961 it was a promise to the professional military that U.S. forces would be used if necessary and to the degree necessary to defend South Vietnam.

—To the professional U.S. diplomat, it meant letting allies know that Washington cared about their fate and was reliable.

—For the presidents themselves, it laid the groundwork for whatever action was at hand and showed that they were prepared to take the next step.

Words and deeds were making Vietnam into a showcase—an Asian Berlin. Consequently it became a test case as well of U.S. credibility —to opponents and to allies but perhaps most essentially to Americans themselves. Public opinion polls seemed to confirm the political dangers.

Each successive President, initially caught by his own beliefs, was further ensnared by his own rhetoric, and the basis for the beliefs went unchallenged. Presidents neither encouraged nor permitted serious questioning, for that would have fostered the idea that their resolve was something less than complete.

There was an undeniable strand in the history of U.S. Vietnam decisionmaking that seemed to stop short of an unalterable commitment not to lose. John McNaughton described this strand in a memorandum in 1964 arguing that the United States would "keep slugging away," but if it ultimately became necessary to leave, would "be sure it is a departure of the kind which would put everyone on our side, wondering how we stuck it and took it so long."[16] The United States should act as a good doctor, perhaps having to accept the patient's eventual death but acting responsibly helpful in the meantime.

The "good doctor" lineage runs from 1949 to early 1965. In expressing his opposition to an aid cutoff to China in 1949, Senator Vandenberg refused responsibility for the last push. In a December 1954 conversa-

16. Ibid., pp. 683–84. See also Daniel Ellsberg, *Papers on the War* (Simon and Schuster, 1972), pp. 86–90.

tion with State Department officials, Senator Mansfield said that the United States had to commit its resources "even if it will cost a lot, to hold Vietnam as long as possible."[17] Indirect evidence stemming from Kennedy's belief that the effort in Vietnam could not survive as "a white man's war" provides another link.[18] The 1964 McNaughton memorandum develops the theme further. The main objective, McNaughton wrote, was "to reverse the present downward trend. Failing that, the alternative objective is to emerge from the situation with as good an image as possible in US, allied and enemy eyes." He urged that any chance should be taken "to back the DRV down" or "to evolve a tolerable settlement," but that "if worst comes and South Vietnam distintegrates or their behavior becomes abominable," the United States should " 'disown' South Vietnam, hopefully leaving the image of 'a patient who died despite the extraordinary efforts of a good doctor.' "[19]

The theme appears again in the critical days of February 1965. In his memo to the President recommending the initiation of "sustained reprisals" against the North, McGeorge Bundy argued that "even if it fails to turn the tide—as it may—the value of the effort seems to us to exceed its cost."[20] Failure might be acceptable but not without first paying a high price to *try* to avoid it; commitment had to be strong but not unalterable in the sense of being unlimited.

There is only one instance on the available record when the principals actually discussed this "good doctor" theme. That was in November 1964 when it was advanced in an NSC working group paper. Rusk rejected the idea that the United States would get credit "merely for trying." McGeorge Bundy and McNamara disagreed. Ball sided with Rusk.[21] No evidence reveals what the presidents thought of this approach to the problem. Maybe it characterized their thinking and maybe not. But whichever, as a practical matter it was a distinction without a difference. Operationally, the proponents of "good doctor" thinking and the opponents came out in about the same place. They all advocated

17. "Memorandum of Conversation," Department of State, December 7, 1954, *United States–Vietnam Relations*, bk. 10, pt. V.B.3, p. 806.

18. Arthur M. Schlesinger, Jr., *A Thousand Days: John F. Kennedy in the White House* (Houghton Mifflin, 1965), p. 547.

19. *Pentagon Papers*, vol. 3, pp. 556–59. See also the memorandum for William P. Bundy from Henry Rowen, Office of the Assistant Secretary of Defense, ibid., p. 643.

20. Ibid., p. 687.

21. Ibid., pp. 237–38.

escalation, and paradoxically, the proponents, especially in the 1964–65 period, urged greater escalation than the opponents. It was again the basic objective of *not losing* that drove U.S. involvement ever more deeply each step of the way.

If this analysis is correct, two conclusions follow. One is that the investment trap model for U.S. involvement is only a subsidiary factor. The other is that the "turning points" so many writers allude to were not *likely* turning points at all.

The investment trap model derives its persuasiveness from retrospection. Looking back on the war, it seems that U.S. leaders must have gotten involved through inadvertence, through aid program piled on aid program, with a growing corps of advisers piled on top, and with high-blown rhetoric used to sell aid packages to a reluctant Congress carrying everyone away. Each new investment, because of the previous investments, seemed a prudent, if not mandatory, way of saving the sunk costs. And so U.S. leaders more or less found themselves throwing good money after bad—"in for a penny, in for a pound." Or at least the calculus of acceptable costs was modified as the ledger was filled. To be sure, there is an important logic in the sunk costs argument. If in 1965 the choice had been either to commit 500,000 troops or to stay out, many of those who later defended the war might not have chosen to go in.

The years of involvement did have a cumulative impact. But two facts conspire against making too much of this. First, the available record shows few instances when anyone employed the sunk cost argument. Surely opponents of further involvement, if not advocates of it, would have used this argument more often if it had been on their minds. Second, the basic international and domestic stakes were present from the start, since 1950. The objective of preventing defeat to which these stakes gave birth was the same in 1950 as in 1954, 1961, and 1964, and the language used to justify this objective remained strikingly similar throughout. All of which leads to this conclusion: Vietnam was not a story of involvements driving commitments but of involvement coming into line with commitment as the need arose.

This conclusion, in turn, casts doubt on the notion of "turning points."[22] If turning points were really meaningful, analysis would have to show that the chances were about even, or at least that the decision

22. For an example of this sort of analysis, see Theodore Draper, *The Abuse of Power* (Viking Press, 1967).

had a reasonable chance of going one way or the other. To argue that American leaders *could* have withdrawn or had the opportunity to begin U.S. disengagement from Vietnam at various stages is not sufficient. Of course, they could choose, but that does not mean that they possessed *real* choice. At every so-called turning point, the odds were so heavily weighted against disengagement that the direction of the decision never seemed in doubt. It was always a matter of how much and what to do and not a matter of whether to stay in or get out, until the 1974–75 debate on cutting military assistance.

This leads to a final conclusion. U.S. stakes and goals in Vietnam did not dictate the strategy for fighting the war nor the tactical scope and character of the war. The latter, as discussed earlier in this chapter, sprang mainly from the bureaucratic organizations that ran the war in the field. The programs for and in South Vietnam derived mostly from their leadership, their interests, and their organizational standard operating procedures. These programs derived from but did not drive the separate decisions on grand strategy made by the political leadership in Washington and subject to pressures and constraints in addition to preventing the loss of Vietnam to communism. How American leaders carved out grand strategy is the grist of part III of this book.

PART THREE

*Means: The Minimum Necessary and
the Maximum Feasible*

CHAPTER NINE

Constraints

When formal planning for the bombing of North Vietnam began in mid-1964, the Joint Chiefs of Staff pushed for a campaign aimed at destroying the capabilities of Hanoi's leadership to wage war. Bombing to interdict the flow of supplies from North to South Vietnam was necessary for the success of the ground war in the South, but it was not enough. To crush Hanoi's will to continue, the chiefs argued, all targets in North Vietnam except population centers and the dike system should be struck, and struck quickly. To civilian strategists, particularly in the Office of the Secretary of Defense, the way to affect the willingness of the North Vietnamese to continue the war was to give them a taste of U.S. airpower, gradually increasing the levels of destruction but always making sure that Hanoi still had something left to lose. The military argued instead that the only way to affect Hanoi's intentions was to thoroughly destroy its assets. "Self-imposed restrictions," as the chiefs called them, were what was holding the United States back from victory. Their basic position never altered.

In March 1966 the chiefs' position gained support from an unexpected quarter, the Central Intelligence Agency. Previously the CIA had had its doubts about all-out bombing, and by the end of 1966 these doubts would become hardened convictions against ending the war by attacking Hanoi's will. But for the moment—and it was an important junction in shaping the future of the bombing program—the military and the CIA found themselves allied. A CIA study in March 1966 conceded that mining harbors, striking lines of communication between China and North Vietnam, destroying POL facilities, and hitting "highly prized" industrial plants, could not stop the flow of supplies to South Vietnam.[1]

1. *The Pentagon Papers: The Defense Department History of United States Decisionmaking on Vietnam*, Senator Gravel ed. (Beacon Press, 1971), vol. 4, p. 77.

But, the study said, these acts would impede the flow and could influence Hanoi's basic decision to continue the war. To maximize the chances of ending the war, the CIA concluded: "First, the constraints upon the air attack must be reduced. Secondly, target selection must be placed on a more rational basis militarily."[2] President Johnson agreed to striking POL facilities for the first time but rejected substantial further escalation.

This was just one of a series of proposed strategies for winning the war that President Johnson and his predecessors had rejected. Admiral Arthur Radford made his pitch at the early stages of the Dien Bien Phu crisis for U.S. air strikes on entrenched Vietminh positions surrounding the French garrison in order to prevent its fall. But more than that, he argued, the strikes would serve as a signal to Moscow and Peking to either call off the Vietminh or face the greater application of American force. In 1961 after their trip to Vietnam, General Maxwell Taylor and Walt Rostow advanced a strategy for winning by calling for wider American involvement in the war on all fronts, including the dispatch of 8,000 combat soldiers. These actions, Taylor and Rostow averred, were necessary both to forestall the imminent collapse of the Saigon regime and to bolster and stabilize Saigon for a final push against the insurgents. The troops would also serve as a warning to Hanoi to stay out or risk paying the price of destruction. President Kennedy adopted most of the Taylor-Rostow recommendations but not the one on combat units considered critical to victory.

The distinguishing factor in the Radford proposal of 1954, the Taylor-Rostow strategy of 1961, the Joint Chiefs–CIA view of March 1966, and the proposals that were to come after 1966 regarding expanded U.S. ground forces and operations was that they promised more than simply avoiding defeat. They went beyond the negative objective of preventing a Communist victory and held out some prospect of defeating the enemy, of U.S. victory. Each was held to be a winning strategy in that it outlined a course of action that was supposed to be decisive. The Air Force strongly implied that massive bombing would be decisive in the near term. In the Army's more cautious view, much more time would be needed, but with enough effort the Vietcong could eventually be brought under control.

2. Ibid., pp. 71–72.

"Decisive" did not necessarily mean that the war would be completely over. Some guerrilla action, terrorism, and banditry were expected to persist for a long time, but this could be easily managed by the anti-Communist Vietnamese. The war would ultimately fade away. But long before that—and here was the real portent of decisiveness—the corner would be turned, the light would appear at the end of the tunnel, and the final result would become certain. No one, of course, cared to go out on a limb and predict precisely when that corner would be turned. Furthermore, the military's pessimism about success within the tactical constraints imposed by the administration rarely abated; optimism about winning was usually hedged by the condition that much heavier doses of force would be needed. But with these conditions, the estimates and the intimations ran from months to a two-year maximum.

Pacification, it should be noted at the outset, was not considered to be one of these win strategies. In August 1966 White House consultant Robert Komer reported on the status of pacification and defined it.

If we divide the US/GVN problem into four main components, three of them show encouraging progress. The campaign against the major VC/NVA [North Vietnamese Army] units is in high gear, the constitutional process seems to be evolving favorably, and we expect to contain inflation while meeting most needs of the civil economy. But there is a fourth problem area, that of securing the countryside and getting the peasant involved in the struggle against the Viet Cong, where we are lagging way behind. It is this problem area which I would term pacification. . . .

At the risk of over-simplification, I see management of the pacification problem as involving three main sub-tasks: (1) providing local security in the countryside—essentially a military/police/cadre task; (2) breaking the hold of the VC over the people; and (3) positive programs to win the active support of the rural population.[3]

Even its most ardent advocates had to admit that pacification could not win or work without other things working first. Maxwell Taylor had observed in August 1964 that "the present . . . pacification plan is not enough in itself to maintain National morale or to offer reasonable hope of eventual success."[4] While most policymakers at most times conceded that pacification was the key variable, they saw it as a dependent variable nonetheless. Thus the United States could not win by pacification alone, but it could not win without pacification.

3. Ibid., vol. 2, p. 571.
4. Ibid., p. 330.

Four Strategies for Winning

The win strategies were aimed directly at the principal actors in the dispute: at France and later Saigon, at the Vietminh and later Hanoi, and at the backers of the Communist Vietnamese in Peking and Moscow as well. Although these strategies were almost always combined in one way or another and were seen as interdependent, and although a particular action might satisfy several strategies, four such strategies can be identified. Two—the dramatic gesture strategy and the leverage strategy —were aimed at winning by reforming the French and the South Vietnamese. Two—the dramatic threat strategy and the crush strategy—sought to win by destroying the will or capability of the foes.

The Dramatic Gesture Strategy

The strategy of dramatic gestures consisted of actions to galvanize the French before the Geneva accords and the Saigon regime thereafter. The problem, according to many American officials, was that the French and later the Saigon leaders had the capability to win but lacked the will. This lack of will, they reasoned, stemmed from uncertainty about the continuation of American support. The United States could bolster that will by making a dramatic gesture of commitment.

The dramatic gesture approach was used at critical times from the Dien Bien Phu crisis through the first Kennedy year to the beginning of direct American involvement in 1965. In 1954 the U.S. ambassador in Vietnam, Donald Heath, frequently cabled that French doubts about American motives and support were holding back the war effort. This perceived need for bold reassurances can be seen in Kennedy's decision to shift ambassadors in 1961, ordering the new ambassador, Frederick E. Nolting, to develop more rapport with Diem. The major fear then was that the leadership in Saigon would feel that Washington was about to compromise with the Communists in Vietnam as it was compromising in Laos. Diem had to be convinced that events in Laos were not a harbinger of what was to come in Vietnam. The need can be seen at the end of 1961 in Vice President Johnson's report on his Vietnam trip and in Nolting's call for a shot in the arm. General Taylor stressed it in arguing for the introduction of U.S. combat troops in October 1961. He cabled the President: "The size of the U.S. force introduced need not be great to provide the military presence necessary to produce the desired effect on national morale in SVN."[5] Taylor was worried about "a crisis of confidence" and wanted to give Saigon "reassurance." Or as the Joint Chiefs put it in a memorandum to the secretary of defense in early 1962: "It must be made clear to Diem that the United States is prepared and willing to bolster his regime and discourage internal factions which may seek to overthrow him."[6] Behind this flurry of attempts to reassure Diem stood General Edward Lansdale, the prophet of winning through restoring confidence between Washington and Saigon. Lansdale, who carried a lot of influence in the Kennedy circles early in the administration, preached a simple message in January 1961: "We have to show him [Diem] by deeds, not words alone, that we are his friend. This will make our influence effective again."[7]

The dramatic gesture approach came to the forefront again in 1964 when Ambassador Lodge and then Ambassador Taylor urged an increase in the visible American presence in the South and in pressures against the North in order to unify the efforts of the South Vietnamese and reduce their internal quarrels.[8] But most important, this theme reemerged in the critical days of February 1965 in the very influential memo that McGeorge Bundy sent to the President.

We emphasize that our primary target in advocating a reprisal policy is the improvement of the situation in *South* Vietnam. Action against the North is usually urged as a means of affecting the will of Hanoi to direct and support the VC. We consider this an important but longer-range purpose. The immediate and critical targets are in the South—in the minds of the South Vietnamese and in the minds of the Viet Cong cadres.[9]

The name of the game was the restoration of confidence and the achievement of reforms by making a major psychological impact. Advocates maintained that Washington, by applying pressure, could not get Saigon to use its resources sensibly. Pressures had not worked and would not. Reassurance through dramatic deeds would be the only way to make Saigon institute the necessary reforms for victory.

5. Ibid., pp. 90–91.
6. Ibid., p. 665.
7. Ibid., p. 26.
8. See the accounts of Lodge's statements at the Honolulu Conference in June 1964 in ibid., p. 323; and of Taylor's report to Rusk in September 1964 in ibid., pp. 335–38.
9. Ibid., vol. 3, p. 689.

The Leverage Strategy

The leverage strategy, on the other hand, entailed actions to pressure France and later the Saigon regime into a wide variety of political, economic, administrative, and social reforms. Again, the problem was not resources but management and politics. If France would make an unequivocal grant of independence, or after 1954 if Saigon would broaden its political base, the legitimacy necessary for victory would be at hand.

Coaxing, in this view, would not work. Pressures had to be applied, and the French and the South Vietnamese had to be convinced of Washington's seriousness in demanding performance as a condition for continuing assistance. From 1950 through 1955 the U.S. military were the most ardent advocates of reform through pressures, only to get off this bandwagon in 1960 to join forces with the advocates of dramatic gesturing. But in 1961 their refrain was picked up in the State Department by officials such as Averell Harriman and Roger Hilsman and in 1965 by Robert McNamara. Mid-level officials throughout the government pressed for this approach throughout the 1960s.

As early as April 1950 the JCS recommended to the secretary of defense that U.S. military aid "not be granted unconditionally" but be carefully controlled, integrated with political and economic programs, and made contingent on French acceptance of increased American advice and a greater voice for the Vietnamese themselves.[10] Eisenhower's correspondence with Diem after Geneva also stressed the theme of aid being contingent on performance. The movement to dump Diem in 1963 was led by men in the State Department who felt that Diem would never reform himself. The McNamara-Taylor report to the President in October 1963 that recommended the withdrawal of 1,000 U.S. military personnel followed this line of reasoning: "Actions are designed to indicate to Diem Government our displeasure at its political policies and activities and to create significant uncertainty in that government and in key Vietnamese groups as to future intentions of United States."[11] Ambassador Taylor's lecturing to the South Vietnamese generals in late 1964 after they had toppled yet another civilian government also stands out. "I have real troubles on the U.S. side," Taylor said to them. "I don't know whether we will continue to support you after this."[12] Winning

10. Ibid., vol. 1, pp. 365–66.
11. Ibid., vol. 2, p. 251.
12. Ibid., p. 348.

through reforms became such a prevalent theme by 1967 that Ambassador Ellsworth Bunker, always reluctant about applying pressure on Saigon, himself issued a "Blueprint for Vietnam" emphasizing U.S. influence to bring about broader popular support and greater administrative efficiency.[13]

Since pressuring, like coaxing, had little success, a variant of the leverage strategy began to evolve in 1965. This could be called the U.S. "takeover" variant. Those who grew impatient with other approaches saw success only through making Vietnam entirely an American show. This meant joint command (staff integration at the top) and encadrement (mixing U.S. and South Vietnamese forces in the field)—proposals that were rejected.

The Dramatic Threat Strategy

Like the dramatic gesture strategy, the dramatic threat came into vogue in any period of acute crisis when there was not enough time to do anything else. This approach consisted of actions to influence the enemies' will to continue. Until the Geneva settlement, this meant signaling Moscow and Peking that they had better "call off their dogs" or face American intervention. After 1961 it was based on the view that the war in the South would "go away" if Hanoi stopped supporting the insurgents, and that Hanoi would in fact stop if faced with the prospect of a direct attack against its industrial and economic structures. Indeed it was argued that a firm, publicly stated intention to take such actions would be the best way to actually avoid having to employ them.

The thread of this strategy also runs from the Dien Bien Phu crisis through the Kennedy decisions in 1961 to the recommendations made by the Joint Chiefs and Walt Rostow. Behind Admiral Radford's proposal to launch American air strikes at Dien Bien Phu was his belief that the Communists would back away from confrontation if Washington showed that it meant business. Taylor spelled out much the same thinking in a cable to the President preceding his October 1961 report. "The risks of backing into a major Asian war by way of SVN are present but are not impressive. NVN is extremely vulnerable to conventional bombing, a weakness which should be exploited diplomatically in convincing Hanoi to lay off SVN." He went on to say in the letter of transmittal accompanying the report itself that whatever was done in the South,

13. Ibid., pp. 402–03.

"the time may come . . . when we must declare our intention to attack the source of guerrilla aggression in North Vietnam and impose on the Hanoi Government a price for participating in the current war which is commensurate with the damage being inflicted on its neighbors to the south."[14]

As this strategy evolved in 1964, there were actually two, and in a way three, variants—and the participants in these decisions were well aware of the differences. The military variant, from which the JCS never wavered, was a program of continuous and escalating air actions against the North designed to destroy its physical resources, and thereby the psychological will, to support the insurgency in the South. The emphasis here was on destruction in the North "as necessary to compel the DRV to cease" providing support to the insurgency.[15] The second variant, Walt Rostow's, emphasized staying power, determination (as in Berlin and the Cuban missile crisis), and signaling. As he told the secretary of defense in late 1964, "I am concerned that too much thought is being given to the actual damage we do in the North, not enough thought to the signal we wish to send." Rostow wanted it made clear that "we are ready and able to go much further than our initial act of damage," and that "we are ready and able to meet any level of escalation they might mount in response."[16] Like the Joint Chiefs, Rostow agreed with intelligence estimates that Hanoi "probably will avoid actions that would in their view unduly increase the chances of a major US response against North Vietnam (DRV) or Communist China."[17] The chiefs, however, saw the difference between their plan and Rostow's as that between trying to cause and trying to compel Hanoi to stop and believed only mass destruction at the outset would be a sufficient signal.[18] Moreover, the chiefs argued that it was necessary to back up these pressure signals with domestic signals such as economic mobilization and a call-up of the Reserves. This would further show the enemy that the United States would pay the costs of victory.

Ambassador Taylor presented yet a third alternative, arguing that the

14. Taylor's cable and letter are quoted in ibid., pp. 92, 98.
15. Ibid., vol. 3, pp. 550–52.
16. Memorandum from Rostow to McNamara, November 16, 1964, ibid., pp. 632–33. To be exact, Rostow said "we should not go forward into the new stage without a US ground commitment of some kind."
17. Ibid., p. 645.
18. Ibid., p. 172.

Joint Chiefs' proposals were not "an accurate or complete expression of our choices." Taylor urged "demonstrative strikes against limited military targets to show U.S. readiness and intent" to go on.[19] He was soon joined by McNamara and the Bundys, and "demonstration" attacks were converted into "sustained reprisals," which in turn evolved into the "slow squeeze" strategy. But this alternative did not hold the same prospect of being decisive—even to its proponents—as did the other variants.

The dramatic threat strategy remained at bottom a form of compellence, of trying to affect the psychology of the opponent. But for many advocates of this approach, the line between military actions to affect will and those to affect capabilities was very slim indeed.

The Crush Strategy

The crush strategy was invariably the other side of the threat strategy coin. Like the threat strategy, it reflected an impatience with seeking to coax or to pressure reforms from the French or from Saigon. The idea was to get on with the fighting and crush the opponent. Robert Komer, although absorbed in pacification and not an advocate of increasing U.S. ground forces or bombing, gave vivid expression to this concept in August 1966 in his longest memorandum to the President. "Wastefully, expensively, but nonetheless indisputably, we are winning the war in the South. Few of our programs—civil or military—are very efficient, but we are grinding the enemy down by sheer weight and mass. And the cumulative impact of all we have set in motion is beginning to tell.[20]

The crush approach could also be called the "more" strategy—more aid, more advisers, more combat troops, more bombing, and so on. While it was not exclusively a military-backed strategy, the military were its prime exponents. It found expression in the Navarre Plan when the war was being fought by France and later in General William Westmoreland's concept of a war of attrition. Westmoreland talked about it in terms of a "meatgrinder"— search and destroy operations, hitting the enemy in his base areas, more manpower, more fire power, and bigger enemy "body counts." Its proponents recognized that this approach would take a longer time to be decisive than the other strategies, but they also believed that it was more certain to reach that point eventually, usually in about two years from its inception. Grinding the enemy

19. Ibid., p. 179.
20. Ibid., vol. 2, p. 575.

down would take time, but in the meantime the combination of bombing in the North and search and destroy in the South would make the final result inevitable.

The Fate of the "Winning" Strategies

To a considerable degree these four strategies for winning shared a common fate. None was ever implemented unequivocally. Presidents invariably stopped short of doing everything proponents of these strategies maintained was necessary for success. The proponents of winning by bolstering France and Saigon and frightening the Communists never got what they wanted when they wanted it. Radford did not receive authority to launch air strikes at Dien Bien Phu. The French never got reassurance about their interests in Indochina. Taylor and Rostow did not succeed in convincing Kennedy to send 8,000 U.S. combat troops to Vietnam for the purpose of restoring Diem's confidence in Washington. Johnson did not succumb to advocates of calling up the Reserves and placing the economy on a wartime footing. Permission was never granted to bomb "Hanoi's will" decisively. Those who proposed to win by pressuring France, then Diem, and then his successors into making reforms to capture popular loyalty got practically no place. The one recorded instance of Washington being serious about pressuring for reform came in 1963 when Kennedy agreed to suspend the Commodity Imports Program. Finally advocates of crushing the enemy by doing more obtained approval for more, but never for what they considered enough. Johnson pulled in the reins on bombing in the North and on ground force increases and always withheld approval for ground attacks against enemy sanctuaries in Laos, Cambodia, and North Vietnam. Why were all these winning strategies either rejected or never fully implemented?

One explanation might be that the presidents and their senior civilian advisers did not think that the strategies would work. To an extent, and sometimes to a large degree, this was so. Before 1965 proponents of winning strategies had to contend with the argument that they were putting the cart before the horse, and that France, or Bao Dai, or Diem had to put their houses in order before, not after, greater American involvement. There also were doubts about being able to win colonial, or "white man's," wars. According to Arthur Schlesinger, Jr., Kennedy's reason for turning down the Taylor-Rostow combat proposal in 1961 was of this genre. Kennedy, he recalled, had said that "the war in Vietnam . . . could be won only so long as it was *their* war. If it were ever converted into a white man's war, we would lose as the French had lost a decade earlier."[21] And beginning in late 1966, McNamara did argue that Hanoi's will could not be broken by bombing (here he was backed by the CIA once again) and that Westmoreland would not be able to wear down the North Vietnamese forces because (1) they and not the Americans retained the battlefield initiative and therefore the choice of where and when to fight, and (2) statistical and demographic projections indicated Hanoi could continue to replace manpower even when its losses were astronomical. In most instances, however, there is no evidence that feasibility was the major reason advanced for presidential rejection or reluctance to fully implement a winning strategy.

Whether these winning strategies would have worked is debatable. What is more significant is that the presidents did not adopt them, although they were the only ones put forward that could have had decisive results, and soon. At best, the other strategies or chosen courses of action portended a lengthy war, and at worst, a war of indeterminate outcome. It was not, then, simply a matter of presidents trying to win at the cheapest possible cost. It seems to be a matter of presidents not wanting to run the risks or to pay the full price of winning. Again, why?

Forms of Constraint

Just as a panoply of pressures impelled the presidents to avoid losing Vietnam, a slew of constraints kept them from doing "what was necessary" to win.

One kind of constraint was particularistic. At times certain fleeting circumstances militated against choosing winning strategies. In part Kennedy rejected the Taylor-Rostow proposal of an 8,000-man combat team because of the critical situation in Laos. He wanted to settle affairs in Laos by negotiations and without recourse to force. He was trying to get those negotiations under way and felt that sending U.S. troops to Vietnam would scuttle that effort.[22] The 1964 elections were obviously a factor in President Johnson's decision to avoid or postpone further

21. Arthur M. Schlesinger, Jr., *A Thousand Days: John F. Kennedy in the White House* (Houghton Mifflin, 1965), p. 547.

22. See ibid., pp. 544–50, and Theodore C. Sorensen, *Kennedy* (Harper and Row, 1965), p. 653.

American military actions in Vietnam that his advisers argued were essential not only to winning but to staving off defeat. With the elections impending, word appeared to have gone out from the White House to keep tough decisions from the President. In the face of growing Communist successes, not doing more could only encourage Hanoi in the belief that Washington did not have the political stomach for seeing the war through. In 1966–67 inflation in South Vietnam became a key limitation on the buildup of both American and South Vietnamese armed forces. Many officials in Saigon and Washington felt it was necessary to do both in order to assume the offensive in the war. Yet U.S. dollars were driving up prices, and Saigon force increases were drawing down civilian manpower. In a message to the State Department in October 1966, Ambassador Lodge stated that the United States should "bring as massive an American military force to bear in Vietnam" as possible, but added "so long as this can be done without a wildcat inflation and other lethal political effects."[23] Combined with others, this argument had a telling effect against force increases requested by the military.

A second constraint can be categorized as strategic doctrinal. How presidents reacted to Vietnam proposals would be conditioned, at least in part, on their global national security and defense policies. This was not a limiting factor for Kennedy and Johnson. Their adopted doctrine of flexible response not only allowed for intervention in a Vietnam-type war but also called for meeting threats on the level at which they were posed. The Truman and Eisenhower strategic doctrines, however, were relatively restrictive. For Truman, Asia was a sideshow to Europe. As Truman recalled Defense Secretary George Marshall's view: "Our entire international position depended upon strengthening Western Europe."[24] Thus Truman did not fight the Korean War to win it.

The Eisenhower case is more complicated. He was in a sense, trapped by the cross-purposes of his approach to global strategy. Glenn Snyder has noted that "the New Look was not isolationist about the *ends* or objectives of policy, but rather about the *means* and application of means for supporting these objectives."[25] New Look objectives held that

23. *Pentagon Papers*, vol. 4, p. 343.

24. Harry S. Truman, *Memoirs*, vol. 2: *Years of Trial and Hope* (Doubleday, 1956), p. 419.

25. Glenn Snyder, "The 'New Look' of 1953," in Warner R. Schilling, Paul Y. Hammond, and Glenn H. Snyder, *Strategy, Politics, and Defense Budgets* (Columbia University Press, 1962), pp. 495–96.

both Europe and Asia were essential to American security, requiring U.S. military intervention if necessary. On the other hand, New Look strategy, which stressed fiscal solvency, the "long haul," holding defense spending in check, relying on American air and sea power for defense, and the threat of massive retaliation for deterrence, strongly argued against intervention. The whole thrust of the strategy ran counter to American ground force involvement in an Asian land war. If intervention were to be decided upon, it would have to be restricted to air and sea power. This in turn meant that ground force requirements would have to be filled, or at least heavily supplemented, by allies.

Eisenhower made it plain in March 1954 that he would not intervene without allied participation. French forces had to stay, and the British and a number of Asian nations would have to join in. While Eisenhower showed some indications of fudging on British participation, he did not budge from the principle of major allied involvement. Johnson did not condition his decisions in early 1965 to intervene directly either on a major role for allies or any role for allies. He wanted allies, and in the spring and summer of that year and again in 1967 he made a special effort to corral allied support but without any indication that his decisions hinged on this support. The framers of the flexible response doctrine did not predicate U.S. moves, particularly outside Europe, on the expectation of alliance action. If anything, their expectation was that allies, particularly European ones, could not be counted on. Senior officials in Washington rightly anticipated that the domestic opposition in these countries to what they regarded as U.S. interference in a Vietnamese civil war would forestall allied help. The most that could be hoped for from the French, British, and Japanese was that their governments would provide some favorable public rhetoric.

For domestic reasons, however, and in order to neutralize U.S. domestic criticism, it was deemed highly desirable to have the flags of Asian allies flying with that of America. It would not be easy to explain to the American people that the United States was fighting in Vietnam for Asian security unless the Asians were a part of that fight. Accordingly President Johnson applied pressure in Asian capitals. South Korea, Thailand, the Philippines, New Zealand, and Australia chipped in troops or aid, but only after agreements, particularly with the first three, to provide generous American subsidies.

A third kind of constraint falls under the heading of internal policy conflicts. This entailed prohibitions or limitations on a promising course of action because doing it would violate other agreed to policy lines or objectives.

Thus before 1965 all strategies for pressuring France, Diem, and his successors into reforms foundered on the controlling imperative to keep it their war rather than make it an American war. A State Department paper of 1948 sounded this warning, which was to be repeated until the end of the Geneva Conference. "We are naturally hesitant to press the French too strongly or to become deeply involved so long as we are not in a position to suggest a solution or until we are prepared to accept the onus of intervention."[26] Or as a memo signed by Under Secretary of State Bedell Smith stated in 1953: "The 'use of influence' . . . may be assumed to fall short of pressure of any type where such pressure might be self-defeating."[27] In late 1964 Ambassador Taylor told Dean Rusk that a threat to Saigon that Washington would "withdraw unless" would be "quite a gamble."[28] Here, Taylor was reflecting the dual nightmare of the pressure strategy: either the United States would be thrown out of Vietnam, thereby jeopardizing the basic "don't lose" objective, or would be thrown into the war directly, thereby crossing the unwanted threshold into an Asian land conflict.

The last thing U.S. presidents wanted was to have the war laid squarely on the American lap. While pressuring for reforms made consummate sense, it was not deemed wise to try winning this way at the risk of direct involvement. Besides, it was widely believed that Saigon had to do the job, for if the United States took over the war, it was bound to be lost. This was the assumption behind a statement by a Defense Department representative at an NSC meeting in January 1954 that "the commitment of U.S. forces in a 'civil war' . . . will be an admission of the bankruptcy of our political policies re Southeast Asia and France."[29] There was also McNamara's injunction in the otherwise bullish memorandum of March 17, 1964, that became NSAM 288: "the South Vietnamese must win their own fight."[30]

26. "Department of State Policy Statement on Indochina," September 27, 1948, in *United States–Vietnam Relations, 1945–1967*, Study prepared by the Department of Defense for the House Committee on Armed Services, 92 Cong. 1 sess. (Government Printing Office, 1971), bk. 8, pt. V.B.2, p. 148.

27. "Memorandum for Executive Secretary, National Security Council," August 5, 1953, ibid., bk. 9, pt. V.B.3, p. 118.

28. *Pentagon Papers*, vol. 3, p. 242.

29. Ibid., vol. 1, p. 90.

30. Ibid., vol. 3, p. 51.

Another internal policy inhibition against pressuring Saigon concerned the perceived need for stability. As the United States began taking over the war there seemed to be less need for immediate GVN effectiveness and more need for long-term political stability. The United States would take care of the war in the short run, providing a shield for the flimsy client regime, and after that the government of Vietnam would reform itself. The long-run nation-building policy that resulted from this thinking blanketed almost all proposals for reform with programs for elections and constitution-making. Pressures for reforms now, so the argument ran, would unnecessarily and prematurely risk sinking the boat by trying to improve it at a time when it was necessary only to keep it afloat.[31]

Just as the winning-by-pressuring-Saigon strategy fell to other policy considerations like nation-building and keeping it "their" war, the strategy of trying to win by pressuring North Vietnam bumped up against considerations about negotiations and the South Vietnamese government's stability. In a senior strategy meeting on September 7, 1964, the principal conferees agreed to defer the JCS recommendation to provoke Hanoi into taking some kind of action that could then be answered by a systematic bombing campaign "in the immediate future while the GVN is still struggling to its feet."[32] Hanoi could strike back on the ground in the South before the GVN was ready This argument turned out to be the key constraint on beginning the bombing campaign until it was brushed aside in early 1965. Also important, however, was the argument that bombing at that time would evoke pressures for premature negotiations, that is, before Hanoi felt the pain and Washington could establish a bargaining advantage. Opponents of the JCS bombing strategy after 1965 often used the concern for negotiations to argue that the United States should not kill the hostage. All-out bombing, they maintained, would give Hanoi no incentive to negotiate. Only the threat to bomb more could do that. But the strategy of winning through bombing and mining North Vietnamese ports had additional obstacles to surmount. After late 1964 the most prominent quick-win strategy of curbing Hanoi's will in the North through bombing and mining was held in check by the President and his senior civilian advisers because they thought it would run the risk of both widening the war and undermining domestic support for the war.

31. Ibid., p. 124.
32. Ibid., p. 193.

A fourth area of constraint, then, centered around fears of certain actions leading to a wider war. In practice this meant that U.S. leaders would be reluctant to pursue any course of action that ran a high risk of direct military confrontation with the Soviet Union or China in Indochina or increased Soviet pressure elsewhere (Berlin, for example) that might also lead to confrontation.

Lyndon Johnson clearly had such risks on his mind, but this was not always the case with other presidents. Indeed much of the contingency planning during 1954 proceeded on the assumption that only a wider war was worth fighting. While principals and staff haggled and devised ambiguous formulas for dealing with a French defeat at the hands of the Vietminh, agreement was implicit on the need for U.S. military action if Peking intervened.[33] Nor did fears of a wider war seem to be a live concern in 1961. Taylor accompanied his recommendation for U.S. ground troops with the judgment that "the risks of backing into a major Asian war by way of SVN are present but are not impressive. . . . There is no case for fearing a mass onslaught of Communist manpower into SVN and its neighboring states, particularly if our airpower is allowed a free hand against logistical targets."[34] Taylor's assertions went unchallenged. If anything, the assumption seemed to be that fear of a wider war would be more of a constraint on the Communist superpowers than on the United States. Thus Rusk and McNamara concluded their memo of November 11, 1961, to the President by saying that given strong committing actions by Washington, their "expectation" was that Moscow would exercise restraint on Hanoi and Peking.[35]

Leaders in the Johnson administration never actually abandoned this notion of using Moscow's fears of direct confrontation as a lever on Hanoi and Peking but gave it a new twist. For example, opponents of mining North Vietnamese harbors frequently contended that such action would increase Hanoi's dependence on China thereby making Hanoi even more intransigent. They saw Moscow as the potential good influence and Peking as the actual bad influence and did not want to play into the hands of the latter. But as American involvement proceeded apace, Johnson and his senior advisers often emphasized the risks of a wider war rather than the opportunities.

These risks were used to rule out using nuclear weapons, invading

33. See the NSC policy statement of January 16, 1954, in ibid., vol. 1, pp. 435–43.
34. Ibid., vol. 2, p. 92.
35. Ibid., p. 116.

North Vietnam, destroying the dyke system, bombing civilian population, striking at lines of communication near the China border, mining North Vietnamese ports, and stepping up clandestine operations in, or invading, Cambodia and Laos. The prohibitions against the first four of these actions were so strong that they were never even proposed (although in 1967 Westmoreland did commission a study of the potential for use of tactical nuclear weapons).[36] In 1964 some military men mused about using tactical nuclear weapons in extremis and about attacking the dykes, and in 1968 the military received authorization to conduct operations in the demilitarized zone between North and South Vietnam, but both matters ended there. The Joint Chiefs and others made formal proposals for the remaining items on the list above and were rejected each time.

The risk of a wider war was also used to postpone air strikes against POL facilities, power stations, airfields, and surface-to-air missile sites. The President made these decisions in the face of a very credible military argument that delays would afford Hanoi the chance to disperse these facilities, put them near population centers, build up their air defenses, and thus increase the costs of the bombing to the United States in men and aircraft. But the President seemed sufficiently concerned about possible Soviet and Chinese reactions to want to feel his way up the escalatory ladder while watching for those reactions. Throughout the course of the bombing campaign Johnson seemed guided by the language of a memorandum written by McNamara in July 1965: "The program should avoid bombing which runs a high risk of escalation into war with the Soviets or China and which is likely to appall allies and friends."[37]

"Friends" was probably a veiled reference to a fifth set of constraints stemming from domestic politics. Politics imposed civilian hardship and moral, time, and cost limitations on all proposed winning strategies.

Civilian hardship was defined in terms of the disruption of lives resulting from calling up the Reserves and extending tours of duty in Vietnam beyond one year. Disrupting the lives of many American families had proved a none too popular move when Kennedy had issued a Reserve call-up during the Berlin crisis in 1961. Thus Johnson chose to raise the draft calls instead. This meant subjecting many men who did

36. General William C. Westmoreland, *A Soldier Reports* (Doubleday, 1975), p. 338.
37. *Pentagon Papers*, vol. 4, p. 29.

not want to go to Vietnam in the first place to prolonged personal risk and also raised the possibility of a public outcry over social and draft inequities. But Johnson chose maximum twelve-month tours, and in this he was supported by the Army, which wanted to give actual combat training to as many officers as possible. Both of these decisions undercut proposed winning strategies. By not calling up the Reserves, Johnson refused to take the kind of penalty in domestic opposition that might have shocked Hanoi into believing that Washington was committed all the way. By not extending duty tours, Johnson crippled the development of expertise necessary to know the Vietnamese culture, run a delicate pacification program, and fight a complicated war.

Moral restraints somewhat mitigated the devastation inherent in warfare, thereby hindering the crush strategy. The television cameras and the press phalanx were watching the war close up to ensure that it was "clean." While as in any war, atrocities were not uncommon, the military did exercise caution in conducting ground and air operations in order to minimize civilian casualities. The difference can be seen in the "gloves off" bombing in Laos where the cameras were not watching.

Domestic politics also put the leaders of the Johnson administration in a bind by impelling them to become fire fighters. Actions in Vietnam were often shaped, if not dictated, by daily criticisms at home. The many false starts on the pacification program came in response to charges by legislators and journalists that LBJ was not doing enough about "the other war"—pacification, nation-building, and political development. If legislators insisted that Saigon's forces do more of the fighting willy-nilly, the size of those forces was increased. No matter that the issue was quality, not size. Problems of size could be fixed faster. And so it was with many other issues as the administration sought vainly to paper over critical television reports and front-page news stories with short-run solutions. Pressures to "produce now" to gain immediate relief from critics militated against all long-range win strategies—pacification, reform of the South Vietnamese government, and compelling the Saigon forces to do more of the fighting. Self-reliance strategies would have to take time.

Finally, the potential domestic costs of the war imposed a fundamental constraint on the perennial proposal of the Joint Chiefs to win through mobilization. The chiefs argued that calling up the Reserves and placing the American economy on a wartime footing with controls and taxes would send a message of unity and resolve that Hanoi could not miss or resist. President Johnson, however, sought to delay the impact of the war on the pocketbook and on domestic programs as long as he could.[38]

Johnson wanted guns and butter. As he told Congress on January 12, 1966, in a speech followed by thunderous applause: "Time may require further sacrifices. If so, we will make them. But we will not heed those who will wring it from the hopes of the unfortunate here in a land of plenty. I believe that we can continue the Great Society while we fight in Vietnam."[39] To ensure that he would have both, he did not encourage his chief defense officials to be candid with his chief economic advisers in 1965 as the critical escalation decisions were being made.[40] He resisted pressures for increased taxes throughout 1966. Finally, in late 1967 he asked for a 10 percent surtax, but this fell far short of paying for the mounting costs of the war. Moreover, he refused to let congressional leaders call it a war tax. Short-run prosperity was purchased at the price of long-run inflation—as Johnson himself admitted in his memoirs.[41]

Building and Breaching "Firebreaks"

All the constraints—the particularistic, the doctrinal, the internal policy conflicts, the wider war, and the domestic political—were a matter of judgment. To be sure, each possessed plausibility to varying degrees, that is, each seemed to be a reasonable judgment about the possible adverse consequences of pursuing a winning strategy. But at bottom they were no more and no less than arguments against taking certain courses of action, sometimes based on thoughtful assessments and sometimes concocted simply to stymie further escalation. As the Joint Chiefs noted, these constraints were self-imposed.

Once stated as constraints, however, arbitrary arguments became real constraints. For example, when the President and others said privately or publicly that mining Haiphong harbor would lead to Chinese inter-

38. For an account of financing the war during Johnson's presidency, see David Halberstam, *The Best and the Brightest* (Random House, 1972), pp. 603–10.

39. "Annual Message to the Congress on the State of the Union, January 12, 1966," *Public Papers of the Presidents of the United States, Lyndon B. Johnson, 1966* (GPO, 1967), p. 4.

40. Halberstam, *The Best and the Brightest*, p. 604.

41. Lyndon Baines Johnson, *The Vantage Point: Perspectives of the Presidency, 1963–1969* (Holt, Rinehart and Winston, 1971), pp. 342–43.

vention, the no-mining barrier became harder to breach. Taking that action with a full appreciation of the risks would have been tantamount to an admission of irresponsibility. The question would always be asked —if it was risky and irresponsible before, why not now? When Nixon finally took that action in response to the North Vietnamese invasion of the northern provinces of South Vietnam in 1972, he did so precisely because he wanted to make a dramatic response.

The presidents and most of their senior civilian advisers created the stakes against losing as well as the constraints against doing what was necessary to win, and accepted them. But the presidents could and did dissolve the constraints, break the self-imposed barriers, and get away with it. (When, how, and why they did so will be discussed in the following chapter.) Congress and the public went along and even endorsed the breaches, and neither Moscow nor Peking intervened in Vietnam as a result. Yet American leaders had to pay a price. As thresholds were crossed, domestic opposition to the war increased. As natural or clear-cut dividing lines were violated, new constraints were not easy to impose. Thus when Kennedy went beyond the 650-man advisory limit set by the Geneva accords, it became difficult to post a new advisory ceiling, and the number of advisers ran up to 17,000 under Kennedy and 26,000 under Johnson before 1965. When Johnson finally authorized ROLLING THUNDER in March 1965, it was only a matter of time—although each step would follow heated internal debate—before POL facilities, airfields, industrial facilities, and the like were placed on the strike list. And when Johnson ordered those first Marine battalions into Danang in March 1965, the issue of whether troop levels would reach half a million or a million came up for grabs. In order to control these processes, even more arbitrary constraints had to be introduced.

The Gap between the Professionals and the Politicians

And yet there was an essential consistency about who was arbitrary about what. In analyses of the critical issue of how Hanoi, Russia, and China would respond if the United States crossed certain "firebreaks," a consistent gap divided the intelligence community and the senior civilian advisers to the President.

On what Hanoi would do in response to increasing advisers, introducing ground combat troops, and starting the bombing, the consensus of the intelligence community was that Hanoi would step up its own role in the South and stick it out, while the senior advisers were likely to dismiss

Hanoi's doggedness (the Taylor-Rostow report in 1961) or play down Hanoi's reactions (McNamara and McGeorge Bundy with respect to getting the bombing under way in March 1965). By 1966, however, McNamara and his principal assistant on Vietnam, John McNaughton, also began stressing the near certainty that Hanoi would meet escalation with escalation.

On the wider war issue, on the other hand, the intelligence community attached a rather low probability to Chinese and Russian intervention in response to Washington's crossing most firebreaks, whereas the senior civilians persistently maximized the probabilities. After 1953 the intelligence agencies gave little credence to Soviet or Chinese intervention except in response to U.S. efforts to invade and overthrow the government of North Vietnam and in the case of bombing near the China-Vietnam border. But in 1954 Dulles scampered to London and Paris to round up a coalition to resist possible Chinese intervention, while the intelligence agencies were saying it would not happen. On October 5, 1964, Under Secretary of State George Ball wrote:

The October 3 SNIE [Special National Intelligence Estimate] concludes that in the face of sustained U.S. air attacks on North Viet-Nam, "a large-scale Chinese Communist ground or air intervention would be unlikely." But we would be imprudent to undertake escalation without assuming that there was a *fair chance* that China would intervene. We made a contrary assumption in Korea in October of 1950 with highly unfortunate consequences.[42]

The difference in emphasis appeared in discussions of the recurrent issue of mining the North Vietnamese ports. The CIA repeatedly concluded that the Soviet Union would be in a real dilemma, but that given its geographic position and the local military superiority of U.S. forces, would not force a confrontation and would settle for vigorous protest. McNamara joined often by Rusk and the American ambassadors in Moscow, accepted the judgment that the Soviet Union would not force a confrontation but "should be expected" to dispatch volunteers, even pilots, provide more and better aid to Hanoi, and take action "elsewhere."[43]

The gap between those with professional expertise and those with political responsibility could have been expected. Analysts can afford to

42. George Ball, "Top Secret: The Prophesy the President Rejected," *Atlantic Monthly*, July 1972, p. 40. Ball went on to argue that "there is no reason to expect Soviet military intervention at an early stage of a U.S. air offensive" (p. 42).

43. *Pentagon Papers*, vol. 4, p. 173. In a memorandum to the President on March 2, 1968, William Bundy essentially argued the CIA line (the "A to Z" review), ibid., pp. 238–46.

be cool and calm. Political appointees and presidents above all have to live with the responsibilities and are therefore bound to emphasize the risks. But it was more than that. The civilian advisers enjoyed a comfortable consistency between their predictions and their predilections. While it is impossible to untangle which ruled which, it is clear that these advisers were skeptical for the most part about the beneficial effects of escalation and did not want the war to get out of control.

The military sided with the analysts on some of these issues. In the various plans the soldiers presented to increase pressure on North Vietnam, they would admit that these actions entailed "some additional risk" but maintained that the "overt introduction" of Chinese and Soviet forces was "remote."[44] Indeed the military often argued that the risks were precisely the reverse of those seen by the senior advisers. For example, in January 1966 the Joint Chiefs wrote in a memo to the secretary of defense that restraint in hitting lucrative targets might lead Peking to miscalculate U.S. intentions, thereby leading to Chinese intervention.[45]

But the curious thing was that being right about the reactions of Hanoi, Moscow, and Peking did not seem to make a great deal of difference. The Joint Chiefs turned out to be right in discounting the wider-war risks in the bombing campaign. And in a sense their hand was strengthened in gradually removing targets such as POL facilities and airfields from the restricted list. But their being right as each of these firebreaks was breached did not give them the added influence to convince the President to remove virtually all bombing restrictions, mine the harbors, and invade Laos and Cambodia. Similarly, those who argued correctly that Hanoi would match more force with more force had little success in preventing or curtailing American force increments. Having a good track record in predicting enemy reactions undoubtedly helped, but it did not tip the scales in any internal debate about crossing new thresholds. New decisions were fought out anew—with the scales preweighted by other considerations in the direction of escalation. Deeper elements were at work than good track records.

Two-Way Constraints

One gets a sense of these deeper elements and the dilemma they established when it is realized that several of the key constraints cut both ways—that is, they were not only reasons against doing what was

44. See the JCS recommendations to the President in mid-October 1967, in ibid., p. 536.
45. Ibid., p. 41.

necessary to win but reasons against incurring increased risks of losing. This was true of the central constraint against beginning the bombing in 1964. On the one hand, the bombing might scare off Hanoi, but on the other hand, Hanoi might step up the pressure and Saigon might collapse entirely. It was true of the wider war constraints. Taking off the military wraps might finish Hanoi or it might lead to Chinese intervention and the defeat of American forces in Indochina. And beyond that, the movement toward a wider war might cause the American public to reverse its opinion and demand complete American withdrawal. It was true of the constraints on increasing U.S. ground forces. More U.S. troops would produce more North Vietnamese troops, which in turn would produce more American casualties, again risking continued domestic support for the war. The Great Society constraint was also a double-edged sword. A meeting in McNamara's office on February 6, 1966, illustrates the point. Chief of Staff of the Army Harold K. Johnson made the case for economic mobilization and a reserve call-up. He argued that these acts "might be an important factor in the reading of the North Vietnamese and the Chinese with respect to our determination to see this war through." McNamara maintained that the economy was near capacity, with the probabilities of shortages and controls, "all of which will add fuel to those who say we cannot afford this [war]."[46]

Those who wanted to keep the risks of winning and losing in balance were always introducing new constraints to meet new pressures. To stifle the demands for winning generated in the wake of the Tet offensive in 1968, the task force headed by Defense Secretary Clark Clifford arrayed the following arguments in early March: "We will have failed in our purpose," the task force memo to the President stated, if the war spreads to the point where (1) there is a direct military confrontation with China or the Soviet Union; (2) other commitments, especially NATO, are no longer credible; (3) the slogan "no more Vietnams" brings other commitments "into question as a matter of US will"; and (4) other nations will not want American commitments "for fear of the consequences to themselves as a battlefield between the East and the West."[47]

Winning strategies always had to have tunnel vision, dismissing the costs and dangers they would entail. Presidents could not afford that kind of partiality. Sensitivity to trade-offs made the middle road the inevitable course for the leaders with final authority.

46. Ibid., p. 314.
47. Ibid., p. 580.

CHAPTER TEN

Pressures and the President

President after President found himself hemmed in on Southeast Asia. One set of international, domestic, and at times bureaucratic imperatives made it unthinkable to lose Vietnam. Another set of constraints militated against choosing strategies that promised victory. Pressured to move clearly in one direction or the other, convinced that both choices were dangerously wrong, U.S. presidents dipped into the bag marked "Rules For Successful Leadership" and came out with the most tried and successful formula of them all—"keep your options open." There was nothing devious, mysterious, or unexpected about it. But as Theodore Sorensen has noted:

. . . too often a President finds that events or the decisions of others have limited his freedom of maneuver—that, as he makes a choice, that door closes behind him. And he knows that, once that door is closed, it may never open again—and he may then find himself in a one-way tunnel, or in a baffling maze, or descending a slippery slope. He cannot count on turning back—yet he cannot see his way ahead. He knows that if he is to act, some eggs must be broken to make the omelet, as the old saying goes. But he also knows that an omelet cannot lay any more eggs.[1]

The tugging at the presidents at times reached formidable proportions, and it is easy to conjure up the image of Prometheus chained. That is undoubtedly the way it looked from the White House. But whereas in the Promethean myth the game of life was stacked in favor of the gods, in the Vietnam tale the political system was tilted toward the presidents. Although nothing was easy for Truman, Eisenhower, Kennedy, and Johnson in guiding their Vietnam policies through the labyrinth of

1. Theodore C. Sorensen, *Decision-Making in the White House: The Olive Branch or the Arrows* (Columbia University Press, 1963), p. 21.

American politics, those who tried to push the presidents off course found that task nearly impossible.

Pressures to Do Both More and Less

The pressures to do more and to achieve victory came mainly from the inside and were reflected on the outside. From inside the administrations, three forces almost invariably pushed hard.

1. Individual military leaders and later the military establishment generally initiated requests for broadening and intensifying U.S. military action. After the 1950s the professional military placed great weight on the strategic significance of Vietnam; they were given a job to do and their prestige was involved. The Joint Chiefs of Staff, CINCPAC, the MAAG chiefs, and later the commander of U.S. forces in Vietnam—and in the early sixties the civilian leaders in the Pentagon—were the chief sources of these pressures.

2. Ambassadors in Saigon, supported by the State Department, occasionally pressed for, and even more often supported, big steps forward. Their reasons were similar to those of the military.

3. An ever-present group of "reformers" made urgent demands to strengthen and broaden the Saigon government in order to achieve political victory. Every executive agency had its reformers. They were usually able men whose entire preoccupation was to make things better in Vietnam.

From outside the administration, pressure came from liberal legislators, Catholic organizations, and the establishment press in the earlier years. After 1964 there were powerful groups who wanted to win—or at least to decide firmly either to win or get out. Capitol Hill hawks and the conservative press stood in the forefront. Paris and later Saigon applied pressure for more as well.

The pressures for deescalation and for disengagement derived mostly from the outside, with occasional and often unknown allies from within. These forces, although small for most of the Vietnam years, grew steadily in strength from 1965 onward. Isolated congressmen and senators led the fight. First, they did so on anticolonialist and anti-Asian-land-war grounds. Later, complementing the cost-benefit arguments, their objections developed moral aspects (against interfering in a civil war and supporting an unpopular regime). This position combined arguments about the war being unwinnable, domestic priorities, and the "senselessness" of the war. Peace organizations and student groups in particular came to dominate headlines and air time. Journalists such as Homer Bigart, David Halberstam, Seymour Hersh, and others played a critical role, especially through television reports when the war became big news. In each administration opposition could be found (1) within the leadership of the military establishment in the early years (Matthew Ridgway, James Gavin) and later among isolated military men who did not want the United States in an Asian land war, or among middle-level officers who became disillusioned through service in the field; (2) among some State Department intelligence and area specialists who knew Vietnam and believed the U.S. objective was unattainable at any reasonable price; and (3) within the civilian agencies of the Defense Department and among isolated individuals at the State Department, particularly after 1966, whose efforts were trained on finding a politically feasible way out. Each of these groups and individuals employed different techniques in pressing their views. Each also possessed distinctive bargaining advantages.

The American allies in the war, France and the GVN, applied pressure basically through the U.S. bureaucracy (especially through the organizations as they were represented in Vietnam), Congress, and various lobby groups (especially in the early days of Diem's rule). Neither Paris nor Saigon wanted U.S. combat troops until late 1961 (and even then only hesitantly on Diem's part), but they always asked for more American money and equipment. France and the GVN also always argued against the United States pressuring them for reforms; the former threatened to dump the war in Washington's lap, and the latter claimed that pressure would bring about political collapse and defeat. Their advantages were their own weaknesses and their ability to play on American anticommunism.

Congress and the Press

Congress and the press tried to keep the President's feet to the fire and had several other pots boiling for him no matter which way he jumped. While some legislators and journalists displayed a remarkable consistency in what they urged, the net effect of the pressures from these quarters was to try to have it both ways—or all ways. The typical speech on Capitol Hill and the typical editorial implored the President not to lose but to avoid further American involvement, to negotiate but to give nothing away, to win but not to run the risks of a wider war. Their speciality was general discourse demanding "action," or "peace," or "answers." They could call for action either way, since the President would be the one to take the responsibility. The whole climate fostered posturing. And when the President was not confronted with this kind of posturing he was being buffeted by diametrically opposed views. In the summer of 1967, for example, Senator Fulbright was urging a total bombing cessation, and Senator Stennis's Preparedness Investigating Subcommittee was issuing a report that concluded: "What is needed now is the hard decision to do whatever is necessary, take the risks that have to be taken, and apply the force that is required to see the job through . . . logic and prudence requires that the decision be made with the unanimous weight of professional military judgment."[2] The net effect of this, it should be emphasized, was not the neutralization of legislative and press opinion but constant pressure on the President to do everything demanded of him.

The Military

Every President, with the exception of Eisenhower, had to contend with constant pressure from the military to use increasing doses of force. The obvious military bargaining advantage was the relative ease with which the military could take their complaints to sympathetic congressional committees, which would then translate them into news stories. When U.S. security was deemed to be at stake, and especially when American men were dying, the military possessed a real bludgeon over debate. Their way, they insisted, based on their professionalism, was the best way to save lives, and "tying their hands" would lead to more American deaths, not fewer. Moreover, in thinking about a compromise settlement, the President would have to measure those compromises against the possibility that the military might charge that Americans "had died for nothing."

The Joint Chiefs excelled at making points for the record. Year after year they promised little or nothing unless they were given everything they recommended. When the President fell short in meeting their demands, they could say only that they would try their best. Limited wars in the sense of limitations on conventional tactics, rather than in the

2. *Air War against North Vietnam,* Summary Report of the Preparedness Investigating Subcommittee of the Senate Committee on Armed Services, 90 Cong. 1 sess. (Government Printing Office, 1967), pp. 9–10.

sense of nonnuclear, particularly grated on the military mind. As Roger Hilsman has written of the Kennedy era: "Not all of the Joint Chiefs fully subscribed to the 'Never Again' view, but it seemed to the White House that they were at least determined to build a record that would protect their position and put the blame entirely on the President no matter what happened."[3]

A more subtle source of military leverage was their well-developed capacity for demonstrating how to get from here to there. The military specialized, as they had to, in plans, and plans sometimes provided the illusion of control over events. It usually proved difficult for the intangible reservations, feelings, and intuitions of the diplomat to stand up against the concrete designs of a paper that said that so many men and dollars employed in such and such a manner would achieve x, y, and z results in six months. The reservations appear as "details" or "administrative wrinkles." While presidents learned to develop a healthy skepticism about this, the allure of the plan remained. Thus the military held high cards with Congress and in internal debates that presidents could reject but not ignore.

Civilian Advisers

Not the least of the pressures with which presidents had to cope were those from their senior civilian advisers. While these men were the President's own appointees, loyalty and influence is a two-way street. Sorensen said that "almost every President is as reluctant to overrule the determined opposition of his advisers as he is to veto an act of the Congress. He rules, to a degree, not only with their advice but with their consent."[4] And as with Congress and the press, advice from senior advisers came from all directions.

Those who wanted more used three sets of arguments. One was that time was running out. Thus in order to get prompt and favorable action from President Kennedy, Taylor said in the conclusion of his 1961 report: "It cannot be emphasized too strongly, however, that time has nearly run out for converting . . . assets into the bases for victory."[5] Unless the President accepted the recommendations quickly, so it was

---

3. Roger Hilsman, *To Move a Nation: The Politics of Foreign Policy in the Administration of John F. Kennedy* (Doubleday, 1967), p. 129.

4. Sorensen, *Decision-Making in the White House,* p. 81.

5. *The Pentagon Papers: The Defense Department History of United States Decisionmaking on Vietnam,* Senator Gravel ed. (Beacon Press, 1971), vol. 2, p. 93.

implied, there would be no tomorrow. A second technique was to frame the President's choice in either-or terms. For example, Johnson recorded that on January 27, 1965, McGeorge Bundy sent him a memo reflecting McNamara and Bundy's opinions and giving him two alternatives: either to "use our military power in the Far East and to force a change of Communist policy" or to "deploy all our resources along a track of negotiation, aimed at salvaging what little can be preserved with no major addition to our present military risks." Bundy said that he and McNamara had "fully supported" the President's "unwillingness, in earlier months to move out of the middle course. We both agree that every effort should still be made to improve our operations on the ground and to prop up the authorities in South Vietnam as best we can. But we are both convinced that none of this is enough, and that the time has come for harder choices."[6] This could well have been read in the White House as a threat. A third technique was to confront the President with a "consensus option." In this case most or all of the senior advisers would band together, evidently before consulting with the President, in recommending a certain course of action. This happened when McNamara, Roswell Gilpatric, and the Joint Chiefs sent a memo to the President endorsing the Taylor recommendations of 1961 and when the NSC Principals Group in 1964 presented a nearly united front (after submerging the objections of Robert Johnson and assuaging those of Admiral Lloyd Mustin) on the "slow squeeze" approach to bombing North Vietnam.

Those senior civilian advisers who pressed for doing less often used feasibility arguments. Some seized on General Ridgway's conclusion that Radford's plan to save Dien Bien Phu with air strikes would not work. Opponents of direct U.S. combat involvement in the early 1960s argued that white faces could not win Asian wars. Opponents of initiating air strikes against North Vietnam in late 1964 warned that Saigon would be unable to cope with Hanoi's likely military response. Adversaries of escalating the bombing in the North claimed that it would not destroy Hanoi's will to resist. The "force levellers" of the late 1960s insisted that U.S. force increments would not improve the situation, since Hanoi would match the increases. The "do-lessers" challenged the means and not the ends of policy.

Both groups sought to embrace domestic political reactions for their causes. The hawks would say that domestic support would be jeopar-

6. Lyndon Baines Johnson, *The Vantage Point: Perspectives of the Presidency, 1963–1969* (Holt, Rinehart and Winston, 1971), pp. 122–23.

dized if more were not done, and the doves said the reverse. As the war dragged on, the case for both viewpoints was enhanced.

Reformers

Special note has to be taken of the reformer group. While accounts of the early 1960s give the impression that these men were the doves of their day, this is misleading. The evidence suggests that they were actually hawks who wanted to do it a different way by pressuring for reforms before deepening the American involvement. For example, Roger Hilsman, a key figure in the early reformer group headed by Averell Harriman, wrote a memo to Rusk on March 14, 1964, in which he argued for a security approach as opposed to a killing-Vietcong approach but went on to urge that once Saigon attained political stability, then enemy infiltration and training areas should be attacked.[7] Actually, the very meddling in Saigon politics that the reformers proposed was a form of doing more because it reflected the assumption that Washington had the right and responsibility to so involve itself. Furthermore, like the military who stood on the other side of the fence, they were never at a loss for plans by which to bring about reforms. The difference was between military hawks, who saw more force as necessary and political reforms as unworkable, and political hawks, who saw reform as necessary and more force as unproductive. Nevertheless, the reformer-hawks of the early 1960s became the inside doves of the late 1960s, joined by McNamara and his key subordinates. It was the overmilitarization of the war that led to their conversion.

Presidential Responses

Presidential responses to these pressures followed two patterns: from 1949 through the spring of 1965, doing what was minimally necessary not to lose; and from the summer of 1965 until March 1968, doing the maximum feasible to win, *within certain domestic and international constraints.*

The Minimum Necessary

In the period before direct massive American involvement, each President was essentially doing what he thought was minimally neces-

7. *Pentagon Papers*, vol. 3, pp. 43–44.

sary to prevent a Communist victory during his tenure of office. Since every several years the floor on the minimum necessary was being raised by conditions in Vietnam, the process became the functional equivalent of gradual escalation. Each President had to do more than his predecessor in order to stay even.

Constraints gave way one by one in order to stave off defeat. In late 1949 Truman and Acheson instituted the program of direct U.S. military and economic aid to the French effort in Indochina. After years of carefully avoiding direct support for what they believed to be the losing cause of French colonialism, they decided they had to step into the breach, since France could not or would not continue to bear the costs of the war alone. In early 1950 they crossed another self-imposed line by granting recognition to the French puppet regime of Bao Dai and beginning direct aid to the states of Indochina as well. With the outbreak of the Korean War, they violated yet a third constraint by linking the struggle in Indochina to American security in order to bolster French morale and deter possible intervention by China.

Eisenhower and Dulles made the war even more evidently an American cause. Whereas under Truman the French still bore the bulk of the war costs, Eisenhower upped both the U.S. share of the costs (to 80 percent) and the volume of Washington's rhetoric. He also authorized the dispatch of U.S. ground crews when Paris said it could not fulfill its own airpower requirements. Most significantly, when France decided to withdraw militarily from Indochina in 1955, Eisenhower ordered American advisers to take their place.

Kennedy made the decision to exceed the limit on foreign military advisers stipulated in the Geneva accords. He then sanctioned the use of U.S. military personnel in combat support operations, such as flying helicopters, and of CIA personnel in covert operations. It was perhaps of greater consequence that Kennedy meddled in Saigon politics, supported the anti-Diem coup, and thereby hiked the U.S. responsibility for the existence of the Saigon regime by an order of magnitude.

Lyndon Johnson, of course, crossed the barriers of ground combat and air war against the North, barriers that had greater visibility but not necessarily more saliency than the previous ones. These were decisions the others did not have to face seriously, perhaps with the exception of Eisenhower at the time of Dien Bien Phu.

At times the presidents shaded the minimum necessary on the down side and at other times, on the high side. Thus when it came to meeting requests for military and economic assistance, they invariably erred on the side of caution and gave the extra millions of dollars whether or not they were convinced that the extra was justified. But when some advisers argued that the minimum necessitated the introduction of U.S. combat forces, the presidents were inclined to take their chances and reject the recommendation. Eisenhower in April 1954, Kennedy in late 1961, and Johnson at the end of 1964 resisted strenuous pleas from their senior advisers to send in the troops or start bombing the North—even though the advisers maintained that doing less than that would almost certainly mean defeat.

The reason the presidents shaded these kinds of requests on the down side reveals a lot about their thinking and is therefore worth dwelling upon. Why were they willing in these instances to reject the military logic that minimal steps would risk losing? The step they were being asked to take was a big one, to be sure, and inhibiting in itself, but the explanation seems to go deeper. Presidents got to the top by gambling, by playing long shots against their numerous competitors and against the odds, and in these instances they were prepared to run the odds that their advisers were exaggerating. No one gets to the White House without being surrounded by Chicken Littles breathlessly exclaiming that "the sky is falling" and that if such and such is not done, all will be lost. Thus the man in the White House comes to discount the Chicken Littles with a "strong belief in his lucky star, a confidence that he can get away with what looks like chance-taking where others might not, confidence that 'something will always turn up' for him."[8]

The Maximum Feasible

The second pattern of presidential response, which evolved in the summer of 1965, was for Johnson to do the maximum feasible to win without using nuclear weapons and attacking the Communist sanctuaries in Laos, Cambodia, and North Vietnam with U.S. ground forces, and without calling up the reserves at home and mobilizing the economy by imposing a war tax. In effect the maximum feasible meant the minimum necessary disruption of domestic life and running the minimum necessary risks of a wider war. Having taken the seminal actions in 1965, Johnson thereafter did not remove any additional major constraints, but

8. Daniel Ellsberg, *Papers on the War* (Simon and Schuster, 1972), p. 79. This point was originally made by Richard Moorsteen to Ellsberg.

he did sanction vast expansion of all authorized actions. As was the case during the minimum-necessary period, after breaching a barrier it became difficult, if not impossible, for the President to establish a new firebreak in that action that could stick. For example, when Truman started direct aid to France of under $100 million, there was no stopping the climb to nearly $1 billion a year under Eisenhower. When Kennedy went over the Geneva limit of 600-plus advisers, the total soon climbed to over 16,000. And once Johnson committed combat troops, their number climbed to a half-million.

But there was an important difference between the two periods in this respect. During the minimum-necessary phase, more aid and more advisers were sufficient because the pressures were directed mainly at avoiding defeat. Vietnam was an issue of low public visibility, and in a sense few were looking at the problem. But during the maximum-feasible phase, when expenses leaped to over $20 billion a year and when hundreds of Americans were being killed and wounded, the costs of not seeking to win increased immeasurably. Sunk costs did have some constraining effect. Given these human and dollar costs, Johnson wanted to do everything he could to damp down the charge that he was not trying to consummate the war. This explains why George Ball's argument that bombing the North would only enlarge the war rather than win it did not sell and why the argument from 1967 of McNamara, Katzenbach, and McGeorge Bundy for leveling off the U.S. effort did not sell either. These arguments missed the point of Johnson's political problem—that the country would not sustain an obvious stalemate indefinitely. Johnson reasoned that he could not keep the spigot open steadily and maintain public support for the war.

Keeping to the Middle of the Road

Whether in doing the minimum necessary or the maximum feasible, presidents tried to stay in the middle of the road, within wider or narrower margins. Their main aim was to avoid the high-risk alternatives of either losing or doing what was really necessary to win. Their chore and their skill was in carving out a third choice.

Truman, caught between the anticolonialism of his Asian specialists and the pro-French and anti-Communist attitudes of his Europeanists, moved from a hands-off approach, to evenhanded diplomacy seeking to reconcile France and the Vietminh, to a blessing of the French effort, while urging France to grant independence to the states of Indochina. In

early 1954 Eisenhower found himself torn between the forces represented by Radford, who favored unilateral U.S. intervention, and the
forces represented by Ridgway, who wanted to keep out, and he chose
the middle way of indicating he would go in if Congress approved,
allies joined the effort, and the French remained to fight on the ground.
In 1955 he found himself pulled one way by the military, who opposed
assuming the French role, and another way by Dulles, who believed the
assumption was mandatory, and he chose to delay the decision until
Diem had demonstrated his survivability.

President Kennedy had to face three basic general decisions. First,
was top priority to go to political reform or to getting on with the war?
Could the war be effectively pursued without making sure of its political
base in Saigon? Would pressures for political reform undermine and
even risk everything in the military effort? On this issue the reformers,
who wanted to give priority to political reform, were arrayed against
the military. Second, should the line of involvement be drawn at combat
units? Was this militarily necessary? Would it make U.S. influence with
Diem stronger or weaker? What would be Hanoi's reaction? On this
issue the reformers were more quiet than in opposition. The military and
the country team pushed hard, even urging the President to threaten
Hanoi with U.S. bombing. Some counterweight came from the State
Department and the White House staff. Third, should the President
make a clear, irrevocable and open-ended commitment to prevent a
Communist victory? Would this strengthen or weaken the U.S. hand in
Saigon? Would it frighten away the Communists? What would be the
domestic political consequences? Here, it seemed that Rusk and Ball
were alone in opposition to virtually everyone else.

In both tactics and decisions the President kept to the middle of the
road by doing what was minimally necessary. On the issue of political
versus military priorities, Kennedy did not make increasing military assistance definitively contingent on political reform, but he pointed to the
absence of reform as the main reason for limiting the U.S. military role.
On the combat unit issue, according to Sorensen, "Kennedy never made
a final negative decision on troops. In typical Kennedy fashion, he made
it difficult for any of the pro-intervention advocates to charge him privately with weakness."[9] On the third issue, he avoided an open-ended
commitment but escalated his rhetoric about the importance of Vietnam.

9. Theodore C. Sorensen, *Kennedy* (Harper and Row, 1965), p. 654.

While he did authorize an increase of U.S. military personnel from 685 to 16,000, he did so slowly and not in two or three big decisions. He gave encouragement to bureaucratic planning and studying as a safety valve —a valve he thought he could control.[10] He kept a very tight rein on information to the public about the war. According to Pierre Salinger, the administration "was not anxious to admit the existence of a real war."[11] By minimizing U.S. involvement, Kennedy was avoiding public pressures either to do more or to do less.

At Johns Hopkins in April 1965 President Johnson told the American people: "We will do everything necessary to reach that objective [of the independence of South Vietnam and its freedom from attack], and we will do only what is absolutely necessary."[12] In order to hold domestic opinion on his side, however, the minimum necessary became the maximum feasible but still in the middle of the road. The Air Force and CINCPAC pressed hard for full systems bombing—the authority to destroy ninety-four key North Vietnamese targets in a blitz of a few weeks. Johnson, backed and pressured in the other direction by Secretary McNamara, doled out approval for new targets over three years in a painstaking and piecemeal fashion. Johnson accommodated dovish pressure and the advice of the many pragmatists who surrounded him by making peace overtures. But these overtures were either accompanied with or followed by escalation. Johnson moved in the direction of those who wanted three-quarters of a million U.S. fighting men in Vietnam, but he never got there. Influenced by domestic repercussions and again by McNamara, the President made at least eight separate decisions on U.S. force levels in Vietnam over a four-year period. For the "fixers" who felt that U.S. conduct of the war ignored its political essence and for the doves who wanted to see something besides destruction, Johnson placed new emphasis on "the other war"—pacification, nation-building, and political development—in February 1966. Johnson referred to this whole complex of actions and the air war in particular as his attempt to seduce rather than rape the North Vietnamese.

As the President crossed the old barriers, he established new ones in order to preserve his options. While he ordered the bombing of North

10. Hilsman, *To Move a Nation*, p. 424.

11. Pierre Salinger, *With Kennedy* (Doubleday, 1966), p. 320.

12. "Address at Johns Hopkins University, 'Peace without Conquest,' April 7, 1965," *Public Papers of the Presidents of the United States: Lyndon B. Johnson, 1965* (GPO, 1966), p. 395.

Vietnam, he would not approve the bombing of targets that ran the risk of confrontation with China and Russia. While he permitted the U.S. force level in Vietnam to go over one-half million men, he would not agree to call up the Reserves. While he was willing to spend $25 billion in one year on the war, he would not put the U.S. economy on a wartime mobilization footing. But the most important Johnson barrier was raised against invading North Vietnam. This limitation was also a cornerstone in the President's hopes for a compromise settlement. He would agree to the permanent existence of North Vietnam—even help that country economically—if North Vietnam would extend that same right to South Vietnam.

Johnson's memoir reconstruction of the bombing debate in the spring of 1967 gave a detailed picture of how he approached a problem:

Both proposals, and the justifications for them, had merit. A stronger air program might further weaken the North militarily and might help convince Hanoi that a peaceful settlement was to its advantage. . . . On the other hand, cutting back to the 20th parallel would concentrate our attacks on a principal objective: impeding the flow of men and supplies into the South. . . . There were other factors [pressures from senators and congressmen] as well. . . . I decided to steer a course midway between the proposal of those who wanted to cut back our air action and the plan advanced by those who believed we should step up strikes in the North. I felt that a cutback to the 20th parallel at that time would have been misunderstood in Hanoi as a sign of weakness. I also believed that strikes in the Hanoi-Haiphong vicinity were costing more than the results justified. Beginning on May 22, I ordered a halt to air attacks on targets within ten miles of the North Vietnamese capital.[13]

The middle of the road was the logical place for the presidents to seek out for ideological, political, and policy reasons. By personality and by ideology, the presidents were political centrists who had gained power by successfully labeling their opponents as extremists and by capturing the middle. None of them were ideologues but working political pragmatists who bridled at grand principles and the systematic exposition of one set of ideas—like most of the men around them, only more so.

The tactic of the small middle-of-the-road decision made optimum sense for the politics of the presidency. Even America's strongest presidents have been inclined to shy away from decisive action. It has been too uncertain, too risky. They derived their strength from movement, the image of a lot of activity, building and neutralizing opponents. Too

13. Johnson, *The Vantage Point*, p. 368.

seldom has there been forceful moral leadership; it may even be un-
democratic. The small step that maintains the momentum gives the
President the chance to gather up more support politically. It gives the
appearance of minimizing possible mistakes. It keeps both extremes on
board, both disgruntled but not alienated enough to jump ship. It allows
time to gauge reactions. It serves as a pressure-relieving valve against
those who want to do more. It can be doled out. Above all, it gives the
President something to do next time.

Rusk, always the President's man, had this very much in mind in the
deliberations of the NSC Principals Group in November 1964. As related
in the Pentagon Papers, the discussion went as follows:

The only basic issue between the options on which the Principals did not
arrive at a consensus was the question of the relative risks of major conflict
entailed by Options B [full fast squeeze] and C [slow squeeze]. General
Wheeler stated that there was less risk of a major conflict before achieving
success under Option B than under Option C. Secretary McNamara believed
the opposite to be true. Secretary Rusk argued that if B were selected, there
would be no chance to apply the JCS variant of C, whereas under the Working Group's C, this would still be left available.[14]

The presidents determined where in the middle of the road they
would land by trial and error and by their own political judgment. During the minimum-necessary period they might have done more and done
it more rapidly if they had been convinced (1) that the threat of a Communist takeover was more immediate, (2) that U.S. domestic politics
would have been more permissive, (3) that the government of South
Vietnam had the requisite political stability and military potential for
effective use, and (4) that the job really would have gotten done. During the maximum-feasible phase Johnson might have exceeded his own
constraints if he had believed that victory could be achieved so quickly
that the Communist superpowers would not respond and that public
opinion at home would have held despite the risks. But the presidents
could not bank on any of these conditions. They could not be confident
about how their actions would turn out, and they sensed that either
nothing would work fully or that the costs of winning would be too high.
Again, the tactic of keeping their options open made perfect sense to
them. Accordingly the presidents reacted to the pressures as brakemen,
pulling the switch against both the advocates of decisive escalation and
the proponents of leveling off and disengaging.

14. *Pentagon Papers,* vol. 3, p. 239.

Presidential Management of the Political System

The interesting thing is not that the presidents adopted the role of centrist brakemen, of keeping their options open (it would have been remarkable had they not done so), but how they made their decisions stick politically despite the forces trying to pull them out of the center. One can concede the formidable powers of the President to get his way on policy and marvel at the juggling and high wire acts nonetheless.

The Left and the Right

Presidents employed a wide range of techniques for neutralizing critics outside the executive branch of government. For those on the Left, the characteristic devices were adoption and scrambling. First, the President could undercut them by adopting their proposals in words (such as publicly calling for reforms or placing new rhetorical emphasis on pacification) and in deeds (like ordering a bombing halt of the North). The latter case has some interesting facets, for the bombing halt that was used in the first instance to placate the Left was at times also used to ready the public for future escalation. Thus in a memorandum to the President on November 30, 1965, recommending a bombing pause precedent to both a troop increase and stepped-up bombing, McNamara argued that American leaders had to "lay a foundation in the mind of the American public and in world opinion for such an enlarged phase of the war."[15] This was a persuasive argument in 1965, but Johnson later developed great caution about bombing halts precisely because he sensed they would fail to bring Hanoi to the negotiating table and would therefore lead to unwanted pressures for escalation—which shows how tricky this whole game was. A second technique was to scramble all critics on the Left into a single "omelet." Johnson frequently lumped together the likes of Fulbright, Mansfield, Martin Luther King, Stokely Carmichael, Benjamin Spock, and the flag burners. It was an easy omelet to make, since in America dissenters are regarded usually as eccentrics or as well-intentioned but naive. The critics could respond to this discrediting by association only with complicated arguments about the origin of the war or the ineffectiveness of the bombing, arguments the administration simply dismissed by rejecting them as untrue. And when it came down

15. Ibid., vol. 4, p. 33.

to a test between the reasoning of the Left and the authority of the administration, the winner usually would be a foregone conclusion.

Controlling the Right was always a more complicated affair than controlling the Left. One way of doing it, as Kennedy and Johnson discovered, was to attack the Left. The attendant complications of this technique arose acutely on the question of how to talk publicly about the war. Popular frustration or passion might well prompt irresistible demands to make means consistent with ends. The U.S. goal of an independent non-Communist South Vietnam was in effect as unlimited an end as unconditional surrender in World War II, and unlimited ends in time are bound to lead to a call for unlimited means. As the ends of the war themselves came into question, President Johnson was faced with a delicate choice. On the one hand, he could have chosen to wave the "bloody flag" and infuse the war with popular emotion. This, in the President's estimation, would have gained him right-wing support, but it also would have lit right-wing fires to win the war, thus eroding barriers against the all-out use of force. And once these barriers were torn down, so LBJ apparently reasoned, right-wing demands could not be controlled. Such a strategy also would have gone against the grain of the President's political style, a style that sought consensus, not divisiveness. On the other hand, he could have run parallel to this line by challenging his critics with innuendo and with the argument that fighting locally in Vietnam was preventing the outbreak of large-scale aggression elsewhere. LBJ picked this course. Instead of insinuating that his critics were traitors or Communists, he called them "nervous Nellies" and "prophets of gloom and doom." Instead of holding parades down Pennsylvania Avenue, he held award ceremonies in the Oval Office. As the war went on from year to year, however, none of this was sufficient to quell the growing opposition.

Johnson nevertheless could call on a second technique to hold the line. This was to paint the alternatives to what he was doing as irresponsible and reckless. Every once in a while Johnson would let drop such a comment as "I won't let those Air Force generals bomb the smallest outhouse north of the 17th parallel without checking with me. The generals know only two words—spend and bomb."[16] Following the paths of either the "nervous Nellies" or the generals, according to the Johnson rhetoric, would result in a greater risk of a future world war.

16. Quoted in Rowland Evans and Robert Novak, *Lyndon B. Johnson: The Exercise of Power* (New American Library, 1966), p. 539.

Presidents were able to fend off pressures from whatever quarter with a retinue of additional maneuvers. First, the President had it in his power to make short-run fixes to get over the immediate hump of criticism. Whatever the charge, a speech could be given a week later saying it was already being taken care of. Second, from Eisenhower on, the presidents manipulated time horizons. Just as Hanoi tried to portray the war as never-ending, Washington had to feed the impression of a near-term win and allow it to grow. The public would not stand for incrementalism that promised only open-ended fighting with continued U.S. fatalities. Thus was born the policy of controlled optimism. Pressure filled the pipelines throughout the government, into the field, down to the very bottom of the command structure. Show progress! But the dilemma of this strategy could not have been lost on American leaders. Optimism would work only so long; after that, it would serve as midwife to the credibility gap. Third, the President, as Kennedy showed, could preserve his options by hiding the war from the public, by making U.S. involvement covert. This was a relatively cheap way to send a signal to the Communists without sending it to the American Congress, press, and public. Finally, each President could and did make most decisions so small that they were difficult to argue against. Only after all the small steps had been tabulated could the pattern be seen and attacked.

None of these techniques and counterpressures proved very successful, it should be emphasized, on the American allies in Paris or Saigon. Their weaknesses and the basic U.S. commitment permitted them the luxury of relative independence at American expense. Of all the forces outside the administration itself, allies were the most difficult to control.

Doves and Hawks

The President's management of pressures from within his own bureaucracy also fell into several definable molds. With respect to the inside doves, the initial effort invariably would be to try to "domesticate" them. James Thomson said that this "arose out of a twofold clubbish need: on the one hand, the dissenter's desire to stay abroad; and on the other hand, the nondissenter's conscience."[17] Everyone would be happy if the dissenter was prepared to state his piece, have his hearing, and then lose and be quiet about it. If the dissenter proved rambunctious, he

17. James C. Thomson, Jr., "How Could Vietnam Happen? An Autopsy," *Atlantic Monthly*, April 1968, p. 49.

could then be cut off the cable traffic or lose his access to the higher-ups, as was the case with Clark Clifford after March 1968.

Managing the inside hawks required another set of techniques. First, as Hilsman remarked about Kennedy's years, "The President. . . . felt he had to keep the JCS on board, [and] that the only way to keep them on board was to keep McNamara on board."[18] (Under Johnson, however, keeping the chiefs on board ultimately required clipping McNamara's wings.) This meant that all the presidents had to avoid handing down a *final* "no" on a military proposal, to always allow the planning to go forward, and to seldom pinch hard enough to make the Joint Chiefs scream outside the conference room. To frost the cake a bit, presidents went out of their way to praise the military. When this showed scant hope of working, the presidents would try to maneuver someone other than themselves into making the fight against escalation. Eisenhower wheeled in congressional leaders to veto the Radford plan, going so far as to stay away from the meeting despite its being held in the White House. Kennedy staved off the recommendations of Taylor, Rostow, and the Pentagon in 1961 by having their final recommendations come to him in a Rusk-McNamara memo that left out the objectionable request for combat troops. Johnson used Ball as devil's advocate in 1964 and 1965 to tone down the recommendations of his other advisers and to promote a more desired middle option. Finally, despite tight monitoring of the air war, Johnson sought to mitigate inevitable military discomfort with a limited war by not interfering in how they ran the war in South Vietnam.

Inside hawks and doves alike could be placated by the dynamics of "Option B" (or "C"—whichever was the option between opposite extremes). This is the technique of giving leeway to the bureaucracy to find its own common denominators. It meant policy papers loaded with false options—two patently unacceptable extremes of humiliating defeat and total war, and Option B. Option B encompassed most of what everyone wanted to do or the essence of their recommendations. It was a concession to expertise and direct responsibility. Few could complain that their advice was not taken. It was, above all, the means by which the policy consensus was preserved.

Because Option B was the basis of consensus, it was full of contradictions, the consequences of which were disastrous for U.S. Vietnam pol-

18. Hilsman, *To Move a Nation*, p. 508.

icy. Washington tried both to bomb more and to negotiate seriously, even though bombing prevented negotiations. Washington wanted the South Vietnamese to do more of the fighting and felt that the United States must have a larger direct combat role for itself, even though the latter gave the South Vietnamese the perfect excuse not to do the former. Washington sought both to reform the Saigon government and to give the Saigon leaders whatever they asked for, thus leaving itself without any leverage. The result was a hodgepodge that could not work in Vietnam but did work in Washington.

Presidential clout and maneuvering influence, it should be noted, were much more of a factor in policy debates in Washington than in implementation in Vietnam. By and large, presidents got their way in the concepts and words that shaped policy, but those who carried out the policy in field programs could, within wide margins, still do their own thing. The ambassador could be instructed to hit the table in Saigon, but whether he slammed it or tapped it would be perforce at his discretion. The military could be ordered to place increased resources in the pacification effort, but the accounting of which resources went where was their own.

Legislators and Journalists

There were still other pressures with which the presidents had to contend, namely the institutional force of Congress and the general impact of the press. Presidents had to do what they could to neutralize the advantage enjoyed by Congress and the press in having it both ways. The men in the White House therefore sought means to implicate legislators and journalists in the presidents' policies. Hugh Sidey analyzed the Johnson technique on the press: "Things are to be represented as Johnson wants them to be, not as they are, and by the time his small hoaxes are discovered he has accomplished his purpose, the theory goes, and nobody will really care about his methods." Sidey noted that Philip Potter, a *Baltimore Sun* reporter, had quoted a Johnson aide as saying that "fundamentally [Johnson] believes what he reads in the papers . . . and he thinks the way to change things is to change what is printed in the papers."[19]

Implicating Congress brought another series of devices into play, all of which boiled down to getting Congress as an institution to share

19. Hugh Sidey, *A Very Personal Presidency: Lyndon Johnson in the White House* (Atheneum, 1968), pp. 162–63.

responsibility for what was being done. Eisenhower brought the Senate on board through the SEATO treaty. Johnson built on this with the Tonkin Gulf Resolution. Johnson could and did entice legislators to go to Vietnam to "observe the free elections," thus trapping them into blessing the results. Every one of the presidents forced Congress to choose sides in the annual appropriations votes. Despite all their criticisms, were the legislators prepared to deny France and later Saigon the funds to fight communism? Despite legislative qualms about U.S. forces fighting an Asian land war, was Congress about to deny the boys in the field what they needed? Again, the President's arsenal of counterpressures was more than equal to the task.

How the System Helped the President

The political system and simply the circumstances of getting along in official Washington reinforced the middle position of the presidents. While the extremes always made the news, it was in the center ground that access and influence resided.

The press was a prime example, as any comparison of the Washington and Saigon press corps would show. The Washington press corps and editorial writers wrote as if they shared the concerns of the policy-makers, dutifully reporting the "cautious optimism" and the hints of possible progress on negotiations. While most Washington-based journalists struck critical notes about certain aspects of the war, by and large they underlined the unacceptability of alternatives to the President's policy and played up the President's problems sympathetically—at least until 1968. The Saigon press corps, on the other hand, adopted a muckraking stance, often punching holes in stories emanating from Washington.

Washington journalists helped readers understand the problems of the decisionmakers. This was the basis of their relationship with official-dom. If they did not write with understanding, they could look forward to reduced access to their friends and sources. The journalists in the field had a different problem. Access to their sources, middle- and lower-ranking officials, could be sustained only by reporting the bad news and what was not being done properly. Moreover, if a good story tempted a journalist to go beyond the bounds of gentlemanly criticism, he might restrain himself or be restrained by his editors for fear of having the rug pulled out from underneath. The President always could do something or reveal something tomorrow that would make the story of yesterday look foolish or irresponsible or both.

Like the press, Congress as an institution found itself impelled to fall in behind the President. On one level, the explanation for this was simple: forever in a time bind, legislators get caught up in the conventional wisdom, or politicians on Capitol Hill feel safer hiding behind the President and "going along with the flag." On a deeper level, until the 1970s Congress lacked effective institutional means of expressing opposition to presidential policies without seeming to endanger American security and the lives of American soldiers. It was unthinkable for most legislators to vote against military and economic aid to Vietnam in the earlier years, and it became impossible for them to oppose war appropriations once U.S. servicemen were in the field and fighting. In practice, until the balance of sentiment shifted decisively after the Johnson administration, Congress could not check or balance the executive on Vietnam policy; so far as its legislative powers were concerned, it could act only as a rubber stamp.

Bureaucratic dissenters, particularly those on the left, found themselves bound by other sorts of strings. Dissenters rarely, if ever, questioned fundamental assumptions. The foreign policy community had become a "house without windows." Since American leaders had the same educational background and outlook, they developed the same views of the world. It was for them a world full of dominoes. But even those who escaped this view in later years, such as McNamara, were trapped by their past support of those assumptions and did not believe they were in a position to make such challenges. Since they continued taking the assumptions as given, they trapped themselves by making arguments only within the framework of the President's policy. They had to show that in effect the marginal changes they were proposing were not only consistent with established goals but a better way of attaining them. Dissenters sometimes prevailed using this technique, but at the price of perpetuating the basic assumptions that kept the war going. Tactical arguments, not fundamental ones, were the order of the day. Those deciding foreign policy argued, not what they believed was right, but what they thought would be persuasive. As Thomson said, they wanted to maintain their effectiveness for the future debates. Now was never the right time to fight.[20]

20. Thomson, "How Could Vietnam Happen?" p. 49.

Friendship and loyalty to the President played an important part in these dynamics as well. David Halberstam related the story of Thruston Morton, assistant secretary of state for congressional affairs, informing Senator Richard Russell in September 1954 of Eisenhower's determination to go ahead and replace French advisers with Americans. Although Russell pronounced this "the greatest mistake this country's ever made" and said that he "could not be more opposed to it," he added that Morton was to tell the President "that if he does it I will never raise my voice."[21] Lyndon Johnson recalled two similar comments by George Ball and Senator Mike Mansfield during the July 1965 debates. At a meeting with Johnson on July 21 Ball said: "I can foresee a perilous voyage. I have great apprehensions that we can't win under these conditions. But let me be clear. If the decision is to go ahead, I'm committed." And with respect to Mansfield: "He thought the best hope was 'a quick stalemate and negotiations.' But he concluded by saying that as a Senator and Majority Leader he would support the President's position."[22] This was high-mindedness, to be sure, but it also totally equated the good of the nation with the fate of the President.

Public opinion, taking its cue from the President, Congress, and the press, also went along with the President's middle-of-the-road policy. As the pollsters put the issue to the public, the alternatives of winning or withdrawing never commanded the support of those who indicated they basically approved what the President was doing. Whichever way presidents turned—more aid, more advisers, peace offers, escalation, bombing halts—the majority stayed with the President until 1968. This did not mean that the public was not frustrated, confused, disgusted, and even angry at the presidents for getting the United States involved and for their management of the war. All these emotions were present, but the public seemed to express them more against the man than the policy. While support in the polls for Kennedy and Johnson's Vietnam policy remained relatively constant, their personal popularity waned.

Thus the reason the executive branch managed to make its policies stick amid strong countervailing pressures was that virtually everybody and every institution ended up in the acceptance column. Congress and the press were full parties to this system. Congress rarely asked for more information or consultation than it was given. That would have meant

21. David Halberstam, *The Best and the Brightest* (Random House, 1972), p. 146.

22. Ball and Mansfield quoted in Johnson, *The Vantage Point*, pp. 147, 151.

more responsibility than legislators cared to shoulder. While the press periodically blew the whistle, it generally cooperated in the selling process. The American people largely felt that foreign policy was the President's business. All hid behind the argument that the President had "all the facts" and knew best. Of equal importance, most agreed with the anti-Communist ends of policy.

Strategy and Politics: The Presidents' Dilemmas

Each postwar President sought to steer a middle course between the costs and risks of losing and the costs and risks of trying to win. Each sought out a strategy for fighting the war that would at once avoid those costs and risks and command domestic support at home. The choices came down to these—another China, the risks of another world war, or another Korea.

Each President unhesitatingly ruled out courses of action that would lead to the first two alternatives. Until 1965 each chose to fight another Korea through the surrogates of France and later South Vietnam. Each received varying degrees of criticism for their choice of strategy, but the criticism was readily manageable so long as U.S. combat forces were not directly involved in the conflict. But Lyndon Johnson in 1965 no longer could choose a surrogate Korean war policy and prevent another China since direct U.S. involvement was required to prevent defeat. Nor would he choose to run the risks of a wider war. This left him with the pure Korea alternative and with the problem of maintaining political support for the unpopular strategy of gradualism or incrementalism. How did he do it?

On a surface level, the strategy of gradualism did face toward the right wing. As the war endured, gradualism became the equivalent of escalation, and escalation in turn was supposed not only to meet the increasing military needs in the field but to appease the right wing at home as well. Yet the right wing was not satisfied. It always wanted much more than Johnson would give, and the President must have known this would be the case, for the strategy of incrementalism was much more complex than a simple effort to placate the right.

On a deeper level, incrementalism was designed to control both the Right and the Left. With respect to the management of domestic aspects of the war, it rested implicitly on the belief that asking the public to swallow the war whole would lead to irresistible pressures either to win or get out. Incrementalism was the product of the old consensus game. Everyone was to be given the illusion that the war might soon be over. The Right was to be given escalation. The Left was to be given occasional peace overtures. The middle would not be asked to pay for the war. The Right would be assured that South Vietnam would not be lost. The Left would be frightened into submission by the specter of McCarthyism. But the key to the whole strategy was phasing.

Until the jolt of Tet, the right-wing reaction was the ultimate nightmare. This was to be forestalled and the right wing controlled by not losing, by escalation, and by promising victory. But given these parameters the immediate problem was to keep the doves, the liberals, and the Left in line.

In the short run Johnson seemed more wary of the Left than the Right. The McCarthyite nightmare might come true if the United States lost Vietnam. But the nightmare could only come true only if the doves and the Left gained the ascendancy, only if their opposition to the war spread to the middle and across to the Right. The Left and the liberals were his friends and political allies, and that counted in itself. But more important, these groups were the only ones who would openly press for withdrawal, for "losing." The Right would be unhappy and disgruntled, but they would never press the case for withdrawal to the public. The Left and the doves would and eventually did.

Thus President Johnson's trilemma was stark. He would not try maximum force to win, because that would risk World War III. He would not replay Vietnam as China in 1949, lose it and take the case to the public, because that would risk another round of McCarthyism. He would, as a last resort, replay Vietnam as Korea, hoping to outlast the enemy and get it to agree to stay on its side of the line—and risk wearing America down at its seams.

President Johnson could look back at the Korean War and think it was bad, but not as bad as losing China. Harry Truman was roundly attacked for his self-restraint in fighting the Korean War—and yet most Americans saw it as a courageous decision, and the history books were filled with praise for the beleaguered President. China ruined President Truman. That is, it ruined him politically at that time—and its loss did ignite McCarthyism. But in the perspective of those same history books,

President Truman's decision to back away from the corrupt regime of Chiang and accept the tide of Mao was being hailed as Truman's most courageous and wisest hour.

Lyndon Johnson did not see it that way. He would continue with middle-course actions in Vietnam and with playing the Left and the Right off against each other at home. This strategy neither satisfied hawks or doves nor faced down the North Vietnamese, but it prevailed.

PART FOUR

Perceptions: Realism, Hope, and Compromise

CHAPTER ELEVEN

Optimism, Pessimism, and Credibility

The centerpiece of Kafka's *The Trial* is the parable of the law wherein a priest sets out to explain the mysteries of life to the character called K. The priest and K discuss the parable and disagree about its meaning. Kafka ended the exchange thusly:

"No," said the priest, "it is not necessary to accept everything as true, one must only accept it as necessary."

"A melancholy conclusion," said K. "It turns lying into a universal principle."[1]

K both got the point and missed it, for what Kafka was driving at was that the world of man defies a single compelling exegesis and that life at its very essence is doomed to different interpretations.

In Vietnam there were thousands of Americans filing reports on what was "really going on," hundreds more sifting and refining the raw materials, scores of analysts molding finished products, dozens of journalists reporting and making the news, and high-level officials and legislators scurrying out to the field for an on-the-spot look—all seeing and creating their own realities. Never before have the platters of the political leadership been so filled with the minutiae of a war. Perhaps never before in war have the facts been so indigestible.

But American leaders had to guess whether the situation in Vietnam was bad or good and getting worse or better, and they did. What was reality in Vietnam to them became the basis of decision. The question of whether and when these leaders were optimistic or pessimistic about the war is the only route to answering some of the pivotal issues and puzzles of Vietnam. Was belief in the credibility gap a justifiable public reaction to official prognosis? What was the basis for optimism in a struggle that

1. Franz Kafka, *The Trial*, trans. Willa and Edwin Muir (Knopf, 1970), p. 276.

never seemed to end? Who believed what and why? Were escalatory decisions made from hopes or fears?

Contradictions and Hedging

What were the presidents being told about the situation in Vietnam? Here are some samples.

In November 1953 three different analyses (a report and two criticisms of it) were received from three separate military sources. From the highest ranking military officer in Indochina, General John W. O'Daniel, the report was glowing. French Union forces "held the initiative" and the Navarre Plan would bring "decisive victory." From CINCPAC, Eisenhower heard that O'Daniel's report was overoptimistic, that it understated political and psychological factors, and that victory would not be possible until the people were won over. The Army military attaché in Saigon and the assistant chief of staff for intelligence were even more pessimistic. They believed that the French were on the defensive, and that there were no signs of being able to win in the future.[2]

It was not unusual for the President to receive a single report that contained contradictions. Kennedy could pick up the Gilpatric Task Force study in May 1961 and read: "Thus, the situation is critical but not hopeless." The South Vietnamese people might be anticolonial and antiforeigner, but they were seen to be generally "pro-American." The Saigon armed forces might be miserably led and organized, but they were "increasing [their] capabilities to fight."[3]

Contradictions abounded among the bureaucracies, as related in one oft told story. On September 10, 1963, Major General Victor C. Krulak and Joseph Mendenhall (a senior Foreign Service officer with Vietnam experience), returned from Vietnam after a whirlwind four-day trip to present their reports to the President at an NSC meeting. Krulak's report stressed that the war was being won and that while there was certain dissatisfaction in the military with the government, no one would risk

2. *The Pentagon Papers: The Defense Department History of United States Decisionmaking on Vietnam,* Senator Gravel ed. (Beacon Press, 1971), vol. 1, p. 79.

3. "A Program of Action to Prevent Communist Domination of South Vietnam," May 6, 1961, *United States–Vietnam Relations, 1945–1967,* Study prepared by the Department of Defense for the House Committee on Armed Services, 92 Cong. 1 sess. (Government Printing Office, 1971), bk. 11, pt. V.B.4, p. 92.

his neck to remove Diem. If present policies under Diem were continued, the United States would achieve victory. Mendenhall gave a totally opposite view of the situation. He said that the possibility of a breakdown in civil administration was strong and that a religious civil war was possible if Diem were not replaced. The war certainly could not be won with Diem. Rufus Phillips, director of Rural Programs of the U.S. Operations Mission, and John Mecklin, director of the U.S. Information Service in Saigon, supported Mendenhall with variations. Frederick Nolting, U.S. Ambassador to Vietnam, agreed with Krulak. In the face of all this disagreement, President Kennedy asked pointedly: "You two did visit the same country, didn't you?"[4]

Lyndon Johnson quickly became aware of the contradictions between Washington and the field. In a report to the President in late 1963 McNamara wrote that the political situation was "deeply serious." But he added that he might be "overly pessimistic, inasmuch as the ambassador, COMUSMACV, and General Minh were not discouraged and looked forward to significant improvements in January."[5]

Such contradictions were to be expected because at any given period some of the war planners were optimistic and some were pessimistic. But beyond contradictory reports, the presidents had to face inevitable, unavoidable, and honest hedging and qualifications, especially when it came to predicting the future. Hedging came in two varieties—the "but's" and the "if's."

The "but" hedge, which included the "probably's," the "appear to be's," the "although's," and the "also's," popped up during periods of both pessimism and optimism. Thus an NSC report at the time of Dien Bien Phu held that the military situation was "deteriorating" but not critical.[6] At the height of optimism in the early 1960s Roger Hilsman and White House aide Michael Forrestal reported to the President: "Our overall judgment, in sum, is that we are probably winning, but certainly more slowly than we had hoped. At the rate it is now going, the war will probably last longer than we would like, cost more . . . and prolong the period in which a sudden and dramatic event could upset the gains already made."[7]

4. *Pentagon Papers*, vol. 2, p. 244.
5. Ibid., pp. 164–65.
6. "Possible U.S. Intervention in Indo-China (NSC Action 1074-a)," April 6, 1954, *United States–Vietnam Relations*, bk. 9, pt. V.B.3, p. 361.
7. Roger Hilsman, *To Move a Nation: The Politics of Foreign Policy in the Administration of John F. Kennedy* (Doubleday, 1967), p. 464.

The "if's," which encompassed the "provided that's" and the "on the assumption that's," quite sensibly accompanied all predictions. Johnson recorded that McNamara told him in October 1963 that the principal job would be over in about two years "on the assumption that political confusion in Vietnam would not affect military operations."[8] Or as William Bundy put it in May 1967: "If we go on as we are doing, if the political process in the South comes off well, and if the Chinese do not settle down, I myself would reckon that by the end of 1967 there is at least a 50–50 chance that a favorable tide will be running really strongly in the South, and that Hanoi will be very discouraged."[9] General Westmoreland reported on January 24, 1967: "If we can neutralize the enemy base areas and prevent replenishment of the material captured or destroyed, we will have taken a long stride toward ultimate victory."[10]

It is hard not to be sympathetic with this tendency to hedge. Honest estimates have to be just that. But there can be little doubt that at least some of the hedging was of the protective-covering genre. Sticking one's neck out to make a concrete prediction usually led to getting it chopped off. Like O'Daniel, McNamara, and Rostow, those who went out on a limb could be shown to be wrong, and when they were, they lost in credibility. Penalties also could be invoked against those who did not qualify their pessimism. For example, a State Department intelligence brief of October 22, 1963, sketched such a bleak picture that McNamara and the Joint Chiefs lodged a protest with Rusk, and Rusk ended up apologizing for his errant estimators, who turned out to be exactly right.[11]

But while the hedging aspect of estimates is understandable, what of the contradictions? Why were some always either optimistic or pessimistic, and why the swings from one to the other?

The Roots of Internal Estimates

Optimism and pessimism are loaded words and can refer to a wide variety of perceptions and attitudes. Most people who reported on the

8. Lyndon Baines Johnson, *The Vantage Point: Perspectives of the Presidency, 1963–1969* (Holt, Rinehart and Winston, 1971), p. 46.
9. *Pentagon Papers*, vol. 4, p. 446.
10. Ibid., p. 402.
11. Ibid., vol. 2, p. 770.

war and made estimates on how it was going no doubt believed they were being objective. And at times the evidence seemed to point so strongly in one direction or another that most observers could agree. But for the most part optimism and pessimism were rooted in the sources of information, the aspects of the war being analyzed, confusion about goals, the practice of linking assessments with recommendations, and personal and organization factors.

Sources of Information

Data or statistical indicators served as a basis for both optimism and pessimism. The indicators that pointed in a positive direction included the size and firepower of friendly forces, the number of hamlets pacified, the number of free elections being held, the absence of riots and coups, and the numbers of Communists being killed. By these standards, many periods by comparison with previous years yielded a sense of real improvement and encouraged at least cautiously optimistic assessments. The indicators that pointed in a negative direction included incidents of terror, assassination, the number of enemy weapons captured (this could serve as a check on body count claims), enemy desertions, friendly desertions, and the disproportionately large number of hamlets that were rated as "borderline" controlled.

But statistics by their very nature could not go deeply enough. Much of the most important information about Vietnam was essentially unquantifiable, and even when it could be quantified the dangers of misinterpretation and overinterpretation were ever present. Comparison with years past was an illusory measure when it was not coupled with judgments about how far there still was to go and how likely it was that the goal could ever be reached. It was all too easy to confuse short-term breathing spells with long-term trends and to confuse "things getting better" with "winning." Many of those who derived genuine hope from these indicators suffered from either a lack of knowledge about Vietnam or a lack of sensitivity toward politics, or both. On balance, data generally made Americans unduly optimistic.

In the early days of the war, assessments about what was happening in the countryside came almost entirely from French and Vietnamese sources. The French in Indochina vigorously opposed any proposals to get American military observers out in the field to see what was going on. In order to make their objections stick, they had to show that the Americans were not needed. Accordingly the French grossly underesti-

mated the strength and staying power of the Vietminh and grossly overestimated their own efforts. This in large part accounts for the optimism
of U.S. military men in Indochina such as General O'Daniel. They had
no other source of information about the fighting. The French would
display pessimism only when their position became absolutely desperate; this in turn often panicked their American military counterparts.

Even after the United States took over from France in 1955, language
and cultural difficulties led Americans to place reliance on South Vietnamese sources who behaved very much as the French had. As the
United States geared up its involvement in the early 1960s, the commander in Saigon, General Paul Harkins, decided he did not want any
defeatist reporting from American officers in the provinces. The dissident lieutenant colonels who saw the rot in ARVN, such men as John
Paul Vann, were purged. Harkins preferred to believe the more upbeat
reports of the Vietnamese themselves. Only after disasters, and particularly after the Diem coup, did U.S. officials begin to investigate seriously
the accuracy and reliability of the Vietnamese sources on which they had
been basing much of their policy for so long. One of the first realizations
of this was shown in McNamara's memo to the President on December 21, 1963: "Viet Cong progress has been great during the period since
the coup, *with my guess being that the situation has in fact been deteriorating in the countryside since July to a far greater extent than we had
realized because of our undue dependence on distorted Vietnamese
reporting.*"[12]

Newspaper and television reports constituted another pool of information. It is not unusual for political leaders in Washington to spend
more time garnering information from the press than from official
sources. Ironically, however, these same leaders often accepted the inside estimates and rejected the journalistic accounts. They needed to
read the press to see what the people were being told and to gauge the
political problems they would have to face at home. Press reports, they
reasoned, either could be dismissed or needed "to be put in perspective."
They judged, and not without some foundation, that the business of the
press was to ferret out troubles and scandals and to exaggerate for
effect, highlighting the bad and slighting the good. Nevertheless, a good
case can be made that press reports over time painted a more accurate
picture of the war than the consensus of official reporting, especially

12. Ibid., vol. 3, p. 494 (emphasis added). See also David Halberstam, *The Best
and the Brightest* (Random House, 1972), pp. 187–88.

during periods of overabundant official optimism. Thus, for example, a story by David Halberstam that appeared in the *New York Times* on August 15, 1963, maintained that the situation had deteriorated seriously over the past year and was growing worse. The official refutation by the secretary of defense and the Joint Chiefs denied everything: "The military situation is improving throughout the Republic of Vietnam, not as rapidly in the Mekong Delta as in the North, but improving markedly none the less. *The picture is precisely the opposite of the one painted by Mr. Halberstam.*"[13]

Informal contacts provided yet another source. From the early 1960s Vietnam had more than its share of wandering minstrels—colonels and majors, junior Foreign Service officers, and AID personnel anxious to tell their tales of woe and their solutions to the problems. Journalists sought them out and they sought out the journalists. Some of these men found their way into the highest councils of Washington and Saigon. Extremely pessimistic about the present, they were very optimistic about the future if U.S. leaders would only do as they suggested. They, however, could be dismissed as "junior people" who did not see the big picture.

Aspects of the War Being Analyzed

From the beginning the United States was fighting the war on a number of different but interrelated fronts:

—To minimize North Vietnamese support to forces in South Vietnam (primarily by bombing).

—To quell the insurgency in the South (by direct use of U.S. forces, aid, and increasing ARVN effectiveness).

—To win the hearts and minds of the people (primarily through pacification).

—To increase political reform and stability in the South (primarily by exerting pressure on the Vietnamese leaders to institute democratic forms of government and increase popular support).

—To minimize the support of Russia and China and to avoid their direct intervention in the war.

—To achieve some sort of acceptable diplomatic solution to the conflict.

13. *United States–Vietnam Relations*, bk. 3, pt. IV.C.1, p. 10 (emphasis in original).

Thus people were apt to interpret the situation differently, depending on what aspect of the problem they were analyzing or emphasizing.

Quite often the optimist-pessimist split occurred along the lines of military versus political emphasis. In the early 1950s the Joint Chiefs emphasized the political side of the war (Bao Dai's weakness and French unwillingness to institute reforms) and saw little hope, while the State Department focused on French military capability and found threads of progress. By the early 1960s they had reversed roles. Sometimes the optimist-pessimist split appeared in the same report. The McNamara-Taylor memo of October 2, 1963, stated that "the military campaign has made great progress and continues to progress" but warned that "further repressive actions by Diem and Nhu could change the present favorable military trends."[14]

Divergencies might also arise depending on whether one was looking at the Communist forces or at Saigon's growing military capabilities. During February 1965 McGeorge Bundy said: "The prospect in Vietnam is grim. The energy and persistence of the Viet Cong are astonishing." He predicted that without additional U.S. action, the GVN would collapse within the next year.[15] Other reports, however, were more favorable. The January MACV report, for example, said: "*Review of military events in January tend to induce a decidedly more optimistic view than has been seen in recent months.*"[16] This divergence took on new forms in 1966 when controversy over the effectiveness of the bombing of North Vietnam arose. The military favored the intensive bombing of the North on the grounds that it had a substantial impact psychologically as well as in terms of interdiction. Some civilian advisers, including notably a growing number of civilians in the Pentagon, disputed the psychological effectiveness of the bombing. More important, they stressed that bombing the North was not getting at the heart of the problem—winning the war in the South, which in large part meant winning the *people* of the South.

At times optimists seemed to be clutching at straws. For example, Ambassador Taylor reported to the President in March 1965 (when the CIA, William Bundy, and John McNaughton were all giving deeply pessimistic assessments) that even though the political support of the

14. *Pentagon Papers*, vol. 2, pp. 751–52.
15. Ibid., vol. 3, p. 311.
16. Ibid., vol. 2, p. 545 (emphasis added by Pentagon Papers analysts).

GVN was still missing, "With the growing pressure on North Vietnam, the psychological atmosphere continues to be favorable."[17]

Time was another factor in assessments. Those who changed their positions frequently often did so according to whether they emphasized current aspects or future prospects. Advocates of the long-haul policy, particularly those with vested interests in the pacification program often made the time distinction, stressing that while success was not yet clearly evident, it would become clear in the longer term.

Confusion about Goals

Administration leaders persistently failed to clarify U.S. objectives in concrete and specific terms. Uncertainty and ambiguity in reports were therefore bound to emerge, for no one could be certain what he was measuring progress against or how victory would be defined.

The range of goals seemed endless. With respect to France and Saigon, was the goal to strengthen them to deal with any Vietnamese Communist threat without requiring direct American intervention? To build a stable South Vietnam now, or fight the war and build a nation later? Or to prevent military or political collapse in the near term? Was the U.S. goal with respect to the Communists to bring about a psychological-political recalculation of aims in Hanoi? To smash their military capabilities, destroying them as a conventional military threat? To merely avoid humiliation? Or to weaken both the North Vietnamese and the Vietcong to the point where they would fade away, and the Saigon government could handle the rest readily?

Some of these goals were quite difficult to attain, others seemingly modest, and still others so intangible that it was hard to gauge progress or retrogression. Indeed the direction of the curve seemed more important than the point on the curve; the sense of moving toward or away from the goals usually established the measure of improvement more than did the estimate of how much longer it would take to attain the goals.

Linking Recommendations to Assessments

If a new program or course of action was desired, proponents portrayed its prospects glowingly, and opponents did the reverse. It is im-

17. Ibid., vol. 3, p. 345.

possible to tell whether assessments were tailored to fit recommendations or the other way around. In most cases it is likely that proponents believed in their product for one reason or another and oversold its prospects in order to maximize the chances of its adoption.

One example of deliberate oversell appeared in a JCS memorandum of August 11, 1953, to the secretary of defense. After pointing out the weaknesses of the Navarre Plan, the chiefs declared that "if vigorously pursued militarily in Indochina and supported politically in France, the Navarre concept offers a promise of success sufficient to warrant appropriate additional U.S. aid required for implementation." However, when the Joint Chiefs learned that the secretary of defense planned to forward their memorandum to the secretary of state, they asked to modify certain "overly optimistic" statements concerning "promises of success offered by the Navarre concept."[18]

While nothing so blatant occurred again, two recognizable patterns did emerge. One was the view that the situation could be improved or disaster sidestepped only if a certain recommendation were adopted. The conclusion of the Gilpatric Task Force was typical: "Barring a significant increase in the present level of guerrilla infiltration and military aggression, the G.V.N. armed forces . . . have the capability of continuing the suppression of the insurgency and even making considerable headway against it. This capability will, of course, depend on a major acceleration of the present retraining program."[19] The other pattern was to utilize the bargaining strengths of both pessimism and optimism. This meant being somewhat optimistic about the present, pessimistic about future progress if no changes were made, and optimistic if new policies were set. On November 27, 1967, the Joint Chiefs asserted that "there are no new programs which can be undertaken under current policy guidelines which would result in a rapid or significantly more visible increase in the rate of progress in the near term." But they also declared that if the U.S. effort were expanded to permit a fuller utilization of American military resources, the trend could become much more favorable: "Any action which serves to reduce the pressure will be detrimental to the achievement of our objectives."[20] This tactic left the chiefs

18. The two memorandums appear in *United States–Vietnam Relations*, bk. 9, pt. V.B.3, pp. 134, 138.
19. "Annexes to a Program of Action for South Vietnam," May 8, 1961, ibid., bk. 11, pt. V.B.4, p. 96.
20. *Pentagon Papers*, vol. 4, p. 537.

in a good position to argue later that the reason for slower progress was that their proposals were not fully adopted and implemented.

Personal and Organizational Interests

Most of the people who were writing reports about the situation in Vietnam were under varying degrees of pressure, both explicit and implicit, to produce certain *kinds* of assessments. Whether they biased their reports in a certain direction because someone else told them to do it or because they knew this would be best for them in the long run (pessimism did not help professional careers) is not particularly important in this context; the fact is that the pressure was there nonetheless.

Optimism in the assessments was part of the gamesmanship of Vietnam. Optimism had a purpose. Career services tacitly and sometimes explicitly pressured their professionals to impart good news, which was seen as a job well done; bad news represented a personal failure. Moreover, optimism bred optimism so that it was difficult not to continue it. People told their superiors what they thought they wanted to hear; the American ethic is to get the job done.

Pessimism also had a purpose. It helped justify requests for expanding or intensifying programs, and it supported previous predictions that a certain idea or project would not work (particularly that of a rival organization in direct competition for a certain program).

The military, for example, was often deliberately optimistic, even to the point of falsification. It has been reported that the Air Force consistently exaggerated the effects of the bombing, in many cases not so much as a deliberate lie but because of the way the military and the military intelligence systems were organized.[21] Although the Air Force had remarkably accurate methods of measuring bomb destruction in its photo intelligence techniques, this information was consistently played down in favor of the pilots' reports, which owing to human error as well as never-corrected duplication gave a grossly inaccurate overall picture of the military effects of the bombing. Why did the Air Force do nothing to change this system (and thus implicitly encourage it)? First, because

21. "Based on what I saw in my little corner of the air war," said Captain Morris Blachman, an Air Force intelligence officer, "the actual destruction was often less than half what the Air Force claimed." ("The Stupidity of Intelligence," in Charles Peters and Timothy J. Adams, eds., *Inside the System: A Washington Monthly Reader* [Praeger, 1970], p. 272. Blachman's chapter first appeared as an article in *Washington Monthly*, September 1969, under the pseudonym "Ariel.")

of the intense competition among the services, and second, because of the pressures regarding promotion. This was emphasized bitterly in the report of an Air Force Intelligence officer.

The Air Force exists only to fight in the air or to bomb. The Air Force had to have the bombing of the North—it was the only real Air Force show in the Vietnam war. . . . The Navy had horned in on the air war, and, even if the bombings were to stop, the sailors could always go back to their ships. But for the Air Force, it was bomb—or do nothing. Without the bombing, the Air Force would hope for little publicity and glory—which would mean smaller appropriations and perhaps less attention to Air Force desires. To criticize the bombing claims meant, therefore, to hurt your own organization and to benefit its rivals. Stopping the bombing could be seen as a failure for the Air Force. . . .

The promotion system created exceptional pressures for conformity on career officers. Promotion depended heavily on the evaluation report of one's commanding officer; one unfavorable mention in the report could postpone promotion for many years and, perhaps, permanently blight a career. . . . So it would have taken a certain amount of courage for the colonel to tell the general that the air strike the general had ordered—and for whose success the colonel felt he would be held responsible—was a failure. (One Air Force general who criticized the bombing was reportedly removed from command and booted upstairs.)[22]

Other parts of the bureaucracy followed a similar pattern—the Army with its body counts, the Navy on bombing, and the Army in competition with the CIA operators and State Department and AID personnel with respect to the pacification program. Despite the attacks of each group on the prospects of the others, this pattern resulted in a whirlpool of optimism—tainted, to be sure, but effective nonetheless.

The Cycle of Highs and Lows

Examining the various explanations for optimism and pessimism, the contradictions, and the hedging is essential to answering the question of what U.S. leaders thought was going on in Vietnam. It is also interesting to note the distinctive periods of ups and downs during the war, dominant or prevailing moods that set the direction of policy. When seen in the light of public statements about the course of the war, these dominant moods give a fuller portrait of the context in which American leaders were operating.

22. Ibid., pp. 275–76.

The Truman Years

From 1947 through 1952 the prevailing mood in the Truman administration was one of continuing pessimism based more on the politics of the situation than on military factors. France was not winning the war, and prospects were dim that it ever would, given the clash of colonialism and nationalism and the unwillingness in Paris to harness the forces of nationalism by granting true independence. Intelligence reports stressed serious weaknesses in French manpower, leadership, and intelligence and warned that the Vietminh were building up for large-scale offenses to seize complete control of Indochina. The best that could be said was that U.S. aid was propping up a dangerously deteriorating anti-Communist position. Public statements, however, gave no hint of this. Dean Acheson, who had said privately on June 17, 1952, that it was "futile and a mistake to defend Indochina in Indochina," made the public announcement the following day that Communist "aggression has been checked" and that the "tide is now moving in our favor."[23]

Dien Bien Phu, Geneva, and Diem: 1953–61

While most of the internal assessments remained pessimistic in 1953, there seemed to be a desire to be cautiously optimistic. No one was saying that the basic political issues had been solved or were likely to be, but a sense of relative quiet plus the influx of large amounts of American aid gave hope to many despite the recognized continued deterioration of the situation. U.S. military personnel in Indochina, in particular, found themselves caught up in a wave of optimism about the Navarre Plan and its prospects for decisively defeating the Vietminh by 1955. The fighting seemed to be leveling off in Indochina, but leaders in Washington began to worry whether the French leaders still had the heart to persist.

The few public statements were mixed but hopeful.

After General Giap's victories in Laos in late 1953 and beginning with his investiture of Dien Bien Phu, the mood dissolved into deep pessimism. In some quarters the feeling persisted that the French had the resources to win if they would only try, but the best that could be said was that while the military situation was deteriorating, it was not

23. Acheson quoted in an unsigned State Department account in *United States–Vietnam Relations*, bk. 8, pt. V.A.2, p. 516; and in "Conversations on Indochina: Press Conference Statement by Secretary Acheson," June 18, 1952, *Department of State Bulletin*, vol. 26 (June 30, 1952), pp. 1009–10.

hopelessly critical. Dulles's statements did not reflect this view. Only Eisenhower admitted to deep inner doubts when he told reporters that the situation in Indochina had always been critical.

The fall of Dien Bien Phu and the signing of the Geneva accords sent Indochina stock plummeting. The only questions were how much territory the Communists would eventually control and when. When Dulles was dispatching General Collins to Saigon in November 1954, he said, "Frankly, Collins, I think our chances of saving the situation there are not more than 1 in 10."[24] The handful of official pronouncements downplayed the seriousness of the situation and sought to provide confidence that Washington could manage the results. Dulles, for example, stated on April 17, 1955: "The situation is difficult but at present problems are neither unexpected nor insoluble."[25]

By mid-1955, with Diem still holding onto power and with the intelligence community estimating that North Vietnamese aggression against the South was now unlikely, a period of cautious and then high optimism took root. By the end of 1956 Diem had consolidated his power; the elections promised by the Geneva accords had not been held, thus denying the Communists their chance to win; and the insurgency activity had become very light. It looked as if the situation might stabilize, and more important, the United States was now in Vietnam, not the French, and so it was hoped that the colonialism issue would vanish. Intelligence assessments pointed to developing executive leadership and improving Saigon's armed forces; some went so far as to say that Communist capabilities in the South had been "neutralized."

The public echoed and enhanced this optimism, with Eisenhower saying on April 21, 1956, that Diem was "doing splendidly," and that he was "a much better figure in that field than anyone even dared hope."[26]

The year 1961 witnessed the flare-up of the Laotian crisis and the vitalization of the insurgency in South Vietnam. More basically, it also revealed the essential weaknesses and instability of the Diem-Nhu regime. Internal documents noted that the Vietcong had capitalized on

24. General J. Lawton Collins, USA (Ret.), John Foster Dulles Oral History Project Interview, quoted in Chalmers M. Roberts, "New Documentation Reinforces View: Dulles Made Key Vietnam Commitment," *Washington Post*, March 26, 1967.

25. "Recent Developments in Foreign Relations," Statement by Secretary Dulles, April 17, 1955, *Department of State Bulletin*, vol. 32 (May 2, 1955), p. 727.

26. "Address at Annual Dinner of the American Society of Newspaper Editors, April 21, 1956," *Public Papers of the Presidents of the United States, Dwight D. Eisenhower, 1956* (GPO, 1958), p. 423.

substantial political opposition to Diem to gain control of most of the countryside. The words "deterioration" and "critical" began to appear as they had at the time of Dien Bien Phu. But the low was not quite as deep as in 1954 when the issue was how to mitigate inevitable defeat, not how to prevent it. In late 1961 the pessimism was somewhat alleviated by the sense that the United States would do something.

Public pronouncements were riveted on Laos, which was called a crisis, but those about Vietnam in early 1961 were muted. Kennedy spoke of Vietnam as a problem and stressed that the Diem government had been endorsed by 75 percent of the South Vietnamese in free elections. By the end of 1961 Kennedy would acknowledge that a war was going on and that it was of growing concern. The only unabashedly pessimistic statements came from Admiral Harry D. Felt, and the welling up of pessimism at this time provoked the Taylor mission.

Rising Hopes Precede Long Downhill Slide: 1962–65

Optimism gradually returned to the assessments in 1962, peaking probably in the first half of 1963. During 1962 real political opposition to Diem was absent, and the Vietcong generally lay low. At least all the statistical indicators of their activity (prisoners, deaths, recruitment, and so on) went down, and even the enemy called 1962 "Diem's year." It can almost be said that there was a feeling of exhilaration because the United States had finally decided to do something about the situation, and the "something" was working. The unanimous consensus was that Communist progress had been blunted and that the situation was improving. Although the end of the war itself was not in sight, many began to see the time when American advisers could be removed.

The public statements made at the subcabinet level of the State and Defense departments during this whole period were uniformly optimistic. High-level pronouncements evinced more caution. Kennedy frequently talked of Berlin and Indochina as "grave crises" but was referring mostly to Laos. On March 7, 1962, he said: "I don't think you could make a judgment [on Vietnam]. It's very much up and down . . . from week to week, so it's impossible to draw any long-range conclusions."[27] And on December 12: "So we don't see the end of the tunnel, but I must say I don't think it is darker than it was a year ago, and in some ways

27. "The President's News Conference of March 7, 1962," *Public Papers, John F. Kennedy, 1962* (GPO, 1963), p. 199.

lighter."[28] On April 22, 1963, Dean Rusk waved an even more cautionary flag, calling the situation "difficult and dangerous" and emphasizing that the United States could not "promise or expect a quick victory."[29] But this period ended with optimism in the air when on July 17 Kennedy reassured everyone that "it is going quite well" despite the clash between Diem and Buddhists.[30]

By the fall of 1963, however, the realization that much of the earlier optimism had been mainly illusory hit hard. The repressions of the Diem-Nhu regime, the Buddhist crises, and the Diem coup, followed by continual political instability and coups and countercoups, raised the specter of the imminent collapse of the Saigon government. Later the assessments would also raise the specter of military defeat. By the end of 1963 the Vietcong, having spent a year and a half adjusting to the increased American presence in Vietnam, now appeared to be a formidable military organization. They not only were getting bolder and attacking American air bases and officers' quarters but were also routing the ARVN, still plagued by corruption and ineffectiveness, at practically every encounter. In addition, the pacification program had come to a halt. By the turn of the year almost all observers expected defeat on both the military and political fronts. This was the period of deepest pessimism in the history of the war to that time.

The public record at this point begins to sound a lot like early 1954. The initial tone is set by the White House statement of October 2, 1963, on the McNamara-Taylor report. The paragraph that received all the attention was the one promising that "the major part of the U.S. military task can be completed by the end of 1965." Little noticed, however, was the next prophetic paragraph (shades of Dulles on the Navarre Plan): "The political situation . . . remains deeply serious. The United States has made clear its continuing opposition to any repressive actions in South Viet-Nam. While such actions have not yet significantly affected the military effort, they could do so in the future."[31] Like Dulles and Eisenhower, the leading figures of the Johnson administration began

28. "The President's News Conference of December 12, 1962," ibid., p. 870.

29. "The Stake in Viet-Nam, Address by Secretary Rusk before the Economic Club of New York, April 22, 1963," Department of State Bulletin, vol. 48 (May 13, 1963), pp. 727, 731.

30. "The President's News Conference of July 17, 1963," Public Papers, Kennedy, 1963 (GPO, 1964), p. 569.

31. "White House Statement Following the Return of a Special Mission to South Viet-Nam, October 2, 1963," ibid., pp. 759–60.

what was to become a standard refrain. Vietnam, they intoned in speech after speech, was the victim of aggression and was of critical importance to the United States (shades of Eisenhower and the domino theory), and America had no alternative but to see it through. On direct questioning from the press or congressional committees, senior officials would acknowledge a "grave" situation. Again, as in 1954, administration leaders made no effort to alert the public either to what insiders called the "imminence of defeat" or to the U.S. actions then impending.

The Optimism of Action: Spring 1965

The spring of 1965 brought with it a brief resurgence of optimism. But as was the case in 1953 and early 1962, the actions of the United States rather than the concrete results they produced served as the launching pad. It was the optimism of doing something, of finally having crossed an important threshold and of hoping, even believing, that it might work. Like Taylor and Rostow, some officials ventured thoughts of winning the war, but most, like McGeorge Bundy, confined themselves to claiming that morale had improved and that therefore both the political and military aspects of the war looked more hopeful.

During their forays into the public domain officials seemed to purposefully avoid commenting on the situation. In his Johns Hopkins University address on April 7, President Johnson merely noted that the war effort was not futile. Later, on April 23, Rusk stated,"There is no evidence that the Viet Cong has any significant popular following in South Viet-Nam."[32]

Mixed Optimism and Another High: Summer 1965–Fall 1967

The two-year stretch between the summers of 1965 and 1967 began with a low, followed by an extended period of mixed views, and ended with a vague sense of hope. Throughout the summer of 1965 all strata of the bureaucracy were reporting that military conditions had worsened considerably, and many resumed the refrain that only a massive increase in the U.S. effort could save Vietnam. That winter and through the fall of the following year, new lines of optimism and pessimism grew and generally persisted until the end of 1968. The pessimists' side included the civilians in the Pentagon, a few high-ranking officials in the State Department, the CIA analysts, and sundry midranking military officers

---

32. *Pentagon Papers*, vol. 3, p. 735.

and Foreign Service officers. They stressed their belief that no level of U.S. effort would have much effect on Hanoi or Vietcong resolve, that the enemy felt the tide was running in its favor, and that it would never give up. To them, the future only held the prospect of military stalemate. The optimistic side included all high-ranking U.S. officials in Vietnam, senior military officers back in Washington, most Foreign Service officers working on the problem at the State Department, and Robert Komer and Walt Rostow. They visualized the prospect of unrelenting and irreversible progress with a crossover point to success somewhere not too far down the road. These two groups contended over the state of every major war issue: bombing, ground operations, and pacification. They never reached agreement, but sometime in early 1967 the optimists appeared to be gaining the upper hand. Most important, these groups did reach a consensus that the United States could no longer be defeated.

The public record varied little from the internal one. On May 9, 1965, McNamara stated, "We are a long way from turning the tide and we certainly have a long, hard row ahead of us. But there is clear evidence of improvement.[33] McNamara especially stressed that he did not "wish to overemphasize the progress . . . it is far too early to state the degree to which [U.S. efforts have] affected the North Vietnamese either in terms of their morale or their capability."[34] His deputy, Cyrus Vance, cautioned on October 16, 1965, that militarily "matters continue to turn toward a more favorable tide. But the road ahead appears long and steep."[35] Even the upbeat statements in 1966 remained controlled. For example, on July 12 Dean Rusk said. "We are not over the hump yet."[36] By mid-1967 officials in the field and some back in Washington had succeeded in filling press stories with glowing accounts of progress. In May Lieutenant General Leonard Chapman, chief of staff of the Marine Corps, announced, "We are winning. And I say that with no doubt whatsoever."[37] In July McNamara commented that "in the political field the progress was dramatic. . . . In the economic field. . . . [there is] evidence

33. Interview, *New York Journal-American,* May 9, 1965.

34. Ibid.

35. Speech at the 19th Annual Banquet of the National Association of Supervisors, Department of Defense chapters 12, 40, and 58, October 16, 1965.

36. "Secretary Rusk's News Conference of July 12," *Department of State Bulletin,* vol. 55 (August 1, 1966), p. 165.

37. Remarks at the Armed Forces Day Luncheon, Chamber of Commerce, Atlanta, Georgia, May 18, 1967.

of considerable gain. . . . In the military field. . . . there has been a very clear indication of the success of General Westmoreland's large unit actions."[38]

The optimism of the last half of 1967 was unlike the previous highs that had derived either from the Communists' relative inactivity or new U.S. escalatory actions. The high developed even though Washington was crossing no new military thresholds nor was Communist military activity abating. To boot, the political situation appeared relatively stable, with coups seemingly a thing of the past, and statistical indicators suggested that pacification was working at last. Significantly, reports from the field emphasized for the first time the Communist problems in recruiting, morale, and resources control, rather than the South Vietnamese and American problems that had characterized the history of reporting. The pessimists did not change spots or cease stating the counterview, but they found themselves overwhelmed by the preachers of progress. The typical public statement featured less reserve than before. On November 21 General Westmoreland saw the light at the end of the tunnel and told the National Press Club, "I see progress as I travel all over Vietnam."[39] This unadorned message stuck in many American minds.

Shock and Recovery: From Tet to the End of 1968

The Tet offensive that began in February 1968 plunged the American leadership into perhaps its darkest moment of pessimism ever. Deluged by terrifyingly bleak news accounts and CIA reports, official Washington was stunned. After years of being battered, the Communists had been able to mount an enormous offensive with great success, especially against the Saigon forces, and had seemingly wiped out a whole pacification program in three months. The pessimists, apparently vindicated at last, briefly reached the pinnacle of their influence in pointing out that if the Communists could do it once they could do it again and again. But the optimists had not given up, nor were they doomed to a permanent loss of influence. They quickly regrouped themselves to argue that Tet was the enemy's last gasp and that the Communists would never be able to recover from their attempt to win it all in one final orgy of killing. As

38. Remarks to the press on arrival at Andrews Air Force Base from a visit to Vietnam, July 11, 1967.

39. Address to the National Press Club, November 21, 1967.

1968 wore on and the ARVN forces reconstituted themselves and moved back into the vacated hamlets, and as the Thieu regime held together, defeat, it seemed, could be survived once more.

Dean Rusk told the Senate Foreign Relations Committee on March 11 that "both sides suffered some severe setbacks in the course of the Tet offensive," and asserted as in times past that abandoning Vietnam would be "catastrophic."[40] But on March 31 Maxwell Taylor told a television audience: "I can't prove my case any more than the other side can be proved, but the indicators certainly are that the Tet offensive was not as destructive to the provinces as we feared at the outset; that the ARVN has not suffered the setback it looked as though it might have had and, indeed, we are resuming the offensive whereas the other side is avoiding combat."[41] Ambassador Bunker on April 9 struck what was to be a lingering public note: "I think it [the Saigon government] has made very substantial progress since this Tet offensive. . . . also, our forces now are on the offensive."[42]

Estimates and Escalation

Other accounts have described the cycle of ups and downs in sawtooth fashion, with highs and lows of roughly equal intensity, but this is misleading.[43] There were, in fact, a great variety of internal moods, with never quite the same blend of reasons for optimism or pessimism, both of which recurred with varying intensity. The substance and frequency of change in these dominant internal moods lead to certain conclusions about the overall assessment of the war and the relation of estimates and escalation and provide a basis for grappling with the credibility gap issue.

First, while the internal moods went up and down, the center of gravity remained essentially pessimistic. With few exceptions, optimists always had to strain and hedge. Their prognosis rested on quicksand—on

40. See Rusk's testimony in *Foreign Assistance Act of 1968*, Part 1: *Vietnam*, Hearings before the Senate Committee on Foreign Relations, 90 Cong. 2 sess. (GPO, 1968).

41. Interview, "Meet the Press," NBC-TV, March 31, 1968.

42. "News Conference, Camp David, April 9," *Department of State Bulletin*, vol. 58 (April 29, 1968), p. 551.

43. See the analysis by Daniel Ellsberg in *Papers on the War* (Simon and Schuster), p. 121.

the exhilaration that comes with taking new actions and crossing thresholds, on "statistical progress," on the holding of elections, on the mere fact that the Buddhists were not rioting or that the generals were not planning another coup, and on the relative inactivity of the Communists for reasons unknown. Only in late 1967 was progress being made despite the active, full-scale opposition of the Communists. *On only three occasions—at the beginning of the Navarre Plan, after the McNamara-Taylor report in October 1963, and in some vague statements by Westmoreland in late 1967—did the optimists carry their estimates to the point of predicting a possible end to the war.* And even on these occasions, whether those who said "out in two years" actually believed it is doubtful. The weight of evidence falls on the side of their having believed it for reasons to be discussed below. Of equal importance, in none of these periods did any of the optimists maintain that the actions actually taken were likely to bring Hanoi to its knees or cause it to cry uncle.

The basis for pessimism, the warning signals, and the underlying realities of the struggle were always present. The political instability of the friendly Vietnamese, from Bao Dai, through Diem, to President Thieu, had always been apparent. The fundamental weaknesses of the Vietnamese armed forces—high desertion rates, poor leadership, and the like —were common knowledge, whatever progress these forces made. Few years went by when the fighting did not gain in intensity. U.S. leaders did not have to know much about Vietnam to see all this. It was going to be a long war, as almost every internal estimate recognized.

Second, despite this underlying pessimism, dominant internal moods did change rapidly. The frequency of change reflected the sensitivity at high levels of government to single events or happenings. The intelligence and informal reports (not through the bureaucratic chain), which almost uniformly depicted deterioration or stalemate, and the formal reporting from the military and the State Department, which was usually on the bright side, did not receive much attention at the top. Their overall effect would have been to level expectations. But there were always too many reports to read, let alone digest. Consequently only a single dramatic event could bring the men at the top to the realization that the tide was changing. This in turn meant that changes in dominant moods came as jolts, with the attendant propensity to overreact one way or the other.

Third, and related to the second point, U.S. leaders made their principal escalatory moves in periods of deep pessimism. This again underlines the argument that their primary motivation was to prevent defeat, not to pursue decisive or near-term victory. In other words, they only moved into previously restricted areas of action to avoid defeat. But it also reveals why optimism reached such highs in certain follow-on periods. As Daniel Ellsberg wrote: "U.S. aims may change significantly in the atmosphere of optimism, especially in the last stage, going beyond the goal of avoiding defeat . . . to that of achieving a victory. . . . All of these responses lead to toleration of rapidly rising costs, and hence to a feeling . . . that the stakes, the investment, the commitment have become still higher than before."[44] Once some wraps have been taken off, it becomes difficult to resist pressures for more of the same; military actions expand and hopes and aims climb.

All of which uncovers a basis for making some observations about the correspondence between public and private assessments of the war—the credibility gap. The point that leaps out when internal estimates and high-level public statements are compared is that the two were not very far apart. With few exceptions, they went up and down together from phase to phase. U.S. leaders hedged public utterances in much the same way they hedged their internal memorandums. Genuine optimists displayed their hopes outside much the same as they did inside. Pessimists and others who had not quite made up their minds openly admitted the problems and the seriousness of conditions. A number of senior officials, such as Dulles, Rusk (numerous times), and McNamara (after 1965), cautioned against overoptimism during the up periods. Formal statement after formal statement was replete with references to a long war.

What, then, was the credibility gap all about? In large part, it was not really a gap but a matter of emphasis. It also involved duplicity (though less than critics believed): denying that the struggle was essentially a civil war, denying that certain advice and recommendations had been given (a frequent occurrence especially about military requests), denying that instructions had been given for expanded military operations (as in April 1965 when the President authorized offensive operations going beyond the defense of base areas), seeking to hide increased American involvement (as Kennedy did with respect to covert operations and U.S. personnel accompanying Saigon forces into combat), and toward the end the deep suspicion that the circumstances of the Tonkin Gulf incident and resolution might have been fabricated. No ad-

44. Ellsberg, *Papers on the War*, pp. 121–22.

ministration would ever admit a mistake even if the mistake was self-evident. The pretense of perfect consistency had to be upheld even when inconsistency was blatant. This was the stuff of the credibility gap.

But the twists and turns of this issue do not end here. At the same time U.S. leaders gave a creditable public accounting of their inside estimates and duly noted the long road ahead, they also fostered precisely the opposite impression—that things were going well and that the end was in sight. To be sure, the right cautionary words appeared in the formal statements, but the stress was on the brighter side, the upbeat note. In a few instances some officials made outrageously optimistic predictions, such as the one that U.S forces would be out by the end of 1965, which tended to linger in the public mind. Of equal importance, leaders in Washington did nothing to damp down the perpetual outpouring of optimism from the field. They also went out of their way to attack deeply pessimistic press accounts of the war such as the stories about ARVN hopelessness in 1963 and stalemate stories in 1967. These, too, became the stuff of the credibility gap, especially as the war dragged on.

The justification for this is obvious. Optimism is psychologically necessary for dedicated and energetic performance; analytical defeatism becomes operationally counterproductive. According to John Mecklin, for example, press policy backed by authorization from the State Department was: success in Vietnam was a given; since success depended on Diem's heeding American advice, and since Diem blamed American press criticism on the U.S. government, press critiques of Diem had to be managed. Accordingly the embassy passed out only good news. "To the best of my knowledge," Mecklin said, "no responsible U.S. official in Saigon ever told a newsman a really big falsehood. Instead, there were endless little ones. They were morally marginal and thus difficult to dispute."[45]

Thus public policy optimism sprang from several rational needs:

—To keep up the morale of America's French and Vietnamese allies and to build some confidence and trust between them and Washington.

—To stimulate military and bureaucratic morale to work and fight hard.

45. John Mecklin, *Mission in Torment: An Intimate Account of the U.S. Role in Vietnam* (Doubleday, 1965), p. 113; see also Ellsberg, *Papers on the War*, pp. 104–11.

—To maintain domestic support for the war, for without this support
the war would be lost.

Although there were genuine optimists and genuine periods of optimism, both optimism and pessimism were a part of the gamesmanship of
the war. They were means to gain other ends and were used as key in-
gredients in the larger strategy of the war. As the priest told K, "It is not
necessary to accept everything as true, one must only accept it as necessary."

CHAPTER TWELVE

The Strategy of Perseverance

"The American people knew what they were voting for in 1964," Lyndon Johnson asserted in *The Vantage Point*. "They knew Lyndon Johnson was not going to pull up stakes and run." But one has to wonder whether Johnson himself fully believed this, for in the paragraph immediately preceding this assertion, he wrote: "A good many people compared my position in 1964 with that of . . . Barry Goldwater, and decided that I was the 'peace' candidate and he was the 'war' candidate. They were not willing to hear anything they did not want to hear."[1] The former President was right on the mark. In large measure he was misunderstood in 1964 and after because of his own wheeling and dealing. Even a close observer, however, finds it very difficult to understand what any President is doing.

Conflicting presidential pronouncements, the contrapuntal signals dispatched from the White House to maintain presidential maneuverability, and the fog of the political scene all conspire to blur perceptions of what is actually going on. So all contemporary observers, inside and outside government, invariably settle for indirect perceptions—the easy way. All heard, as Johnson wrote, what they wanted to hear. Instead of looking hard at what the President was saying, they sought out whom he was saying it against and who was against him. By focusing in this way, the American people were bound to see Johnson as the peacemaker and Goldwater as the warrior in 1964.

By 1966 another set of inclinations were in place to deflect the observer from seeing the obvious. While Johnson kept on announcing that he would do whatever was necessary to meet American commitments,

1. Lyndon Baines Johnson, *The Vantage Point: Perspectives of the Presidency, 1963–1969* (Holt, Rinehart and Winston, 1971), p. 68.

even saying that it would be necessary for the United States to do more and more, pundits insisted the "political realities" would compel Johnson to end the war in Vietnam one way or another before the 1968 elections. He could not be elected, so the judgments of most ran, if he still had the war around his neck. In a way, these judgments proved right. President Johnson did not choose to run. But the judgments were wrong about his having to alter course in Vietnam.

Neither Johnson nor his predecessors would face the choice of either winning or getting out, and the mainstream of the American political system never asked them to. Pundits and political professionals understood the Presidents' problem with this choice. What they did not understand, or could not imagine, was that the consequence of not making this choice would mean that the war would go on forever. Thus they assumed that "something would happen" or that "the President would have to do something" to begin bringing the war to an end by victory or by a peace settlement.

In sum, contemporary observers saw the problem but not its consequences. Most did not understand that the war was essentially a stalemate, that given the exclusion of the extremes—withdrawal or a Carthaginian peace—simple perseverance became the only plausible strategy, that the war then came down to a test of wills between Washington and Hanoi, and that concluding the war at any foreseeable point in time was at best a long shot.

The Stalemated War

The presidents and most of their advisers saw the Vietnam quagmire for what it was. Optimism was by and large put in perspective and was under control. This meant that many knew that each minimally necessary decision would be followed by another. Most seemed to have understood that more assistance would be required either to improve the relative position of America's Vietnamese allies or simply to prevent a deterioration of their position. Almost each year, and often several times a year, key decisions had to be made to prevent deterioration or collapse. These decisions were made with hard bargaining but rapidly enough to suggest that there was a preconceived consensus to go on. Sometimes several new steps were decided at once but announced and implemented piecemeal. The whole pattern conveyed the feeling of more to come. The fact that most of those in and close to the White House from 1947 on perceived the war as a stalemate is of central importance. It is therefore necessary to document this contention carefully.

On February 3, 1947, Secretary of State George Marshall signed a cable that said he could not "overlook" French colonial methods as an obstacle to ending the war, but that the United States did not want to see France supplanted by the Kremlin through Ho, nor did Washington favor United Nations intervention. The plaintive conclusion followed: "Frankly we have no solution of the problem to suggest."[2]

In May 1950, before Korea, Secretary of State Dean Acheson announced that the United States would provide military and economic assistance to the French and their Indochina allies for the direct purpose of combating Communist expansion. After years of hesitating, Truman finally had decided that anticommunism was more important than anticolonialism in Indochina.

This aid was provided with full awareness of the Indochina problem.

On the one hand, Acheson wrote: "All of us recognized the high probability of [a Communist victory] unless France swiftly transferred authority to the Associated States and organized, trained, and equipped, with our aid, substantial indigenous forces to take over the main burden of the fight." Then, on the other hand, he wrote that "the Western European Office [of the State Department] doubted that there was any chance that pressure would induce the French leaders to move further, and thought that it would only stiffen and antagonize them."[3]

Acheson admitted that U.S. policy was being criticized as a "muddled hodgepodge."

The criticism, however, fails to recognize the limits on the extent to which one may successfully coerce an ally. . . . Furthermore, the result of withholding help to France would, at most, have removed the colonial power. It could not have made the resulting situation a beneficial one either for Indochina or for Southeast Asia, or in the more important effort of furthering the stability and defense of Europe. So while we may have tried to muddle through and were certainly not successful, I could not think then or later of a better course.

2. *United States–Vietnam Relations, 1945–1967,* Study prepared by the Department of Defense for the House Committee on Armed Services, 92 Cong. 1 sess. (Government Printing Office, 1971), bk. 8, pt. V.B.2, pp. 99–100.

3. Dean Acheson, *Present at the Creation: My Years in the State Department* (Norton, 1969), pp. 672–73.

One can suggest, perhaps, doing nothing. That might have had merit, but as an attitude for the leader of a great alliance toward an important ally, indeed one essential to a critical endeavor, it had its demerits, too.[4]

Acheson later recalled the warning of an "able colleague" several months after the Korean War began: "Not only was there real danger that our efforts would fail in their immediate purpose and waste valuable resources in the process, but we were moving into a position in Indochina in which 'our responsibilities tend to supplant rather than complement those of the French.'" But Acheson decided "that having put our hand to the plow, we would not look back."[5]

In December 1952, according to Acheson:

The Department noted the rising uneasiness in France about Indochina and a large gap in our government's information about the situation there and about French military plans, and it recognized as no longer valid an earlier French intention to so weaken the enemy before reducing French forces in Indochina that indigenous forces could handle the situation. It seemed clear to our observers that Vietnamese forces alone could not even maintain the existing stalemate.[6]

Eisenhower's recollections of the 1953–54 period fit into the same mold. "I am convinced," he wrote in his memoirs, "that the French could not win the war because the internal political situation in Vietnam, weak and confused, badly weakened their military position." About the military situation, he said: "In the earlier stages of the conflict, the fighting was mostly conducted where rough terrain made it impossible to seek out the enemy and bring him to a pitched battle. Later, even when the battle lines became so located that the *groupes mobiles* could be effective, there still existed within the Red River Delta a condition in which the French could control even the main roads for only about two or three hours a day." Then, the crux: "American aid could not cure the defect in the French-Vietnamese relationship and therefore was of only limited value. The decision to give this aid was almost compulsory. The United States had no real alternative unless we were to abandon Southeast Asia."[7]

But Eisenhower also wanted to make it clear in retrospect that he was not prepared to see the French defeated militarily. "Had the Chinese adopted a policy of regular air support for the Vietminh, we would have

4. Ibid., p. 673.
5. Ibid., p. 674.
6. Ibid., pp. 676–77.
7. Dwight D. Eisenhower, *The White House Years: Mandate for Change, 1953–1956* (Doubleday, 1963), pp. 372–73.

assuredly moved in to eliminate this blatant aggression from without. This would have necessitated striking Chinese airfields and would have created some risk of general war with China. As it was, I feel confident that our capability to operate in this fashion had a decisively deterrent effect on the Chinese."[8]

In his critical wrangle with General Lawton Collins in the post-Geneva period when it looked as if all of Indochina might be lost, Dulles cabled: "We have no choice but continue our aid Viet-Nam and support of Diem."[9] The quiet of the ensuing years in Vietnam may have led Eisenhower and Dulles to think beyond stalemate, but no evidence exists one way or the other. What is clear is that they knew they were still mired down in Indochina because of the volatile situation in Laos in which the right-wing group, the Communists, and the neutralists all seemed unable to gain the upper hand.

With the exception of much of 1962, the principal Kennedy decisions were made in an atmosphere of deterioration. This feeling of deterioration explains why Kennedy dispatched so many high-level missions to Vietnam. As Kennedy's biographers have written, the President was not really being told he was winning but how much more he would have to do. Kennedy's often expressed sense of the dilemma of not being able to cure the fatal flaws of Diem without making Vietnam "a white man's war," yet knowing that a white man's war was fundamentally unwinnable, indicates that he also caught the essence of the stalemate.

Theodore Sorensen has summed up the White House view of events following the Diem coup in November 1963.

The President, while eager to make clear that our aim was to get out of Vietnam, had always been doubtful about the optimistic reports constantly filed by the military on the progress of the war. . . . The struggle could well be, he thought, this nation's severest test of endurance and patience. . . . He was simply going to weather it out, a nasty, untidy mess to which there was no other acceptable solution. Talk of abandoning so unstable an ally and so costly a commitment "only makes it easy for the Communists," said the President. "I think we should stay."[10]

President Johnson knew he had inherited a serious and deteriorating situation in Vietnam. Vietcong military successes and constant changes in the Saigon government from 1964 to 1966 were not secrets to anyone.

8. Ibid., p. 373.

9. Cable for Lawton Collins and Douglas Dillon, December 24, 1954, *United States–Vietnam Relations*, bk. 10, pt. V.B.3, p. 854.

10. Theodore C. Sorensen, *Kennedy* (Harper and Row, 1965), pp. 660–61.

Throughout the critical year of 1965 he struck the themes of endurance and more-to-come. In his requests for Vietnam supplemental appropriations on May 4, 1965, he warned: "Therefore, I see no choice but to continue the course we are on, filled as it is with peril and uncertainty." In his press conference on July 28 he announced a new 125,000-troop level and went on to say: "Additional forces will be needed later, and they will be sent as requested." What was really driving Lyndon Johnson during these early years is, however, best captured by two private remarks. In November 1963 he is quoted as having said: "I am not going to be the President who saw Southeast Asia go the way China went."[11] Lady Bird Johnson quoted him as saying in the spring of 1965: "I can't get out. I can't finish it with what I have got. So what the Hell can I do?"[12] Bill Moyers, Johnson's press secretary, confirmed that the President carried these feelings into early 1966: "I believed the President began to expect the worst. More and more he would talk about a long war with no end in sight."[13]

At that time several of Johnson's key subordinates were conveying messages that could only contribute to the President's feeling of being trapped. John McNaughton, McNamara's principal Vietnam adviser, put the issue quite starkly in a subsection of a memo: "We are in an escalating military stalemate." McNaughton went on to say: "There is an honest difference of judgment as to the success of the present military efforts in the South. There is no question that the US deployments thwarted the VC hope to achieve a quick victory in 1965. But there is a serious question whether we are now defeating the VC/PAVN [People's Army of (North) Vietnam] main forces and whether planned US deployments will more than hold our position in the country."[14] In April 1966 the Priorities Task Force headed by Ambassador William Porter in Saigon reported to the President: "The war will probably increase in intensity over the planning period (two years) though *decisive military victory for either side is not likely*."[15]

11. Johnson quotations are from Tom Wicker, *JFK and LBJ: The Influence of Personality upon Politics* (William Morrow, 1968), p. 208.

12. Lady Bird Johnson, *A White House Diary* (Holt, Rinehart and Winston, 1970), p. 248.

13. "Bill Moyers Talks about the War and LBJ: An Interview," July 1968, in Robert Manning and Michael Janeway, eds., *Who We Are: An Atlantic Chronicle of the United States and Vietnam* (Little, Brown, 1969), p. 269.

14. *The Pentagon Papers: The Defense Department History of United States Decisionmaking on Vietnam*, Senator Gravel ed. (Beacon Press, 1971), vol. 4, p. 47.

15. Ibid., vol. 2, p. 580 (emphasis in original).

With the flush of optimism that accompanied 1967, Johnson's assessment seems to change. "By early 1967," he wrote in his memoirs, "most of my advisers and I felt confident that the tide of war was moving strongly in [our] favor."[16] McNamara confirmed this in the summer of that year. "I asked McNamara about reports that the the military situation was really a 'stalemate,' as some observers claimed," Johnson wrote. " 'There is not a military stalemate,' he answered. He said that 'for the first time' since we committed troops to combat in 1965, he was convinced we could achieve our goals and end the fighting if we followed the course we had set."[17] But other memos by McNamara during the same period indicate that he still believed that the weak political situation in Saigon and Hanoi's will to persist continued to herald a long war.

Nevertheless, it is perfectly reasonable to assume that Johnson and most of his advisers did feel genuinely optimistic by the summer of 1967, for indeed the tide of the war had changed militarily and there was no longer the danger of defeat. But it is one thing to equate optimism with progress, and even progress with eventual success, and another to see the light at the end of the tunnel. By late 1967 President Johnson may no longer have worried about being the first President to lose a war, but he still had to worry about whether it would all end and when. As Johnson himself is quoted as saying after the Guam Conference in March 1967, following his rhetoric about "turning points": "We have a difficult, a serious, long-drawn-out, agonizing problem that we do not have an answer for."[18]

Like his predecessors, then, Johnson essentially found himself in a stalemate. It was not the kind of stalemate that precluded both the sense and the reality of winning or losing but one in which the major participants realized that whoever was winning or losing, the game would not be over in the ninth inning; they were locked into an extra-inning game from the start. It was not a matter of holding out until the ninth inning, since there were no agreed upon rules as to when the war would end. Only one aspect of this dynamic stalemate could be certain: from 1949 onward each President knew that he would probably have to do more and not less next year. This is not to deny the possibility that one side or

16. Johnson, *The Vantage Point*, p. 257.
17. Ibid., p. 262.
18. Henry Brandon, *Anatomy of Error: The Inside Story of the Asian War on the Potomac, 1954–1969* (Gambit, 1969), p. 102.

the other could gain a victory but merely to state that the odds always were that the struggle would be going on the next year and at higher costs to all parties.

But stalemate was not the result of the situation inherent in Vietnam itself. It is highly likely that the Vietminh would have defeated the French militarily if the French had been without American aid and that Hanoi would have defeated Saigon even with American aid as long as Washington eschewed direct massive participation. The Communists were always better led, motivated, and disciplined than their opponents, and were more cohesively organized; to boot, they historically possessed the mantle of nationalism—as Asian scholar Paul Mus argued, the classical "mandate of heaven."[19]

The roots of stalemate lay buried in Washington, not Vietnam, and led back to a succession of presidents who perceived and arranged policy imperatives and constraints in such a way as to avoid the costs and risks of both winning and losing. Perhaps one-quarter of the population of South Vietnam actively opposed the Communists (which was at least as many as favored the Communists). Given some solid basis of support from these South Vietnamese, the presidents always could and did do enough to prevent a Communist victory. But neither the minimum necessary until the summer of 1965 nor the maximum feasible, given the constraints thereafter, were sufficient to bring about Communist defeat —at least in anything approaching the near term.

It is possible, perhaps even probable, that some combination of the following actions would have produced a Communist defeat in the sense of deterring further support of the Vietcong by Hanoi and of reducing the Vietcong to a negligible threat that could be managed by Saigon: using nuclear weapons, dispatching a million men to fight, removing all sanctuaries and bombing restrictions, running a nearly perfect pacification program with 1,000 men the caliber of John Paul Vann, and demanding and receiving a range of fundamental political reforms. But none of these actions was ever sanctioned by any president for reasons discussed in previous chapters. *Presidents never bought the maximum proposals advanced by their advisers.* This is a critical fact because *only* those proposals for the maximum use of force or the maximum use of pressure for reform on Saigon (with the exception, at times, of the

19. Paul Mus, *Viet Nam: sociologie d'une guerre* (Paris: Editors du Seuil, 1952). A translated version of the discussion of the mandate of heaven appears in John T. McAlister, Jr., and Paul Mus, *The Vietnamese and Their Revolution* (Harper Torchbooks, 1970), chap. 3.

pacification program) were accompanied by promises of victory. Presidents Eisenhower, Kennedy, and Johnson may well not have believed what the military and others were proposing would work, but there is no reason to think that they believed that doing less would lead to victory.

There is, of course, a difference between choosing the unwinnable and choosing a course of action that *could* win. Presidents, and particularly Lyndon Johnson, did the latter, choosing action that would not necessarily win but would increase the chances of winning. That hardly constituted a strategy for ending the war. Yet there was such a strategy, there had to be, for no president would have ventured into the Vietnam trap so aware of its contours and its grip without conceiving of some way to unbind himself.

Elements of the Strategy

The strategy was to persevere in the hope that eventually Hanoi would have to break and negotiate, or that after years of grinding the Communists down they simply would begin to fade away, thus becoming manageable by the Saigon forces alone. In either case, once the U.S. role had ended, the situation in South Vietnam would be as follows: the Vietcong would not be completely eliminated, but they would not be afforded safe haven for their military operations; the Vietcong in effect would be reduced to banditry in unpopulated jungle and mountainous areas much as the guerrillas had been in Malaya and the Philippines; the GVN would control 80–85 percent of the population; and "former" Communists and "neutralists" would be allowed to participate in the political life of the country within this framework.[20] This was how many U.S. leaders visualized the war could end and may have made it easier for presidents not to choose strategies with a high promise of early victory.

The strategy of perseverance was a compound consisting of one part test of wills and one part buying time.

The Test of Wills

The test of wills shaped up this way. Neither the United States nor the Vietnamese Communists had good odds for a traditional military

20. Lodge cable to the President, October 21, 1965, *Pentagon Papers*, vol. 2, pp. 532–33. This was Lodge's particular vision, but it was shared by most of the military, Komer, and Rostow.

victory in Vietnam. Most American leaders—and a good guess would be most of the Vietnamese Communist leaders as well—recognized this by the fall of 1965 and probably much earlier. Washington and Hanoi experienced periods of genuine and general optimism about victory from time to time, but the dominant perception in both capitals was that given the mutual will to continue the war and self-imposed American restraint in the use of force, stalemate was the most likely outcome.

This common perception had a critical effect on the strategies of both sides. It meant that the "winner" would be determined by whose will to persist gave out first. Hanoi's will was much less malleable than Washington's because of the nature of the North Vietnamese government, society, and economy, but most of all because the Communists were fighting in and for their own country. Washington's will, because of the vagaries of American politics and the widespread dislike of interminable and indeterminate Asian land wars, presented an inviting target. For both sides, then, U.S. politics—public support and opposition to the war—was to be the key stress point.

The common strategic syllogism was quite simple. If American public opposition could be contained within manageable proportions, and if U.S. forces were thereby allowed to continue grinding down Communist forces in the field, Hanoi would either have to accept U.S. terms or lie low and risk the destruction of its cadres in the South. If opposition to the war reached the point where it became politically unacceptable to continue the fight, Washington would either have to withdraw or reduce its forces. What was important was not so much what was going on in Vietnam but what was happening in America.

American leaders knew with high confidence that the United States could not lose the war in Vietnam itself. The United States was too strong for that. The war could be lost only if the American public turned sour on it. American public opinion was the essential domino. U.S. leaders knew it. Hanoi's leaders knew it. Each geared its strategy, both rhetorically and in the conduct of the war, to this overwhelming fact.

Hanoi's leaders could bank on controlling the essential elements of their own situation in the North. They could control their own domestic politics. While Hanoi's politburo undoubtedly had its pro-Moscow and pro-Peking wings, every sign pointed to remarkable leadership unity on the pursuit of the war. There had not been a major purge in the last twenty years, and Ho reigned supreme. Hanoi's leaders also knew they could control their rate of loss in the fighting in South Vietnam. The option to engage or not to engage in ground combat was largely theirs. Of course, the less Hanoi's leaders chose to fight, the more risk they ran of Saigon's extending its domain, but that was a risk they were prepared to run—and on occasion they ran it successfully. They also knew that as long as the Soviet Union and China maintained the supply lines and the United States restrained itself from bombing the major cities, they could sustain their war effort with minimum disruption of the lives of their countrymen—and they did.

From the vantage point of Hanoi's leaders, the problem was not their own political situation; it was turning around the American leadership. And according to all indications they did think that such a turnaround would be difficult to achieve. Most of the statements made by the Hanoi leadership from 1965 on harped on a single theme: U.S. leaders would never leave South Vietnam of their own free will. Hanoi could not conceive of the "leaders of American imperialism" spending billions of dollars, losing thousands of American lives, building modern bases, and then simply pulling out. To make the imperialists bend to historical necessity, a shock would have to be administered. Dien Bien Phu was the shock that ended the first Indochina war. While Dien Bien Phu did not spell military defeat for French forces, it did decisively crack what was left of the shell of French public endurance and tolerance for the war.

It probably became clear to Hanoi's leaders that American forces and resources were too powerful and mobile for a Dien Bien Phu. The siege of Khesanh, which was ultimately broken by massive American air bombardment, turned out to be a diversion from the Tet offensive. The North Vietnamese needed to produce a shock with much more sustained or wide-ranging effects to dislodge the American leadership. Hanoi saw that the proportions of the problem demanded a Tet offensive, a countrywide jolt, and not a single pitched battle. But this was not enough. Although some evidence later suggested that in 1968 the Communists were aiming at a popular uprising throughout South Vietnam, it is not certain that Hanoi's strategy was to have the Tet offensive be a finale to the war, but Tet might well have been the key element in that strategy.

Tet 1968, like Dien Bien Phu 1954, was a symbol. It signified that Washington-Saigon progress toward ending the war was without foundation and could be swept away in weeks. While Hanoi paid a dear military price for Tet—the decimation of the southern infrastructure of the Vietcong—the political shock in America was even more profound.

Tet turned out to have a two-pronged effect, causing U.S. disengagement from Vietnam by playing on American domestic politics.

The first effect was the driving of a wedge between the American government and the American people. This could be done, so Hanoi's leaders may have reasoned, by using the U.S. press to tell the people the "truth" about the war. They would paint a hopeless portrait of corrupt Saigon leadership and an ineffective South Vietnamese army—a portrait that many involved American observers saw as real. They would show themselves as peace-seekers but willing to match force with force at ever increasing levels. Above all, they would convince Americans that unless U.S. forces withdrew, the killing of Americans would never end. If the American public, or significant minorities in the public, could be brought to this conclusion, continuation of the war by the leadership would become bad politics.

The political costs of a never-ending war in which U.S. troops were being killed were self-evident. Hanoi had only to look back to the American experience in the Korean War to see the effects of an Asian land war that offered no prospect of victory. It meant a bad press, diversion from domestic legislative concerns, economic troubles, political charges that had to be answered again and again, risky electoral prospects, agitation in Congress, and bad public opinion polls for the President. If Washington's leaders would not change their minds on their own about the war by virtue of the "facts" of Vietnam, they would be compelled to do so by the "facts" of politics at home.

The second effect was the provision of a face-saving exit for American leaders. It was not enough—indeed it might have been dangerous—to push official Washington flat up against the wall. That might possibly have led to unlimited escalation of the war. Some kind of exit with a red carpet, albeit tattered, had to be provided as well. It would have been helpful if American leaders could have been assured that withdrawal could take place without severe withdrawal symptoms. The Vietnamization of the U.S. Saigon war effort did that in effect.

Beginning in late 1965 the government of North Vietnam tacitly allowed President Johnson to believe that the pain of withdrawal could be muted, that withdrawal might be made to appear as something other than defeat. At one time or another, privately and publicly, directly or indirectly, Hanoi's leaders conveyed the following suggestions: after U.S. withdrawal, they would not move immediately to conquer South Vietnam by direct military means; elections under a provisional coalition

government would be held; South Vietnam would, for a time, be a separate Socialist entity with a neutral foreign policy; unification of North
and South Vietnam would occur over time and by means of negotiations; and to mitigate the domino vision, they would not move militarily
against Cambodia and Laos. As a package, this should have had some
appeal. But it did not appeal to American leaders because they probably
did not believe it (and as it turned out, Hanoi did not fully adhere to
this scenario in the mid-1970s). But more important, this package did
not appeal to American leaders because they were not looking for a face-
saving way out; they were looking for a non-Communist South Vietnam.

Without a North Vietnamese equivalent of the Pentagon Papers, no
one will ever really know what Hanoi's strategy was in detail. But nothing in the available evidence contradicts the foregoing hypotheses. The
two-pronged strategy of the never-ending war and withdrawal without
withdrawal symptoms may seem too sophisticated for leaders of a small
underdeveloped Asian country, but contacts with these leaders indicate
a high degree of sophistication about the United States. Westerners
came away from meetings with them impressed by their up-to-date
knowledge of American literature and newspapers, and with a sense of
having spoken to people who knew what was going on. Hanoi's public
statements repeatedly played on such issues as race relations, student
unrest, and the credibility gap. But perhaps the surest sign that Hanoi's
leaders knew what they were up to was that U.S. leaders also believed
that American politics was the Achilles heel.

Buying Time

American leaders did not have to worry a great deal about the Communists turning U.S. public opinion around on the war before 1965.
Washington could keep pace during the minimum-necessary period because the costs of the war were relatively low and the war was not a
major domestic political issue. During this fifteen-year stretch, the buying-time element of perseverance came to the fore. Dulles specifically
characterized the strategy as such when he cabled General Collins in
late 1954: "Investment Viet-Nam justified even if only to buy time build
up strength elsewhere in area."[21] The idea of persisting, feeling the
way step by step, and looking for an opening encompasses virtually

21. Cable, December 24, 1954, *United States–Vietnam Relations*, bk. 10, pt.
V.B.2, p. 854.

everything Kennedy did with respect to Vietnam. During the discussion in November 1964 about whether the United States should start bombing North Vietnam, the following views were set forth:

Westmoreland said bombing should be delayed until Saigon rested on firmer ground. McNamara said that the political situation would not become stronger, but that Washington still had to go ahead. Taylor said that "stronger action would definitely have a favorable effect" in Saigon, but that he "was not sure this would be enough really to improve the situation." McNamara concluded that "the strengthening effect [of the bombing] could at least buy time, possibly measured in years."[22]

William Bundy and two of his key aides struck a similar theme in notes prepared for a meeting with Rusk in January 1965. They argued that stronger action was unlikely "to induce Hanoi to call it off." Yet, "on balance," they went on, "we believe that such action would have some faint hope of really improving the Vietnamese situation, and above all, would put us in a much stronger position to hold the next line of defense, namely Thailand."[23] McGeorge Bundy struck hard on this point in his critical memorandum of February 7, 1965, to the President urging him to begin the bombing even though he realized that it might fail. Damping down the charge that the United States was not doing all it could do, he argued, was vital because "this charge will be important in many countries, including our own." And then to stress that he was not talking about a disguised pullout, he added: "We must recognize, however, that [the ability to deter other such wars] will be gravely weakened if there is failure for any reason in Vietnam."[24]

This buying-time approach succeeded in holding down domestic criticism for fifteen years. But during the maximum-feasible phase, with war costs and domestic opposition rising, public support did come into question. In October 1966 McNamara formulated the problem when he wrote to the President that the enemy offensive had been blunted, that the situation was "somewhat better," but that the enemy was waiting for America's will to cave in. "I see no reasonable way to bring the war to an end soon," he said. He recommended that Johnson adopt "a posture that makes trying to 'wait us out' less attractive." He called on the President to stabilize U.S. forces in the South and the Rolling Thunder pro-

22. For Westmoreland, McNamara, and Taylor opinions, see *Pentagon Papers*, vol. 3, p. 242.
23. Ibid., p. 296.
24. Ibid., p. 314.

gram in the North, to *"pursue a vigorous pacification program,"* and to make a renewed effort at negotiations "to increase our credibility." Success in the next two years was unlikely, but American leaders "should recognize that success . . . is a mere possibility, not a probability," gird for "longer war," and make the costs to the American people "acceptably limited." He concluded that if the American people were to go on supporting the war, they must be convinced that the "formula for success has been found and that the end of the war is merely a matter of time."[25]

McNamara continued in this vein into 1967 and found allies in McGeorge Bundy (who had left government) and, to some extent, Dean Rusk. Bundy wrote Johnson a letter in May 1967 arguing that "escalation will not bring visible victory over Hanoi before the election. Therefore the election will have to be fought by the Administration on other grounds." With the war still going on and negotiations not in sight, he concluded, "what we must plan to offer as a defense of Administration policy is not victory over Hanoi, but growing success—and self-reliance —in the South."[26] The matter of strategy came to a head in the fall with considerable disagreement among Johnson advisers. Johnson weaved along a middle course, but one closer to McNamara than to the military —despite increasing the authorized number of bombing targets. He would not institute a bombing pause, but he would hold missions down below maximum levels and "remove as much drama as possible from our bombing effort."[27] He would not level off the troops, but he would ensure that they did not increase by much. He would not announce these moves publicly for fear of showing a weakening resolve to the enemy, but he would sound the theme that the formula for success had been found. Domestic opposition to the war increased, nonetheless.

The Question of Compromise

American leaders thus sought to match wills with the Vietnamese Communists from 1950 onward, but what did they expect would come of it? Did they expect the Communists to negotiate or fade away in the first fifteen years? In 1947 Secretary of State George Marshall expressed the hope that "a pacific basis of adjustment of the difficulties" between France and the Vietminh could be found.[28] After that, Truman's policy

25. Ibid., vol. 2, pp. 595, 597 (emphasis in the original).
26. Ibid., vol. 4, p. 159.
27. Johnson, *The Vantage Point*, p. 377.
28. Pentagon Papers, vol. 1, p. 31.

gradually hardened to the point where negotiations were no longer even discussed. Truman and Acheson expected the war to spiral. No evidence indicates that in the pre-Geneva days Eisenhower thought the Vietminh would fade away, but right from the start of the Geneva Conference he saw that the Vietminh would settle for a territorial compromise. The President and Dulles stepped back from the Geneva accords with no illusions, refusing to sign them in full anticipation that the Communists would shortly resume the battle and were likely to win. They could only have been pleasantly surprised, indeed amazed, by the years of quiet that followed. They may even have been tempted to speculate that Hanoi would remain quiescent, but everything they thought they knew about communism had to tell them that Hanoi would come back, and everything they knew about Diem had to lead them to believe that the Saigon regime would be an inviting target. Eisenhower's greeting to Diem on October 26, 1960, closed with a pledge of continued American assistance "in the difficult yet hopeful struggle ahead."[29] President Kennedy had all he could do to prevent the complete collapse of the GVN, and no one in his administration ventured into musings about a negotiated settlement. Indeed part of the rationale for a coalition government in the Laotian settlement was to make the stand in Vietnam, and thoughts of a Communist fadeaway in 1962 quickly vanished in the Saigon political turmoil of 1963.

Was it different for Lyndon Johnson? Did he and those closest to him believe that Hanoi would agree to American terms or, failing that, would fade away? The answers are much more complicated than for the Johnson administration's predecessors.

President Johnson preferred a compromise settlement, which by all odds he believed Hanoi would have to accept. By traditional diplomatic standards of negotiations between sovereign states, the possible compromises would not have been fatuous. One was to guarantee that the Communists could remain in secure control of North Vietnam. The United States would not seek to overthrow this regime. The other compromise was to allow the Communists in South Vietnam to seek power in the same way Communist parties seek it in France and Italy.

But the real struggle in Vietnam was not between sovereign states. It

29. "Message to President Diem on the Fifth Anniversary of the Independence of Viet-Nam, October 15, 1960," *Public Papers of the Presidents of the United States, Dwight D. Eisenhower, 1960* (GPO, 1961), p. 808.

was between Vietnamese. It was a civil war and a war for national independence.

Herein lies one of the paradoxes of and miscalculations about Vietnam. Most American leaders (and their critics) saw that Vietnam was a quagmire but did not see that the real stake—the question of who would eventually govern Vietnam—was not negotiable. Free elections, local sharing of power, international supervision, separate states within one nation—none of these could serve as a basis for settlement. What were legitimate compromises from Washington's point of view were matters of life and death to the Vietnamese. For American leaders, the stakes were keeping their word and saving their political necks. For the Vietnamese, the stakes were their lives and their lifelong political aspirations. Free elections meant both bodily exposure to the Communist guerrillas and likely surrender to the anti-Communists in Saigon. Neither side would rest its fate in the throw of some electoral dice. The risk was too great. There was no trust, no confidence.

The Vietnam War could no more be settled by traditional diplomatic compromises than any other civil war. President Lincoln could not settle with the South. The Spanish republicans and General Franco's nationalists could not conceivably have mended their fences by elections. None of the post–World War II insurgencies—Greece, Malaya, and the Philippines—ended with a negotiated peace. In each of these cases only the logic of the war could put these civil differences to rest.

It is commonly acknowledged that Vietnam would have fallen to the Communists in 1945, in 1954, and in 1965 had it not been for the intervention of first the French and then the Americans. The Vietnamese Communists, who were also the most dynamic of the Vietnamese Nationalists, would not accept only part of a prize for which they had paid so heavily. They had even more sunk costs than did the United States. The anti-Communist Vietnamese, protected by the French and the Americans, would not put themselves at Communist mercy.

It may be that American presidents understood this better than their critics. The critics, especially on the liberal Left, fought for "better compromises," failing to realize that Hanoi was as uninterested in compromise as Saigon was. The critics fought for broad nationalist governments, unaware that no really viable middle force existed in Vietnam. American presidents, it seems, recognized that there was no middle ground in Vietnam and that better compromises would frighten Saigon allies without bringing about a compromise peace. And they would not compromise South Vietnam away to the Communists.

But while Johnson and those close to him probably miscalculated the *ultimate* susceptibility of a civil war to a negotiated end, they did not miscalculate the time factor. Hanoi, they thought, would have to capitulate *eventually*, but they never seemed to have believed that that eventuality would come to pass before the 1968 presidential elections. From year to year hardly anyone, and particularly not Johnson, considered the odds good that Hanoi would come to the table. Indeed it was Johnson's acute consciousness of these odds that led him to be wary of all proposals for bombing halts. Bombing pauses, he repeatedly counseled, would fail to bring Hanoi to the table, leaving him to face renewed and strengthened pressures for escalation, pressures that he would be less able to control. Even the partial bombing halt he announced on March 31, 1968, was premised on Rusk's judgment that it had to be done to quiet the doves, but that Hanoi certainly would reject it.[30] The reaction in and around the White House when Hanoi responded that it would "talk" can be described as profound surprise, if not shock.

Wishful Thinking

By March 1968 the prospects for a negotiated settlement seemed so remote that Johnson and most of his advisers already had begun to pin their hopes on the fadeaway solution alone. But did they think that if they persevered the odds were favorable for forcing this solution? The answer is again yes, but not before the 1968 elections. Even in the brightest days of optimism, one of the more celebrated optimists made a point of drawing back from easy promises and solutions. Robert Komer, Mr. Pacification, concluded the introduction to his "Vietnam Prognosis for 1967–68" with: "In sum—slow, painful, and incredibly expensive though it may be—we're beginning to 'win' the war in Vietnam. This is a far cry from saying, however, that we're going to win it—in any meaningful sense." Komer's list of "imponderables" included in part: Will Hanoi escalate the fighting? Will the GVN fall apart politically? (His answer: "I expect plenty of political trouble.") Will the new pacification program work? (His answer: "We've got nowhere to go but up.") Will the U.S. settle down for the long haul? ("This is hardest to predict.") Komer's memorandum ended as follows: "By themselves, none of our

30. See Johnson, *The Vantage Point*, pp. 399–421.

Vietnam programs offer high confidence of a successful outcome (forcing the enemy either to fade away or to negotiate). Cumulatively, however, they *can* produce enough of a *bandwagon psychology* among the southerners to lead to such results by end-1967 or sometime in 1968. At any rate, do we have a better option?"[31]

In microcosm Komer's memo said it all: no need to worry about losing anymore, about progress, about imponderables and "if's." At least there was a bandwagon psychology, and the most salient point was the question about a better option. As long as the imagined costs of losing or winning exceeded the actual costs of pursuing the war, Johnson would persevere. It could almost be said, in fact, that the strategy of perseverance was chosen more for the means it employed than the ends it was expected to achieve, more for the problems it avoided than the ones it solved.

Presidents take problems one at a time, often without a clear conception of where they will come out, buying time to see how the whirlpool of pressures is evolving. In Vietnam they took each step expecting to do more but hoping that the worst would not happen. If the roof was falling down, however, they would shore it up and muddle through. This is the timeworn method of leaders and diplomats through history when confronted with an intractable problem, a problem that seems to brook no near-term solution. The skill needed is that to surmount the immediate crisis and keep the situation going (maybe status quo, maybe ameliorate it somewhat) without having it blow up—and wait for the breaks. And presidents of the United States are used to getting the breaks.

It is the inner belief of things working out for them that sustains them, and similarly, it was wishful thinking, not optimism, that sustained them in Vietnam. True optimism is rooted in the analysis of a problem. The problem is poked, weighed, and observed, and a set of judgments is given or odds laid. Wishful thinking springs from something inside the observer rather than from the problem. It is a feeling one has despite the facts. In Vietnam the analysis pointed toward stalemate most of the time, losing some of the time, and at times winning—but never to victory in any two-year period or within any term of a president.

Wishful thinking, or call it self-delusion, was required to sustain them, to bridge the gap between analysis and prognosis. Thus Komer provided a keen description of a number of nearly insurmountable difficulties and

31. *Pentagon Papers*, vol. 4, pp. 390–91 (emphasis in the original).

imponderables, predicted it could be over by 1968, and justified this with a psychological bandwagon. In 1961 William Bundy could write: "An early and hard-hitting operation has a good chance (70% would be my guess) of *arresting* things. . . . Even if we follow up hard, on the lines the JCS are working out . . ., however, the chances are not much better that we will in fact be able to *clean up* the situation. It all depends on Diem's effectiveness, which is very problematical."[32] The intelligence community could provide estimates from 1953 onward that no action could cripple enemy capabilities to persevere because the main sources of Communist strength in South Vietnam were "indigenous"[33] and still maintain, for a brief moment in the spring of 1966, that more bombing could help to change Hanoi's policy.[34] Thus McNaughton could write in January 1965 that the "best present estimate is that South Vietnam is being 'lost'," but could go on this way: "The situation could change for the better overnight, however. This is what happened in the Philippines. This is another reason for d———[sic] perseverance."[35] Those who were deeply pessimistic about the prospect of negotiations could look to Moscow, of all places, to help out. As Bill Moyers recalled: "The President—well, most of us shared this at the White House—we felt that he could reason with the Russians and they would deliver. We overestimated their influence in Hanoi or their willingness to help us off a painful hook."[36] Thus it went with McNamara, McGeorge Bundy, and most other high officials (with the exception of Rostow and the military). Moyers described it this way: "There was a confidence—it was never bragged about, it was just there—a residue, perhaps, of the confrontation over the missiles in Cuba—that when the chips were really down, the other people would fold."[37]

Denis Warner, a reliable and experienced journalist on Vietnam, captured the point squarely in an interview with an unnamed senior civilian official who said: "Sure we hoped things would go much better, but, intellectually I doubt that we ever believed they would." Warner conceded this truth as far as the political situation was concerned but

32. Ibid., vol. 2, p. 79 (emphasis in the original).

33. See, for example, the synopsis of the Special National Intelligence Estimate of May 25, 1964, in ibid., vol. 3, pp. 124–25.

34. See the account of the CIA's recommendations in ibid., vol. 4, pp. 71–72.

35. Ibid., vol. 3, p. 683.

36. "Bill Moyers Talks about the War," p. 270. This strain can be found going back to 1961.

37. Ibid., p. 262.

registered his doubt that Americans were not surprised at the Communists' ability to absorb the military pounding.[38]

With a sense of tragedy and "no exit," American leaders stayed their course. They seemed to hope more than to expect that something would happen. The hope was to convince the Vietnamese Communists through perseverance that the United States would stay in South Vietnam until they abandoned their struggle. This hope in a sense was the product of disbelief. How could a tiny, backward Asian country *not* have a breaking point, *not* have a price when opposed by the might of the United States? How could they not relent and negotiate? The hope was also a product of despair—the need to find some solution, some way out. The alternatives were deemed always to be unacceptable. Thus to American leaders perseverance did not seem so irrational.

The question of whether these leaders would have started down the road if they had known this would mean over half a million men in Vietnam, over 50,000 U.S. deaths, and the expenditure of well over $100 billion is historically irrelevant. Only President Johnson had to confront the possibility of these large costs. The point is that each administration was prepared to pay the costs it could foresee for itself. No one seemed to have a better solution. Each could at least pass the baton on to the next.

The presidents, given their politics and thinking, had nothing to do but persevere. But the Communists' strategy was also to persevere, to make the United States go home. It was civil war for national independence. They simply had more reason to persevere than did the United States.

38. Denis Warner, "Report: The War in Vietnam," September 1967, in Manning and Janeway, *Who We Are*, p. 116.

PART FIVE

Conclusions

CHAPTER THIRTEEN

The Lessons of Vietnam

In April 1975, Marine helicopters swooped down on the rooftops of the American Embassy in Saigon to carry away the last of the American officials and some of their Vietnamese friends, marking the end of the U.S. commitment to save South Vietnam from communism. When the helicopters were airborne, the passengers could look down and spy Vietcong and North Vietnamese flags flying throughout the city. Ten years before, the Marines had splashed ashore at Danang, the beginning of an American armada that was to reach almost 550,000 troops in South Vietnam and countless aircraft flying to bomb North Vietnam. Twenty years before, the last of the French troops had departed from the divided country, only to be followed by scores of American advisers and hundreds of millions of dollars in American aid. Twenty-five years before, as North Korean troops raced toward Seoul, President Truman had made the commitment that brought all those Americans to Vietnam.

It was as if destiny had been suspended since that day in 1945 when French forces returned to Indochina to reclaim their colonies. What virtually everyone who knew about Indochina at that time predicted would happen eventually did happen. The French and the Americans would be driven out; the strongest of the Vietnamese factions would face each other undisturbed by outsiders and one would win. It would not have surprised many even back then that one day Saigon might be renamed Ho Chi Minh City.

But that day had been postponed for thirty years, and the price of holding back destiny is always great. The millions of Vietnamese who perished, the more than 50,000 Americans killed and the many more thousands wounded, attest to that. But while small nations such as Vietnam must suffer even in victory, great powers like the United States are given the luxury of learning lessons. As the Vietnamese are rebuilding their ravaged country, Americans are rethinking their country's role in the world and retouching their institutions to prevent another Vietnam. The lessons of the Vietnam War for the United States—they are few in number, but of critical importance—are the subject of this chapter.

Coming to terms with what happened and deciding what to do about it will go on in the United States, explicitly or implicitly and intuitively, for decades. This is because Vietnam's civil war became America's civil convulsion. The more the United States did to preserve an independent identity for South Vietnam, the more America's own identity changed. The events and battles of the Vietnamese civil war seemed then and now inextricably bound to the Americans' own turmoils and grief: the assassinations of President Kennedy and President Diem less than a month apart in 1963; the massive American troop buildup in Vietnam in the summer of 1965 and the beginning of frank congressional inquiries and frontal questioning of twenty years of American foreign policy; the Communist Tet offensive in February 1968 and the bloodied heads of the March on Washington in 1969; President Nixon's Cambodian "incursion" in 1970 and the victims of Kent State; the struggle to keep President Thieu afloat as American troops withdrew; and President Nixon's "enemies list" and use of the federal police and intelligence apparatus to harass war critics, leading to the final spasm known simply as Watergate. The downward slide toward defeat in Vietnam was a central ingredient in the process that led to the impeachment of a president. The White House became the ultimate domino.

Nixon's and Ford's Policies

This book was not intended to cover the Nixon administration or the final days of South Vietnam under the Ford administration. It was meant to be the story of how the United States became progressively involved in Vietnam and not the tale of withdrawal. But the policies of involvement and withdrawal were really tied to the same roots of commitment and credibility. They were different means toward the same end of preventing a Communist victory in Vietnam. Thus a brief excursion into the Vietnam policies of the Nixon and Ford administrations before going directly into lessons learned is excusable.

On May 14, 1969, President Nixon stated his objective in almost precisely the same words as his predecessors: "We seek the opportunity for the South Vietnamese people to determine their own political future without outside interference."[1] This seemed to suggest that if the North Vietnamese would withdraw from the South and allow the Vietcong and the Saigon regime to slug it out on the battlefield or in the ballot box, the United States would accept the verdict whoever the victor might be. Indeed given the decimation of the Vietcong over the years, this would not have been a very risky course for Nixon and his then national security adviser, Henry A. Kissinger, to adopt. But it seems fair to assume that precisely because this risk was readily acceptable to them, it was clearly unacceptable to Hanoi. Hanoi would not agree to withdraw its troops from the South, and the Nixon administration did not insist that Hanoi do so when the Paris cease-fire accords were signed in 1973.[2] Thus to state an objective the adversary was certain to reject in negotiations was to indicate that the objective would be imposed on the adversary by force majeur.

This apparently was the goal of the policy of Vietnamization of the war. The strategy of Vietnamization was to phase out American forces slowly enough not to jeopardize the battlefield situation but fast enough to assuage American political opinion. The idea was that if Hanoi would not agree to a negotiated settlement that allowed the South Vietnamese to settle their own affairs, its leaders would be faced with a Saigon regime armed to the teeth and able to defend itself without compromise.

Another interpretation of Vietnamization is that Nixon and Kissinger intended only to ensure that Saigon's defeat was delayed long enough to place the responsibility solely on Saigon's shoulders. This "fig leaf" interpretation, however, cannot be made consistent with the total record. President Nixon, in the four years preceding the Paris accords, did reduce American forces in Vietnam from 550,000 to 24,000. American deaths and casualties fell from hundreds each week to under 25. Spending on the war declined from about $25 billion a year to a projected $3

1. "Address to the Nation on Vietnam, May 14, 1969," *Public Papers of the Presidents of the United States, Richard M. Nixon, 1969* (Government Printing Office, 1971), p. 371.

2. The Agreement on Ending the War and Restoring Peace in Vietnam was signed in Paris by William P. Rogers, representing the United States, and Nguyen Duy Trinh, representing the Democratic Republic of Vietnam, on January 27, 1973. The text of these so-called Paris accords appears in the *Department of State Bulletin*, vol. 68 (February 12, 1973), pp. 169–88.

billion. This vast reduction did entail some risk of losing the war, but the point is that it was a policy of reductions, not a policy of complete withdrawal. The Nixon administration never pledged total withdrawal unless Hanoi would agree to American settlement terms. Even after the Paris cease-fire accords were signed, it never promised to remove the aircraft carriers from Indochina waters or not to use American aircraft stationed in Thailand and Taiwan in further military action. It was Congress that prohibited any further American military action in and over Indochina after the accords were completed. The Nixon administration always sought to keep these hedges against losing.

Vietnamization, in practice, was a strategy designed to do two things: to decrease American forces in Vietnam to a level that would be tolerated by American politics and to use the prospect of endless American presence or assistance to persuade Hanoi to accept the proferred negotiating terms. To repeat, these terms were tantamount to a North Vietnamese surrender. But the discussion of the ultimate intentions of Nixon and Kissinger is so complicated and convoluted that it cannot end here either.

The fact was that when Secretary of State William Rogers and Vietnamese Foreign Minister Nguyen Duy Trinh put their signatures to the Paris cease-fire accords on January 27, 1973, the Nixon administration did take real risks. The essence of this agreement was that all American forces were to be withdrawn in return for the release of American prisoners, and Hanoi's forces could stay in the South. Further, the accords called for a cease-fire in place leading to free elections conducted by a National Council of Reconciliation and Concord. The risk was allowing North Vietnamese forces to remain in the South. The answer to the puzzle about Nixon's ultimate intentions, then, turns on how much of a risk he actually believed he was running.

The secret files have not been made public, but almost all contemporary news accounts recorded that the leaders of the Nixon administration believed that Saigon's forces stood a better than even chance of holding their own against the North Vietnamese if. There were two"if's." One was if Congress would continue to approve substantial amounts of military and economic aid to the Saigon regime. In 1975 Congress cut the administration's aid request by half. The other was if Congress would do nothing to jeopardize the threat of American military reinvolvement should Hanoi violate the agreement. In particular, Nixon and Kissinger wanted to hold open the option of bombing North Vietnam once again. In 1974 Congress legislated a ban on all future American military reinvolvement.

What changed from the time of the Truman administration to the advent of the Ford administration was not the goals of presidents but the attitudes in Congress. In early 1975, a new congressional majority had emerged that was prepared to use legislative power to end American involvement in the war. The motives within this majority were mixed. Some believed that it was historically just for the Communists to take over South Vietnam. Others became convinced that ending the aid and dumping President Thieu would lead to a truly neutral and national government in Saigon. Still others did not pretend to be able to divine who would rule Saigon, and did not care; they simply wanted the United States to wash its hands of the whole affair. That this majority was able to legislate its will without any evident political backlash indicated that the American people also had had enough.

The Ford administration clearly tried to develop that backlash with its public rhetoric. Down to the last days of the Phnom Penh regime in Cambodia and the Saigon regime, some of the strongest rhetoric ever emanated from the White House and the State Department. In his message to Congress in January 1975 requesting emergency aid for Cambodia and South Vietnam, President Ford stated: "U.S. unwillingness to provide adequate assistance to allies fighting for their lives would seriously affect our credibility throughout the world as an ally. And this credibility is essential to our national security."[3] To those who thought the administration had finally abandoned the domino theory, Secretary of State Kissinger made clear that quite the opposite was true. He said, "We must understand that peace is indivisible. The United States cannot pursue a policy of selective reliability. We cannot abandon friends in one part of the world without jeopardizing the security of friends everywhere." He added that if the Saigon regime were allowed to fall, "then we are likely to find a massive shift in the foreign policies of many countries and a fundamental threat over a period of time to the security of the United States."[4]

The United States, they were all saying, had a commitment. This is

3. "Special Message to the Congress Requesting Supplemental Assistance for the Republic of Vietnam and Cambodia, January 28, 1975," *Public Papers, Gerald R. Ford, 1975* (GPO, 1977), p. 119.
4. "Secretary Kissinger's News Conference of March 26, 1975," *Department of State Bulletin*, vol. 72 (April 14, 1975), pp. 461, 463.

where the story of American involvement in Vietnam ended and where it began. From Truman to Ford, six presidents felt that they had to do and say what was necessary to prevent a Communist takeover of Vietnam. While other perceived threats to peace came and went, Vietnam was always there—a cockpit of confrontation, a testing place.

And there were always two battles going on for those twenty-five years: one out there and one back home. There, it was the Promethean clash of colonialism, nationalism, communism, and Americanism. Back home, it was the clash of imperatives not to lose a country to communism and not to get embroiled in an endless Asian land war, a struggle to walk the line between not winning and not getting out. The battle would be endless in Vietnam until it was no longer viewed as necessary in Washington.

How the System Worked

It is in Washington and to the policymaking process, and specifically to the process of making commitments, that one must look for the lessons of Vietnam. This whole book has been an attempt to explain why American leaders felt it was necessary to prevent defeat in Vietnam, to fight the war by gradual escalation, and to persevere despite pessimism about the final outcome. They saw no acceptable alternatives to what they were doing. They really believed they had no choice. To deduce lessons from this experience, one must ask what it was about the system of decisionmaking that took *choice* away. Again, as Kafka's priest said in *The Trial:* "It is not necessary to accept everything as true, one must only accept it as necessary."[5]

This approach to the subject of lessons sidesteps the more profound question of whether the Vietnam War was "good" or "bad." No final answer to that question emerges from this research. It will be debated as long as people are interested in truth. The dominant view now is that the war was a tragic mistake, that its costs were too horrible to be offset by any conceivable outcome. Revisionists will come along to argue that the war provided time and a period of safety for the adjustment of the world order from a period of bipolarity and cold war to another era of multipolarity and international fluidity. Still others will maintain that apart

5. Franz Kafka, *The Trial,* trans. Willa and Edwin Muir (Knopf, 1970), p. 276.

from the immediate human costs, the war altered the broad flow of history only imperceptibly for twenty-five years.

If Vietnam were a story of how the decisionmaking system failed, that is, a story of how U.S. leaders did not do what they wanted to do, did not realize what they were doing, did not understand what was happening, or got their way principally by lying to Congress and the American people, it would be easy to package a large and assorted box of panaceas. There are many examples: fix the method of reporting from the field to stress incentives for accuracy rather than bureaucratic sycophancy; fix the way progress is measured in a guerrilla war; improve the analysis of intelligence; concentrate more on the political and economic dimensions of conflict and less on the military side; tell the American people more of the truth to prepare them for sacrifices and the long haul; make sure the President sees all the real alternatives; involve Congress more; and so forth. These are all interesting and some are of consequence, but it is the thesis of this book that improvements in any of these respects would not have appreciably altered the thrust of the war. At most they would have altered tactics. In the end they were all third-order issues because the U.S. political-bureaucratic system did not fail; it worked.

The point seems paradoxical, if not whimsical. But it is nothing more than a direct conclusion from one simple and unassailable fact: American leaders were convinced that they had to prevent the loss of Vietnam to communism, and until May 1975 they succeeded in doing just that. It can be persuasively argued that the United States fought the war inefficiently with needless costs in lives and resources. As with all wars, this was to be expected. It can be persuasively argued that the war was an out-and-out mistake and that the commitment should not have been made. But the commitment was made and kept for twenty-five years. The shared values were pursued consistently. That is what the system— the political and bureaucratic mechanisms and pressures—was designed to do, and it did it.

At each critical juncture the governmental debate centered on *how* to contain communism in Vietnam. Decisionmakers perceived the immediate costs of maintaining the commitment, and the President always refused to pay enough of the costs to make clear or quick victory possible, but until the end they always paid the costs of preventing *Communist* victory. The commitment in principle always determined the scale of the commitment in fact, not the reverse. The escalation of involvement was not a blind slide down a slippery slope; it was the response to the progressive escalation of the price of keeping the commitment. The minimum-necessary price grew, but it was always paid. In 1950 the price was aid to France; in 1954 it was accepting partition in exchange for what appeared to be a more easily defensible anti-Communist bastion in the South; in 1961 it was a vigorous infusion of American materiel and advisers; in 1963 it was dumping Diem, who seemed the principal obstacle to more productive South Vietnamese effort; and in 1965 it was using American forces.

At each of these junctures decisionmakers disagreed about exactly how much action was advisable, or what kinds of action were appropriate, or which aspects of action should receive more emphasis than others. But they agreed that action was required. The few who questioned the commitment itself were either principals such as Robert Kennedy, whose questioning was only offhanded, tentative, and overridden by his visceral commitment until he left the executive branch, or low-level officials such as Kattenburg, or isolated figures such as George Ball, who almost never went so far as to say explicitly that the United States should accept the demise of the Saigon regime. The system facilitated decisionmaking on means to reach the end of containment; that end remained virtually unchallenged within the executive branch. The system facilitated decisionmaking on ways to keep the costs of commitment as low as possible; the problem was the progressive inflation of the lowest possible costs of preventing Communist victory. The bureaucratic system did what it was supposed to: select and implement means to a given end. The political system did what a democracy usually does: produce a policy responsive more to the majority and the center than to the minority or the extremes of opinion. And strategic thought, from that of the limited war theorists to the counterinsurgency specialists, did what it was supposed to do: support the general policy of worldwide containment with specific ideas and programs for containment in Vietnam.

Two Schools of Thought on the Lessons of Vietnam

Two broad schools of thought have emerged to draw lessons from this experience. One, which might be called the Win School, holds that if the United States is to make a commitment and intervene with force once again, it must win quickly and decisively. The other, which might be called the Reformist School, seeks to alter institutions and policies to prevent another Vietnam.

The Win School includes both people who retrospectively feel that American involvement in the war was a mistake and those who believe that it was necessary. What unites members of this school, then, is not their shared belief in the wisdom of the commitment, but their shared conviction that the war was fought the wrong way. Mostly composed of military men and political conservatives, this school is divided in its concern about how future commitments should be set but unanimously convinced that once American prestige and credibility are committed, the United States should swiftly and fully employ its technological advantages in battle.

The Reformist School consists of people who believe that the war was a mistake and that ways must be found to prevent its recurrence. Composed of liberals and moderates, it is united by the desire both to curb the war power and to frame policies with a restricted view of what is vital to American security. It is concerned principally with the politics and substance of ends more than with the question of means. Interestingly, in the late 1970s most members of both schools seem to agree that the United States should not intervene with force in the developing world.

Neither school conclusively addresses the critical element in the Vietnam experience, the elements in the system that made the war and the way it was fought "necessary," and neither seriously gets to the related problem of how to deal with a "mistake" after it is made. But before developing these points, the arguments of the two schools need to be explored more closely.

The Win School

The Win School looks to the differences in military strategy between President Johnson and President Nixon for the basis of its argument. Johnson's strategy rested on three interrelated principles: gradual escalation, a highly restrictive list of permissible operations (no mining of harbors, no population bombing in North Vietnam, no large-scale conventional cross-border operations, and the like), and a declaratory policy that made clear that America had no intention of threatening the existence of the North Vietnamese regime. The purposes behind the strategy were both to give Hanoi some added incentive to negotiate and to avoid a wider war. Avoiding a wider war meant specifically doing nothing that ran a high risk of bringing about counterintervention by the Soviet Union and China.

Nixon, on the other hand, chose a military strategy anchored to massive and quick military action, to a less restricted bombing target list, coupled with a declaratory policy that was ominously silent about what might happen to the North Vietnamese regime if it persisted. Accordingly he invaded Cambodia in 1970, ordered U.S. forces to support Saigon's thrust into Laos in 1971, and in 1972 restarted the bombing of North Vietnam on a large scale, mined the harbors, and then approved the bombing of Hanoi itself.

Nixon, like Johnson, had to make his military moves without serious risk of intervention by Peking or Moscow. But while Johnson did this by restricting military actions in Indochina, Nixon did it by enlarging his diplomacy. Nixon's "insight," or plan, was that the way out of Vietnam was through Moscow and Peking, not Hanoi. By playing on Sino-Soviet rivalry and by initiating the policy of détente with both countries, he hoped and calculated that they would restrain Hanoi and thus prevent an American defeat.

Was the Nixon approach successful? In many respects, it seemed to work. Despite the reescalation of the war, Moscow and Peking did not intervene. Startlingly, the Russians wanted détente badly enough that they even welcomed Nixon to Moscow after he ordered the mining of the harbors. But quite apart from jeopardizing the benefits of détente with Washington, intervention could not have looked very attractive to the Communist superpowers. By the time of the reescalation in 1972, the United States had 8 aircraft carriers, some 200 B-52 bombers, and numerous other aircraft in and near the Indochina theater. The U.S. Air Force also had just begun to use so-called smart bombs with astronomically higher probabilities of knocking out targets than ordnance used in all previous bombing. The United States thus had overwhelming conventional superiority in the area.

Nixon's decisiveness also seemed to have a tangible effect on the battle in South Vietnam. Mining the harbors and knocking out the railway links between North Vietnam and China clearly curtailed the flow of supplies from Hanoi's friends. This in turn reduced the flow of supplies going into South Vietnam. The upshot was that the North Vietnamese offensive was impaired, and the battlefield situation in the South seemed to stabilize.

Nixon's strategy also worked politically in 1972. By the spring of that year it appeared that the antiwar movement was growing irresistibly and that Congress would legislate a terminal date for American participation in the war. Senator George S. McGovern had become the Democratic Party's presidential nominee largely on the strength of his strong stand against the war. Nixon's escalation in May did not silence the liberals, but it did contain them. It also hastened a transformation of the basic liberal argument against the war, as did the strategy of Vietnamization that reduced the number of Americans being killed. Instead of stressing the hopelessness of winning the war, liberals now began to emphasize its immorality. This transformation probably weakened the antiwar movement with the American people, although the evidence on this point is not conclusive. Nonetheless, from the time of the escalation right down to Henry Kissinger's statement in October 1972 that "peace is at hand,"[6] Nixon had captured the support of most Americans in the middle and on the right.

Thus Nixon's strategy helped keep Moscow and Peking at bay, adversely affected North Vietnamese military operations·in the South, and gained the backing of most Americans. But this still does not prove that it was successful. To demonstrate success, it would have to be established that Nixon's military decisiveness caused Hanoi to accept settlement terms that it would not have accepted otherwise. Here, the evidence and arguments become quite murky and the answer depends on judgment.

The essence of the Paris accords of January 1973 was North Vietnam's agreement to return U.S. prisoners of war in exchange for complete American withdrawal from South Vietnam. Why was not this agreement hatched years earlier? Because until 1973 the Nixon administration was unwilling to settle for that exchange. For a long time the United States, with Thieu anxiously nipping at Nixon and Kissinger's heels, held out for the withdrawal of North Vietnamese troops from the South. The administration finally abandoned this condition, buying Thieu off with secret assurances of U.S. support in the event of North Vietnamese violation of the truce. Kissinger and others maintain that Hanoi's demands for Thieu's removal from power—demands that were dropped at the end of 1972—were what held up the agreement. Having Washington eliminate Thieu would have been a bonus, but it was not the basic issue for Hanoi. Hanoi's aim all along was to rid the South of outside military forces and

6. "Dr. Kissinger Discusses Status of Negotiations toward Viet-Nam Peace," *Department of State Bulletin,* vol. 67 (November 13, 1972), p. 549.

support and to face Saigon one-on-one. To be sure, the Paris accords did not prohibit the United States from reintervening, but Hanoi had good reason to calculate that this would be unlikely for political reasons. On balance, it would seem that Nixon's approach succeeded only in causing Hanoi to abandon the Thieu bonus and in damaging North Vietnamese forces enough to give Thieu a better chance of survival with the Americans gone.

Some will still judge this as sufficient reward to validate the lesson that once a commitment is made, military decisiveness is required. But a contrary lesson suggests itself with at least as much persuasiveness. Only when terms that reflect the long-range battlefield and political realities are offered can an agreement be concluded. If it is true that Nixon succeeded in getting Moscow and Peking to pressure Hanoi into signing the Paris accords, certainly neither he nor they pressured Hanoi into dropping its central demand—that North Vietnamese forces be permitted to stay in the South and that American forces leave.

The quick and massive use of force has appeal in certain limited situations. It did when Johnson employed the Marines in the Dominican Republic in 1965 and when President Ford used sea and air power to rescue the cargo ship *Mayaguez* from the new Communist government in Cambodia in 1975. In both instances American political opposition did not have time to form; to the contrary, both operations gained general public approbation while eliciting some criticism from the intelligentsia and allied groups.

But to make broader deductions from these experiences would seem futile. Presidents are unlikely to inculcate general lessons about the use of force. They and Congress will want to look at each case. Decisiveness may have been the right way to dislodge a handful of Communists in the Dominican Republic or to regain a ship from the Cambodians. But Nixon rejected this course when the North Koreans shot down the EC-121 spy plane in 1969. If there were to be another Korean War, would decisive escalation be the best way to deter Chinese intervention or would it compel such intervention? And at a time when the Soviet Union is building up its capability to project conventional force beyond its borders, would decisive military action be an advisable strategy in Africa?

More important from the viewpoint of lessons, the Win School has little to add to a discussion about how to judge vital interests and make commitments. Its advocates appear less interested in the question of when to fight than of how to fight. Its tendency is to perceive a challenge as meriting either no response or a nearly total one. Gradations become unacceptable. Moreover, the school appears to be indifferent to the issue of what to do about a mistaken commitment. Some advocates of this school come close to implying that honor and credibility must be upheld whatever the merits of the commitment. This seemed perilously the case in the manner in which the Ford administration handled the Angolan civil war in 1975. The Win School ultimately makes a virtue of necessity and thereby allows U.S. policy to be driven by the weakest features of the system that brought about the Vietnam War in the first place.

The Reformist School

While the Win School makes a virtue of whatever appears necessary, the Reformist School would have the United States adopt a new set of values and constraints—in sum, a new necessity. The majority of the members of this school—and they are mostly liberals and moderates in both parties—were early supporters of the American commitment to South Vietnam. Gradually most came to see the war as a mistake that they did not want to see repeated, to state the problem in terms of intervention, and to believe that controlling intervention meant changing policies and governmental structures.

The policy prescriptions of the Reformist School vary considerably; all basically hold that the United States should be prepared to engage in war in Europe and Japan, but they differ on Israel and South Korea. It is with respect to the developing world that their differences are most noticeable. Some would not exclude direct American intervention if the attackers included the Soviet Union and China. Others would limit U.S. intervention to air and sea power and leave the ground fighting to others. Some would categorically preclude direct involvement.

Whatever the variants, all seem motivated by the same fundamental thinking about world politics. Earl C. Ravenal, who goes beyond most members of the school in his detachment from Europe and Japan, summarized some of these fundamentals. All the new presumptions, he said, should

add up to a strong orientation of nonintervention—a skepticism of exercising control of the international order. It is an orientation against exercises of deliberate violence to prevent or pre-empt future danger, to anticipate future disadvantages, to wage long-range defense, to reinforce credibility in large matters by intervening in small ones. Thus, a set of antipresumptions that establish a structured bias against intervention would result in a profound change in the direction of our foreign policy.[7]

In the earliest stages of the Reformist School critique of past policy, its advocates fastened onto the issue of bilateral foreign aid. This kind of aid, they argued, created U.S. security interests where none previously existed and magnified those that did exist. Their point was that bilateral economic and military aid deepened American involvement in Vietnam, increased the stakes for the United States, and generated new incentives to support the existing regimes regardless of their visibility. That aid programs have these effects is doubtless true. Aid does deepen involvement. But to go further and contend that aid was the grease on which the United States slid into the substantial commitment to the Saigon regime is to misread the bulk of the evidence. Increased bilateral aid to Diem, Ky, and Thieu followed rather than preceded the basic commitment to a non-Communist South Vietnam. The aid programs were essentially a reflection of the prior commitment, as well as a way of implementing it.

There may be a host of valid reasons for eliminating bilateral aid programs, which certainly do increase American identification with many repressive regimes and often are the form of aid most resented by the recipients. But to consign these programs to history with the expectation of thus having relieved the problem of intervention is to miss what really drives commitments, namely the institutions of the system and the values that permeate them.

The same objections can be made to the view of reformers who seek to control commitments and interventions by reducing military spending. Here again, it is difficult to see the connection between the Pentagon budget and the commitment in Vietnam. Pentagon spending increased after the start of the Korean War and after the commitment to Vietnam. It leveled off in the latter Eisenhower years, increased somewhat in the early Kennedy administration, and then leveled off again in 1964 and 1965 under Johnson. The decision to acquire nonnuclear limited war options precipitated the rise in spending under Kennedy, not

7. Earl C. Ravenal, "The Strategic Lessons of Vietnam," in Anthony Lake, ed., *The Vietnam Legacy: The War, American Society, and the Future of American Foreign Policy* (New York University Press, 1976), p. 272. See also Ravenal, "After Schlesinger: Something Has to Give," *Foreign Policy,* no. 22 (Spring 1976), pp. 71–95.

the reverse; the decision to get into direct and massive combat in Vietnam precipitated the budget increase under Johnson, not the reverse.

Some reformers have been more specific on this point, suggesting that severe cutbacks in general purpose forces might make it easier for presidents not to intervene. Thus Graham Allison, Ernest May, and Adam Yarmolinsky asserted in *Foreign Affairs:* "For the critical variable is the set of expectations within the bureaucracy, and an apparent leanness in non-nuclear forces would help to persuade the bureaucracy that the President genuinely intended to stand behind the presumptions he had announced."[8] It is difficult to accept, however, that the bureaucracy is the "critical variable" or that "leanness" would deter a president on intervention. As discussed extensively in previous chapters, the bureaucracy (and particularly the military bureaucracy) was not a major force in making the commitment. Indeed to the extent that opposition to the commitment was anywhere to be found, it was in some quarters of the bureaucracy itself. There may be many sound reasons for curtailing defense spending, but curbing commitments is not one of them. Forces so lean as to preclude any intervention in the Third World may well be too lean to intervene credibly anywhere. Moreover, precluding options by limiting capabilities puts the cart before the horse. It is a strategem to prevent a president from being able to do what he may want to do. The U.S. military buildup in the flexible response program of the early 1960s —which made large-scale intervention in Vietnam possible—was the result of administration policy, not the cause. It was a rational strategic adaptation to the containment doctrine, undertaken precisely because the administration *wanted* to be able to use force to prevent the establishment of new Communist governments.[9] The anti-Communist doctrine of containment led the United States into Vietnam, not the strategy of flexible military options, and doctrine and policy, more than the strategy and tactics that flow from them, are the problem for the future.

Most adherents of the Reformist School have come to accept these counterarguments and to focus on broader policy issues and on the institutions and procedures of the system. Members of the Reformist School

8. Graham Allison, Ernest May, and Adam Yarmolinsky, "Limits to Intervention," *Foreign Affairs,* vol. 48 (January 1970), p. 261. See also Allison, "Military Capabilities and American Foreign Policy," *The Annals of the American Academy of Political and Social Science,* vol. 406 (March 1973), pp. 17–37.

9. Richard K. Betts, *Soldiers, Statesmen and Cold War Crises* (Harvard University Press, 1977), pp. 102–03.

have thus proposed curbing the powers of the President and enhancing those of Congress. For reasons that are understandable but unsubstantiated, it has become fashionable in reform circles to blame wars on presidents and to seek wisdom and restraint in Congress.

The arguments about the imperial presidency in foreign affairs are by now well known. Irrefutably, the powers given to Kennedy, Johnson, and Nixon were well in excess of those of their predecessors and perhaps in excess of those allowed in the Constitution. It is also probably true that presidents constituted the main force behind establishing the Vietnam commitment and the main stumbling block to extrication from the war. Thus reformers find it natural to ignore or downgrade the pressures external to the presidents, the beliefs and constraints that impelled the presidents toward commitment.

On similar grounds, the reformers turned to Congress. Never mind that congressional pressures on Truman at the time of the Korean War and after the "loss" of China to prevent Communist gains elsewhere and anywhere were enormous. Congressional leaders were even ready to back an Eisenhower intervention in Dien Bien Phu as long as the United States was joined by allies. The situation was not much different for Kennedy and Johnson. Nonetheless, the reformers turned to Congress, not because they forgot Congress's role in making the commitment, but because they saw hope in Congress's role in ending the war. The question is whether they saw more than was really there. It is true that the main pressures to end the war were centered in Congress. But the fact remains that Congress did not enact restrictive legislation on the war until after all American troops were out of Indochina. Before 1973 the Senate passed bills to set a terminal date for American participation, but the House rejected them.

The new pro-Congress sentiments did produce a rush of legislation, beneficial in the sense of enhancing checks and balances. Congressional review procedures were enacted into law that reduce executive branch secrecy, expose self-serving bureaucratic rationales, and make the conduct of diplomacy more open. The reformers' attitude toward Congress, however, seemed to take on the qualities of a new fashion, just as the policies they were advancing seemed to presage a new doctrine. But if there is one lesson to emerge from the Vietnam War that might withstand the test of time, it is that America needs no new doctrines. New doctrines consecrate new truths, and new truths create new certainties, new compulsions—a new framework of necessity. Anything that becomes necessary to do in the first place becomes virtually impossible to undo thereafter.

To sum up: The Win School would have America vindicate mistakes in victory, while the Reformist School would have it avoid another mistake. Neither is comforting. The former gives promise of only threats and force. The latter suggests a certain naiveté. For if one thing can be counted on as one looks back to Vietnam, China, Munich, and Sarajevo, it is that mistakes will be committed. The problem, then, is not so much prevention as extrication, and the solution is not so much governmental restructuring as changing fundamental attitudes about and within the system.

Recommendations

Specifically, what can be done to the political-bureaucratic decision-making process to make it more likely that if a mistake is made, it can be corrected?

Posing the issue this way raises the question of how to define a "mistake." But this seems more a philosophical than a practical problem. Considerable evidence suggests that on the basis of intuitive cost-benefit analyses and moral values, most of the American people, the foreign policy professionals, the politicians, and the foreign leaders concluded that the Vietnam War was a mistake long before it was over. The same can be said of U.S. efforts to isolate China after 1950, or of Western efforts to appease Hitler in the late 1930s, or of some of the policies that led to World War I. The problem is translating the retrospective awareness of mistakes, turning the policy around, and overcoming the necessities that had overwhelmed the facts.

Many of the proposals advanced by the Reformist School would help to restructure incentives in the system, to make it more thinkable and more politically feasible to change policy. Multilateral as opposed to bilateral aid does make it easier to avoid identification with a particular regime. Congressional review of such actions as arms sales often brings to the surface embarrassing facts and sloppy executive branch thinking and thus makes it more difficult to continue policies that make little sense.

In general, any proposal that fosters checks and balances and competing power centers serves this purpose. What may be lost in leadership potential is at least balanced by what is gained in promoting escape routes. Those who worry about leadership usually believe that this quality inheres only in the President and are fearful of damaging presidential authority. These fears are exaggerated. With few exceptions, the chief executive has been able to prevail in foreign affairs over the past thirty years. Even in the past few years, with new restrictive legislation on the books, he has generally been able to follow his desired course.

Competing centers of power, however, allow for a greater sharing of responsibility, and this sharing is essential for extrication. Political costs are bound to be attached to any reversal of policy. Judging by the Vietnam experience, presidents seemed to have been more concerned about these costs than many congressmen were. Particular constituencies of individual congressmen turned against the war before the President's national constituency. It was politically safer for these congressmen to come out against the war than it was for the man in the White House. When they became a majority in 1973, these congressmen began to mandate a declining American involvement. Their actions were a signal to the President and the American people that Congress was prepared to share the blame for whatever might subsequently happen in Indochina. Although Nixon and Ford rejected these entreaties, other presidents might find them a welcome cover for retreat and change. Thus the notion that Congress should play a larger role in foreign affairs is a healthy change in the system.

The War Powers Resolution of 1973 is a case in point.[10] Congressmen came to see that putting together a majority to vote against the President was impossible until after all American troops were withdrawn. Based largely on that experience, Congress framed the War Powers Resolution in such a way that it did not require a majority vote against the President. By this law the President cannot continue military action beyond sixty days unless Congress votes with him. Failure to support him constitutes a veto.[11] This may be a small matter, and perhaps once the President commits forces Congress will go along anyway. But the act does address a weakness in the system, the difficulty of opposing the President

10. 87 Stat. 555. The resolution was enacted November 7, 1973, when Congress overrode President Nixon's veto.

11. In the event that Congress does not approve the deployments, the resolution allows the President thirty days beyond the original sixty days to complete the extrication of U.S. forces if he certifies in writing that such an extension is required by military necessity.

when troops are in the field, and that is a plus in itself. It is easier to do nothing than to undue something.

Presidents can do two things to give themselves similar flexibility. One is to nurture dissent. The other is to present Congress and the public with a realistic list of policy alternatives.

Dissent and Policy

Once a president sets policy, it becomes a herculean task for senior officials and bureaucrats to argue against it. Presidents have to make clear up and down the line that they want to hear criticisms and alternatives from their subordinates before they read them in the press, and that dissenters will be rewarded as well as team players. This does not mean that presidents and their senior officers should penalize team players or not seek agreement on policies. They should press for agreement on coherent policies but also leave the door open to revising judgment. Nor does it mean creating separate "dissenting staffs" in the various departments; that would serve only to isolate and tame dissenters. Dissent should be institutionalized by rewards and promotions, not domesticated. Subordinates will perceive quickly whether or not the President is serious.

Related to this is the manner in which the President speaks to the American public about his choices. Presidents have made the unholy trilogy of two extremes and the Aristotelian mean their standard fare— an inaccurate reflection of the options given to a president by his subordinates. The middle way subsumes many separable choices, which would certainly be difficult to break out for public inspection, but the alternative is having these options aired by outside critics, and what comes from outsiders is bound to be less acceptable. Moreover, the very fact of a president speaking about these other alternatives in serious and realistic terms might make it more possible for him to choose them if he should change his mind.

Doctrine and Consensus

Above all, Presidents should eschew ambitious new conceptual and overall policy doctrines supported by a new consensus. Doctrine and consensus are the midwives to necessity and the enemy of dissent and choice. They breed political paranoia and intellectual rigidity. Opposition to a policy is tolerable; disagreement with revealed truth is close to treason. Facts are transformed into serviceable commodities; they are either ignored or forced to fit the theory. To define policy in terms of necessity, as doctrines do, is to preclude choice by definition.

While an overall doctrine embodied in political consensus does not end dispute, it makes the outcomes a certainty. There was little chance that President Roosevelt could have the United States weigh in the scales against Hitler before the Japanese attack on Pearl Harbor, given the doctrine of isolationism. There was no way President Truman could avoid the commitment to Vietnam, given the doctrine of containment. The street demonstrators, the academic critics, and congressmen had no power to reverse that commitment; they could only affect how the war was conducted.

As long as the general doctrine of military containment of communism remained the consensus, the specific military intervention in Vietnam followed logically. The domino theory saw any conflict with Communists as a testing ground of Western resolve and credibility. Communists had threatened, or had seemed to threaten, to take over "Free World" territory in Greece, Berlin, Korea, Iran, Guatemala, Lebanon, and the Dominican Republic. Actions to prevent these changes were seen by majorities in the public and within government as the American successes of the cold war. When Communists did gain control in China and Cuba, these were seen as American defeats. When containment was interpreted flexibly and modified, as it was in the secondary scene of conflict in Indochina (Laos) in 1961, this made affirmation of commitment in the primary Indochina scene (Vietnam) all the more necessary. Vietnam was another arena in the cold war, another domino, and as such it was covered by the doctrine that Communists would not be allowed to take over territory by force, that salami tactics that succeeded in the 1930s would not succeed in the postwar era. Doctrine dictated commitment.

Opposition to unyielding doctrine need not degenerate into a pragmatic nihilism or an anarchy of standards that paralyzes decisionmaking. Some doctrine is of course necessary and valuable. It lends coherence and direction to policy; it puts particular challenges in perspective; it enables the bureaucracy to handle routine problems without constant and enervating debates; it translates values into objectives. But goals have to be balanced against the possibility that they may be wrong or unattainable at acceptable costs. The need is for doctrine with escape hatches, doctrine that is susceptible to easy adaptation, that guides rather than constrains, and that does not take on a life of its own. Pragmatism does not produce paralysis or sterility in domestic policy; it need not in foreign policy. In short, there is a need to avoid overarching doctrines and to seek more particular, more adaptive, and more conditional ones. Rusk and Kissinger argued that commitments cannot be met selectively; if this is so, it is all the more vital that they be *made* selectively.

The objection here is not to a consensus on a particular policy for a particular part of the world. The problem is with a conceptual or doctrinal consensus—the Truman Doctrine, the Eisenhower-Dulles doctrine of massive retaliation, or the Nixon Doctrine. These in time acquire the character of a political imperative. It is only possible to dissent successfully on a particular policy so long as it is not encased in Holy Scripture.

The compulsion to have conceptual doctrine embodied in consensus is strong. Most of the best foreign policy minds in the country devote themselves to promoting new doctrines. In Henry Kissinger's most influential book, *Nuclear Weapons and Foreign Policy,* he rejected pragmatism as improvisation and ended with a chapter on "The Need for Doctrine." A strategic doctrine, he wrote, "is the mode of survival of a society" and is the only basis for achieving purposeful action, defining work responsibilities, giving direction, and defining challenges and responses. "By explaining the significance of events *in advance* of their occurrence, it enables society to deal with most problems as a matter of routine and reserves creative thought for unusual or unexpected situations."[12]

Years later, after Congress passed the ban on further American military action in Indochina, Secretary of State Kissinger said: "The present ordeal of the whole nation is too obvious to require commentary." His solution: "The consensus that sustained our international participation is in danger of being exhausted. It must be restored."[13]

There are two unspoken assumptions here: that effective leadership requires doctrine and consensus, and that doctrine and consensus allow more effective control. That leaders have sought to establish an overall

12. Henry A. Kissinger, *Nuclear Weapons and Foreign Policy* (Harper, 1957), pp. 403–04.
13. Quoted in Leslie H. Gelb, "Dissenting on Consensus," in Anthony Lake, *The Vietnam Legacy: The War, American Society, and the Future of American Foreign Policy,* p. 102.

doctrine bearing their names is unquestionably true. That they could not have been effective without that doctrine is questionable. Leaders could have argued the merits of each policy on a case-by-case basis. This certainly would have been more difficult, which serves to point out that the main lure of doctrine and consensus is indeed control. Kissinger did not idly italicize the phrase "in advance" when writing of the virtues of doctrine. To the extent that doctrine is embodied in consensus, it virtually eliminates the chance of seriously debating the significance of an event in advance. By this means, bureaucrats come to know what to expect and dissenters come to understand the futility of resistance.

Control and power, however, are purchased at a high price. In obtaining them a leader or a president not only stymies potential opponents but entraps himself as well. In the end it is the President himself who is most bound by his own doctrine and who most deprives himself of choice.

Stanley A. Hoffmann saw this quite clearly: "The tendency to analyze issues in terms of set formulas or analogies instead of tackling them on their merits encourages the continuance of policies long after they have outlived their usefulness, and then a rather abrupt dismissal of them once their counter-productiveness has become damaging (at which point they are replaced with new dogmas that have the same effect); hence, the alternation of rigidity and radical change noted by observers."[14]

The need for pragmatism more than doctrines, formulas, and ideologies is the basic lesson of the Vietnam War. Americans are rightly known as a pragmatic people in their internal affairs and in their thinking. That so pragmatic a people have followed such ideological foreign policies is paradoxical. While Americans by and large spurned ideology in their domestic politics, they embraced it in their foreign policy. Somehow the United States had to be better, purer, and cleaner abroad than it was at home.

The Vietnam War brought an end to the consensus on containment. New doctrines are now contending for a new consensus. This is not the place to discuss their merits or weaknesses. Suffice it to say that if the Vietnam War can teach anything, none should be accepted. Doctrine demands a dangerous consistency; a workable policy requires discrimi-

14. Stanley Hoffmann, *Gulliver's Troubles, or the Setting of American Foreign Policy* (McGraw-Hill for the Council on Foreign Relations, 1968), p. 140.

nation and choice. Americans have been so mesmerized for the past thirty years by calls for leadership and creativity in the conduct of foreign policy that they have neglected the need for adaptation and change. They always talk about "the changing world" but too rarely of the related need to change policies. It is to this end—to think of policy-making as an act of adjustment as well as an act of creativity and leader-ship—that the system must work.

Documentary Appendix

CLARK M. CLIFFORD
815 CONNECTICUT AVENUE
WASHINGTON, D.C. 20006

May 17, 1965

The President
The White House

Dear Mr. President:

I am returning herewith the letter of the Director of Central Intelligence, dated May 8, 1965, together with enclosures.

I wish to make one major point.

I believe our ground forces in South Vietnam should be kept to a minimum, consistent with the protection of our installations and property in that country. My concern is that a substantial buildup of U.S. ground troops would be construed by the Communists, and by the world, as a determination on our part to win the war on the ground.

This could be a quagmire. It could turn into an open end commitment on our part that would take more and more ground troops, without a realistic hope of ultimate victory.

I do not think the situation is comparable to Korea. The political posture of the parties involved, and the physical conditions, including terrain, are entirely different.

I continue to believe that the constant probing of every avenue leading to a possible settlement will ultimately be fruitful. It won't be what we want, but we can learn to live with it.

Respectfully yours,
/S/Clark

This letter is in LBJL/NSF-VNCF, box 11, 1965 Troop Decision folder, item 14.

THE WHITE HOUSE

WASHINGTON

Saturday, July 24, 1965
8:15 p. m.

MEMORANDUM FOR THE PRESIDENT

SUBJECT: The History of Recommendations for Increased US Forces in
Vietnam

This story relates almost entirely to 1965. When you became President, US
forces in Vietnam totalled 16,000. On 31 December 1964, they totalled
23,000. Today they are between 75 and 80,000, and you are considering
increases of another 100,000 between now and November.

In December and January, our attention did not focus upon increased ground
forces. We were trying to get the Huong Government to pull up its socks,
and we were preparing to authorize air strikes at the right moment. We had
no recommendations from the military for major ground force deployments.

At the end of January, after Bob and I discussed with you our growing
doubts, you sent me to Vietnam. During that trip, the attack on Pleiku occurred and in February, you put into effect the program of limited air strikes
against North Vietnam, and unlimited air action in South Vietnam. It is in
this connection that the Joint Chiefs of Staff recommended, and you approved, the deployment of Marines in Danang. Two battalion landing teams
were approved for such deployment on February 25.

The bombing did not reverse the situation and we did not expect it would.
In the first week of March, you sent General Harold Johnson to Vietnam. He
returned with three basic recommendations:

> First, a 21-Point program of small actions which was promptly ap-
> proved;

> Second, a deployment of a tailored division force either to the high-
> lands or to certain bases; and

> Third, a four division ground force to contain infiltration by land.

The last two recommendations were tentative in form and were not pressed
to a decision. General Taylor, in an important dispatch on March 16 (Saigon
3003) weighed the pros and cons of a single US division and recommended
that judgment be reserved.

At the end of March, General Taylor visited Washington and there was discussion of a possible three-division force, as suggested by the Joint Chiefs
of Staff, but Taylor himself was skeptical and reported a similar skepticism

in Prime Minister Quat. The Secretaries of State and Defense recommended that the decision be deferred and that instead we should approve deployment of two additional Marine battalions and an 18–20,000 man increase in other US support forces. This recommendation was accepted in the first days of April.

The study of ground-force deployment continued in April, and on Tuesday, April 20, McNamara, Taylor, Wheeler, Sharpe [sic], Westmoreland, McNaughton, and William Bundy met in Honolulu. At that point there were 2,000 Koreans and 33,000 US troops in the country, and an additional 18,000 were already approved. After the Honolulu discussions, McNamara recommended additional deployments leading to a total strength of 82,000—including 13 combat battalions. Part of this recommendation was given formal approval on April 21; and other parts, on May 15. This set of recommendations was the most important between January and the present, and I attach McNamara's memorandum of April 21.

Early in May, you requested $700 million for Vietnam, and our defense of this request and related statements made it clear that additional forces were being sent. On June 16, McNamara gave a full public exposition, announcing the planned deployment of 15 battalions, with a total military strength of 70–75,000.

Meanwhile, on June 11, after discussions with MACV and Ambassador Taylor, the Joint Chiefs recommended additional deployments to a total of 116,-000. The most important element in this recommendation was the air-mobile division. On June 19 you gave approval to the necessary preparatory steps for these deployments, without deciding on the deployment itself.

On July 2, the Joint Chiefs produced a further recommendation for a total troop strength of 179,000, again in coordination with MACV and Ambassador Taylor. Before approving this recommendation, you sent McNamara to Vietnam. With marginal modifications, it is this recommendation which is now before you for decision.

The essence of this history, I think, is that initially we all had grave objections to major US ground force deployments. Even those in favor, (like my brother Bill), wanted to try other things first, and none of us was prepared to urge on Westmoreland things he was not urging on us.

Then when we got major bases of our own, largely for air action, we moved quite promptly to protect them. These deployments did not give us bad reactions, and it became easier for Westmoreland to propose, and for us to accept, additional deployments. Thus, between the end of March and the beginning of July—a period of only three months—we moved from recommended force levels of 33,000 to recommended force levels of 180,000. We also moved from the mission of base security to the mission of active combat in whatever way seems wise to General Westmoreland.

I have found this review instructive. It suggests to me that McNamara's Plan

3 is better than his other two plans. I think we should now approve the recommended deployments through November. I think that at the same time we should explicitly and plainly reserve decision about further major deployments. After all, we have not yet had even a company-level engagement with Viet Cong forces which choose to stand their ground and fight.

McG. B.

This memorandum is in LBJL/NSF-VNCF, box 11, 1965 Troop Decision folder, item 3a. It was declassified on May 14, 1976.

Bibliographical Note

The essential source of information about U.S. decisions on Vietnam is the official Defense Department history, popularly known as the Pentagon Papers, compiled by a task force in the Office of the Secretary of Defense in the late 1960s. These papers have been published in three forms, but none is complete and none fully subsumes any of the others.

First was the series of stories in the *New York Times* in 1971 that included excerpts from the original documents and commentary in the Defense Department study. This compilation appeared subsequently as *The Pentagon Papers as Published by the New York Times* (Quadrangle, 1971). The *Times* version of the papers is the one most widely circulated and read, but it is the least comprehensive of the three. For this reason it is rarely cited in this book.

The second version is the collection read into the record of the Senate Subcommittee on Public Buildings and Grounds by Senator Mike Gravel on June 29, 1971, and published subsequently in four volumes as *The Pentagon Papers: The Defense Department History of United States Decisionmaking on Vietnam,* Senator Gravel ed. (Beacon Press, 1971). This collection includes most but not all of the original study. Since it is nearly comprehensive and is both more clearly organized and more widely available than the third version, it is the one most frequently cited in this book.

The third version was the official declassified edition, consisting of reproductions of the original papers (with deletions) and published in twelve volumes under the original title: *United States–Vietnam Relations, 1945–1967,* Study prepared by the Department of Defense for the House Committee on Armed Services, 92 Cong. 1 sess. (Government Printing Office, 1971). This edition is the most definitive, though it lacks some material in the Gravel edition.

Several sections of the original study were not published in 1971 because they dealt with the history of U.S. contacts with North Vietnam and, because the negotiations were still in progress at that time, they were considered too sensitive for declassification. These sections were later entered as evidence in the trial of Daniel Ellsberg and have since been largely declassified. At the time this book was completed these negotiations volumes had not yet been published, and we are indebted to Morton Halperin for access to his copy of them (cited here as USVNR, Negotiations Volumes).

Portions of this book are also based on material in the John F. Kennedy and Lyndon B. Johnson presidential libraries. The most important documents in these libraries are memorandums from White House files, to which the Defense Department analysts compiling the Pentagon Papers did not have access. It should be noted, however, that large portions of these files remain classified and may not be released for years to come. We made use of those portions of the files that were available as of mid-1977, citing them as JFKL/ NSF-VNCF and LBJL/NSF-VNCF.

Index

Escalation, 27; alternatives to, 112–16; analysis of, 19–20, 23–24; by bombing and reconnaissance in Laos, 100, 116, 117–20; decisionmakers' strategy for, 131–33; gradual, 3, 139, 144; by ground forces deployment, 120–24; phases of, 109, 113; rationale for, 110–12; risks of, 136–37; step-by-step deployment, 131–32; and Tonkin Gulf incident, 101, 103, 212

Ethnocentricity, 18–19

European Defense Community (EDC), 47, 53–54

Evans, Rowland, 97n, 117n, 137n, 160n, 287n

Expenditures, military, 284, 349–50, 360–61

Fairlie, Henry, 71, 149n

Fall, Bernard B., 5n, 20, 65n

Felt, Harry, 74

Fitzgerald, Frances, 19n, 83n

FLAMING DART raids, 115, 136, 138, 139, 140

Ford, Gerald R., 5, 364; commitment to Vietnam, 351

Foreign aid: criteria for bilateral, 360; to France, 43, 44, 46, 51, 191, 279, 325, 330; multilateral, 363; to South Vietnam, 67, 83, 117, 191, 350–51

Foreign policy, U.S., 1; against losing war, 221–22; cold war, 22–23, 204; conservatives' effect on, 214–20; criteria for, 2–3; dilemmas, 11–13; on escalation, 131–33; on Korea, 113; moderates' and liberals' effect on, 205–14; politics and, 221–26; resolve in, 78–79. See also Commitment; Containment of communism; Involvement

Foreign Service, 228, 239; diverse views on Vietnam, 233–36, 316; professionals versus political appointees in, 237

Forrestal, Michael, 81, 87, 88, 100n, 301; on China's aggressiveness, 107; dovish approach, 149–50; low-profile strategy, 98

Foster, William C., 51n

Fowler, Henry H., 177

France: and DRV, 37–38; and EDC, 53–54; military forces, 9; pressures on U.S., 274; reforms in Vietnam, 12, 254; trusteeship for Indochina, 35–36; underestimate of enemy's power, 303–04; U.S. aid to, 43, 44, 46, 51, 191, 279, 325, 330; U.S. leverage on policy of, 47, 254–55; and U.S. State Department, 39–40; win strategies aimed at, 252, 253

Free, Lloyd A., 78n

Frizzell, Donaldson D., 14n, 83n, 84n

Fulbright, J. William, 14n, 72, 176n, 275; defense of Diem, 208; on negotiated settlement, 216; and Tonkin Gulf Resolution, 103, 212

Galbraith, John Kenneth, 87, 88, 93

Gallucci, Robert L., 17n, 77n, 82, 94, 99n, 124n, 130n, 137n, 175n

Gallup, George H., 129, 173n

Gavin, James, 57, 134

Gelb, Leslie H., 191n, 367n

Geneva Conference, 53, 55, 68, 114; Laos settlement, 64–66; pessimism following, 312; press reaction to, 206, 207, 208; Vietnam settlement, 61

Gettleman, Marvin E., 57n

Geyelin, Philip, 115n

Giap, Vo Nguyen, 53, 139, 311

Gilpatric Roswell, 76, 86, 277; Task Force, 72, 300, 308

Goldberg, Arthur, 141, 174

Goldman, Eric F., 117n

Goldwater, Barry, 128, 212

Goodman, Allen E., 5n, 83–84, 108n

Goodwin, Richard, 150, 217, 218n

Goulden, Joseph C., 100n, 103n, 104n, 116n

Goulding, Phil G., 157n

Government of (South) Vietnam (GVN); corruption in, 145; escalation contingent upon reforms of, 112, 113, 254, 263; fighting by forces of, 266; leverage strategy aimed at, 145–46, 254–55, 263; political system, 84–86, 145; pressures on U.S. presidents by, 274; problems in, 98, 99, 112–13

Graff, Henry F., 82n, 91n, 106n, 108n, 111, 128n, 129n, 147n, 156n, 157

Graham, James C., 133n

Gravel, Mike, 40n, 69n, 97n, 146n, 229n, 249n, 276n, 300n, 328n

Gray, Cecil W., 33n

Great Society, 97, 117, 267; effect of war on, 96, 160, 223

Greene, Felix, 116

Greene, T. N., 211n

Greene, Wallace M., Jr., 109

Gronouski, John, 152

Ground forces deployment, 120–24, 131–32, 142, 154–56, 170, 173–74, 177, 250; strategy for, 133–35

Gruening, Ernest, 101, 102, 211, 212